The Eighteenth-Century British Verse Epistle

Also by Bill Overton

FICTIONS OF FEMALE ADULTERY 1684-1890: Theories and Circumtexts

A LETTER TO MY LOVE: Love Poems by Women First Published in the Barbados Gazette, 1731-1737

THE NOVEL OF FEMALE ADULTERY: Love and Gender in Continental European Fiction, 1830-1900

THE WINTER'S TALE: The Critics Debate

THE MERCHANT OF VENICE: Text and Performance

THE UNOFFICIAL TROLLOPE

From Dorothea Du Bois's *The Lady's Polite Secretary* (London: for J. Coote and T. Evans, [1771]).
Reproduced by kind permission of the British Library.

The Eighteenth-Century British Verse Epistle

Bill Overton

palgrave
macmillan

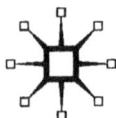

First published 2007 by
PALGRAVE MACMILLAN
Houndmills, Basingstoke, Hampshire RG21 6XS and
175 Fifth Avenue, New York, N. Y. 10010
Companies and representatives throughout the world

PALGRAVE MACMILLAN is the global academic imprint of the Palgrave Macmillan division of St. Martin's Press, LLC and of Palgrave Macmillan Ltd. Macmillan® is a registered trademark in the United States, United Kingdom and other countries. Palgrave is a registered trademark in the European Union and other countries.

ISBN 978-1-349-52098-5   ISBN 978-0-230-59346-6 (eBook)
DOI 10.1057/9780230593466

A catalogue record for this book is available from the British Library.

A catalog record for this book is available from the Library of Congress.

10   9   8   7   6   5   4   3   2   1
16   15   14   13   12   11   10   09   08   07

Transferred to Digital Printing

Contents

Preface

The verse epistle was a key form in eighteenth-century Britain. My research with printed and online sources indicates that, at a conservative estimate, at least five percent of the poems printed in the period were epistolary. These poems were of many different types, extending well beyond those inherited from Horace (the verse letter and verse essay) and Ovid (the heroic epistle). It is surprising, therefore, that no attempt at a comprehensive study of the form exists, even though it has attracted several excellent articles and chapters, along with a single book – dedicated, however, chiefly to the variant that Pope called the ethic epistle.[1] The aim of this book is to provide such a study. It sets out to address all kinds of eighteenth-century epistolary verse, it considers how to define and theorize the form, and it discusses and analyses examples of its various sub-types in detail.

The approach that the book takes is to a significant extent empirical. At the most basic, this means that I have done my best to read as many verse epistles as I could within the time available, to analyse a good number in detail, and to compare different types as well as different examples. But it also means that the book is driven by no particular thesis, except for the obvious one that the verse epistle was an important form in eighteenth-century Britain, and also, as I hope to show, one of great interest and complexity. In other words, I have aimed at producing a survey and an analysis rather than an argument. I would justify this by the need to avoid tendentiousness in such a project, especially in the absence of much critical or scholarly inquiry about it. Particularly in the first two chapters, that aim will involve more use of statistics than is common in critical studies. I have done my best to make these accurate within the limits of the data available; I hope readers will not find them irksome.

In two key respects, however, my approach is not wholly empirical. First, any critical method will be inflected, even biased, by various kinds of critical and ideological assumptions – in my case, to put it reductively, historicist, formalist, socialist and feminist. Empirical data are important partly as the main way of redressing any bias of this type. Second, the main motivation for the study is a delight in and fascination with verse. Such a statement is unfashionable nowadays, and it may seem to sit oddly with, for example, the analysis of numerical data that will be found in parts of the first two chapters. But a study of a kind of writing in verse is properly, in one fundamental respect, a study of poetry and of specific poems. It is, of course, essential to approach these as historical artefacts, products of a particular time, place and culture, and to use all the resources of literary and historical research to do so. Yet they cannot be sufficiently understood without knowledge of what makes them poems: how, in particular, they use verse form as well as language. This includes what makes them pleasurable and successful – or the reverse. For, in order to understand how good a poem is, especially as an example of a specific form, it is necessary to compare it with poems that are less good: Pope's 'Eloisa to Abelard', for example, with most of the responses it attracted, or, to cite a less familiar example, William Dunkin's *Epistle to Charlemont* with any of the obsequious complimentary epistles of the period.[2] Only in such a way is it possible to develop anything approaching an adequate understanding of the form and its various potentials. For that purpose, objections about the arbitrariness of value judgements are beside the point, although, of course, the grounds on which such judgements are reached always stay open to argument.

This book offers, then, both a wide-ranging survey of the verse epistle in eighteenth-century Britain and detailed analysis of how specific examples work. It considers not only the different shapes that the form took, but also their development and their embeddedness in the culture and history of the period. I am only too aware that these are large aims, aims that entail a high risk of error. Those that have got by are mine rather than those of the various friends, colleagues and other contacts who have kindly given advice and help.

Acknowledgements

It is a pleasure to thank people and institutions who have helped with this project. To begin with individuals, Roger Lonsdale's work on eighteenth-century verse has been a constant inspiration; Christine Gerrard started the project by inviting me to write an essay on 'The Verse Epistle'; Karina Williamson stimulated my thinking with her essay 'Voice, Gender, and the Augustan Verse Epistle'; Stuart Gillespie gave valuable information on Dryden's miscellany; Peter Cogman and Derek Connon advised on French versification; Anthony Barker has allowed me to quote from his thesis; Thomas Bonnell, Audrey Carpenter, David Fairer, Simon May, Juan Christian Pellicer and Adam Rounce gave useful information or suggestions; Warren Chernaik, Isobel Grundy and Donna Landry have backed and encouraged me; colleagues at Loughborough University have been helpful and supportive, especially Neal Swettenham, who introduced me to the work of George Lakoff; while Grace, Keith, Gisela, George, Julie and Henry Overton, and Rachel Barton, have also provided much-appreciated support and encouragement. To Elaine Hobby, however, I owe most, for advice, companionship and help during the whole period of research and writing, for much of it in difficult circumstances.

Among institutions, I am grateful to the staff of libraries at which I have carried out research, particularly the British Library and the libraries of Loughborough, Cambridge, Leicester, and Nottingham Universities. My applications to the usual sources in Britain for research funding – the Arts and Humanities Research Council, British Academy and Leverhulme Foundation – fell on stony ground. I am therefore all the more thankful to Loughborough University for granting me two semesters of study leave, especially to the support of the Dean of Social Sciences and Humanities, Terry Kavanagh, and of two Heads of Department, Nigel Wood and Elaine Hobby. Without these periods of leave, the study would have taken much longer, if indeed it could have been completed at all. To Nigel Wood I am also indebted for obtaining University access to Chadwyck-Healey's *Literature Online*, which helped me get my research off the ground, and to Gale's *Eighteenth-Century Collections Online*, invaluable in the later stages. I record my gratitude, too, to the anonymous reader for helpful comments on the original proposal for the book and for the report on the final draft, and to Paula Kennedy and Christabel Scaife at Palgrave Macmillan for their always prompt advice and constructive responses.

I acknowledge permission from Blackwell Publishing to reproduce material from my essay 'The Verse Epistle' in *The Blackwell Companion to Eighteenth-Century Verse*, ed. by Christine Gerrard (Malden, MA and Oxford: Blackwell Publishing, 2006), pp. 416–28, including Appendix 2, giving details about my database of verse epistles from *Literature Online*. The image for the book jacket is reproduced by permission of the Syndics of Cambridge University Library from the Rev. George Brown's *The English Letter-Writer* (London: for Alexander Hogg, [1779?]), shelfmark 7240.d.102; the image for the frontispiece by permission of the British Library from Dorothea Du Bois's *The Lady's Polite Secretary* (London: for J. Coote and T. Evans, [1771]), shelfmark 10920.aa.11.

Note on References

Titles of works cited are standardized with respect to capitalization and italicization but not punctuation. Where appropriate, they are shortened for convenience. Titles of works first published separately are italicized, but when they are cited from a collection they are given in quotation marks. However, titles of works first printed as part of another publication are given in quotation marks even if they were later printed separately, or, like Pope's 'Eloisa to Abelard', have gained equivalent status. Where line numbers are provided in references to poems, these are from the editions cited; references to poems without lineation are by page number. Standard editions are used where available; where they are not available and where alternative editions exist, references are normally to those most likely to be accessible. Glosses are from the editions cited or from *OED*.

To facilitate identification of poems from the period 1700–1750 that are little known, the Bibliography provides the reference term in David F. Foxon, *English Verse 1701–1750: A Catalogue of Separately Printed Poems with Notes on Contemporary Collected Editions*, 2 vols (Cambridge: Cambridge University Press, 1975). Details of better-known poems are given without this term.

The standard abbreviations are used for the *Oxford English Dictionary* (*OED*) and *Oxford Dictionary of National Biography* (*ODNB*). In both cases I have used the online editions, accessed at various points during 2006, because they were the most up-to-date.

1
Definition

'A literary work, usually in poetry, composed in the form of a letter.' The definition in the *Oxford English Dictionary* of the form that is the subject of this book is simple enough, yet it begs two questions. These consist in a tension between the word 'literary' (amplified by 'poetry') and the word 'letter'. There are two main elements in that tension. The first, the much-debated question of how to define 'literature', may be addressed by applying Gérard Genette's distinction between the 'constitutively' and the 'conditionally' literary.[1] A work that is 'constitutively' literary has aesthetic effect as its primary aim. Such a work is produced either within an accepted literary form or in a manner that reworks or seeks to replace one. Examples are sonnets, pastoral elegies and novels. According to this definition, such works could never constitute anything other than 'literature', whatever their quality. The latter qualification is important, because it rules out as irrelevant the value judgements that otherwise complicate the issue endlessly. But value judgements come into decisive play when defining the 'conditionally' literary, for this category consists of work that has come to be regarded as having aesthetic merit, whether or not it was originally produced with that aim. Examples of works that are now often read as literature, though they were never intended as such, are Jonathan Swift's *Drapier's Letters* (1724), a series of highly effective political pamphlets, and Edward Gibbon's *Decline and Fall of the Roman Empire* (1776–88), a monument of historical scholarship.

Genette's distinction provides a solution to the question of how to treat letters that were written in verse but were not intended as 'literature', for such letters may be regarded as conditionally literary. There are many examples, some of which are discussed in this book.[2] But the second part of the problem is more intractable. It stems from the fact that many poems that have the title 'Epistle', or that are understood as epistolary, bear little

1

if any relation to actual letters. Examples go back to Horace's *Art of Poetry*, written as an epistle to the Piso family;[3] and they include many essay-epistles and complimentary epistles of the eighteenth century, some of which I will also discuss. Such poems seldom carry the usual markers of non-literary prose correspondence. They frequently lack salutations (though Horace addresses the Pisos at the end of his fifth line), and, even more often, valedictions (Horace's ends quite abruptly); they also rarely state formally their time and place of writing. Indeed, they often distance themselves still further from actual letters through the use of epigraphs or even annotations. It is difficult to understand in what sense such works might conform to the second part of the *OED* definition, though it is as essential as the first: 'composed in the form of a letter'. What further compounds the problem is that almost any kind of poem may be written as an epistle, from panegyric to satire, or epithalamium to elegy; that an epistle may be as short as two lines or as long as over a thousand; and that some examples show considerable variety in verse form.

In a brilliant essay on the Augustan verse epistle, Karina Williamson confronts such difficulties as these by emphasizing what she calls 'a fact so obvious as to be tautological, but forgotten or ignored surprisingly often in critical discussion: the verse letter is a letter'.[4] On that basis she argues that, 'In terms of its discursive properties, the epistle is in fact more, not less, distinct as a kind than satire, verse essay or lyric.' She goes on to define those properties by drawing on an article about non-literary prose letters by Patrizia Violi. However, although Williamson points out that verse epistles 'proclaim their difference within the broad parameters of the letter form by using the artificial medium of verse',[5] she does not give sufficient weight to the fact that they are also, crucially, poems. It is because they are poems that, as with the Horatian essay-epistle and its various derivatives, verse epistles do not necessarily share with non-literary prose letters such discursive properties as salutations, valedictions, set forms of address, or details of the time and place of writing, or carry them only in highly diluted forms. It may be objected that, if they lack such properties, or render them residual, poems of those types should be understood as only nominally epistolary. But such an objection does not help with eighteenth-century usage: the fact that, in the period, many poems were entitled epistles, or understood to be such, even though they resemble letters very little. This chapter will therefore follow a double approach. Much of it will examine eighteenth-century usage by considering how the form was understood in the period – not only in critical discussion, but also through its representation both in the form of titles for poems and in that of subtitles and subdivisions of collections of poetry. But it will also draw on recent cognitive science in order to develop a more adequate way of defining and classifying the verse epistle.

Eighteenth-century usage with regard to titles is too often inconsistent to provide a basis for definition. For instance, while some poems are named epistles, whether or not they look like actual letters in any respect, others are simply called letters; and others still bear neither term in their titles. The latter class of poems, often with titles in the form of the word 'To' and the name of addresser, addressee, or both, sets special problems for anyone trying to collect verse epistles. Pope's 'Eloisa to Abelard' is a famous example, but there are many more. As I shall demonstrate later in the chapter, such titles offer ample latitude for identifying poems as epistolary that are only marginally or dubiously so.

Whether a poem is entitled 'epistle' or 'letter' poses a problem of a different kind. Because the latter is a more everyday term than 'epistle', it might be thought that a poem entitled 'letter' would be more likely to resemble a genuine written communication. But eighteenth-century poets observed such a distinction only on occasion. Among them was Elizabeth Tollet, who used the title 'epistle' only twice, in both cases for formal, serious poems: the first a protest at a fallen world that ends by finding a solution in the example of Horace, the second, 'Anne Boleyn to King Henry VIII', an heroic epistle.[6] In both cases, her choice of the word followed classical precedents: the Horatian moral reflection on the one hand and, on the other, the fictional letter to a lover from a mythical or historical figure, usually female, in the tradition of Ovid's *Heroides*. Tollet used the word 'letter' in none of her titles, although 'To my Brother at St. John's College in Cambridge',[7] is an Horatian verse letter, and although the second edition of her *Poems on Several Occasions* contains three complimentary epistles.[8] In contrast, women writers whose status, unlike Tollet's, was marginal tended to avoid the title 'epistle', especially in the earlier part of the period. For example, Mary Barber, Mary Chandler and Mary Savage refrained from applying the word to any of their epistolary verse. This was probably on the assumption that the word 'epistle' – as opposed to 'letter', or the simple indicator 'to' – implied a more prestigious form than any that their status might have been expected to authorize.[9]

Two male poets whose titles generally reflect a distinction between 'epistle' and 'letter' are Samuel Wesley the younger and John Byrom. Of the 12 poems by Wesley entitled 'epistle', three are addressed to Lord Oxford and one to Lord Orrery; four are political poems, in two of which he writes as an imaginary Tory opponent; while there is one poem each to his brother Charles, his sister Martha, himself, and a friend.[10] All but one are in iambic pentameter couplets, the standard form for serious verse at the period. Five of Wesley's poems are entitled 'letter'. Two of these are occasional letters to friends, one is 'A Letter from a Guardian to a Young Lady', and the other two are satirical: one mocking Edmund Curll for having been tossed in a blanket, the other a riposte to Thomas Tickell's *Epistle from a Lady in England; To a Gentleman at Avignon*, the title of which it reduces, perhaps as part of its satire, to 'Letter'.[11] With one exception, then, Wesley seems to have reserved the title 'epistle' for poems to noblemen and members of his family, and for mock-formal political controversy; the word 'letter' for poems to friends and two satires. The exception, 'A Familiar Epistle to a Friend', is alone among his poems entitled 'epistle' in that it is in tetrameter, not pentameter, couplets; the reason it has the word 'epistle' in its title is probably that it is on the whole serious. Two of the five poems entitled 'letter' are also in tetrameters, one the squib about Curll, the other an informal familiar epistle. Wesley used the simple title 'To [. . .]' for nearly all of his more than 20 other epistolary poems. The great majority of these are familiar, and most are in pentameter or tetrameter couplets.[12] These provide further evidence that he kept the title 'epistle' almost exclusively for verse letters to addressees whom he wished to distinguish.

Samuel Wesley's care in choice of titles reflects habits of mind that he may have got from his father, who, a generation earlier, had used the more formal term for his Horatian essay *An Epistle to a Friend Concerning Poetry*.[13] John Byrom, who followed suit with 'An Epistle to a Friend on the Art of English Poetry', showed similar discretion. One of the most prolific writers of verse letters in the period, Byrom's collected poems include 19 entitled 'epistle', 13 entitled 'letter', and at least 19 others that are epistolary. Thirteen of the poems entitled 'epistle' engage in doctrinal controversy.[14] Some are arranged in a series of several poems, in one case consisting of six with the sub-title 'Letter', reflecting the use of the term for scholarly and scientific discourse. Eight of these 13 are in iambic pentameter couplets, while the remaining five, including a series of four poems, are in the other main form Byrom favoured for this type of verse, huitaines of anapestic tetrameter couplets. Of the other six poems entitled 'epistle', the subject of four, including a series of three, is scholarly disputation; one is an advisory epistle to his sister; and the other is the essay on the art of poetry already mentioned.[15] The 13 poems entitled 'letter' include two renderings in verse of historical letters written in prose, and one answer to an epistolary request; all three are in iambic pentameter couplets, in two cases arranged in stanzas.[16] Four further poems styled as 'Letter' are familiar, one a humorous account of a highway robbery in which the poet yielded only a few shillings and the thief took superstitious flight on seeing characters of his shorthand. Two of these are in stanzas of anapestic tetrameter couplets, one of iambic tetrameter couplets, the other of iambic pentameter couplets.[17] Of the other six poems, one, a response to a request to revise the poems of Bishop Ken, may also be classed as a familiar letter despite its serious tenor; one is satirical; and two of the remaining four are familiar in tone though they deal, respectively, with matters of history and religion, and with scriptural interpretation. This informality is clear from the way they begin: 'Will you please to permit me, my very good Lord', 'If you remember, Rev'rend Sir, the Talk'.[18] In contrast, all of Byrom's poems entitled 'Epistle' that begin with salutations use more formal terms of address, for example: 'Sir', 'Reverend Sir' (not elided, as above), 'Dear Vicar', and *'Mr. Bl—k—n'*.[19] Yet the two poems entitled 'letter' that remain show that not even Byrom's choice of titles was always consistent. 'On the Same Subject, in a Letter to Mr. Ponthieu' is a disquisition, as the cognate title shows ('On the Disposition of Mind Requisite for the Right Use and Understanding of the Holy Scriptures'); and so is 'Enthusiasm; A Poetical Essay. In a Letter to a Friend in Town', the word 'Essay' in its title indicating its actual nature.[20]

Unlike Wesley and Byrom, most poets of the period did little to observe consistent distinctions between the titles 'letter' and 'epistle'. Some used the term 'letter' for serious verse, among them Joseph Addison (*A Letter from Italy, to the Right Honourable Charles Lord Halifax*), Laurence Eusden (*A Letter to Mr. Addison, on the King's Accession to the Throne*), and William Congreve (*A Letter from Mr. Congreve to the Right Honourable the Lord Viscount Cobham*).[21] In using the more everyday term, such writers probably meant to convey a greater degree of familiarity with their addressees than its formal equivalent tends to carry. But the Horatian type is inherently familiar, and many writers also used the word 'epistle' rather than 'letter' for familiar or humorous verse. In doing so, they sometimes followed such conventions of normal correspondence as salutations, valedictions, and details of place and date; and, in the humorous examples, use of the word 'epistle' in the title is often tongue-in-cheek. It follows that the most to be said of eighteenth-century usage in this respect is that choice of the word 'letter' rather than 'epistle' in the title of a poem may connote actual communication, and also greater informality, but that there are far too many exceptions to make this a rule. Conversely, the word 'epistle' may connote a more formal poem that is further from genuine correspondence – or it may not.

Nevertheless, although titles can identify types of epistolary verse no more reliably than examples of such verse themselves, the distinction between verse letter and verse epistle is simple and, for critical purposes, useful. The distinction may be extended by ranging epistolary verse on a spectrum extending from the actual letter written in verse – an example is considered later in this chapter – to the essay-epistle or complimentary epistle. Poems bearing the most explicit markers of real correspondence would come at one end of the spectrum; those that bear the least explicit markers, or, in extreme cases, none at all, would come at the other. 'Verse letter' reflects the greater closeness of the former to genuine written messages, while 'verse epistle' helps reflect the derivation of essay-epistle and heroic epistle directly from Horace and Ovid.

It is the distinction between Horatian and Ovidian epistles that has done most to influence the verse epistle – and also discussion about it. As Karina Williamson points out, Ambrose Philips set the pattern in 1714 with a *Spectator* paper on what he called 'the *Epistolary* way of writing in verse'.[22] This, he claimed, was 'a *Species* of Poetry by it self' that had not 'so much as been hinted at in any of the Arts of Poetry' he had met (p. 112). He went on to distinguish between 'Love-Letters, Letters of Friendship, and Letters upon mournful Occasions', and, on the other hand, 'such Epistles in Verse, as may properly be called Familiar, Critical, and Moral; to which may be added Letters of Mirth and Humour'. He added: '*Ovid* for the first, and *Horace* for the latter, are the best Originals we have left.' Whether or not, as he claimed, Philips's was the first printed discussion in English of the epistle as a literary form,[23] it was a roughly accurate account of it to date. Ovid's *Heroides* had been printed in 1680 in translations by John Dryden and others that remained popular for over a century; and, nearly a century earlier, Michael Drayton's *Englands Heroicall Epistles* (1597) had given it a distinctively British turn that also proved influential. Going back almost as far as Drayton, Ben Jonson and John Donne had produced verse letters modelled on Horace's, and the form had developed further during the seventeenth century in the work not only of Dryden but of Alexander Brome, Charles Cotton, Sir George Etherege and others.

Printed at the time it was, and in a collection continually reprinted and read through the period, Philips's discussion is very likely to have guided thinking about the verse epistle and practice in it. An example from later in the century is one of the chapters in *The Art of Poetry on a New Plan*, printed by John Newbery in 1762 but probably a revision, perhaps by

Goldsmith, of a manual dating from the 1740s.[24] This is of special interest because the chapter on the epistle is new. As it does not appear in the earlier version, it confirms the status that the form had achieved. It also strikes a different note from the *Spectator* paper. Whereas, half a century earlier, Philips had declared that key qualities for epistolary verse are 'a good Fund of strong Masculine Sense', along with 'a thorough Knowledge of Mankind, together with an Insight into the Business, and the prevailing Humours of the Age' (p. 113), Newbery's handbook, reflecting a different cultural moment, gave greater weight to civility: 'the poet is still to consider that the true character of the Epistle is ease and elegance; nothing therefore should be forced or unnatural, laboured, or affected, but every part of the composition breathe an easy, polite and unconstrained freedom' (p. 116). This emphasis left no room for the heroic epistle, which the handbook wholly ignores. The writer goes on to declare that the form 'is suitable to every subject; for as the Epistle takes place of discourse, and is intended as a sort of distant conversation, all the affairs of life and researches into nature may be introduced'.

As with the other chapters, and in keeping with the aim to instruct rather 'by example and practice, than by precept' (p. 117), such remarks preface several examples. These consist of five complete poems, starting with two examples of a type that Roger Lonsdale has called 'the verse letter from abroad',[25] Addison's 'Letter from Italy' and George, Baron Lyttelton's 'Epistle to Mr. Pope, from a Young Gentleman at Rome', but ending with an example of the more familiar type of epistle, Pope's 'Epistle to Miss Blount, on her Leaving the Town, after the Coronation'.[26] The fourth poem, Philips's 'To the Earl of Dorset. Copenhagen, March 9, 1709', is a further verse letter from abroad.[27] It not only shows that Philips could practise what he was later to preach, but also illustrates a new type of epistle that developed in the eighteenth century and is, as the handbook observes, 'entirely descriptive' (p. 125). These four poems all conform to the writer's definition of the verse letter as 'a sort of distant conversation', but the remaining example, the third of the five, does not. This is Pope's 'To Mr. Addison, Occasioned by his Dialogues on Medals', one of those poems that scarcely seem epistolary at all, because it bears no indication that it was written at a distance as part of a correspondence. All the same, Pope had included it as 'Epistle III' in the 1735 edition of his *Works*,[28] and this, as well as its inclusion in the handbook, is further evidence of the wide definition that eighteenth-century writers gave to the form.

With its emphasis on 'ease and elegance', Newbery's handbook omits not only the Ovidian epistle but also the humorous variant derived from Horace. Writing a generation earlier, John Bancks had taken a more eclectic view. In the Preface to his *Miscellaneous Works, in Verse and Prose*, he distinguishes between 'the several Species of Poetry and Prose' of which they consist, disarmingly explaining that he has not had time to arrange them accordingly.[29] Bancks divides his poems into 'Odes, Songs, Stanzas, Ballads, Tales, Fables, Epistles, Occasional Verses, Epigrams, and Inscriptions' (p. iii), and discusses each in turn. His main point about the epistle is its variety:

> the Word Epistle has a very extensive Signification. There is no Subject, no Stile or Manner whatever, but may be proper to Pieces with this Title. Horace, Boileau, and Mr. Pope, have given us moral and satirical Epistles in great Number. Ovid and Old Drayton have written Epistles, under feign'd Names, in the amorous Way; and they have had many Imitators in their respective Languages. (p. xv)

In considering the familiar epistle he went even further:

> there may be a thousand Occasions given us of writing to our Friends, and every Occasion may make some Variation in the epistolary Character. Most of the Poems that come out on public Occurrences, or on Matters of Condoleance and Congratulation, are address'd to particular Persons. And do they not, on that very Account, become a Sort of Epistles? Even Prologues and Epilogues, by the same Rule, are they not a Species of Epistle address'd to the whole Town? (p. xvi)

Bancks's Preface is to a large extent an attempt to explain and justify a decidedly heterogeneous collection. For this reason he had a vested interest in offering so promiscuous a definition of the epistle – the familiar form of which, I shall argue in Chapter 2, he was able to exploit cleverly. His remarks show again how loosely epistolary verse could be defined in the period. They are interesting because they also reflect a sporadically developing tendency to arrange collections of verse by type.

Bancks refers to that tendency two pages later when, further defending the miscellaneous nature of his collection, he points out that 'we find in most of our modern Poets, who have ranged their Works into Books, that they have their *Sylvae, Miscellanea, Poesies diverses*, as well as their Odes, Satires, Epistles, Elegies, and Epigrams' (p. xviii). The practice of arranging collections by genre stems from editions of classical authors. It was followed by Jonson in his Folio edition of 1616, which includes, as well as plays, his *Epigrams* and the various types of poem that make up *The Forest*.[30] However, although Jonson clearly ordered the 15 poems of

The Forest with care, gathering songs separately from the two epistles, and although *Underwoods*, printed after his death, also shows what George Parfitt calls 'obvious signs of purposive grouping',[31] he did not go so far as to set out his work according to the traditional genres named by Bancks. One of the earliest vernacular collections arranged explicitly according to types of poem was John Gay's *Poems on Several Occasions* of 1720. This has in its first volume a georgic, a mock-epic, a pastoral, an urban eclogue and a farce; and, in its second, separately titled sections for epistles, tales, eclogues, miscellanies, and a pastoral tragedy.[32] If it was Gay's example that Allan Ramsay followed in the first volume of his *Poems* in the following year, he improved on it by providing an Index classifying the contents under the headings 'Serious, Comick, Satyrick, Pastoral, Lyrick, Epistolary, and Epigrammatick'.[33] As with Jonson over a century before, Ramsay's motive was probably in part to stake a claim to classic status – especially important to a poet determined to assert Scottish national identity and the rights of his own language alongside standard English.[34] At the same time, the fact that he chose the epistle as one of his seven categories both underlines the importance it was acquiring culturally and provides clues about how the form was understood in the period. Although he did not classify the poems of his second volume, simply listing them in the table of contents in order of their appearance,[35] later poets, and also editors, followed the precedent he had set in 1721. The editors included George Chalmers, who, collecting Ramsay's poems in 1800, extended his 1721 categories to them all.[36]

But Alexander Pope is the best known example of a poet who arranged his works according to the traditional genres. The first volume of his *Works* (1717) begins with his *Pastorals* and proceeds through *Windsor Forest* (representing the related genre of georgic), *An Essay on Criticism, The Rape of the Lock* and *The Temple of Fame* to 'Translations' and finally 'Miscellanies' (under which category are grouped 'Eloisa to Abelard' and three other epistles).[37] The second volume (1735), subtitled *Containing his Epistles and Satires*, begins with the four epistles of *An Essay on Man*, and follows them with four 'Ethic Epistles' (later to be known as 'Moral Essays') and seven further 'Epistles [. . .] to Several Persons'.[38] Warburton's edition of 1751 retains much the same groupings, though it refines upon them, eliminating the category of 'Miscellanies'.[39] Unlike Ramsay's, the example proved influential. First, in 1756 the Glasgow booksellers Robert and Andrew Foulis brought out a two-volume edition of Dryden's poems, dividing them into 'Poems on Several Occasions' in the first volume and part of the second, followed by 'Epistles', 'Prologues and Epilogues', 'Elegies and Epitaphs', and

'Songs'.[40] As Paul Hammond has pointed out, during Dryden's lifetime there had been 'no systematic attempt to keep his works in print, or to assemble a clearly defined *oeuvre* under his own name'.[41] After his death this certainly applied to his verse, for, while the plays had been collected in two volumes in 1701, and in six volumes edited by Congreve in 1717,[42] the poems had taken second place. The Foulis edition is therefore significant, not least because arranging most of Dryden's poems by genre was implicitly to affirm his classic status. Soon afterwards the Tonson house followed suit, printing a four-volume edition of Dryden's *Miscellaneous Works* in 1760.[43] Without using the Foulis subtitle 'Poems on Several Occasions', this placed in the first volume and part of the second what could be understood as miscellaneous verse, from 'Upon the Death of Lord Hastings' to *Mac Flecknoe*, but arranged most of the poems in the second volume under the headings of 'Epistles'; 'Elegies and Epitaphs'; 'Songs, Odes, and a Masque'; 'Prologues and Epilogues'; and 'Translations'. The remaining two volumes contain Dryden's 'Tales from Chaucer' and further translations.

For the purposes of the current discussion, however, John Bell's multi-volume edition *The Poets of Great Britain* was the most critical venture.[44] For it was this edition that, as Thomas F. Bonnell has pointed out, not only published a canon of English verse but also ordered all the poems it included by genre. Staking a claim against the rival collection, *The Works of the English Poets*, to which Samuel Johnson contributed the biographical essays later to be known as *Lives of the Poets*, Bell 'deplored the printing of poems "without any order or method observed in arranging the different pieces, epistles, tales, ballads, odes, epigrams, &c. being indiscriminately jumbled together, circumstances at the same time inconvenient to the reader of taste and judgement"'. Instead, he announced that the poems in his edition would be 'classed and arranged according to their several kinds; so that the whole of the same species of writing falls under the reader's eye in one and the same department of the book only'.[45] To cite a few examples, the first volume devoted to the verse of Matthew Prior, published early in the series in 1777, is divided into 'Odes', 'Songs and Ballads', 'Tales', 'Prologues and Epilogues', and the second into 'Epistles', 'Hymns', 'Epigrams', and 'Miscellaneous Poems'; while the third has two long poems, 'Solomon on the Vanity of the World' and 'Alma; or, the Progress of the Mind', and two shorter ones, favourites among readers, 'The Nut-Brown Maid' and 'Henry and Emma'.[46] Among poets represented by a single volume, that allotted to Sir John Denham is divided into 'Miscellanies', 'Epistles', 'Songs', and 'Translations, &c.'; that to John Pomfret into 'Miscellanies', 'Pindaric Essays', and 'Epistles';

and that to George, Baron Lyttelton, into 'Miscellanies', Epistles', 'Songs', 'Epitaphs', 'Inscriptions', and 'Imitations'.[47]

Like that of his Glasgow colleagues twenty-odd years earlier, Bell's example proved influential. Various examples could be cited, but an interesting early one is the six-volume anthology entitled *Choice of the Best Poetical Pieces of the Most Eminent English Poets*, published in Vienna by Joseph Retzer, which divides its contents into 'Odes', 'Songs', 'Epistles', 'Elegies', 'Pastorals', 'Tales', 'Fables', 'Epigrams and Epitaphs', and, of course, 'Miscellanies'.[48] Similarly, the volume allotted to Congreve in Charles Cooke's pocket edition of select British poets arranges his work into 'Epistles', 'Irregular Odes', 'Pindaric Odes', 'Pastorals', 'Elegies', 'Prologues and Epilogues', and 'Miscellanies';[49] while, as an example of a poet collecting his work for the first time, Bryan Waller grouped his *Poems on Several Occasions* of 1796 into 'Epistles', 'Imitations &c.', 'Elegies, Epitaphs, & Inscriptions', 'Sonnets', 'Epigrams', 'Descriptive Poems', 'Sacred Poems', and, once more, 'Miscellaneous Poetry'.[50] These samples illustrate the centrality of the epistle in verse collections of the period, while also providing evidence of the kinds of poems that, not styled as epistles by their titles, could nevertheless be represented as such. For instance, John Cunningham's 'To a Young Widow', which might be better classed as an amatory ode, is entitled 'Epistle to a Young Widow' in Retzer's collection, the probable source for which is Bell's edition, where it bears its original title but is indexed under 'Epistles';[51] and Cooke's edition of Congreve places 'To Mr. Dryden, on his Translation of Persius' under 'Epistles', although, as a poem first published with the work it praises, it would have been more accurate to have classed it as commendatory.[52] In this respect Cooke's compiler was in good company, for most of the poems by Dryden classed as epistles fall into the same category, a fact with important implications that I will consider below.

But, for the verse epistle, including the question of how to define it, the single most important collection is another one published by Bell. The initial seven volumes of his *Classical Arrangement of Fugitive Poetry* are an enterprising attempt at a partial anthology of the form. First issued in 1789, they were followed over the next eight years by a further eleven volumes containing elegies, monodies, imitations of Spenser and Milton, and odes.[53] Bell's aim was to supplement his *Poets of Great Britain* with a collection of poems by authors whose work was not thought substantial or extensive enough to be included in it. It is for this reason that, as an anthology of the verse epistle, the seven volumes are incomplete, for they exclude standard authors such as Pope and Prior who had appeared in the larger collection. Nevertheless, the *Classical Arrangement* has much to contribute to understanding of the form and how it was seen in the period. Not only are the various kinds of 'fugitive poetry' arranged in different volumes or parts of volumes, following the practice introduced by *Poets of Great Britain*, but, extending it further, the first seven volumes, containing a total of 180 verse epistles, arrange them too by genre. Bell honours the distinction between Horatian variants, as well as between the Horatian and the Ovidian form, by devoting each volume to a different type of epistle, according to the following titles: Ethic; Familiar and Humorous; Critical and Didactic; Descriptive and Narrative; Satirical and Preceptive; Panegyrical and Gallant; Heroic and Amatory. The first five volumes and part of the sixth represent variants of the Horatian epistle, especially the essay-epistle and the familiar verse letter; the seventh represents the Ovidian epistle; while Volume VI also includes poems that seem more closely related to the ode than to the epistle.

Bell's collection is significant for several reasons. First, it was produced at the point when the verse epistle had reached the point of its greatest popularity and was already in decline. Second, because it contains little verse by canonical writers, it better represents what might be seen as standard verse practices of the period. Third, by the phrase 'classical arrangement' in his title, Bell meant poems arranged by classes (*OED* sense 8, 'Of or belonging to a class'). This was especially apt for the inherently miscellaneous form of the verse epistle, and it enabled his anthology not only to reflect the established distinction between Horatian and Ovidian epistles, but also to represent and categorize the different variants of the Horatian type that had developed, some during the eighteenth century. Fourth, the anthology demonstrates some of the difficulties that an attempt to define and classify the form has to face. In these respects it is especially useful, even though, unlike Newbery's book or Philips's essay, it offers no discussion.

Of the 180 poems contained in the anthology, 21 are not attributed. The remainder are assigned to a total of 86 named authors, though these include some false and dubious attributions.[54] Making no allowance for the latter, among the 86 named authors 48 are represented by one poem and 38 by more than one. Assuming that all the unattributed poems are by different authors, and that none is represented elsewhere in the collection, the number represented by a single poem rises to 69. Only 8 authors, none canonical, are represented by more than 3 poems.[55] The anthology drew heavily on collections that were already in print. No fewer than 71 poems appear in the final edition of the most famous and successful eighteenth-century miscellany, Dodsley's *Collection of Poems by Several Hands*;[56] others probably came from John Nichols's *Select Collection of Poems*; and, as Harold Forster has pointed out, others still from supplements to Dodsley, especially by Francis Fawkes, Moses Mendez and George Pearch.[57] The taste it reflects is strongly metropolitan. Though it represents six Irish writers, it has only one Scot; none of its poems by Irish or Scottish writers gives any hint of nationality; and the Scottish verse epistle, though well established long before Burns, is absent.[58] Confirming one of Roger Lonsdale's findings about eighteenth-century anthologies, it also greatly under-represents verse by women.[59] Though women wrote many epistles in the period, it includes only five that are definitely female-authored; and one of these it attributes to a man.[60]

The attempt to classify the verse epistle undertaken by Bell's compiler provides important evidence for the way in which the form was seen at the period. For this reason, a brief analysis of each volume is necessary. The compiler took from Pope the title he gave to the first volume, 'Ethic Epistles'. As the adjective indicates, this is a discursive type of epistle dealing with questions of morality and behaviour. It is often seen as especially characteristic of the eighteenth century, for example by William C. Dowling;[61] and the series probably begins with it because it sets a suitably serious tone. The volume contains 21 examples, though none by Pope himself because of the limitation to poems not published in standard editions. Among these are the first, Soame Jenyns's 'An Essay on Virtue'; the fifth, John Brown's 'On Honor'; and the twelfth, Robert Craggs Nugent's *An Essay on Happiness* (untitled in Bell).

Two other types of epistle in the collection stem from a related Horatian tradition, the 'Epistles Critical and Didactic' of Volume III, and the 'Epistles Satirical and Preceptive' of Volume V. Volume III has 15 poems, ranging in date from Thomas Parnell's 'On the Different Styles of Poetry', first printed in 1713, to a poem without attribution but by William Combe entitled 'To Sir Joshua Reynolds' (1777).[62] As these two examples show, the subjects include not only literature, as with Horace's *Art of Poetry*, but also painting; other poems address the theatre and acting ('The Stage', attributed to James Webster, and Robert Lloyd's 'The Actor'), and architecture and landscape gardening (John Dalton's 'On Building and Planting'). Volume V has eleven poems, beginning with John Brown's 'An Essay on Satire', and including others following the lead given by Pope for satirical epistles, such as James Bramston's 'The Man of Taste', and Joseph Warton's 'Fashion'. It ends with Benjamin Stillingfleet's 'Essay on Conversation', which inclines more to the preceptive than the satirical.

While the three volumes discussed so far represent variants of the Horatian essay-epistle, two others stem from the other main Horatian form, that of the familiar letter. Opening his collection with the most prestigious type of epistle, the ethic, Bell devoted the second volume to the most popular. Entitled 'Epistles Familiar and Humorous', Volume II contains 35 examples, beginning with 'From Soame Jenyns, Esq. in the Country, to the Lord Lovelace in Town', and ending with Matthew Green's 'The Spleen. To Mr. Cuthbert Jackson'. In these the note of personal address is much stronger than in most others in the collection, as befits their more informal subject matter and tone. Several, like the one by Soame Jenyns that opens the volume, take up the stock Horatian contrast between country and city; while two follow another Horatian variant, that of the invitation: indeed, a note points out that Christopher Pitt's 'To the Honourable George Doddington' 'was written in allusion to the 5th Epistle of the First Book of Horace' (II, 167), the much-imitated dinner invitation to Torquatus.

Most of the 15 poems in Volume IV, 'Epistles Descriptive and Narrative', also stem from the Horatian familiar letter. Some are narrative in that they recount journeys, such as John Whaley's 'To a Friend, [. . .] Recapitulating the Particulars of a Journey to Houghton', or Sneyd Davies's 'Describing a Voyage to Tintern-Abbey, in Monmouthshire'; while others, such as William Julius Mickle's *Almada Hill* (rendered as 'Written from Lisbon'), or Goldsmith's 'The Traveller', are further examples of Lonsdale's 'verse letter from abroad'. The best example of a descriptive epistle is Gilbert White's 'The Naturalist's Summer Evening Walk', a reminder that *The Natural History of Selborne* was written in the form of letters;[63] but the volume also has room for industrial subject-matter with Thomas Yalden's 'To Sir Humphry Mackworth, on the Mines, Late of Sir Carbery Price', and John Dalton's 'Addressed to Two Ladies, at their Return from Viewing the Mines Near Whitehaven'.

Since the Horatian epistle was such a protean form, and since it was so popular in the eighteenth century, it is not surprising that it and its derivatives dominate Bell's collection. As mentioned earlier, however, just as Bell opened the series with the classic kind of Horatian epistle, he closed it with a volume devoted to the alternative tradition deriving from Ovid. By the later eighteenth century this had also developed several variants, and the volume is arranged accordingly. The first six follow the tradition established by Drayton in taking their subjects from English history; then there are seven motivated by classical and other literature: four by Lord Hervey, one without attribution but by Edward Lovibond, and the two most famous responses to Pope's 'Eloisa to Abelard' – which, like nearly all the poems already available in standard editions, is not itself included. The volume ends with adaptations of the form to contemporary material: two poems by William Dodd between an enslaved African Prince and his beloved, and 'The Dying Negro', unattributed but by Thomas Day and John Bicknell.

The 67 poems in Bell's sixth volume, 'Epistles Panegyrical and Gallant', are the most difficult to classify, and also the most difficult to define as epistolary. As the title suggests, some are of the complimentary type especially common earlier in the century, and deriving loosely from those by Horace to a patron. Others are poems of gallantry, and the fact that most of these are at the end of the volume seems intended to link them with the 'Epistles Heroic and Amatory' of Volume VII, though few are genuine love poems. Instead, most of the volume consists of light occasional verse, often addressed to a friend. No fewer than 12 poems are of a type almost peculiar to the period sent with a gift of some kind, such as John Sican's 'To Dean Swift on his Birth-Day, with Pine's Horace Finely Bound', or William Harrison's 'To a Lady, with a Bough of an Orange Tree'.

In representing such a variety of poems, Bell's 'Epistles Panegyrical and Gallant' raise two questions that occur to a lesser extent in all volumes of the collection but the last. The first question is one of classification, and it arises because the Horatian epistle proved such an adaptable and versatile form. For example, several of the epistles collected as 'Critical and Didactic', including William Combe's to Sir Joshua Reynolds, might better be called complimentary poems. An obvious reason for this is that epistles about a particular art most often address one of its practitioners, whom such a poem can hardly avoid praising. Nevertheless, at least two of the poems in the volume – James Dalacourt's 'To James Thomson' and the anonymous 'To the Celebrated Beauties of the British Court' – are much more concerned with praise than with critical principles. Similarly, essay-epistles occur in several volumes. Examples are Abel Evans's 'Vertumnus' and Bainbrigg Buckeredge's 'To Signior Antonio Verrio', both of which raise political questions as well as complimenting their addressees, but which appear as 'Epistles Descriptive and Narrative'; and John Duncombe's 'The Feminead' and Thomas Seward's 'On the Female Right to Literature', which open the 'Epistles Panegyrical and Gallant'.

Bell's 'Epistles Familiar and Humorous' illustrate a further way in which poets had developed the Horatian form. Evolving from the familiar epistle in the later seventeenth century, the humorous type was almost as popular. The link between the two forms is clear from the many poems in which they overlap – for example, in the engaging series of poems from letters addressed by Thomas Lisle from Marseilles, Smyrna and Cairo to his sisters in Hampshire. Others are straightforwardly humorous, as with three poems by Isaac Hawkins Browne. The first is entitled 'Isaac Hawkins Browne to Himself'; the second, 'From Celia to Cloe', plays a variation on the country/city theme ('I rural life enjoy, the town's your taste'); while the third, 'To Corinna, from a Captain in Country Quarters', not only takes up the same theme but turns it to risqué effect as the captain asks his mistress to leave town in order to join him – and also a friend with whom he proposes to share her. All three poems are discussed in detail in Chapter 3.

One explanation for the mixture of poems in some volumes is the sheer variety of epistolary verse. A note to the final poem in Volume III, Joseph Spence's 'To a Swiss Officer. From his Friend at Rome', illustrates the point: 'This Epistle being ethical, critical, and descriptive, the Editor was in some doubt how to dispose of it' (III, 184). But a further, more taxing, problem is what the collection suggests about the definition of the epistle as a form. Those that come closest to actual letters are, of course, familiar epistles, and this is often clear from the way they begin. Anthony Alsop opens his epistle to Sir John Dolben, a doctor of divinity, with the salutation: 'Sir John, or Doctor, choose you whether'; while Francis Fawkes begins his 'Journey to Doncaster', addressed to his wife, 'Dear Anne, / In prose I've wrote you many a journal'. Yet discursive epistles often adopt the same convention, even when they bear the word 'Essay' in their titles. Eighteen of the 21 'Ethic Epistles' specify the addressee in their titles, 12 have titles in the form 'To' the addressee or 'From' the poet, and most salute the addressee in the first line – for example, 'Yes, you condemn those sages too refin'd', 'What? Sir, – a month, and not one line afford!', or 'My Lord, / "What is Nobility?" you wish to know'.[64]

The two poems most surprisingly included in the collection are Samuel Johnson's 'London' and 'The Vanity of Human Wishes'. Indeed, referring to the two, a contemporary reviewer objected: 'we cannot see why they are classed with Epistles'.[65] One possible explanation is that the aim was to fill a volume that contains fewer poems than any other, but this seems unlikely. Instead, though it may appear easy to dismiss the inclusion of two satires as a category error, more is involved. First, in the eighteenth century, satirical epistles are often difficult to distinguish from satires, especially where epistolary format is nominal. An example in the same volume is Thomas Warton's 'Newmarket', which not only bears an epigraph – a common feature of satirical epistles, but hardly of personal letters – but has no named addressee. The compiler of Newbery's *Art of*

Poetry points out the difficulty, explaining: 'Satires either of the *jocose* or *serious* kind, may be written in the epistolary manner, or by way of dialogue. *Horace, Juvenal,* and *Persius,* have given us examples of both. Nay, some of *Horace*'s Satires may, without incongruity, be call'd Epistles, and his Epistles, Satires' (II, 101). Probably for similar reasons the compiler discusses Pope's *Essay on Man* not in his chapter on the epistle but on that on 'Didactic or Preceptive Poetry', though it is written in the form of epistles, and refers to *Epistles to Several Persons* – entitled *Moral Essays* by Warburton – in the same place (I, 158–70). Second, an essay-epistle that is 'didactic or preceptive' may be classified by subject rather than genre. Writing a manual on the art of poetry, Newbery's compiler chose the latter; while Bell's, consulting form as well as subject, divided his examples differently: 'Epistles Critical and Didactic', and 'Epistles Satirical and Preceptive'. The inclusion of Johnson's two satires could therefore be said to reflect the form's heterogeneity: not only are there various kinds of epistle, but of essay-epistle too.

Yet the problem is also part of a larger one. Although the reviewer who questioned the representation of Johnson's two satires as epistles did not challenge any of the other selections, various of Bell's 'Epistles Panegyrical and Gallant' bear little or no relation to actual letters. Examples are Walter Harte's 'To the Prince of Orange' (VI, 24–5), which compliments its addressee on recovering from illness; Elizabeth Carter's 'To a Friend, Occasioned by an Ode Written by Mrs. Cath. Philips' (VI, 50–2), which is more of an ode itself; and the anonymous 'To a Lady, Who Sent Compliments to a Clergyman upon the Ten of Hearts' (VI, 138), a four-line epigram. Like the last example, the complimentary and amatory epistles included in the same volume are often only nominally epistolary. It could be argued that Bell exploited the heterogeneity of the epistle to fill out his seven volumes, yet, with the one exception noted above, I have found no evidence that contemporaries protested. Instead, it is more likely that the idea of the epistle dominated occasional verse of the period, rather as – on a much larger scale – the idea of the novel has tended to eclipse other forms of narrative, even of literature, in our own.

William Dowling argues a wider version of just such a case, calling the eighteenth century 'a literary movement dominated by epistolarity'. He draws attention not only to such obvious examples as Richardson's *Pamela* and *Clarissa,* and Smollett's *Humphry Clinker,* but also to 'the hundreds of minor epistolary novels produced during the period' and, equally, 'the hundreds of works of philosophy, theology, aesthetics, political theory, controversy, conduct and travel whose titles give no hint that they, too, are written in the form of letters or epistles', citing among his examples three works rarely recognized as epistolary, Bolingbroke's *The Idea of a Patriot King*, Goldsmith's *History of England*, and Burke's *Reflections on the Revolution in France*.[66] Of his main subject, the verse epistle, Dowling claims that it emerged 'out of relative literary obscurity to become the dominant poetic mode of its age, giving voice during the period of its formal hegemony to a tremendous range of related moral and imaginative concerns'.[67] Dowling's view requires various qualifications, however. As Karina Williamson has pointed out, it centres 'almost exclusively on letters of the Horatian type', and it largely ignores not only 'the huge number of verse letters by women' but the issue of gender – for example, 'poems in which male writers masquerade as women or female writers masquerade as men'.[68] It may be added that, by confining his attention virtually without exception to what he calls 'literary Augustanism',[69] Dowling also overlooks the work of labouring-class writers, who, as the next chapter will show, produced many epistles; and that he takes for granted the idea of Walpole and his government promulgated by their most famous literary opponents.

These reservations granted, Dowling presents much evidence for the importance of epistolary writing in the period – evidence that expands further when the kinds of verse he omits are added. Though it is not among his aims to identify the material and other conditions that enabled it, these also need recognition. Part of the explanation is the development of postal facilities in the second half of the seventeenth century. For example, summarizing work by Robert Adams Day, James How remarks that 'the key points in the development of fast and efficient postal services were the appointment of a postmaster general by Oliver Cromwell, the establishment of the London Penny Post and the increasing use of stamps'.[70] The Post Office, founded in 1660, How declares, gave 'a legal settlement once and for all to the carriage of private letters by a government body'; and there followed what Williamson calls 'a vast increase in letter-writing of all kinds'.[71] Yet the provision and rapid expansion of postal facilities in the later seventeenth century merely furnished the material conditions for epistolary writing to flourish as it did in the century that followed, aided and abetted by other developments, especially the continuing growth of printing and of the press. The political and ideological changes that accompanied them had at least an equal impact.

Writing on another key eighteenth-century epistolary form, Elizabeth Heckendorn Cook argues that letter-narratives became important at the 'historical moment between manuscript and print, private correspondence and published text', and that they were decisively involved in the creation of 'a *literary* public sphere' that prepared the way for the political public sphere theorized by Jürgen Habermas.[72] Like Dowling's, Cook's argument is limited to only one type of letter form, but it is supported by the massive increase in all kinds of epistolary writing in the period. In the case of the verse epistle, David Fairer makes a point about epistolary writing similar to Cook's and develops it. 'No poetic form', he remarks,

is more obviously 'between manuscript and print' in the ways it entangles private and public, allowing a glimpse of the handwritten letter through the formalities of a printed page. As a sociable communication it is expected to accommodate both wit and politeness – to entertain and surprise without forgetting the presence of an addressee and the decorums that involves.[73]

Fairer here defines the verse epistle as 'between manuscript and print' in its tone and style. Although he qualifies parts of the analysis offered by Habermas, emphasizing that not all communications were 'sociable',[74] his view reinforces Cook's thesis about the role of epistolary narrative in the creation of a public sphere. Such a perspective enables two further propositions, developing both her arguments and his. The first is that the verse epistle, among other epistolary forms, was important to a culture that, empowered by a huge expansion of printed matter, valued public discourse as never before. The second is that the importance of that discourse made it easy to read verse essays as if they were epistles, even when they bore no markers of epistolary form. Similarly, complimentary and amatory verse were also likely to be understood as epistolary because both cultivated the grace, courtesy, and unostentatious wit and learning of civilized discourse at its best. Bell's anthology of the verse epistle is a monument to its prestige, built even as the ideological conditions that had enabled it were dissolving. It is all the more significant in that it shows how far the definition of the form had expanded.

But to try to explain why epistolary discourse was so important in the period does not help in defining the verse epistle – however much it may help clarify why eighteenth-century usage in designating poems as epistolary was so often loose. Instead, it is necessary to develop a more adequate method of classification, based on analysis of the various forms of epistle as they were practised. Work on categorization in cognitive science provides a way of meeting the first of these requirements.

In order to respect eighteenth-century usage and practice, an adequate definition of the verse epistle has to leave room for some of the flexibility with which people treated it in the period. This may be achieved by approaching the issue of classification without assuming that categories are ideal and fixed.

According to the classical view that is still widely accepted, categories are strictly delimited. As a result of research summarized and extended by George Lakoff and various associates, such a view is now untenable. The key reason for this, Lakoff argues, is that 'The classical category has *clear boundaries*, which are defined by *common properties*. Wittgenstein pointed out that a category like *game* does not fit the classical mold, since there are no common properties shared by all games.' Instead, Wittgenstein proposed, there are *'family resemblances'*.[75] The complexity of the research is such that it cannot be described here. However, a concept it has produced that is useful to the present discussion is that of the radial category. This Lakoff defines as a category in which 'there is a central case and conventionalized variations on it which cannot be predicted by general rules' (p. 84). Lakoff's example is the category of mother, in which the central case 'includes a mother who is and always has been female, and who gave birth to the child, supplied her half of the child's genes, nurtured the child, is married to the father, is one generation older than the child, and is the child's legal guardian' (p. 83). Variations that spread out from this core definition are stepmother, foster mother, and surrogate mother. According to Lakoff, who adds other variants too,

> These subcategories of mother are all understood as deviations from the central case. But not all possible variations on the central case exist as categories. There is no category of mothers who are legal guardians but who don't personally supply nurturance, but hire someone else to do it. There is no category of transsexuals who gave birth but have since had a sex-change operation. Moreover, some of the above categories are products of the twentieth century and simply did not exist before [e.g., the surrogate mother]. The point is that the central case does not productively generate all these subcategories. Instead, the subcategories are defined by convention as variations on the central case. There is no general rule for generating kinds of mothers. They are culturally defined and have to be learned. (pp. 83–4)

Such a model is more adequate than the classical theory, which cannot explain how members of a category can vary so widely. This makes it suitable for classifying the peculiarly elastic form of the verse epistle.

In order to begin that task, the form has to be located within what Lakoff calls a taxonomic hierarchy (pp. 46–7). At what is known as the basic level of categorization, the verse epistle is a subordinate member of the category of poetry, the superordinate category for which is literature. This is an important distinction, because it means that a verse epistle is more poem than letter. Conversely, a letter written in verse is a subordinate member of the category of letters, the superordinate category for which is human communications. That there is no category of non-literary letters in verse confirms that the verse epistle belongs more to the domain of poems than of letters. It is also necessary to distinguish between categories in current use and those available from induction. Examples of current categories are the Horatian and the Ovidian epistle. Although these have played so large a role in the tradition of epistolary verse that they cannot be discarded, they cannot describe the form adequately. The most obvious evidence for this is that they represent two different kinds of verse epistle, and there cannot be two central cases. Another means of providing distinctions is therefore needed, and this is where induction is necessary.

The central case in the category of verse epistle may be defined as having the following properties: it is a written communication; it is in a verse form accepted as epistolary; it is addressed from distance; its authorship is single and undifferentiated; and it has a single named addressee. Among these properties, the first is obviously invariable, and the third is also usually constant, as letters are normally motivated by absence. The other three require explanation.

First, while it might seem that a verse epistle could be written in any form whatever, in practice the available forms have been limited by convention. Since the earlier seventeenth century, the most common have been couplets of iambic pentameter or tetrameter, divided, as in a letter, into paragraphs rather than stanzas. In this respect, Ben Jonson's example seems to have been influential, ten of the 13 poems he entitled 'epistle' being in iambic pentameter couplets, and the remaining three in iambic pentameter triplets. Similarly, 18 of the 40 verse letters by John Donne are in iambic pentameter couplets, and another six in iambic pentameter triplets, though some are in stanzaic forms. Perhaps not surprisingly, in light of its greater rigidity and artificiality, the triplet form did not catch on. Of more than 1800 eighteenth-century verse epistles on which I have collected data, only 35 are in irregular forms, but 20 of these are humorous and a further 5 are in the version of French *vers libres* devised by John Gilbert Cooper (iambic tetrameter couplets rhyming irregularly). Seven of the remaining ten poems in non-standard forms use iambic tetrameter or pentameter couplets but also rhyme them irregularly. Further evidence is that the 180 epistolary poems in *Bell's Classical Arrangement*

addressee, which is crucial, most verse epistles are closer to lyric than to narrative, and so are epistolary in different ways from letters in narrative works. In particular, verse form makes a decisive difference. As de Pretis maintains, 'the aim of a verse letter can never be the same as a prose one [. . .]. The choice of different means to convey a message inevitably affects that message.'[87] The same point applies to the differing connotations of specific verse forms, as many examples in this book will show.

It is now possible to set out a taxonomy of the verse epistle, based partly on variations on the central case defined above and partly on the categories used by Bell. Returning to the two basic terms that are in such interesting tension in the *OED* definition of the epistle, the essential distinctions may be clarified by imagining the various types of epistle within a Lakoffian radial pattern. At the centre would be the Horatian familiar epistle, for it contains all the key properties. To repeat these, it is a written communication; it is in a verse form accepted as epistolary; it is addressed from distance; its authorship is single and undifferentiated; and it has a single named addressee. On the periphery would be the most artificial types of epistle, among them complimentary epistles and those essay-epistles that barely refer to an addressee. Such types conform less closely to epistolary form because they bear little resemblance to letters – not least because they imply or overtly address a general readership. Dramatic epistles would occur between centre and periphery, as striking a balance between artifice and the simulation of an actual letter written out of a particular situation. The humorous epistle, which derives from the familiar type, is closer to the centre than the satirical epistle, which derives from verse satire as well as from the essay-epistle. Indeed, some humorous epistles of the period do not appear to have been intended for publication, and so imply a single reader, while satirical epistles almost always address a wider readership, implicitly or explicitly.

Some examples may help flesh out these abstractions. First, among the Harrowby manuscripts at Sandon Hall, Stafford, there is a verse letter sent by Lady Mary Wortley Montagu to Lord John Hervey, probably in October 1734. It was first printed, inaccurately, in the collection of Wortley Montagu's *Works* edited in 1803 by James Dallaway, and it appears not in the modern edition of her poems but of her letters.[88] Second, in Lady Mary Chudleigh's *Poems on Several Occasions* of 1703 there appears a poem entitled 'To Clorissa'.[89] Sarah Prescott remarks that, 'As the title suggests, the poem is framed as an epistle to a female friend',[90] and this is in keeping with Chudleigh's pledge near the end of the poem that she and her addressee will, 'When present, talk the flying Hours away, / When absent, thus, our tender Thoughts convey' (72–3).

Yet in other respects 'To Clorissa' little resembles a letter, even a letter in verse. It has none of the formal properties of correspondence, such as date, address, salutation or valediction, all of which are present or implicit in Wortley Montagu's poem, and its form is that of an irregular ode rather than a verse epistle. Specifically, it is in stanzas of irregular length and rhyme scheme, and line lengths also vary within each stanza: the most frequent is pentameter, but three of the stanzas contain tetrameters and at least one hexameter, and the third contains four trimeters.

'To Clorissa' has four of the five central properties of the verse epistle; the one it lacks is that it is not in a verse form accepted as epistolary. Yet it is clearly epistolary verse, and it might best be classified as an epistolary ode. Chudleigh wrote several similar poems, and, in the same period, Jane Barker also produced two verse epistles in the form of an irregular ode, 'To my Unkind Friend, Little Tom King' and 'A Second Epistle. To my Honoured Friend Mr. E. S.', though most of her other verse letters, including the first one to E. S., are in iambic pentameter couplets.[91] The term I am suggesting seems to have been first used as a title at about the same time, by Thomas Yalden in 'To Mr. Congreve. An Epistolary Ode. Occasioned by his Late Play', first printed in 1693 in *Examen Poeticum*,[92] but it occurs only rarely. Examples are 'An Epistolary Ode to a Young Gentleman, Written in the Late Frost, Translated from the 9th Ode of the 1st Book of Horace' in the *London Magazine* of 1740; Nathaniel Evans's 'Epistolary Ode to a Friend' in his *Poems on Several Occasions* of 1772; and Robert Merry's 'Epistolary Ode. To A . . . . R . . . . . Esq.', in *The Arno Miscellany* of 1784.[93] Significantly, none of these poems is in a verse form recognized as epistolary.[94]

In contrast to Chudleigh's poem, Wortley Montagu's seems an actual letter that happens to be in verse. Though Hervey may have shown it to others, the fact that no copies are known apart from the single one in the Wortley papers suggests that, unlike many verse epistles of the period, it was written primarily, perhaps even exclusively, for him. Its appearance is, instead, that of a private communication. This is an important difference, bearing in mind the distinction set out above from epistles that directly or indirectly address a wider readership. A related difference is that, unlike 'To Clorissa', or even the most apparently personal of Horace's familiar epistles, it addresses no general themes – such as, for example, the attractions of country over city, or advice on how to live.[95] If the term 'verse letter' were not already in general and somewhat promiscuous use, it would be the most logical one for the category to which the poem belongs, which is a sub-type of the familiar epistle. Indeed, the fact noted above that it appears in the modern edition of

Wortley Montagu's letters rather than of her poems suggests that it is less poem than personal letter. A further way to illustrate the differences between a verse epistle and an ode as these forms were understood in the period is to consider examples of two poems that evolved from one form to the other.[96] Perhaps the best known such example is Mark Akenside's *Epistle to Curio*, a satirical attack on William Pulteney, who, though a longstanding adversary of Walpole, not only declined an invitation to form a government when Walpole finally fell but also accepted a peerage. Akenside published his poem in 1744, but later revised it heavily – when exactly is unknown – as 'Ode IX. To Curio. MDCCXLIV', which first appeared in the revised collection of his 'Odes on Several Subjects' in the posthumous edition of his works printed in 1772.[97] The revision has found little favour. Notoriously, Samuel Johnson remarked that Akenside's 'love of lyricks' was such that, 'having written with great vigour and poignancy his *Epistle to Curio*, he transformed it afterwards into an ode disgraceful only to its author'.[98] It is represented as significant, however, by William Dowling, who argues that the rewriting discloses 'an entire set of assumptions about the situation of poetry at midcentury'. According to Dowling, these assumptions involve 'the paradoxical idea of a politics outside history, the Greco-Roman myth of republican freedom as a private source of poetic inspiration ceasing to have any necessary reference to a moral and ideological struggle actually taking place in English society'. The result, Dowling claims, is that the Ode is 'ultimately about the absorption of history into the solitary imagination', in a 'movement toward poetic solipsism'.[99] Such a view is rejected by Dustin Griffin, who cautions: 'we should not read back into [Akenside's] poems of the 1740s and 1750s the impulse to move beyond "history" into "the solitary imagination"'. Part of the evidence for this is the fact that, as Griffin points out, for Akenside 'the ode is by no means always a meditative-rhapsodical exercise in solipsism. It is often a social form – an ode addressed, commonly upon a particular occasion, to a named friend or public figure.'[100] Such a use of the form follows the example of Horace, many of whose odes could be described in the same way. However, as Griffin's observation seems to present special difficulties for anyone trying to distinguish between ode and epistle, it is important to examine the differences between original poem and revision.

Akenside's alterations are drastic. Most strikingly, as Robin Dix points out, 'the meter has been changed, and the number of lines reduced from 348 to 160'.[101] To take these points separately, *Epistle to Curio* is in iambic pentameter couplets: not only the standard form of the period for verse satire, but also the most common form for the verse epistle. Instead, the Ode to Curio is in ten-line stanzas, each consisting of nine lines of iambic pentameter culminating in a hexameter, and with the quite elaborate rhyme scheme of two quatrains, one rhyming alternately, the other in enclosed form, enveloping a couplet (*ababccdeed*). Although the verbal changes are also extensive, the ode largely follows the same course as the epistle, with some passages reduced more heavily than others, a few cut completely, some lines towards the end repositioned, and a quite different conclusion. Akenside retained 21 lines without modification in wording from the epistle, and a further 14 lines with the alteration of a single word.[102] Other key changes are the shift from Roman to British names, including the addition of three traditional British heroes (65–7); the appeal to the nation, not to God, at the end of the poem; and not only a lesser role for the poet within the poem but also a different construction of the addressee (though he is still called 'Curio'). The substitution of British names, and the closing appeal to the nation, support Griffin's rebuttal of Dowling's contention that the ode returns to the classical past in an act of imaginative abstraction that removes it from its actual political and ideological context. On the contrary, Akenside appealed to his readers through references to a specifically British tradition of liberty, addressing them as 'sons of Alfred' (158) at the end.

More relevant to the generic differences between epistle and ode are the changes to the figure of poet and of addressee. While, in the epistle, Akenside plays the role of 'impartial Bard' (24) and 'Judge of Truth' (33), emphasizing his devotion to freedom 'from Reason's earliest Hour' (184), and declaring himself at the end of the poem as 'fated to the studious Shade' (337), in the ode he has a less prominent position. Although he still refers to himself in the first person singular, he does so only twice and with less particularity. Similarly, the ode greatly reduces those parts of the epistle that characterize his addressee, omitting the phrase 'Idiot's price' (80) for Pulteney's acceptance of a peerage, and curtailing a long passage later in the poem in which the appeal is especially *ad hominem*, as when the poet suggests that Pulteney ask himself 'if all be well within' (228). Yet, despite the implication in Johnson's remark that, compared with the epistle, the ode lacks 'vigour and poignancy', it is surprisingly hard-hitting. Among the lines that Akenside retained are some of the most forceful in the original poem: for example, 'To beg the infamy he did not earn' (29/70), 'Is this the man in freedom's cause approv'd? / The man so great, so honour'd, so belov'd?' (75–76/161–2), or 'O lost alike to action and repose!' (81/167).[103] Therefore, though the changes in the presentation of poet and addressee might seem to support Dowling's argument that the ode is more abstract than the epistle, other textual evidence discounts it. Instead, they are to be explained by the different formal requirements of epistle and ode respectively. Because the epistle stems from the personal letter, it usually personalizes writer and addressee more than an ode, which stems from a convention of song. Akenside was very much of his period in the importance he attached to such conventions. Equally important is verse form. As I have already argued, couplets of iambic pentameter or, less often, tetrameter are the most common form for verse epistles in the eighteenth century, whereas odes are most often stanzaic. An example of standard practice is that of Robert Craggs Nugent's *Odes and Epistles* of 1739, in which the five odes are in stanzas and both epistles are in iambic pentameter couplets.[104] Akenside's usage is similar, for, of the 36 odes credited to him, only two are in couplets, a suitably sprightly 'Hymn to Cheerfulness', and 'The Remonstrance of Shakespeare', the verse form of which is explained by the fact that it is, as the title goes on to indicate, 'Supposed To Have Been Spoken at the Theatre Royal' (308). The stanza forms he used for his other odes range in complexity from Pindaric to quatrains of iambic tetrameter. He was especially fond of various kinds of dixaines, writing two further odes in the same form as that of the ode to Curio – both, significantly, also political poems.[105] In rewriting his epistle to Curio as an ode, Akenside was not, therefore, blunting the impact of his attack on Pulteney or his support for the principle of liberty, especially British liberty, behind it. As Griffin has argued, neither was he retreating into lyrical abstraction. The shift is instead significant as evidence of a developing cultural preference for the ode rather than the epistle, reflected in the work of Gray, the Wartons and many others. That preference involved a move towards greater formality, often on broadly neoclassical lines. In the case of the ode to Curio, it also led to Akenside condensing, arguably for the better, a poem that at times slips into all but incoherent syntax in its passion to denounce and condemn.

A second but very different example is Coleridge's reconstruction as 'Dejection: An Ode' of a verse letter to Sara Hutchinson.[106] Instead of bringing out how the forms of the verse epistle and ode differed in poetic practice, as with Akenside's poems to Curio, this revision dramatically shows how quickly such distinctions could dissolve in the Romantic period. The issues in Coleridge's case are quite other. First, the original letter is a deeply private poem. It was never intended for publication, and, though it is known to have been read, probably with some misgivings on Coleridge's part, to William and Dorothy Wordsworth, there is no evidence that it was ever sent to its addressee.[107] Second, although the revision entailed cuts of a similar scale to those that Akenside made in adapting his *Epistle to Curio* as an ode – the verse letter has 340 lines, 'Dejection: An Ode' 139 – there is no appreciable change in verse form. Both poems are, formally speaking, irregular odes; and one of the surviving manuscripts of the verse letter is divided into numbered sections, much as the ode is divided into numbered stanzas. According to J. C. C. Mays, Coleridge's 'purpose was to convert a gesture of love and an appeal for sympathy into a poem about the imagination';[108] it was also to produce a poem that, unlike the verse letter, might be published. Unlike Akenside, who worked chiefly by condensing his original poem, Coleridge adapted his by deleting the most private sections. Comparing the two processes of reconstruction indicates that for Coleridge, as for most other British Romantic poets, the conventions of the verse epistle as it had been practised during the eighteenth century no longer carried any weight. 'A Letter to ——' is, in its content as well as its form, an ode, not a verse epistle. Indeed, although Coleridge wrote two poems that he entitled 'epistle' when they were first published, he retitled both, one as 'Ode', the other as 'Lines',[109] and the only other poems by him that he called 'letter' are *jeux d'esprit* not intended for publication.[110]

The kind of ode that is addressed to a named individual is, then, one of the forms that have affinities with the verse epistle, and the epistolary ode is best characterized as marginally epistolary. Another type of poem on the margins of the form is the complimentary epistle. This poses problems of definition because it stems both from the Horatian familiar letter and also from commendatory verse. According to Franklin B. Williams, Jr., commendatory poems 'are an innovation of the Renaissance humanists', appearing as testimonials among the opening pages of many early modern books.[111] Examples in English date from the late fifteenth century, as Williams shows in a table summarizing the number of books recorded with them from 1478 to 1640. He estimates that 'the vogue reached its peak about 1650', waning in the late Restoration until 'in the eighteenth century the practice lapsed into unimportance' (p. 3). This decline he illustrates with two examples: 'During a writing life of forty years Jonson contributed verses to thirty books, whereas over a span of fifty years Dryden commended fourteen.' He also notes that, from 1560 to 1640, 'the most striking feature of the statistics of literary patronage and commendatory verses is the increasing preponderance of literary works' (p. 4).

Commendatory poems cannot be classed as epistles, though dedications may be so classed when they are in verse form. Instead, they are a form of panegyric. Yet there is a family relationship between many commendatory poems and verse epistles in that, like numerous odes, they belong to the superordinate category of poems addressed by one person to another.[112] In the later Restoration, commendatory verse is superseded by the complimentary epistle. This, too, originated in the Renaissance and it also has its roots in patronage, examples appearing in the verse of Donne and Jonson among others.[113] Dryden had a special influence on its later development, for his move away from commendatory verse, identified by Williams, is at the same time a move towards the complimentary epistle.

The first three commendatory poems published by Dryden are quite conventional. Their imagery and diction place them close to panegyric, as when Dryden addresses John Hoddesdon as 'Young eaglet' (11) and ends the poem by describing his friend's verse as 'pure gold' in comparison to his own 'adult'rate copper' (24–5); or when he assures Walter Charleton: 'Such is the healing virtue of your pen, / To perfect cures on books, as well as men' (41–2).[114] Dryden published several poems of this type, the last clear example being 'To my Friend Mr J. Northleigh, Author of *The Parallel*, on his *Triumph of the British Monarchy*', the 14 lines of which compare its addressee with Joseph, Solomon and Daniel (II, 429–30). These poems may be compared to others not printed as prefatory matter, such as 'To my Lord Chancellor. Presented on New Year's Day' (I, 62–9), 'To the Lady Castlemaine' (I, 80–3), and 'Prologue to the Duchess. On her Return from Scotland' (II, 35–7).

But later in his career Dryden started writing a different kind of poem, recalling and probably drawing on Horace in its wit, informality and avoidance of fulsome praise. 'To Mr. Lee, on his *Alexander*' (I, 341–3), first printed in 1677, marks a shift towards a more familiar style, though the praise is still extravagant. Much closer to the Horatian familiar epistle, however, are 'To Mr Southerne. On his Comedy called *The Wives' Excuse*' (III, 268–70), and, especially, 'To my Dear Friend Mr Congreve. On his Comedy Called *The Double-Dealer*' (IV, 328–35), first printed in 1692 and 1693 respectively. 'To my Dear Friend Mr Congreve' not only opens in a colloquial manner – 'Well then, the promised hour is come at last' – but sounds a genuinely personal note when Dryden refers to himself as 'worn with cares and age' (66), and reaches beyond its occasion to a general theme: a survey of English theatre from Shakespeare to the present. These are qualities associated more with the Horatian epistle than with conventional commendatory verse, and they may also be seen in 'To Sir Godfrey Kneller' (IV, 342–55) and 'To my Friend, the Author [Peter Motteux]' (V, 22–5), first printed respectively in 1694 and 1698. Indeed, 'To Sir Godfrey Kneller' is another poem not written to preface a literary collection but, rather, occasional; and, as Paul Hammond and David

Hopkins point out, it is generically diverse, combining 'elements of the verse-epistle, panegyric, and "progress piece"' (IV, 343).

The fact that, like Donne and Jonson, Dryden blended elements of the Horatian verse epistle into poems of commendation and compliment helps explain why they were seen in the later eighteenth century as epistolary. For example, the 1756 edition of Dryden's *Original Verse* by the Foulis brothers, mentioned above, lists 13 titles under 'Epistles' in its table of contents, nine of which were first printed as commendatory verses; of the remaining four, one is the verse letter to Etherege that Dryden ghostwrote for the Earl of Middleton, and another the poem to Kneller, while another is a presentation piece, and the last not an epistle at all but a prologue.[115] The heading not only reflects the loose definition given to epistolary form in the eighteenth century, and the prestige the form had gained. It also points to recognition of a distinct if hardly new sub-type of epistle, not necessarily written to preface a work by someone else, that is best termed complimentary. While discussion of this type must wait for a later chapter, it is important to register it here because complimentary epistles constitute one of the main kinds of verse that complicate definition of the epistle form. For the reasons just given, it is among the kinds classified as marginally epistolary in the following chapter, which attempts to estimate the frequency of epistolary verse in the period.

To sum up, then, I suggest that there are six basic types of verse epistle: familiar, humorous, dramatic, discursive (the kind I am calling the essay-epistle), satirical, and complimentary. I further suggest that some of these basic types have sub-types, and also that the borders between the various kinds are far from impermeable, resulting in assorted hybrids. Examples of sub-types are the literal verse letter, such as Wortley Montagu's to Lord Hervey, and the invitation, both of which are forms of familiar epistle; the Ovidian or heroic epistle, which is the most important version of the dramatic type; and the various sorts of essay-epistle, which may be distinguished, as they are in *Bell's Classical Arrangement*, according to their subject-matter. Examples of hybrids are the humorous epistle when it is in dramatic form, and the epistle from abroad, which usually draws on more than one type of epistolary form. Verse that is marginally epistolary is some kind of generic compound – for example, between epistle and ode, epistle and satire, or, in the case of complimentary epistles, epistle and panegyric. Alternatively, it may present in verse form an epistolary or quasi-epistolary type of text such as a petition. The rest of this book is organized on the basis of the six main types, taking the heroic epistle as the prime form of the dramatic. But first there is another general chapter, considering the frequency of epistolary verse in the period.

2
Frequency

Although it is generally accepted that the verse epistle was a popular form in the eighteenth century, precise evidence to confirm such an impression is surprisingly sparse. Jay Arnold Levine cites two pointers: Raymond D. Havens's remark that 'Dryden's *Miscellany* (1684–1709) contains but ten verse epistles, while Dodsley's (1748–58) offers forty-five specimens'; and a claim deriving from statistics in a study by Calvin D. Yost that the epistolary content of the *Gentleman's Magazine* declined 'from a peak of thirty-nine in 1731–40 (the period of Pope's activity) to a low of eleven in 1771–80'.[1] This chapter begins by reconsidering the evidence presented by Havens for the two miscellanies and for the *Gentleman's Magazine* by Yost. It then analyses evidence from one printed and one online source in order to estimate approximately what proportion of verse printed in the eighteenth century was epistolary; and it closes with a series of case studies. These analyse the contents of Roger Lonsdale's two anthologies of eighteenth-century verse, along with those of various collections from the period, mostly single-authored and produced by writers of both sexes and various social ranks. The findings demonstrate not only the popularity of epistolary verse in the period but also its special attractiveness for marginal writers; and they outline its growth and decline.

The study by Havens cited by Levine compares the two best-known eighteenth-century collections of verse as a way of identifying changing patterns of taste. Both collections have complicated publishing histories – a fact that casts further light on the question. The first is usually called 'Dryden's Miscellany', though the extent to which the poet was involved in it, rather than the bookseller Jacob Tonson, remains difficult to determine.[2] It appeared in successive volumes from 1684 until 1716, when it reached what was more or less its final state in the second complete edition of what by 1709 had become six parts of *Miscellany*

Poems. The second, *A Collection of Poems by Several Hands*, though often called 'Dodsley's Miscellany' after its main compiler and publisher, was first published in three volumes in 1748, after which three further volumes were added over a period of ten years until it reached the same total of six. Eight subsequent editions ensued, though none made changes of substance till that of 1782, which added explanatory and biographical notes.[3] Comparing the two collections, Havens remarked that 'in Dryden's anthology [. . .] there are 10 epistles, whereas Dodsley's has 45'.[4] But this considerably underestimates the numbers of epistolary poems in both.

The edition of Dryden's miscellany from which Havens compiled most of his comparative statistics was that of 1727. As he points out, this was a reprint of what he called 'the first collected edition', published in 1716, 'except for some transfers from one volume to another and for a very few omissions and additions'.[5] The 1716 edition is the one I will cite.[6] It comprised the fourth editions of *Miscellany Poems* (first published 1684) and *Sylvae* (first published 1685); the third editions of *Examen Poeticum* (first published 1693) and *The Annual Miscellany* (first published 1694); and the second editions of *Poetical Miscellanies: The Fifth Part* (first published 1704) and *Poetical Miscellanies: The Sixth Part* (first published 1709). Although Havens neither indicates his criteria for identifying epistles nor cites titles, it may be inferred that he only counted poems the titles of which include the words 'epistle' or 'letter' (for details, see Appendix 1, section 1A). But, as mentioned in the previous chapter, titles alone cannot adequately identify epistolary verse. One of the examples apparently not included by Havens is a poem by Etherege to the Earl of Middleton that is obviously an epistle because it appears in a series – indeed, though its title does not say so, it is the antecedent of 'Sir George Etheridge's Second Letter to the Lord Middleton'.[7] Among others apparently not included, one has the subtitle 'In a Letter to Signior Verrio at Hampton-Court', another 'An Epistolary Ode'; while a third is an invitation, in imitation of an epigram by Catullus. Eight further poems in the 1716 edition may also be counted as epistolary (Appendix 1, section 1B). Among these, one is a satirical heroic epistle ('Bajazet to Gloriana'); three are familiar epistles by Charles Hopkins; one is an essay-epistle ('An Account of the Greatest English Poets. To Mr. H. S. April 3, 1694. By Mr. Jo. Addison'); one is an imitation of an epistle by Horace (perhaps excluded by Havens on the incorrect assumption that it is a translation); one a ribald verse missive sent to a man who had remarried; and one a further invitation.[8] All eight have characteristics that identify them as epistolary. In the case of seven, these include salutations or valedictions (three have both, and the imitation begins with a salutation lacking in the original, 'Dear Friend, for surely I may call him so'); the other specifies in its title that it was 'sent by a Friend' to the addressee.[9] Such features distinguish the eight from the various amatory or complimentary but not necessarily epistolary poems in the collection, many of which, like most of the epistolary poems, also have titles in the form 'To' with the names of the writer and addressee.[10] Excluding these, but adding the 12 further examples just described to the 10 counted by Havens, the number of epistolary poems in the 1716 edition of Dryden's miscellany rises to 22. This is without including 7 poems in the tradition mentioned in Chapter 1 of verse letters that accompany a gift (in one case, appropriately, of verse letters),[11] and one humorous petition (Appendix 1, section 1C). Taking such less clearly epistolary poems into account would raise the total to 30.

It is more difficult to work out on what basis Havens arrived at his tally of 45 epistles in Dodsley's *Collection*, although the latter's publication history is less complex than that of Dryden's. The six-volume edition first completed in 1758 contains 23 poems that are clearly epistolary and that include the word 'epistle' in their titles, 4 poems by Lord Hervey under the heading 'Epistles in the Manner of Ovid', and a further 10 that style themselves as letters or as answers to letters (Appendix 1, section 2A). In order to bring the total to 45, 8 may be added on the basis that their form and content identify them as epistles. These include some that begin with salutations, such as John Hoadly's 'To the Rev. Mr. J. Straight, 1731'; other familiar epistles, such as 'Captain Lewis Thomas, of Battereau's Regiment, in the Isle of Skie, to Captain Price, at Fort Augustus'; a humorous epistle, Isaac Hawkins Browne's 'From Cælia to Cloe'; and James Bramston's satirical essay-epistle 'The Man of Taste. Occasion'd by an Epistle of Mr. Pope's on that Subject' (Appendix 1, section 2B). But there are many other poems in Dodsley's *Collection* that are also clearly epistolary, and others still that are arguably so (Appendix 1, section 2C). These I will consider according to the categories set out in Chapter 1.

The largest such group consists of essay-epistles. Of this type there are a further 8 in addition to those already counted on the ground that they define themselves as epistles in their titles. All appear as epistles in *Bell's Classical Arrangement of Fugitive Poetry*; indeed one of them, Soame Jenyns's 'An Essay on Virtue. To the Honourable Philip Yorke, Esq;', has the privilege of beginning the collection. The next most numerous group consists of 7 amatory epistles, composing three discrete exchanges. Three that also appear in Bell are verse pleasantries represented as having passed between Sir Charles Hanbury Williams and 'Mrs. Bindon at Bath'.[12] Two of the others – by Lady Mary Wortley Montagu, though the *Collection* gave her credit for neither – are especially interesting in that they are responses in characters other than her own. Her 'Answer' to James Hammond's 'Elegy to Miss Dashwood' is a cogent exposition of grounds on which a woman might refuse courtship; while 'Sir William Yonge's Answer',[13] written in response to a highly indiscreet epistolary overture by the Countess of Hertford, is a caustic put-down, ending as it does with the words: 'But the fruit that will fall without shaking / Indeed is too mellow for me'. Wortley Montagu's two poems are dramatic epistles because in both she adopts a persona – in one case, that of a man. It is bitterly unjust that one of the very poems to which she had written a reply was attributed to her instead. This poem (the one by the Countess of Hertford) is a love letter, and so in a different way is Hammond's – the word 'elegy' in the title refers to the Ovidian love elegy and probably also to the verse form in which it was written, iambic pentameter couplets equating roughly to the elegiac distich.[14]

A further 17 poems that are clearly epistolary belong to various other categories. Four are of the type accompanying a gift, such as John Sican's 'Verses Sent to Dean Swift on his Birth-day, with Pine's Horace Finely Bound'; three are essentially complimentary, such as George Bubb Dodington's 'To the Right Hon. Sir Robert Walpole' (a poem entitled 'Epistle' on its first publication);[15] three are epistolary odes, such as Richard Owen Cambridge's 'To Mr. Whitehead, on his Being Made Poet Laureat'; two are familiar (Lord Lyttelton's 'To my Lord — in the Year 1730. From Worcestershire', and Soame Jenyns's 'To a Lady in Town, Soon after her Leaving the Country'); a further two are satirical (Joseph Warton's 'Fashion: A Satire', first published as *An Epistolary Satire to a Friend*,[16] and James Bramston's 'The Art of Politicks, in Imitation of Horace's Art of Poetry'); one is an epistle from abroad (Lord Hervey's 'To Mr. Fox, Written at Florence. In Imitation of Horace, Ode IV. Book 2'); one is advisory (Lord Lyttelton's 'Advice to a Lady', answered in a witty manuscript couplet by Wortley Montagu);[17] and the last, Richard Owen Cambridge's 'An Elegy Written in an Empty Assembly-Room', is a parody of parts of Pope's 'Eloisa to Abelard'. Even these do not exhaust the number of poems that could be counted as epistolary, especially four on the ground – admittedly not definitive – that they are included as epistles in *Bell's Classical Arrangement of Fugitive Poetry* (Appendix 1, section 2D). Excluding those, but counting the 17 poems just discussed, the 8 discursive and the 7 amatory epistles, the total number of epistolary poems in the first complete edition of Dodsley's *Collection* rises by 32 to 77; if the further 8 poems are included, the total becomes 85.

On Havens's reckoning of 10 to 45, the relative number of epistles in the two miscellanies is strong evidence for the increasing popularity of the form in the first half of the eighteenth century. The more inclusive estimates given above may seem to dilute that evidence, because they identify a greater proportion of additional poems as epistles in Dryden's collection than in Dodsley's. To repeat, Havens's total of 10 in Dryden's rises to 22, or to 30 if the epistles accompanying gifts and the humorous petition are included; while his total of 45 in Dodsley's rises to 77, or to 85 on a more flexible definition of epistolary verse. On these figures, the proportion of verse epistles in Dodsley's collection increases by 450 per cent over Dryden's according to Havens's estimates; but, with a more inclusive tally, only by 350 per cent on the less and by 283 per cent on the more liberal definition. Yet such statistics can offer only the kind of broad-brush picture at which Havens aimed. If the total numbers of poems in the two collections are taken into account, they produce a more accurate estimate – though the result is a ratio between the relative frequency of epistles in each close to that of 10 to 45 arrived at by Havens.

   Counting the poems in the two collections is not the straightforward task it may seem, because it depends on how a separate poem is defined. The tallies given here reckon each translation as a single poem when it is printed with the original, and also each different translation of the same original; and they include dedicatory poems (for example, the three for *Absalom and Achitophel*); poems with separate titles even when they appear under an umbrella title (for example, the three headed 'The Court-Prospect', the 23 in Walsh's *Letters and Poems, Amorous and Gallant*, the six *Pastorals* by Philips, and the four *Pastorals* by Pope).[18] They do not represent as separate items any poem printed in parts except for the two parts of *Absalom and Achitophel*, which are by different writers. On these assumptions, the total number of separate poems in the 1716 edition Dryden's miscellany is 874. As this number is inflated by the 54 poems, all very short, that appear in the fifth volume as *Verses Written for the Toasting-Glasses of the Kit-Kat Club, in the Year 1703*, it could reasonably be reduced to 821 by counting those as a single item. On the same assumptions, the total number of poems in the 1758 edition of Dodsley's *Collection* is 573. This includes as separate items the four parts of Lyttelton's 'Progress of Love' (by analogy with the *Pastorals* of Philips and Pope); Nugent's 'Introduction' to his 'Ode to Mankind' as well as the ode itself; the six parodies in Isaac Hawkins Browne's 'A Pipe of Tobacco'; the four Parts of William Shenstone's 'Pastoral Ballad'; the eight poems by John Hoadly to accompany Hogarth's *Rake's Progress*; two series of songs by Shenstone; a series of inscriptions by him and another by Mark Akenside; and 32 poems entitled epigrams, including two series, one of translations of Martial.[19] As the epigrams in the two series just named are all very short, they could be considered to inflate the total in the same way as the toasting-glass verses in Dryden's miscellany. Counting each series as a single poem would reduce the total number of separate poems in Dodsley's *Collection* to 547.

Before drawing any inferences from these statistics, it is worth adding that both collections accumulated epistolary verse progressively as they evolved and that, between them, they discarded only three such poems. For example, the first edition of what was to become the first volume of Dryden's *Poetical Miscellanies* contained two epistles, unrelated but printed consecutively; and not only were further epistles added in the first editions of each subsequent volume – the three involving Etherege, for instance, appearing only in the third edition of *Sylvae* in 1702 – but they also appeared in later editions.[20] An especially interesting set of additions consists of six of the seven accompanying a gift.[21] These all appeared for the first time in the first edition of *Poetical Miscellanies: The Fifth Part* in 1709, perhaps suggesting an interest in this kind of verse at the period. Additions continued until the collection reached its more or less final form in 1716, when five further epistles were added.[22] The sole epistolary poem omitted from the 1716 edition of Dryden's miscellany is Wentworth Dillon, Earl of Roscommon's translation of Horace's *Art of Poetry*, which appeared only in the second edition of *Examen Poeticum* (1706). Dodsley's *Collection* shows a similar pattern, though over a period of only ten years rather than 32. From the more or less final version of this, only two epistolary poems disappeared: William King's 'Imitation of Horace's Invitation to Torquatus to Supper', and Wortley Montagu's 'Epistle from Arthur Grey [sic], the Footman, after his Condemnation for Attempting a Rape'. King's imitation, and another seven poems by him, appear only in Dodsley's first edition of 1748. These omissions may be explained by the inference that their quality was not considered high enough.[23] Wortley Montagu's 'Epistle from Arthur Grey' appeared in all editions until the third (1755). Its subject may have been thought out of keeping with a collection aiming to appeal to polite taste.

It is now possible to draw reliable inferences from these unavoidably tedious details. The result of taking into account the number of poems in each collection is that a sum of 22 epistles in Dryden's out of a total of 874 produces a proportion of just over 2½ per cent; this rises to nearly 3½ per cent if the seven poems accompanying gifts and the humorous petition are counted as epistles, and further to 3.65 per cent if the toasting-glass verses are counted as a single item. A sum of 77 epistles out of a total of 573 separate poems in Dodsley's *Collection* produces a proportion of almost 13½ per cent; this rises to nearly 15 per cent if the further 8 marginally epistolary poems are included, and further to just over 15½ per cent if the 2 series of epigrams are counted as single items. Whichever set of figures is taken, the evidence for a significantly higher number of epistles in Dodsley's collection than in Dryden's is overwhelming.

The proportion of epistles in each volume of Dryden's miscellany as it developed between 1684 and 1709 shows no increase. This suggests that it was after 1709 that the epistle grew substantially in popularity. The statistics derived from Foxon set out below indicate that this growth began in the 1720s. Dodsley's *Collection*, more or less complete by 1758, and showing a much greater proportion of epistolary verse, confirms such a finding. There is evidence, however, that the epistle began to decline in popularity soon after 1760 or so. A case in point is the most important of the several collections marketed as supplements to Dodsley's. This is the one by George Pearch that first appeared in 1768 as *A Collection of Poems in Two Volumes by Several Hands*, grew to four volumes in 1770, and, after a revised edition in 1775, appeared in 1783 in a further revision issued by James Dodsley. The edition of 1783 was uniform with the 1782 edition of the *Collection*, and it included notes compiled by the same hand (Isaac Reed's).[24] Among the total of 301 poems in Pearch's *Collection*, 11 identify themselves as epistles by their titles and a further 3, all of which are heroic epistles, by their form and content (Appendix 1, section 3A). Another 8 poems, 6 of which appear as epistles in *Bell's Classical Arrangement*, are clearly also epistolary; and to these may be added a further 2, also included by Bell (Appendix 1, section 3B). The number of poems that may be classified as epistles therefore comes to 24. At all but 8 per cent of the total, this is a significantly lower proportion than in Dodsley's *Collection*, though still significantly higher than that in Dryden's miscellany. The finding confirms the view put in Chapter 1 that Bell produced his collection of epistles at the point when the form was already out of vogue – though not, of course, north of the Border.

As mentioned at the start of this chapter, the source from which Jay Arnold Levine cites statistics for the frequency of epistolary verse in the *Gentleman's Magazine* is Calvin D. Yost's study of 1936.[25] Because it was the most successful magazine of the period, the *Gentleman's* is a very useful measure of polite taste. Established by Edward Cave in 1731, it quickly gained a wide circulation and attracted many imitators.[26] Though it drew most of its readers from the growing bourgeoisie and gentry, it catered to a surprisingly wide social range, from artisans to members of the aristocracy. As editor of the *Gentleman's*, Cave styled himself

'Sylvanus Urban' in order to signify interest in country as well as town, culture as well as public affairs.[27] From the start he set out to include not only news and comment but verse. The *Magazine*'s first number contained a three-page section entitled 'Poetical Essays' with ten verse items; and this soon became a fixture, omitted only in the numbers for March and May 1731. By 1733, the 'Poetical Essays' began running to seven or even eight pages. Unlike the rest of the *Gentleman's*, most of which was a digest culled from other publications, by 1733 most of the verse included as 'Poetical Essays' had not first been printed elsewhere. Between 1733 and 1736 Cave further stimulated interest through poetry competitions, but many readers also responded to the chance that his magazine offered to get their work in print for the first time.

During its first ten years of publication, between January 1731 and December 1740, the *Gentleman's* printed over 2300 separate items in verse. These range from a dozen or so ribaldries from the *Glass-Window and Bog-House Miscellany* through riddles, epigrams and various types of occasional poem to piecemeal reprintings of three of the four Epistles of Pope's *Essay on Man*. Some of this verse was already in print, like the *Essay on Man*, or for that matter the items from the *Glass-Window and Bog-House Miscellany*. Most of it, however, was original, especially after 1732, and much was written specifically for the *Gentleman's*. For that reason, and because the *Magazine* enjoyed a wide readership, the verse it published provides invaluable evidence about poetic and other tastes in the period. It showed a special predilection for the verse letter, as is clear from an analysis of the verse it published in its first ten years.

Of the more than 2300 items of verse printed in the *Gentleman's Magazine* from 1731 to 1740, at least 400, or over 17 per cent, may be classified as epistolary. This statistic depends, however, on assumptions not only about what constitutes epistolary verse but also about what constitutes a verse item. For example in the only statistically-based study of verse in the *Gentleman's*, Calvin D. Yost excluded the epigram on the ground that, though it 'was always popular', it was 'seldom artistic'.[28] Popular epigrams certainly were, with over 500 examples published in the *Gentleman's* between 1731 and 1740; a less subjective reason for excluding them would be that, because nearly all are in iambic pentameter couplets, their abundance would distort statistics on verse forms. Because Yost leaves epigrams out of account (and also, it may be inferred, items such as those from the *Glass-Window and Bog-House Miscellany*), his tally of 1476 poems for the period 1731 to 1740[29] is much lower than mine. My count of over 2300 items of verse includes verse of all kinds. Another reason why Yost's total is smaller is that it seems to be limited to verse in the section entitled 'Poetical Essays' that appeared in all numbers of the *Gentleman's* but two in this period. Although relatively few verse items were printed in the section entitled 'Weekly Essays', and in some of the prefatory material, it is better to include them in order to represent as fully as possible the range of verse that the *Gentleman's* made available.

Yost's definition of epistolary verse is also limited: 'poems that are expressly called letters or epistles in verse'.[30] As he admits, the trouble with such a definition is that 'it excludes a number of genuine examples', the most famous being Pope's 'Eloisa to Abelard'. The reason why his restriction might seem acceptable lies in the word that he rightly applies to the form: 'amorphous'. However, even on his own definition, Yost under-represents the number of verse epistles or letters in the *Gentleman's* between 1731 and 1740 – and therefore probably also in the four later decades that he covers. His total for the first ten years of 'poems that are expressly called letters or epistles in verse' is 39. Including only verse published in the 'Poetical Essays' sections with the word 'epistle' or 'letter' in their titles, and counting only once poems spread over one or more issues, the number I find is 54. This increases to 62 if 2 poems are included from elsewhere in the *Gentleman's*, plus a further 6 that are referred to as epistles or letters elsewhere than in their titles – for instance, in the table of contents or index. It increases further to 65 if the three Epistles from Pope's *Essay on Man* are added, ignoring their confusing division into 17 instalments but counting each Epistle as a separate poem.

But it is when epistolary verse in general is included that the numbers really climb. To show this, I will take 1733 as an example, because it was in this year that the 'Poetical Essays' became firmly established as a major part of the *Gentleman's*, running from between four to eight double-columned pages, and with a minimum of 7 verse items in a number to a maximum of 26. Among the poems published in 1733, only one was expressly called an epistle, and only one a letter, yet no fewer than a further 35 may be identified as epistolary. I will categorize these in order to simplify discussion and to clarify further some of the questions at issue in so defining them.

The most obvious category might be called constructively epistolary, as poems of this type contain evidence that they were actually or virtually letters. Eleven examples appeared in 1733, including 'An Irish Miller, to Mr. Stephen Duck', 'The Invitation. To a Poetical Friend in Devonshire', 'A Gentleman in Lapland to his Mistress in England', and 'A Gentleman at Leyden to One at Cambridge'.[31] Part of the evidence that these poems may have been genuine letters is that they address someone who is in a different place from the writer; but the reason I have called them 'actually or virtually letters' is that, with one exception, there is no way of telling whether or not any was really sent as a written message to its addressee. The exception is 'A Gentleman in Lapland to his Mistress in England', because the reason it locates the writer in Lapland is clearly to provide its leading trope, a contrast between what it styles as a 'dreary Clime' and the fire of the poet's love. Similarly, as the other three examples also follow one or another poetic convention, especially that of the Horatian epistle, none need necessarily have been an actual letter. Nor does this matter, since they are presented first and foremost as poems. The one to Stephen Duck is especially interesting. This is partly because, among the many responses to the success of the pirated 1730 edition of Duck's *Poems on Several Subjects*, it is one of those from another labouring-class poet – John Frizzle from '*Corry's Mill* near *Enniskillen*' – and the only one known from Ireland.[32] But the poem is also of interest because, if it was not sent directly to Duck, it is a new type of verse epistle specific to the *Gentleman's* and to publications like it: not a verse letter *to* the editor, but one *via* the editor. Before the advent of the periodical press, such a poem could only have been printed in a collection. Yet, despite the development of publication by subscription, which was already enabling lower-class poets to get their works into print at this period,[33] it is unlikely that Frizzle's would have been published elsewhere than in a journal, unless Duck had chosen to include it in one of his own works.

An epistolary poem that ranks as a letter to rather than via the editor is 'To Silvanus Urban, on the Death of the *Weekly Magazine*'.[34] This rejoices in the downfall of one of the various competitors that Cave's success had attracted, and, like Frizzle's epistle to Duck, it is a new variant of the form brought into being by journalism. Three further examples of constructively epistolary poems consist of an exchange between Mary Barber, whose *Poems on Several Occasions* were to be published by subscription in 1735, and the Earl of Orrery.[35] Their titles are 'Sent to the E. of O—y Half an Hour Past 9', 'Receiv'd for Answer, the Same Hour', and 'Mrs B—r's Reply'. All are brief, and they were printed on the same page of the March number. As the very first epistolary poem in the *Gentleman's* is by Barber,[36] and as other poems by her appear in later numbers, it is clear that Cave was one of her supporters. But the exchange with the Earl of Orrery also provides further evidence of the point made in Chapter 1, that epistolary verse was often complimentary.[37] The poem by Barber that begins it calls on the Earl to seek relief for his distress at bereavement in writing poetry. In his reply he claims that neither Bath, where both were staying, nor the other famous spa at Tonbridge can inspire him, because in losing his father he has also

lost a friend. This gives Barber the opportunity to add to the praise she
has already given for his poetic abilities – not only by blaming him for
'Excess of Virtue', but by telling him that, if he persists in grieving,
'Mankind will lose a FRIEND in you'.

The poems between Barber and the Earl of Orrery indicate by their
titles that they constitute a correspondence. Because this is rarely the case
with complimentary verse proper, it is more difficult to identify such
verse as epistolary. Among the 35 poems in the *Gentleman's* for 1733 that
might be called epistolary, 11 are of this type. The first, entitled 'To the
Rev. Dr Freind, on his Quitting Westminster-School. By Stephen Duck',[38]
illustrates the difficulties of classification neatly. It is clearly not an actual
letter, not only because it lacks such epistolary markers as salutation,
valediction, date and the writer's address, but because its register is too
formal. Nevertheless, equally clearly, it is addressed to its stated recipient
on a specific occasion, Freind's retirement, and, in conformity with a
leading convention of epistolary verse, it is also intended to be read by
others – Duck takes the opportunity of complimenting some of Freind's
ex-pupils as well as the famous headmaster himself.

The problem of classification might be resolved by arguing that the
poem is an example of complimentary but not of epistolary verse. Yet this
does not necessarily help, as many complimentary poems, with diction
and imagery as florid as Duck's, were written and styled as epistles. A few
examples from the same period are Gay's *Epistle to her Grace Henrietta,
Dutchess of Marlborough*, Dodsley's *Epistle to Mr. Pope, Occasion'd by
his Essay on Man*, and Savage's 'The Friend. Address'd to Aaron Hill,
Esq;' (1726) – which, much revised, and retitled 'An Epistle', appeared in
1736 both in the *Gentleman's* and in the *London Magazine*.[39] However,
just as not all epistolary poems include the word 'epistle' in their titles,
not all complimentary poems do so either. This is shown in the discussion
in Chapter 1, including of complimentary epistles in *Bell's Classical
Arrangement*.[40] Indeed, Bell's Volume VI, 'Epistles Panegyrical and
Gallant', contains a complimentary poem that appeared much earlier in
the 1733 volume of the *Gentleman's*, where it is entitled 'To Mr. Thomson
on his Generous Concern for Mr. Dennis's Last Benefit'. This text of the
poem is extensively revised, and it is assigned to Richard Savage, though
C. Lennart Carlson has shown that it is actually by one of Cave's regular
contributors, John Duick.[41] As I have argued above, because complimentary poems often styled themselves as epistles in their titles, and
because Bell's anthology indicates that, even when they did not do so,
they were usually seen as epistolary, it is fair to classify them as such,
though they cannot be counted as central to the epistolary tradition.

Three other types of epistolary poem to appear in the *Gentleman's* in 1733 are amatory – called 'gallant' in the title of Bell's sixth volume – advisory, and satirical. There are also examples of that variant of the complimentary epistle in which the poem accompanies a gift of some kind, such as the Earl of Orrery's 'To the Rev. Dr. Swift, with a Present of a Paper Book Finely Bound', and the anonymous 'To Mrs A— K—Y with a Present of Fruit'.[42] One type that does not feature at all, and rarely appears elsewhere in the *Gentleman's*, is the Ovidian heroic epistle.[43] Presumably it was not to the taste of Cave and his advisers.

As Cave was employed by the Post Office for most of the years in which he edited his magazine, it is apt that so much of the verse he published was in one way or another epistolary. Anthony Barker has shown how his Post Office privileges and connections helped him establish and consolidate the *Gentleman's* as the leading periodical of its day.[44] At the same time, the space he made available to epistolary verse created opportunities for verse-writers of all kinds both to produce verse on almost any subject and to get it published. Here are some examples, still from the magazine's initial ten years.

First, the fact that epistolary verse is by definition occasional was a boon to those who might not feel qualified to write on public affairs or in forms requiring a classical education. Especially interesting examples include not only verse by unprivileged poets such as Stephen Duck, John Frizzle, and Mary Barber, but also Lady Anne Irwin's 'Epistle to Mr Pope. By a Lady. Occasioned by his Characters of Women', a very effective response printed anonymously in 1736.[45] Second, the *Gentleman's* stimulated epistolary verse by virtue of its nature as a journal. Verse letters could be sent to the editor, or, more interestingly, via the editor; and these helped build and maintain reader-interest as well as provide material. Another poem in the 1733 volume, 'To Camilla and Flavia. The Invitation: Or, the Flying Fair',[46] shows particular chutzpah. It is prefaced by a note from two gentlemen explaining that they wish it to be printed in order to make the acquaintance of two ladies whom they see while taking evening walks but whose 'Coyness', as they describe it, has so far precluded meeting them. The fact that they could assume that the ladies would read the *Gentleman's* illustrates the popularity it had achieved by this point. But the best example of epistles stimulated by the magazine itself is a series involving various contributors that ran from 1734 to 1736. This began when an unidentified contributor who wrote as 'Fidelia' from Lincoln humorously took exception to what she claimed was the miserliness of £50 for a poetry prize, and proposed herself as a wife for Swift in consolation.[47] The other main contributors were Jane

Brereton ('Melissa') and Thomas Beach ('Captain Fido'), but others took part too, Beach and Brereton even submitting further facetious exchanges under different pen-names, 'Prudence Manage' and 'Parson Lovemore'.[48] As Barker explains, the series ended when Brereton found out that Beach, who was a friend but whom she did not know to be 'Fido', had been using her drafts, which she had been showing him, to facilitate his responses; and in May 1737 farce turned to tragedy when Beach cut his throat, 'plagued by a morbid guilt' after sexually exploiting a servant-girl.[49]

But a third implication of epistolary verse in the *Gentleman's Magazine* is perhaps the most interesting of all. This consists in what it has to suggest about social relations and their interaction with print at the period. The importance of all kinds of epistolary writing in the eighteenth century is a function not only of developments in communication and technology, but also of the growth of a new social and literary culture, and with it a new reading public. Publications such as the *Gentleman's* helped feed this growth through the unprecedented access to print they afforded, for those who wrote as well as those who read. Further examples from those who wrote are epistles from abroad, such as poems from the 1733 volume addressed to James Oglethorpe on the colony in Georgia, and to Lord Baltimore about Maryland; and 'Cynthio to Leonora: An Epistle from the Cape of Good Hope', printed in two parts in 1738.[50] The historians of the *Gentleman's* have claimed that much of the verse it printed is undistinguished.[51] Although it is difficult to disagree with such a verdict, the magazine provides lively evidence of relations between poetry and print in the period, especially in the prominence it gave to verse in epistolary form.

Useful as the two miscellanies and the *Gentleman's Magazine* are for providing a guide to tastes in verse during the long eighteenth century, this inevitably has limitations. Michael Suarez has demonstrated the processes of selection behind Dodsley's *Collection* and the various interests that they represented;[52] analysis of Dryden's miscellany would probably yield comparable findings with respect to Jacob Tonson; and studies of the *Gentleman's* have shown how small a group chose the verse it printed.[53] Producing more detailed and more accurate estimates requires a much larger store of data. The ideal and properly empirical solution would be to read all the extant verse from the period and record all the epistles. Though such an enterprise is not wholly impracticable – Roger Lonsdale has not only read all the available verse but anthologized it – it is beyond the scope of lesser mortals. However, David Foxon's *English*

Verse 1701–1750 goes some way towards meeting the requirement for the first half of the century; while an electronic source, Chadwyck-Healey's *Literature Online*, offers not only a huge sample of data but also some of the search tools necessary for its analysis.

As resources for studying the verse epistle and other types of poem, Foxon and *Literature Online* are more useful than the English Short Title Catalogue and also, despite its massive collection of texts and its sophisticated search technology, Gale's *Eighteenth-Century Collections Online* (ECCO). In the case of ESTC, this is partly because, by definition, it is confined to works published separately. But a more significant limitation that applies both to ESTC and to ECCO is that they allow only limited searching by genre. *Literature Online* both indexes and contains a large number of poems; and the third edition also enables searches by genre. Because the search methods are not very effective in the case of the verse epistle, I use a database constructed by my own methods from the second edition of *Literature Online*, and I shall occasionally draw on it in this book.[54] The sample that it provides of 867 eighteenth-century epistolary poems is large enough to enable estimates about the nature of the form at the period, though for a fuller picture it must be supplemented by evidence from other sources such as those used in this chapter.

As Foxon's catalogue and *Literature Online* have different functions, the information they offer produces different results. In particular, as his title and subtitle indicate, Foxon covers only half of the century and only separately printed poems; while the scope of *Literature Online* is limited by several factors including copyright. Nevertheless, despite these restrictions, Foxon catalogues nearly 10,000 poems, at least 500 of which, or 5 per cent, may be classified as epistolary; while the 'Search Texts' option in the second edition of *Literature Online*, limited to poetry and to the eighteenth century, produced a total of 1060 poems with the keywords 'epist*', 'letter' or 'letters' in the first line or title. The latter total includes a relatively small number of poems that are not epistles or are duplicates. However, like the statistics cited by Havens, it excludes the much larger number of poems that, like Pope's 'Eloisa to Abelard', are epistles but do not bear the keywords in their titles or first lines. Allowing for such omissions, and with a total of 37,901 poems indexed by *Literature Online* as eighteenth-century, it is likely that the proportion of epistolary verse in the database is similar to that in Foxon. By way of comparison, the only kinds of poem that the same search showed as more numerous were the hymn (2428 poems indexed under 'hymn' or 'hymns' in their title or first line), the ode (2387 under 'ode' or 'odes'), and the song (1560 under 'song' or 'songs'). This suggests just how popular a form the verse epistle was. It far outscores, for example, not only the elegy (614 poems with 'elegy' or 'elegies' in title or first line), the fable (528 with 'fable' or 'fables'), and the satire (170 with 'satir*', 70 with 'satyr*'), but even the ballad (660 with 'ballad' or 'ballads').

Of the two differences mentioned above between poems catalogued by Foxon and those available from *Literature Online*, the more significant is that Foxon lists only those printed separately. In consequence, many of the poems he indexes are occasional or ephemeral, though some – most obviously Pope's – were republished later in collections. A related point is that well over half of the verse epistles he describes were first published anonymously, and in a large number of cases the author remains difficult or impossible to identify. As well as a vital resource for tracking political, religious and literary controversies of the period, Foxon provides the means to assess how many poems of various kinds were published separately in each of the years he covers. In the case of verse epistles, 35 may be classed as such in 1701–10, 97 in 1711–20, 111 in 1721–30 (with 31 in 1730), 176 in 1731–40 (with 28 in 1735), and 92 in 1741–50. This shows a clear rise and decline in popularity, peaking in the early 1730s when Grub Street activity was at its height. It must again be emphasized, however, that the separately published verse epistle is not necessarily the same kind of poem as one that appears in a collection. It is much more likely to engage directly in contemporary affairs, and its content is more often satirical. The fact that the number of verse epistles catalogued by Foxon decreases after 1740 should therefore not be taken to indicate that the form itself declined at that time. It may point instead to a decline in the market for separately published verse of a topical or satirical kind.

Literature Online provides two further indications of the verse epistle's popularity with eighteenth-century writers. The same search options already specified produced totals of 374 poems out of 48,947 for the period 1500–1699 with the keywords 'epist*', 'letter' or 'letters' in the first line or title, 867 poems out of 142,494 for the period 1800–1899, and 850 poems out of 131,575 for the period 1900–1999. This means that, allowing as before for the limitations of the search method, the proportion of epistolary poems identified for the period 1700–1799 is nearly four times greater than that for the period 1500–1699, and over four times greater than that for the period 1800–1999. The second indication is the number of eighteenth-century writers identified by the search method to have written verse epistles. This is 200, 25 of whom were women.

Before leaving this mass of quantitative data, it is possible to use it in combination with data from the Dryden and Dodsley miscellanies to arrive at a closer estimate of the number of epistolary poems printed in the period. Such an estimate is admittedly speculative, but it may be useful pending the development of better methods. As I have mentioned above, a major stumbling-block to identifying verse epistles by their titles is the fact that many do not include the word 'epistle' or 'letter'; indeed, common titles for verse epistles are the simple formulae 'To AB from CD' or 'AB to CD'. These formulae are no more adequate, however, since they are also often used for complimentary, amatory or other verse that is not epistolary. However, the statistics set out above of epistolary verse in the Dryden and Dodsley miscellanies may be used to estimate the ratio in each between epistles that do and do not include the keywords 'epist*' or 'letter' in their titles. These ratios may then be applied to the statistics from *Literature Online* in order to provide a rough estimate of the total number of epistolary poems in the database. Analysis of the titles of all the 30 poems in Dryden's miscellany classified as epistolary produces a total of 13 poems that include in their titles one or other of the keywords specified, and of 17 that do not.[55] The same analysis of the 85 poems in Dodsley's *Collection* produces totals of 39 and 46 respectively;[56] in both cases I have used the more liberal classification of epistolary verse. These ratios are remarkably similar: over 43 per cent of the epistolary poems in Dryden's miscellany contain one or other of the keywords in their titles, and nearly 46 per cent in Dodsley's. If the ratios have any representative validity, they suggest that counting epistolary poems in the period only on the basis of their titles is likely to underestimate their numbers by a factor of at least two. For example, the search of *Literature Online* produced a total of 1060 poems in the period 1700–1799 with the keywords 'epist*', 'letter' or 'letters' in the first line or title. If it is assumed that this identified only 45 per cent of epistolary verse, a more accurate figure might be closer to 2356, raising the estimated percentage of epistolary verse in the database for that period from 2.8 to 6.22. It is therefore reasonable to suggest that, at the very least, 5 per cent of the poems printed in the eighteenth century were epistolary, a figure confirming that already arrived at from Foxon for the first half of the period.

The remainder of this chapter considers the frequency and distribution of epistolary verse in a number of eighteenth-century collections of various kinds. In order to arrive at a fairly accurate picture, it is important to take a range of such sources into account, not least because some, even *Literature Online*, tend to under-represent verse by women and labouring-class writers.[57] This is especially significant, because, for good reason, much epistolary verse was produced by such writers. As Roger Lonsdale remarks in the Introduction to his *Eighteenth-Century Women Poets: An Oxford Anthology*,

> although there were some clear exceptions, women poets, like their unfashionable male contemporaries, were often intimidated by or indifferent to the loftier poetic genres and worked most happily in less self-conscious, sociable forms: most notably, throughout the century, in the familiar verse epistle, in which generic expectations were minimal, polished diction inappropriate, and the writer would be confident of her ability to amuse a friend whose interest was guaranteed.[58]

Moyra Haslett argues similarly that the epistle probably attracted women writers because 'it does not require elevated diction or classical learning, nor does it rank highly in the hierarchy of poetic genres'. She also goes so far as to suggest that, in the eighteenth century, the verse epistle 'may lay claim to being the dominant poetic genre for women writers in particular', stating that 'almost a third of the selections' in Lonsdale's anthology 'are kinds of verse epistle'.[59] Haslett does not specify the criteria by which she identifies these epistles, and such an estimate is probably over-generous. Nevertheless, there is much evidence to suggest that not only women writers but writers of both sexes from the labouring and artisan classes were drawn, including for the reasons stated by Lonsdale and herself, to the verse epistle. Comparison of the two Lonsdale anthologies – the first including men and women writers, the second only women – shows that the ratio of epistolary verse in the latter is indeed high.

In Lonsdale's *New Oxford Book of Eighteenth-Century Verse*, which represents a total of 552 poems, 206 male writers account for 466 items, and 25 female writers for 40, while the remaining 46, of which at least 2 are by the same hand, are anonymous. Of the total of 552 poems, 14 items identify themselves as epistles by including the word in their titles, and 3 by including the word 'letter'. A further 22 poems may be classified as epistolary, including two to accompany gifts, two from abroad, an invitation, an extract from Pope's *Essay on Man*, two humorous petitions, and two that appear in *Bell's Classical Arrangement*: Gilbert White's 'The Naturalist's Summer-Evening Walk', and Samuel Henley's 'Verses Addressed to a Friend, Just Leaving a Favourite Retirement'.[60] Other items, such as Anna Laetitia Barbauld's 'To Mr. [S. T.] C[olerid]ge', seem closer to odes than epistles, and others still, such as Prior's 'A Better Answer to Cloe Jealous', closer to amatory odes. Excluding 10 such marginally and doubtfully epistolary items, the total stock of epistolary verse in Lonsdale's first anthology is 39, or just over 7 per cent; including them, the total rises to 49, or nearly 8.9 per cent. Among items excluded from the count are Chesterfield's 'To a Lady on Reading Sherlock upon Death' (pp. 275–6), which is light amatory verse, and John Winstanley's 'To the Revd. Mr. ——— on his Drinking Sea-Water' (p. 136), which is a humorous squib.

As the estimates just given include items by women as well as men, it is also necessary, for the sake of accuracy, to distinguish them by gender. However, this makes little difference. Of the 466 male-authored items, 12 use the word 'epistle' in their titles, and 3 'letter'; a further 18 are among those classed as epistolary, and 9 among the marginally and doutbfully epistolary. On the stricter definition of epistolary verse, this produces a total of 33, just over 7 per cent of the male-authored items; on the looser definition, a total of 42, or just over 9 per cent. Since these figures are very close to those for the volume as a whole, it is not surprising that the corresponding estimates for female-authored items also differ only slightly. Of the 40 items by women, 2 use the word 'epistle' in their titles, but none 'letter'; while a further 1 may be classed as epistolary, and 1 as marginally epistolary. This produces totals of 3 on the stricter definition and 4 on the looser, resulting in proportions of 7.5 and 10 per cent. While these estimates necessarily exclude anonymous items, it may be added that all 3 of the unattributed epistolary items are clearly by men.

Lonsdale's *Eighteenth-Century Women Poets* contains 323 poems. Of these, 16 designate themselves as epistles in their titles, and 8 as letters. But no fewer than a further 37 may be classified as epistolary, including straightforward examples such as Jane Brereton's 'To Mr Thomas Griffith, at the University of Glasgow', and less obvious ones, such as Anne Finch's 'Ballad to Mrs Catherine Fleming', Esther Lewis's 'Advice to a Young Lady Lately Married', and the anonymous 'Rebuke to Robert Southey'. All the items counted so far produce a total of 61, or all but 19 per cent. On a looser definition of the epistle, a further 20 poems could be added, including 3 by Sarah Fyge Egerton, Mehetabel Wright's 'Address to her Husband', and Sarah Dixon's 'To Strephon'. If these are included in the count, the total number rises to 81, or just over 25 per cent. Among items excluded from the count are Sarah Fyge Egerton's 'To Marina' (pp. 30–1), which seems closer to satirical invective, and Lady Mary Wortley Montagu's 'Addressed to ———' (pp. 68–9), which is an ode. These, along with a few others including Lady Mary Chudleigh's 'To the Ladies' (p. 3), are not quite epistolary, in that they have too little in common with letters.

Of course, evidence of such a kind can only carry broadly indicative value. This is partly because not all epistolary verse is capable of precise definition, as the last three poems mentioned bear witness, and partly because neither anthology aimed, or needed to aim, at any kind of generic representativeness. Yet, though it is difficult to support Haslett's claim that nearly a third of the poems in *Eighteenth-Century Women Poets* are kinds of verse epistle, the contents of the two anthologies show a dramatically larger proportion of epistolary writing by women than by men.

Similar proportions appear in two sample single-volume miscellanies of the period, one of which contains more poems by women than most. Of the 103 poems included in Anthony Hammond's *A New Miscellany of Original Poems, Translations and Imitations* (1720), only 1 styles itself as an epistle in its title, but 3 represent themselves as letters (one in imitation of an epistle by Horace), and at least a further 9 may be classified as epistolary.[61] Those 9 include the verses addressed by Lady Mary Wortley Montagu from Constantinople to her uncle William Feilding, printed apparently as a result of his indiscretion;[62] Susannah Centlivre's 'From the Country, to Mr. Rowe in Town. MDCCXVII'; and 2 poems that first appeared in the second edition (1708) of Dryden's *Annual Miscellany*.[63] Estimates are complicated by a high proportion of social verse, but it is probably safe to classify another 4 poems, all by Martha Fowke, as marginally epistolary. Taking these into account produces a total of 17, or 16½ per cent, which is high for the earlier eighteenth century. It is more than double the proportion in the miscellany of 61 poems compiled by John Husbands 11 years later, containing 5 epistolary poems of which 4 signify that they are epistles in their titles.[64] Most of the verse in Husbands's collection is his own, and what is not by him is almost certainly by other men. Rather than reflecting the coterie world of London, like Hammond's miscellany, it reflects that of the Oxford college.[65]

Analysis of single-authored collections also shows that women favoured epistolary form even more than men, but with the important qualification mentioned above: that, like women of various social ranks, men from the artisan and labouring classes were especially drawn to the verse epistle. To begin with verse epistles by gentlemen in order to provide a standard for comparison, three representative collections published in the first half of the century all contain a modest number among other stock kinds of verse. Eric Rothstein sums up the contents of the first, John Smith's *Poems upon Several Occasions* (1713), as 'A mixture of odes, songs, ballads, epistles, anacreontics, dialogues, and occasional or nonce poems', and declares that Smith's 'variety and cosmopolitanism, and range of tones and styles [. . .] are quite normal for this eclectic period'.[66] Out of a total of 81 poems, the collection contains 3 entitled 'Epistle', all familiar, and several others that are close to epistolary form, including 3 complimentary poems. Such a showing of epistles and other social verse is quite frequent in single-author collections, especially from the earlier half of the century. Another example is Henry Travers's *Miscellaneous Poems and Translations* (1740), revised and expanded from its first edition in 1731,[67] which contains a total of 42 poems. Travers's title advertises translations as well as original poems, but he also includes, along with these and several imitations and paraphrases, 2 poems entitled 'Epistle' and 3 others that could be considered epistolary. Thirdly, Soame Jenyns's *Poems* (1752) musters, among a total of 34 items,[68] 2 poems styled as epistles in their titles, including one Horatian imitation, and 5 more that are epistolary – all appear as epistles in *Bell's Classical Arrangement of English Poetry*. Though the complexion of each of these three collections differs to some extent, all are fairly eclectic and all represent epistolary verse.

The male poet most associated with the verse epistle in the period is, of course, Alexander Pope. In the nine-volume edition of his *Works* produced by William Warburton in 1751, seven years after his death, epistles feature in no fewer than four of the six volumes that include verse. They range from two heroic epistles in Volume II (the translation from Ovid, 'Sappho to Phaon', and 'Eloisa to Abelard'), to the discursive epistles of Volume III (*An Essay on Man* plus five *Moral Essays*, including 'To Mr. Addison, Occasioned by his Dialogues on Medals'), and the Horatian imitations of Volume IV, and finally to the occasional epistles of Volume VI (which contains a further Horatian imitation). Counting as separate poems the four *Pastorals*, the four epistles of *An Essay on Man*, and the four Books of the *Dunciad*, this yields a total of 22 epistles from 93 poems, or over 23 per cent. Yet Pope also wrote many poems, including epistles, not included in the 1751 *Works*. Among the verse excluded from that edition are several familiar and occasional epistles that had entered print without his blessing, such as 'An Epistle to Henry Cromwell, Esq;', 'To Belinda on the Rape of the Lock', and 'Bounce to Fop. An Heroick Epistle from a Dog at Twickenham to a Dog at Court'.[69] Indeed, the only familiar epistles included in the 1751 *Works* are not in verse and appear in the three volumes of prose that end it. According to Warburton, as Pope's literary executor, the aim of the edition was to represent 'all his principal poems [. . .] with his last corrections and improvements'.[70] For this reason, the selection of epistles excludes familiar verse entirely in favour of work in such classic modes as the heroic, discursive, complimentary and satirical.

Two final examples of collections by gentlemen of the period show contrasting patterns but still testify to the importance of the verse epistle. As Stephen N. Brown has pointed out, Edward Young's tendency 'was to shift genres, to experiment with style, to pursue originality almost obsessively – all in an attempt to validate himself'.[71] It was probably owing to this aim of self-validation that, when his *Poetical Works* were brought out by a group of copyright holders in 1741,[72] collecting poems, plays and prose published over a period of more than 20 years, it included work from various classic genres but, anticipating Pope's *Works* a decade later, no familiar verse epistles. Most of the 23 poems by Young in the two volumes are satirical, though there are, too, a few complimentary and discursive poems as well as two tragedies and several odes and other lyrics. Yet the two volumes also include three poems entitled 'Epistle', all of which are discursive, along with one 'Letter'; and, as David Fairer has demonstrated, the seven satires of *The Universal Passion* have an epistolary character.[73] In contrast, another contemporary, Thomas Gilbert, produced a collection more resembling those of Smith, Travers and Jenyns in his *Poems on Several Occasions* of 1747.[74] This contains 36 poems, the longest of which are satirical or discursive, but also 8 poems entitled 'Epistle', most of which are familiar, and a further 3 occasional poems that may be seen as epistolary too. The inclusion of familiar verse makes it clear that Gilbert's literary ambitions were pitched lower than Young's or Pope's.

As Lonsdale and Haslett suggest, however, women cultivated the verse epistle – especially the familiar type – to a greater extent than men. Anne Finch, Countess of Winchilsea, furnishes an especially interesting example. On the one hand, the 81 verse items in Finch's *Miscellany Poems* of 1713 include only 2 entitled 'Epistle' and 1 'Letter', along with a further 4 poems that are clearly epistolary.[75] On the other hand, Finch wrote a large number of poems not included in her collection, and many are epistles. Drawn from manuscript and other sources as well as *Miscellany Poems*, Myra Reynolds's edition of Finch's works adds a further 13 epistles, 1 of which is styled as such by its title, and 1 as a letter.[76] But Reynolds was not aware of the existence of a further important manuscript, the Wellesley. In their critical edition of this manuscript, Barbara McGovern and Charles H. Hinnant state that it 'contains fifty-three poems by Finch, one of which is transcribed twice', and that 'only one had been printed prior to the preparation of the manuscript'.[77] Of the 53 poems by Finch, only 1 is entitled 'Epistle', and 2 'Letter', one of the latter beginning and the other ending in prose. Yet a further 15 poems are clearly epistolary, and so are the 2 by other writers, complimentary responses from Catherine Fleming and Pope respectively. This means that well over a third of the poems in the manuscript is epistolary – just over a third if those not by Finch are excluded.

Most of the poems in the Wellesley manuscript were written after 1713, and so could not have been included in Finch's *Miscellany*. McGovern and Hinnant argue, furthermore, that the manuscript was not intended for print publication. Dating its compilation to the aftermath of the failed Jacobite rebellion of 1715, they suggest that, though only some of the poems have political implications, Finch and her husband probably felt it would have been imprudent to print it at such a time. On related grounds, they also help explain why it contains so many verse epistles in claiming that 'The epistolary form answered to Finch's sense of the loss of an ideal corporate community and to her consequent need for a more informal and intimate use of language.'[78] Such a view does not, however, account for the exclusion from *Miscellany Poems* of a number of verse epistles Finch had written earlier. As Hinnant says elsewhere, the collection was clearly 'intended to represent a generous selection of her poems'.[79] These are in different genres, ranging from fables to two pindarics, translations from French and Italian, various lyrics, occasional poems and a tragedy. Of the two poems entitled 'Epistle', one is heroic ('An Epistle from Alexander to Hephæstion in his Sickness') and one a translation ('An Epistle from a Gentleman to Madame Deshouliers'). For the most part, such a collection is not unlike those of gentlemen at the period. The main differences are that there are no translations from classical languages, that some poems are implicitly female-authored (for example, 'Friendship between Ephelia and Ardelia'), that the tone is always chaste, and that, as Hinnant goes on to point out, the volume 'also contains verses addressed to her husband and intimate circle of friends in Kent'. Hinnant raises the question whether such private verse could appeal to the larger readership opened up by print. But only a small number of poems in the collection are of this type,[80] and it seems unlikely that they could have impaired its fortunes with readers. Instead, the reason why a large number of verse epistles by Finch survive only in manuscript is probably that they were neither written with a view to print publication nor considered subsequently for printing. In the case of some of the poems in the Wellesley manuscript, McGovern and Hinnant are almost certainly right to argue that political motives would have weighed against wider publication. What must also be remembered, however, is that epistolary verse was a social practice of the period, and that, especially for upper-class women, the writing of a letter in verse by no means entailed an intention to publish it.

A similar pattern may be seen in the epistolary verse of Lady Mary Wortley Montagu and others. As Claudia Thomas Kairoff has put it, Montagu's 'desire to share her opinions and talent were countered by strong determination to maintain her status by refraining from print'.[81]

Montagu did, of course, cause some of her work to be printed, concealing her authorship, but few if any poems.[82] Those poems that appeared in print had first been published otherwise, by manuscript circulation. To quote Kairoff again, 'she frequently copied her poems into letters to highly placed correspondents, where she must have known they would circulate among acquaintances. She may have felt that she reached her most significant readership through that process.'[83] But Montagu also wrote at least one complete letter in verse, 'Letter to Lord Hervey from Twict'nam Wrote on the King's Birthday', and parts of others, ranging from 20 lines in a letter to her sister, Lady Mar, and 16 in 'The Conclusion of a Letter to a Freind Wrote 1741 from Italy',[84] to couplets and single lines elsewhere. Appropriately, as remarked in Chapter 1, 'Letter to Lord Hervey' does not appear in the standard edition of her verse,[85] but only in that of her letters.

A further example is the correspondence between Frances, Countess of Hertford, addressee many years before of verse epistles from Anne Finch,[86] and Henrietta Louisa, Countess of Pomfret. First collected and printed in 1805, this had taken place between August 1738 and October 1741, when Lady Pomfret was in Italy with her husband.[87] James How has argued that the two Countesses encouraged 'the mutual belief that their correspondence represented an excellent example of the aristocratic ideal of letter writing', and that they did so in an attempt to distance themselves from an increasingly disreputable court. At the same time, he suggests, they sought 'a refuge in epistolary space, if nowhere else, from the unremitting dissemination of the culture of London' – in other words, that of rising commercialism.[88] One of the means they employed to promote an idea of cultural distinction was the exchange of poems and extracts from poems. Three of the 169 letters between them contain poems that one or the other had written. They also copy for each other 16 poems attributed to other writers, and 6 that are unattributed (1 of which may have been written by Hertford),[89] along with 10 brief attributed verse quotations and a further 5 that are unattributed (2 of which may have been written by Pomfret).[90] These represent verse by, among others, Elizabeth Carter, Lady Mary Wortley Montagu, Pope, and Sir William Yonge, and also translations, especially from Italian, but on four occasions the two turned to verse as the form for their own letters. One complete letter, from Hertford, consists of 81 lines of verse; one from Pomfret consists of 255 lines, following a brief prose introduction; and there is one from each in which verse lines are embedded in prose – 64 of them in the case of a letter from Hertford, 54 in that of one from Pomfret.[91] While these are, technically, familiar epistles, their style is dignified, in keeping with the high-culture designs of the whole correspondence; only once does one of them descend, for part of a letter, from pentameter to tetrameter couplets.[92] As with the poems that Wortley Montagu copied into letters, the two must have expected that these would be shown to others. Indeed, the whole correspondence suggests an intention to impress as well as to please – each other, initially, but also those in each woman's immediate circle, if not the wider public it reached over 60 years later.

The example of Elizabeth Tollet suggests that a woman with serious literary aspirations might be less likely to allow familiar epistles to be printed. In this she anticipated her male contemporaries Young and Pope. The 54 poems in Tollet's *Poems on Several Occasions* of 1724 include only 2 entitled 'Epistle'. Both are in serious modes. As I have indicated in Chapter 1, the first, 'An Epistle', is an Horatian reflection, while the second, 'Anne Boleyn to King Henry VIII', is an heroic epistle. Only one other poem, 'To my Brother at St. John's College in Cambridge',[93] is epistolary, but its learning, style and measured gravity distinguish it from the familar epistles that Jane Brereton was writing, but not for print publication, at the same period.[94] Even when Tollet increased the number of poems to 120 in an expanded edition of 1755, she included no familiar verse, though she did add three complimentary epistles.[95]

Women writers of lower social rank were less averse to publication in print, especially from the 1730s when opportunities expanded. Mary Barber's *Poems on Several Occasions*, also mentioned in Chapter 1, is a good example. The collection contains 132 poems, 112 of which are attributed to her. As many as 75 of these, or nearly 67 per cent, may be considered as epistolary, though not one calls itself an epistle in its title. The likely explanation for this paradox is that, as a lower-middle-class Irishwoman, Barber felt it prudent to disclaim assocations not only of the grander type, especially the essay-epistle, but also of its less respectable cousin, the familiar epistle, which often descended to bawdiness at the period. Only 10 of her epistolary poems even identify themselves as such by including the word 'letter' in their titles; and, of these, three represent themselves as written on behalf of others, two as parts of letters, and two as accompanying other letters.[96] However, although in ways such as these Barber did her best to avoid hinting at pretensions above or descents below her station, the collection also displays her ingenuity in creating opportunities for verse. A large number of her titles begin with the word 'To', followed in some cases simply by the addressee's name, but more often specifying the occasion – such as 'To Mrs. Mary Caesar, upon Seeing her Just after the Marriage of her Friend, the Lady Margaret Harley' (pp. 236–7), or 'Written at Tunbridge-Wells, to the Right Honourable the Lady Barbara North, Occasion'd by Some of the

Company's Saying They Would Go to Faint-Fair, and Act a Play' (p. 45). Many of her epistolary poems, including the two just cited and the two to the Earl of Orrery discussed above, are complimentary, and most are quite short; indeed, 62 of her 112 poems have fewer than 20 lines. Others accompany gifts, including in one case her son 'as a Present, to Dr. Swift, Dean of St. Patrick's, on his Birth-Day' (pp. 71–2); or are apologies of some kind, five using the word in their titles; or refer to social occasions, often invitations but in one case a remonstrance 'Upon Seeing a Raffle for Addison's Works Unfilled' (p. 46). Especially interesting are those written on behalf of another person – often her son, once her daughter, but also including 'The Widow Gordon's Petition' (pp. 2–5), two poems associated with it (pp. [1]–2, 6), and 'To the Right Honourable the Lady Elizabeth Germain, upon Seeing Her Do a Generous Action. Written as from the Person Reliev'd' (pp. 116–17). Precluded from attempting subjects or genres that would have been found unbecoming for one of her sex and station, Barber specialized in occasional verse that was often epistolary in character though rarely avowed as such. It was a shrewd and, for its purposes, successful solution to the problem not so much of being able to write verse at all, but of fitting it for publication and modest profit.

A second example is Jane Brereton's *Poems on Several Occasions*, published with a much more modest subscription list in 1744, four years after her death. It contains 98 poems, 67 of which are by Brereton. Of those 67, 27, or just over 40 per cent, are clearly epistles, although only 3 style themselves as such by using the word in their titles. A further 10 could be classed as epistolary, which would raise the total to 37 and the percentage among Brereton's verse to just over 55 per cent. Over a third of the verse in the collection was first printed in the *Gentleman's Magazine*, including a total of 30 poems, 11 by Brereton, in the correspondence sparked by 'Fidelia' mentioned above. The collection gains a still more epistolary character from five of Brereton's prose letters that, along with an account of her life, preface the verse. Sarah Prescott has argued convincingly that this prefatory material, especially Brereton's biography, is modelled on that in Elizabeth Rowe's *Miscellaneous Works*, also published posthumously, in order to present the author 'in the most attractive light to a potential readership'.[97] A good example is the sentence introducing her five prose letters: 'As nothing better expresses the true Characters of Persons, than their Epistolary Correspondence with their Friends, in which the Mind opens itself without Reserve, the Editor has thought proper to insert a few of Mrs. *Brereton*'s Letters, which may serve to show, at once, her Sincerity, easy Elegance of Expression, and the affectionate Warmth of her Friendship.'[98] One reason for the number of epistles, especially familiar epistles, in the work of eighteenth-century women poets is that they would have supported similar claims.

Another reason, however, is that it had become much more acceptable for women to collect and publish familiar and occasional verse and prose letters. That Brereton, for instance, had ambitions as a poet is clear from her first publications, *The Fifth Ode of the Fourth Book of Horace Imitated: and Apply'd to the King* (1716), and *An Expostulatory Epistle to Sir Richard Steele upon the Death of Mr. Addison* (1720), not to mention *Merlin: A Poem*, which she dedicated to Queen Caroline in 1735.[99] But it is unlikely that her early verse epistles, such as 'Epistle to Mrs Anne Griffiths. Written from London, in 1718', 'To Mr Thomas Griffith, at the University of Glasgow. Written in London, 1720', and 'Epistle to Mr Tho. Griffith, 1720',[100] were written with a view to print publication. Instead, they would have been written for her own entertainment and that of her immediate circle, and they were only published when her verse and the five exemplary prose letters were assembled for printing after her death.

Mary Jones's *Miscellanies in Prose and Verse* is comparable in several ways. Published in 1750 with an even longer and more prestigious subscription list than Mary Barber's,[101] it contains 53 poems, all but 1 by Jones. Four of her poems are entitled 'Epistle'; 9 further poems are clearly also epistolary, and another 7 could be considered so, producing a total of 20, or nearly 38 per cent. As its title indicates, the collection also contains prose, mostly in the form of letters – 30 to an unidentified correspondent, probably Charlot Clayton, and a further 38 to the addressee of many of the poems, Martha Lovelace, later Lady Beauclerk. These play a different role from the letters prefacing Brereton's collection. Though they follow the verse, they occupy more pages; and, rather than offering a kind of character reference, as Brereton's do, they demonstrate the same intelligence, wit and vivacity as the poems themselves. Similarly, the opening poems are carefully chosen to present Jones's work at its best. Beginning with 'Epistle to Lady Bowyer' – modelled, as David Fairer and Christine Gerrard have pointed out, on Pope's *Epistle to Dr. Arbuthnot*[102] – it continues with two discursive epistles, 'Of Patience' and 'Of Desire', followed by an elegy in memory of Lady Beauclerk's brother-in-law, before shifting into lighter verse. The first four poems demonstrate their claim to seriousness in their length – all over 100 lines, one nearly 300 – and their form of iambic pentameter couplets. The only other poem styled as an epistle, 'Epistle, from Fern-Hill', appears much later in the volume, probably because it is familiar and its humour is rather broad. Most of the other poems are social verse and therefore quite short: 37 of the total of 53 by Jones have 50 lines or fewer, and 17 have fewer than 20. It is easily conceivable that these, like many occasional poems of the period, were never intended to be printed. Indeed, it is not difficult to imagine 'Epistle, from Fern-Hill' being sent as an actual letter, though the discursive epistles were probably written with higher ambitions.

But it was labouring-class poets of both sexes who exploited the epistle most – especially the familiar type. A rough idea of how often this kind of verse featured in their work may be gained from the fact that, among the 322 poems represented in the superb anthology *Eighteenth-Century English Labouring-Class Poets*, at least 86, or nearly 27 per cent, are epistolary, with 29 styling themselves as epistles in their titles, 1 as a letter, and 1 as an 'epistolary answer'.[103] One reason the form attracted so many such writers was probably, as Lonsdale and Haslett suggest with women poets, that the familiar epistle is an unpretentious form that requires no special erudition or an elevated style. Yet many artisan and labouring-class writers were well informed about classical literature, though rarely in the original, and those that found their way into print were fully capable of producing verse according to the conventions of the period. It is therefore likely that they had other motives too for favouring the epistle. One of these was probably the fact that in the eighteenth century, as I have been emphasizing, the verse letter was not just a literary genre but an occasional social practice, even at non-genteel social levels. Another is that, as print publication expanded in the 1730s, it became clear that occasional verse, including familiar epistles, could be printed for profit.

Among the first of the labouring-class poets to seize the opportunity offered by the marketability of epistles was John Bancks.[104] Although the 11 poems of Bancks's first book, *The Weaver's Miscellany* (1730), include no items entitled 'epistle', 2 are epistolary and a further 2, both informal amatory odes, are close to epistolary form. Bancks went further in his next book, *Poems on Several Occasions* (1733),[105] advertising the presence of epistles as well as 'Songs, Odes, Epigrams, and other Miscellaneous Pieces' in his subtitle, and including, out of a total of 66 verse items, 7 poems entitled 'Epistle' and a further 4 epistolary poems, all of which are familiar, amatory or humorous. In his *Miscellaneous Works* of 1738, his final publication as a poet,[106] he raised the proportion of epistolary verse by including, among a total of 165 poems in its two volumes, 17 entitled 'Epistle', 1 'Letter in Verse and Prose', and 13 further items identifiable as verse epistles from page headings or other contextual indicators. This produces a total of 31, or nearly 19 per cent. In the same year he also had one of the epistles from his first volume printed separately. *Love Atones for Little Crimes: An Ethic Epistle, by Way of Apology for a Darling Passion* is a humorous plea for tolerance in sexual matters, set off by jaunty iambic tetrameter couplets, tongue-in-cheek *Cum notis variorum*, Horatian epigraph, and a sly appropriation of Pope's adjective for a verse epistle on social morality.[107]

It is not just the number of epistles in Bancks's output that distinguishes his contribution to the form. Not only did he offer his own views on how it might be defined, as I have shown in Chapter 1, but he also gave witty demonstrations of how a writer such as he could turn it to gain. A case in point from his second collection is 'A Very Critical and Moral Epistle, to the Same' – the addressee of the previous poem, 'Mr. J. W.' (probably John Winship). This begins by making fun of the fact that familiar letters need not necessarily aim to say anything in particular:

> The Subject? prithee, what dost mean?
> In Letters, when are Subjects seen?
> If I write on, and write to please ye,
> In Name of Goodness *John*, be easy.[108]

Claiming that 'we may write for writing sake' (p. 113), Bancks produces 236 lines of whimsical verse. Part of the joke is his recognition that his verse is not very good, and that he is spinning it out for fun. Referring, for instance, to one of the best early eighteenth-century writers of light verse, he wryly remarks: 'Had *Prior* not so finely writ, / Mine might have past for Sterling Wit' (p. 114). Yet the poem wanders into a discussion of life in general, including the role of free will and providence, that reads as a kind of poor man's equivalent of Pope's *Essay on Man*, published in epistle form at the same time. Arguing, for example, that what will be probably just has to be, Bancks humorously opines:

> If Freewill in the Creature rest,
> She can but counterplot at best:
> If Things in destin'd Order fall,
> Poor Chance has got no Chance at all. (p. 119)

In the end, the title turns out to be less a joke than it seemed, as the poem goes on to offer homespun philosophy on how to cope with life. Its final lines are surprisingly serious and orthodox: 'Be ne'er transported nor deprest, / And leave to Providence the rest' (p. 120).

But the work in which Bancks showed most fully his ability to exploit the familiar epistle is 'The Progress of Petitioning; in Three Epistles to Mr. Pope', which, along with 'The Author's Picture: A Fourth Epistle to Mr. Pope', enjoys pride of place in Volume 2 of his *Miscellaneous Works*. Here Bancks presents a version not only of the familiar epistle but of its grander relative, the complimentary epistle, often written to ask for financial or other patronage. As William Christmas has pointed out, he also offers a humorous version of the progress narrative that was so popular in the period in painting as well as in literature.[109] Bancks's note to the third epistle provides a sample of his shrewd insight into the relations between poetry, print and patronage, and of his wit:

> For as much as the getting of Money is usually the great End of all laudable Performances and Endeavours (even among Poets themselves, notwithstanding their pretended Disinterestedness with regard to the Affairs of this mortal Life) our Author, after two introductory Epistles, explains himself fully and honestly on this Article, in his third Petition. He proves, by undeniable Arguments, that a good Place, with a certain Salary, is much preferable to the Reputation of being a Poet, or even to the Encouragement of Booksellers and Readers. He shews at large, that Modesty is a great Obstacle to noble Attempts, and should therefore be thrown aside when we have any such in View; by which means he decently excuses this last and highest Degree of the *Progress of Petitioning*.[110]

According to one of Bancks's footnotes, Pope responded with a note subscribing for two sets of his *Works* and a couplet stating his verdict on the poems: 'May THESE put Money in your Purse, / For I assure you, I've read worse' (II, 43). Bancks's skill at enclosing his tongue in his cheek, and his discretion in not claiming any special merit for his writing, enabled him to ply the epistle form to amusing effect and probably also for some profit.[111]

While the epistle was a favourite form among labouring-class poets, others among them employed it differently. For example, the 4 poems entitled 'Epistle' and 2 further epistolary items out of the 24 poems in Robert Dodsley's *A Muse in Livery* (1732) range from the familiar ('The Footman. An Epistle to my Friend Mr. Wright') to the complimentary ('An Epistle to Stephen Duck');[112] but Mary Masters uses the form in a quite different manner. Although her two collections embrace only a few poems entitled 'Epistle', they also contain, along with some religious poems including imitations of Psalms, much social/moral verse that has an epistolary character.[113] This is shown most clearly by the circumstantial titles she gave several pieces in her second collection, such as 'Sent to a Young Lady in Town, Who Had Vow'd to Die a Maid, in Answer to a Letter, Where, in a Copy of Verses, She Signify'd her Resolution, and Desired an Account of the House and its Situation, in Which a New Married Lady of her Acquaintance Settled. Wrote Suddenly at the Request of her Correspondent in a Very Sultry Day'.[114] As its title suggests, the collection also includes prose letters, 31 in all, in keeping with the practice by then well established for female as well as for male poets.

The most gifted and interesting labouring-class poet of the period is now widely and rightly acknowledged as Mary Leapor. Like Mary Barber, Leapor wrote much epistolary verse, though often without drawing explicit attention to its nature in her titles. Her *Poems upon Several Occasions*, published in two volumes three years apart after her tragic early death, contain 103 poems of which 99 are by her. Only 4 of her poems designate themselves as epistles, and only 1 as a letter.[115] Yet a further 23 are clearly epistolary in character, making a total of 28, or over 28 per cent. Unlike Mary Barber's, however, few of Leapor's poems are complimentary. Although, as a domestic servant, she had even fewer social advantages,[116] her ambitions as a poet ran higher. This is clear from such enterprising non-epistolary work as 'The Fields of Melancholy and Chearfulness' (pp. 81–6), 'Man the Monarch' (pp. 159–61), and 'Crumble-Hall' (pp. 206–11), along with the tragedy she completed and a further play that she left unfinished. But much of her epistolary verse shows comparable ambition, even when it is familiar or humorous.

Leapor's most serious epistolary verse is discursive or advisory. Four bear the title 'Essay', proclaiming not only their ethical character but also the inspiration of Pope;[117] yet her advisory and even her familiar poems often have a moral focus too. Examples of advisory epistles are the two entitled 'Mira to Octavia' (pp. 142–4, 202–6); two addressed to Stella, one 'On Discontent' (pp. 95–6), the other 'On Patience' (pp. 157–8); and 'Celadon to Mira' (pp. 77–80), addressed to herself. Examples of familiar epistles that have serious ends are 'An Epistle to a Lady' (pp. 24–6), 'The Consolation' (pp. 192–3), and 'The Visit' (pp. 222–3). Leapor also wrote two fine parodies of the conventional invitation, 'To Artemisia. Dr. King's Invitation to Bellvill: Imitated' (pp. 61–2),[118] and 'The Sacrifice. An Epistle to Celia' (pp. 125–7), along with the mocking 'Strephon to Celia. A Modern Love-Letter' (pp. 59–61), and wry reflections on her position as a woman and poet in poems such as 'The Head-Ach. To Aurelia' (pp. 58–9), 'To Grammaticus' (pp. 69–71), and 'The Epistle of Deborah Dough' (pp. 186–8). Her epistolary verse shows her not only exploiting the form to make occasions for poetry, as Mary Barber had done, but learning from some of its best past practitioners, especially Pope, and extending several of its branches. Had she survived, she would almost certainly have developed it further. Two collections from the second half of the century provide a final example of a woman favouring epistolary verse. Priscilla Pointon was born into somewhat better circumstances than Mary Leapor, but, according to the Preface to her *Poems on Several Occasions* (1770), she lost her sight 'so early as her thirteenth year'.[119] Although the quality of her verse is for the most part undistinguished, it is of interest not only because much of it is epistolary, but also for the special case it presents of how verse of that type, in David Fairer's phrase, hovers 'between manuscript and print'.[120] Some of Pointon's poems evidently circulated in manuscript before her collection was published with a subscription list of well over 1500 names. It contains a total of 69 poems, 65 of which are by her. Most of her poems are of a familiar, social nature, and many have highly circumstantial titles, recalling those by Mary Masters – for example, 'To a Young Tradesman, Who Complained That He Had Secretly Languished for a Lady of Distinction in the Neighbourhood for a Long Time, without the Least Hope of a Favourable Return; and on the Next Day the Author Addressed Him with the Following Epistle' (pp. 23–4). All 6 of her poems that identify themselves as epistles by using the word in their titles are familiar, as is the single poem that styles itself as a letter. A further 21 poems may also be classified as epistolary, most of them verse letters but including 2 valentines and 2 invitations. This reckoning yields a total of 28 epistolary poems, or just over 43 per cent.

The reason that Pointon presents a special case is that her verse not only hovers between manuscript and print but introduces her composing voice too. Her 'Epistle to a Young Lady, Who Greatly Complained to the Author of her Long Silence' (pp. 80–2), indicates that she depended on others to write her poems down – the dearth of companions prepared to do so accounting for the silence of which her friend had complained. For this reason, it is not surprising that she had a special facility for extempore composition. No fewer than 31 of her titles identify poems made in that way, including 4 odes, 3 elegies, 2 enigmas, 2 invitations, a valentine and an epistle as well as a number of addresses delivered orally. Indeed, 7 of her poems bear the title 'An Address', in the sense of 'A discourse specially directed to any one, a formal speech of congratulation, respect, thanks, petition, etc.' (*OED*, 11.a), and 6 of these were clearly oral performances. The exception is one of her best poems, 'Address to a Bachelor, on a Delicate Occasion', which is marked as epistolary by its opening line, 'You bid me write, Sir, I comply' (p. 51).[121] In this she rebukes a male host who had humiliated her in company when she needed help to leave the room to relieve herself while his maidservants were out. The poem must have circulated in manuscript, for it bears the subtitle 'Inserted by Desire'. Its valediction is properly stinging: 'Adieu – enjoy your empty fun' (p. 52).

Pointon published a second collection in 1794 under her married name of Pickering, after her husband had died and she had fallen on hard times.[122] The volume contains 38 of her poems, though it is eked out by a further 59, mostly by two well-wishers, one of whom acted as editor.[123] Consistently with the decline in popularity of the verse letter towards the end of the century, it contains fewer poems of this type than her first collection: 1 entitled an epistle, 1 a letter, and 8 others that may be classified as epistolary, producing a total of 10 or a little over 26 per cent. But this is still quite a high proportion, much higher than that of the poems by other writers in the collection, which includes little further epistolary verse. The proportion of extempore verse, all by Pointon, is also much lower at 4 items, though it includes the single poem entitled an epistle; and, while 1 of her 3 poems styled as addresses is epistolary, neither of the other 2 – to Time and to Patience – indicates that it was delivered orally. These reductions in extempore and oral material are probably not to be explained by her marriage, because that took place relatively late, in 1788.[124] They may have resulted from a decline in public interest after the success of her subscription in 1770. More likely, however, they reflect a gradual move away from the cultural attitudes and practices that favoured epistolary verse, public addresses and extempore performance. No doubt Pointon's blindness encouraged her to produce such kinds of verse. The same fact is further evidence of the popularity of the verse letter in the period, especially among women writers.

Allan Ramsay supplies a final example of the importance of the verse epistle to writers from the margins. Although, unlike several of his compatriots, Ramsay does not feature in *Eighteenth-Century English Labouring-Class Poets*, his early life as a shepherd boy and wigmaker gives him a claim to have been represented there.[125] He was able to advance himself in business, moving from wigmaking to bookselling and publishing, and through his writing. But his position was marginal on account not only of his social rank but of his nationality as a Scot.

As mentioned in Chapter 1, Ramsay showed an interest that was early for the period in arranging his collected verse by genre. The Index to his

Poems of 1721 lists a total of 84 items, of which 80 are by him.[126] Eighteen poems, of which 14 are his, are set down as 'Epistolary', including 'Seven Familiar Epistles Pass'd between Lieut. Hamilton and the Author'; a further 2 poems entitled 'Epistle' are placed under other headings ('Comick' and 'Satyrick' respectively). Although Ramsay did not classify his poems in his second volume, published in 1728, he specified the genre of a large number in their titles. The 100 poems listed in the Contents, 98 of which are his, style 9 as 'Epistle' and a further 2 as 'Answer'.[127] One-volume editions and two-volume editions later in the century dropped the system of classification in their tables of contents, though they often listed Ramsay's songs separately; but it was reinstated and extended by George Chalmers to all of Ramsay's verse known at the time in an edition of 1800 that became the standard one until the twentieth century.[128] Its two tables of contents list a total of 225 poems, of which 35 are categorized as epistles, 27 of them written by Ramsay; in accordance with the Index to his volume of 1721, two of his poems entitled 'Epistle' are placed under other headings. The total includes 2 poems by Ramsay entitled 'Epistle' that were printed but not collected in his lifetime, along with 2 answers to epistles sent to him by others; a further 4 poems entitled 'Epistle' surviving in manuscript, plus 2 fragments, have been published subsequently. Even these do not represent all his epistolary verse, as some of his poems with titles in the form 'To [. . .]' clearly belong to the genre.

At least 20 of the more than 30 epistolary poems by Ramsay are familiar. This is significant, because it demonstrates again how often verse of that kind existed 'between manuscript and print', or was not even intended for print. More significant still is the fact that Ramsay not only anticipated Bancks and others in turning familiar epistles to profit, but also directed them to other ends. As a firm opponent of the parliamentary union with England established by the Act of 1707, he used his verse to promote Scottish interests. His many epistles not only offer another example of the exchange of verse as a social practice, but illustrate a further use to which the form could be put by a writer from the social margins.

In 1719 Ramsay began publishing *Familiar Epistles between W[illiam] H[amilton] and A[llan] R[amsay]*. Begun by Hamilton in compliment to him, the series expanded to six poems and was later capped by a seventh. It is not known whether the two had met before they corresponded, but the first exchange suggests that they had not, and there is no sign that Hamilton expected his epistle to be printed. As an enterprising bookseller as well as poet, Ramsay no doubt saw that opportunity quickly. But, having recently begun to write in Scots as well as in standard English, he also grasped it as a chance to promote Scottish writing. Referring in his first response to Hamilton to several contemporary English poems, including Pope's *Rape of the Lock*,[129] he laid down a challenge:

> The Chiels of *London, Cam,* and *Ox,*   *fellows*
> Ha'e rais'd up great Poetick Stocks
> Of *Rapes,* of *Buckets, Sarks* and *Locks,*
>   While we neglect
> To shaw their betters. This provokes
>   Me to reflect
>
> On the learn'd Days of *Gawn Dunkell,*
> Our Country then a Tale cou'd tell,
> *Europe* had nane mair snack and snell   *none more clever and*
>   At Verse or Prose;   *sharp*
> Our Kings were Poets too themsell,
>   Bauld and Jocose. (I, 120) *bold*

In celebrating the glory days of Gavin Douglas and James I and V of Scotland, Ramsay also looked to bring them back. He therefore not only wrote in Scots but adopted from Hamilton the distinctively Scottish verse form that he named in the same poem as 'Standart *Habby*' (I, 119).[130] And he practised it with dash – the running-on of the first stanza above into the second is surely not, as Allan MacLaine remarks, 'awkward',[131] but an exhilarating demonstration of mastery of the form.

The epistles between Hamilton and Ramsay are important not only in themselves but because they launched a new form of Scottish writing that was to develop during the century and to culminate in the work of Burns. Ramsay also wrote epistles of other kinds – satirical, humorous, and complimentary[132] – and, in some of his familiar epistles, he discussed various social and moral questions as well as promoting Scotland and its literature. But what he communicates at his most characteristic is warmth and friendship. In this respect above all he maintained the spirit of the familiar letter. Even while he was still making his way as a poet and bookseller, he did not print all his familiar epistles;[133] and, when his prosperity in later life removed much of the incentive to publish, he continued exchanging them.[134] Though some familiar epistles by various authors that were not intended for publication exist in manuscript,[135] many more must have been written. Those that survive, not least Ramsay's, underline once more the importance of epistolary verse in the period as a cultural practice.

3
Familiar and Humorous

Most discussions of the eighteenth-century verse epistle chiefly confine themselves, like William C. Dowling in *The Epistolary Moment*, to the discursive variant – what Pope and John Bell called the ethic epistle.[1] The reasons for such a bias stem from the seriousness that such poems claim for themselves, commenting as they do on a wide range of subjects including religion, morality, the arts and poetry itself. A much humbler form, the familiar epistle was often cultivated by people who made no pretensions to social or cultural importance – especially, as I have shown in the previous chapter, by women and by labouring-class writers of both sexes. At a time, too, when writing verse was a social accomplishment, verse letters were often written by people who would not have considered themselves poets, though some of them had enough skill or panache to find their way into print. It is therefore not surprising that, although many occasional epistles must have failed to survive, the type is still the most common in published verse of the period. For example, it makes up over a quarter of the sample in my database of 867 eighteenth-century epistles assembled from *Literature Online*.[2] But, for all its neglect by the academy, and for all its own tendency to depreciate itself, it is a mistake to undervalue the form. It has much to show about literate social relations at the period, and the role played in them by verse-writing, and also about changes in taste and the development of the literary market. Not least, too, as I hope this chapter will show, many are fine poems in their own right. The chapter also considers the humorous epistle, which developed from the familiar type and established its own presence in the period. It does not consider epistles that are primarily discursive in content although familiar in genre or tone, such as the various verse letters from abroad of the period, or Matthew Green's 'The Spleen'.[3] Epistles of this type are discussed in Chapter 4 instead.

The familiar epistle resembles an actual letter more closely than any other variant of the form, and, as mentioned at the end of the previous chapter, some actual letters in verse have survived from the period. Because ordinary prose correspondence is rarely lengthy, most familiar epistles are considerably shorter than discursive, dramatic or narrative epistles. The shortest I have come across, Elizabeth Thomas's 'Laconick Epistle to Clemena', is a mere two lines long, while the longest, the anonymous 'Familiar Epistle, from a Law-Student, in the Country, to his Friend, at the Temple', runs to 476.[4] These, it goes without saying, are unusual. Out of 250 familiar epistles in my database, the average length is just under 98 lines, but 71 have 50 lines or fewer, and 167 have 200 lines or fewer, whereas only 7 have more than 300 lines. Also on account of its relative closeness to normal correspondence, the verse form of most familiar epistles tends to informality. In the same database, the commonest verse form for familiar epistles is iambic tetrameter couplets, often with hypermetrical end-of-line light stresses with double or forced rhymes, followed fairly closely by iambic pentameter couplets – not usually, as with heroic couplets, closed. Familiar epistles in Rochester's *Poems on Several Occasions* of 1680 and in Dryden's miscellany, often reprinted, probably helped set both patterns: especially the exchanges between Etherege and Lord Buckhurst (later Earl of Dorset) in the one and Etherege, the Earl of Middleton and Dryden (ghosting for the latter) in the other, along with Matthew Prior's 'Epistle to Fleetwood Shephard, Esq'.[5] All these are in tetrameter, pentameter being preferred for less informal epistles such as the four in Dryden's miscellany by Charles Hopkins and those by Thomas Otway and Francis Knapp.[6] The verse form next most frequently used in the familiar epistle is the anapestic tetrameter couplet, again often with humorous light endings and rhymes. This comes a poor third at a little over 10 per cent of the sample, followed closely by the Standard Habby at a little under 10 per cent. Familiar epistles rarely employ blank verse, with its more serious associations; but other stanzaic forms than the Standard Habby, albeit used only very occasionally, include quatrains and even, rarely, the 'Song to David' stanza.[7]

Another sign that the familiar variety is closer than other types of epistle to actual correspondence is that it much more often includes salutations, valedictions, and details of the time and place of writing. These may be placed outside or inside the opening or closing verse lines, though they are more often included within them. Those that fall outside the verse line tend to carry a more formal air, as when John Hoadly begins with the word 'Madam' a poem to the Marchioness Grey accompanying his opera *Phoebe*, or when Mary Leapor opens 'To Grammaticus', a poem of ironic apology, with the separate word 'Sir'.[8] Similarly, Alexander Nicol not only provides the salutation 'Sir' for his two epistles to Allan Ramsay but ends both poems with the separate, formal, valediction of his name in full.[9] As an unknown poet seeking to impress Ramsay with one poem in the Standard Habby form and the other in a version of the demanding Cherry and Slae stanza,[10] he maintains a respectful distance. Nicol adopts the same device in two other more serious poems, 'An Epistle to a Friend Newly Married, against the Will of his Wife's Friends', which begins '*Kind Friend*' and ends '*Farewell*'; and 'An Epistle, or New-Year's Gift, to a Young Merchant in Perth, January 1st 1751', which has no salutation but ends with the separate formal valediction 'I am, Yours, &c. / Alex. Nicol'.[11] Further examples of separate valedictions, though less formal, close Josiah Relph's 'To the Printer of the Kendal Courant' ('*Yours* ——'), the anonymous 'To the Author. In Answer to the Foregoing Epistle' ('&c. &c.'), and Lewis Thomas's 'Captain Thomas, of Battereau's Regiment, in the Isle of Skie, to Captain Price, at Fort Augustus' ('C. T.').[12] But a few of Allan Ramsay's poems suggest that valedictions and details of time and place of writing were sometimes omitted when epistles were printed or reprinted. For example, 'An Epistle to Lieutenant Hamilton, on the Receiving the Compliment of a Barrel of Loch-Fine Herrings from him' ends in early editions with the signature 'SIR, / *Yours*, &c. / A. R.';[13] and several poems unpublished in Ramsay's lifetime conclude with subscriptions ranging in formality from 'A. R.' to 'So Sayth, Sir your humble Servt / Allan Ramsay / of Edr. in his Grand Climaterek', along with a drawing of his head in caricature, and 'Your ever obliged, / humble servant, / Allan Ramsay. / Pennycuik, / *May* 9, 1755'.[14]

Details of time and place of writing, and even the writer's name, are not, of course, always easy to versify. For this reason, the most common practice is to give them in prose below the body of the epistle – a practice that nevertheless conveys the impression of an actual letter, whether that was what it was or not. But the more enterprising writers often incorporate salutation and valediction within the poem, and even, albeit rarely, an address and/or a date too. One of Alexander Nicol's correspondents wryly gives up his attempt at the latter as follows, his otherwise fairly fluent Standard Habby stanzas breaking down after the lines 'In verse acrostic my name I thought to sen'; / But waes me now, a hair is in my pen', so that he closes with the deliberately over-formal subscription: 'This, with my compliments to you and your spouse, / is from, / SIR, / Your humble and obedient servant, / D—— L——, A. B. / Teacher of the school of Kinnaird'.[15] Others are more skilful, especially in managing valedictory metre and rhyme. One way of solving one of D—— L——'s problems, adopted quite often, is to rhyme 'servant' with 'fervent';[16] while others contrive rhyming signatures. Among the most ingenious of these are 'I'll own I am sae, / And while my Champers can chew Bread, / Yours — ALLAN RAMSAY' (ending a Standard Habby stanza); 'My pleasurable Labours done, / Subscribe, your Servant PATTISON'; 'And am with ev'ry compliment which due is, / Your most obedient servant, ESTHER LEWIS'; and, in emulation of Ramsay, 'And that your saul may never dive / To *Acheron*, / I'll wish as lang's I can subscrive / ROB. FERGUSSON'.[17] Other devices include the use of initials in rhymes, as several times by Priscilla Pointon (later Pickering, so her initials stayed the same after marriage), and, more subtly, the phrase 'One whom no body knows' (the last word rhyming with 'prose') to end Mary Savage's 'Letter to my Friend E. B.', a poem that comments critically but humorously on the fashionable social scene.[18] In an epistle to the same addressee, Savage managed to find a rhyme for the stock abbreviation '&c.' for the writer's name, through the jaunty expedient of shortening it further by omitting the final syllable ('cet.' rhyming with 'fate').[19]

These examples demonstrate that, just like some familiar prose letters, familiar verse epistles often aimed to amuse as well as to show the writer's skill at versifying. Early in the century Edward Ward has the writer of his 'Letter from a Lawyer in Town, to a New Married Officer in the Country' finding time 'to thus Salute-ye, / And pay in Rhime this Friendly Duty', and ends the poem with an outrageously forced triplet: 'Excuse me Friend, in what I Write t'ye, / And don't forget the *Aqua-Vitae*, / Is all I Beg, and so Good B'y't'ye'.[20] Similarly, Pope begins his 'Epistle to Henry Cromwell, Esq;' with a verse salutation ('*Dear Mr. Cromwell*, / May it please ye!'), and dates it approximately at the end in humorously poor rhyme ('The twelfth or thirteenth Day of *July*, / But which, I cannot tell you truly'); John Smith, after saluting his addressee in his first line ('You left me ill, but, *Sir*, your Letter'), closes 'Epistle to Sir R. E.' with the droll valediction: 'And I'll be, what I ever was, / Your Friend, and Servant / J. S. pos.'; Anthony Alsop hails his epistle to the Rev. Sir John Dolben, D. D., with 'Sir John, or Doctor, choose you whether' and takes his leave with equal brio: 'Thus, having tir'd myself and you, Sir, / I kiss your hands, and so adieu! Sir'; Samuel Derrick begins his 'Epistle to the Reverend Mr. ****' with a salutation within the verse line ('Dear Crape'), ending it not only with a comic valediction but versified address and date ('Advice will therefore be expedient, / To, Sir, your humble and obedient. // From my apartments, June the second, / May twenty first, by old stile reckon'd'); and Francis Fawkes opens his 'Journey to Doncaster; or, a Curious Journal of Five Days. Wrote with a Pencil in a Chaise' with the separate salutation 'Dear Anne', but closes it with the couplet: 'Wrote, dearest Anne, at your commands, / And now it flies to kiss your hands'.[21]

In her short career, Mary Leapor showed special wit and adeptness with the same protocols in epistolary poems. Addressing an aspiring poet, she begins with an elegant salutation, 'Since you, *Myrtillo*, will devote your Time', but ends with a humorous, self-deprecating dampener, 'Still may you scribble on; and in the End / Be just as rich as – Sir, your humble Friend'; and, in one of two poems advising a friend about marriage, opens with 'Fair One, to you this Monitor I send', but, considering it likely that her advice will not be accepted, ends dryly: 'But if there's none but *Florio* that will do, / Write Ballads both, and you may thrive – Adieu'.[22] Leapor also finds a rhyme for 'adieu' at the end of 'The Sacrifice. An Epistle to Celia', which begins: 'If you, dear *Celia*, cannot bear', and ends: 'Yes at your Peril: But adieu, / I've tir'd both myself and you'; but only in two dramatic epistles, 'Strephon to Celia. A Modern Love-Letter', and 'The Epistle of Deborah Dough', did she subscribe a name; both poems are humorous and are discussed more fully below.[23] But it was probably Burns who, among his many familiar epistles, versified the tops and tails of correspondence most vivaciously, even though for some he gave one or both separately in prose.[24] Examples beyond the two already mentioned include 'To William Simson, Ochiltree, May 1785', which begins: 'I gat your letter, winsome Willie', and ends, before a long postscript: 'While Terra Firma, on her axis, / Diurnal turns; / Count on a friend, in faith an' practice, / In ROBERT BURNS'; 'Third Epistle to J. Lapraik. Sept. 13, 1785', which opens: 'Guid speed an' further to you Johny', and closes: 'Then I maun rin among the rest / An' quat my chanter; / Sae I subscribe myself in haste, / Yours, RAB THE RANTER'; and 'To Mr Gavin Hamilton, Esq., Mauchline. Recommending a Boy. Mossgaville, May 3, 1786', which starts with 'I hold it, Sir, my bounden duty', and finishes with 'To phrase you, an' praise you, / Ye ken, your LAUREAT scorns: / The PRAY'R still, you share still / Of grateful MINSTREL BURNS'.[25] Postscripts occur only rarely, even among familiar epistles, though they are a little more common in the humorous and satirical types. Examples in familiar epistles include several from Scottish poets. Hamilton and Nicol, and one of Nicol's correspondents, contribute one apiece, and Burns two; others may be found ending Mary Barber's 'Letter Written for my Son to a Young Gentleman, Who Was Sent to be Educated at the Jesuits College in Flanders', John Byrom's 'Letter to R. L., Esq', on his Departure from London', and Thomas Gilbert's 'Familiar Epistle to Doctor Reeve, in London'.[26] Once more, the inclusion of a postscript in a familiar epistle indicates its closeness to an actual letter.

But crucial to the familiar epistle is a different kind of closeness: a sense of friendship and cordiality. The sincerity of that sense is, of course, impossible to certify, not least because even the most intimate of letters, not written with a view to publication, is unlikely to be innocent of art. It is a question of finding apt words and metre to convey warmth, affection or respect. This is often best done with a light touch, as when Anthony Alsop follows his salutation to Sir John Dolben, already quoted, with the line 'Or Friend, a better name than either', goes on to declare a preference for the 'living furniture' of his friend's estate above the 'costly traffic / That comes from India, Spain, or Afric', and, after complimenting the lady of the house and the three children, ends with a humorous apology for what he claims is the poor quality of his letter: 'For where no better can be had, / Respect is shown, tho' fare be bad'.[27] D. K. Money declares that, 'For at least some contemporaries', Alsop 'was the best Latin poet in the world' (*ODNB*). Though Alsop cultivated verse in English much less, he provides in this ostensibly casual poem, which was almost certainly not written for publication,[28] an engaging example of the type.

Another way to express warmth with evident sincerity is to do so in the teeth of a recognition that it is easily simulated. So John Bancks ends 'The Diurnal', a poem about how he spends his time, with the words:

'Tis not th' epistolary Strain,
Without a Compliment, or twain:
Take then what Love a Verse can bring,
(If Love in Verse be any Thing)
The greatest Part belongs to you;
The rest divide among the Few,
Who best deserve the Name of Friend. –
– 'Tis not amiss with Love to end. (117–24)[29]

Bancks follows 'The Diurnal' with a poem entitled 'Friendship' that takes the same addressee kindly but firmly to task for failing to respond. The ground on which he does so is that letters are important for sustaining friendship over periods of absence:

My gen'rous Friend, forgive the Muse,
Who dar'd this Liberty to use!
She knew the Sparks were still the same,
And only strove to make them flame.
A distant Friendship often lives
But on the Breath a Letter gives:

And still the Passion most improves,
When most the warm Expression moves. (102–9)[30]

The words may be simple and direct, but they enhance the appeal rather than hinder it. Similarly, opening a long journal-letter about his voyage from England to Calcutta via Rio de Janeiro, Thomas Pearson expresses a warmth heightened, no doubt, by long absence and great distance:

> To thee, dear Dan, my better part;
> The kind associate of my heart;
> The friend, which in the boy began,
> Approv'd and settled in the man;
> My long, long journey near an end,
> What pass'd upon the road I send. (1–6)[31]

Pearson ends his account with some poignant lines on how much he misses those he has left behind, whom he may never see again:

> Perhaps a Sister is no more;
> Perhaps my Friend may now deplore
> Some hardship, when my rightful part
> Might ease the sorrows of his heart.
> Such are the fears I undergo;
> Fancy's the Parent oft of Woe. (709–14)

The fact that he writes 720 lines of verse informing and entertaining his friend with his impressions on the voyage itself declares his friendship, especially as he could hardly have expected the epistle to be published.[32]

When Pearson confides his fears at the end of his epistle, he shows the kind of vulnerability that could only be expressed to a friend. In 'The Visit', which Richard Greene describes as presenting 'an unusual picture of Mira simply defeated by the "scolding Dame" and the gossips and physiognomists of Brackley',[33] Mary Leapor does much the same. She addresses Bridget Freemantle ('Artemisia') with an ironic compliment that could only be paid to a close friend – 'O ARTEMISIA! dear to me, / As to the Lawyer golden Fee' (5–6) – praises her warmly in the next couplet ('Whose Name dwells pleasant on my Tongue, / And first, and last, shall grace my Song'), and spends the rest of the poem revealing her misery from malicious comments on her personal appearance, a misery that only her friend's company can relieve.[34] Epistles celebrating friendship may refer to the addressee's troubles as well as the poet's, as the then pedlar, later ornithologist, Alexander Wilson shows in his 'Epistle to a Pedlar' and in a series of three poems to William Mitchell, another aspiring poet down on his luck. The final stanza of 'Third Epistle to William Mitchell' illustrates not only this but also the skilful handling of the Cherry and Slae form that is part of Wilson's tribute:

Adieu, my kind, my wordy chield;	*worthy fellow*
Lang may ye hae a cozie bield,	*snug shelter*
To screen frae Winter's cauld;	
May time yet see ye wi' a wame	*belly*
As fat as J——'s sonsy dame,	*jolly*
Till thretty year thrice tauld;	
An' gin we live to see that date,	*if*
As, fegs, I hope we will;	*faith*
Tho' ye to gang, hae tint the gate,	*go; lost the way*
Yet we sal hae a gill.	*shall have*
Fu' cheary, I'll rear ye,	
And 'neath my burden bend;	
And show fouk, without joke,	*folk*
What it's to hae a friend. (113–26)[35]	

Wilson was inspired by Burns, who supplies an example of how to express bluff affection in his 'Epistle to Dr. Blacklock', in Standard Habby form, which begins:

Wow, but your letter made me vauntie!	*proud*
And are ye hale, and weel, and cantie?	*well, cheerful*
I kend it still, your wee bit jauntie	*knew, small journey*
Wad bring ye to:	*would*
Lord send you ay as weel's I want ye,	*always; well as*
And then ye'll do.—[36]	

For reasons to be considered later in this chapter, it was perhaps the Scots poets who found the finest ways of conveying the sense of camaraderie that distinguishes many familiar epistles.

That sense is a leading example of the 'addressee-consciousness' that Janet Altman defines as a prime characteristic of epistolary texts.[37] In the familiar epistle, it is so important a feature that there is a close relation between the degree of the poem's familiarity and that of its orientation towards its addressee. As a corollary, familiar epistles rarely address other readers either explicitly or by implication, even though the poet may have expected that the addressee would not have been the only reader. In this they differ markedly from discursive and satirical epistles, which usually imply or openly invoke an external readership, as Chapters 4 and 6 will show. Yet the consequence is not that the reader is likely to feel shut out. Instead, because the external reader occupies a position analogous to though distinct from that of the addressee, one of the pleasures of reading a familiar epistle is the sense of participating, by proxy, in an exchange of affection and cordiality. Inflected in various ways, it is a sense that most of the examples to be discussed in the chapter will show.

Like their discursive cousins, familiar epistles may be written on all kinds of subjects. The key difference is that, reflecting again their equivalence or proximity to actual correspondence, their subject-matter almost always concerns the events that occasion them. As familiar epistles may cite events of all kinds as their motive, constructing a typology is difficult. Nevertheless, several broad categories may be distinguished. Excluding the numerous verse letters that chiefly give news about what the writer is doing, and his or her opinions about it, the largest is the advisory epistle, in which the writer offers personal guidance to the addressee. Here, a crucial term of the definition is 'personal' – this type of epistle differs from a discursive epistle in that, though it may invoke general principles or experiences, it is tailored to particular circumstances. Other subtypes stem from special kinds of occasion: familiar epistles may congratulate (for example, on marriage), or condole (for example, on bereavement); or they may give accounts of a journey or an unusual event. Perhaps the most distinct subtype is the invitation. Horace's Epistle V, 'To Torquatus', attracted many eighteenth-century imitators, and naturally led to verse responses too. The type of epistle that accompanies a gift of some kind also often falls into the familiar category; if its tone and language are formal, it might better be classified as complimentary. As examples in Chapter 6 will indicate, complimentary epistles are often informed by relations of material or social disparity between writer and addressee, whereas it is important that, whatever their actual status, the writer of a familiar epistle can relate to the addressee more or less equally. But tone and language cannot alone identify the familiar epistle. The reason for this is that, as a genre, the epistle is at least nominally informal. At the start of the century, Samuel Wesley declared: 'None than th' *Epistle* goes more *humbly* drest, / Tho' *neat* 'twould be, and *decent* as the *best*'.[38] Though he overstated the point, and though some writers of discursive epistles, especially John Byrom, pressed this quality further than others, an epistle concerned with a religious or moral topic, or with scholarly disputation, is more an essay than a familiar letter. The rest of this discussion of the familiar epistle considers examples of the commonest types, and also some others of special interest.

It is appropriate to begin with an example on the subject itself. Though the guidance offered by St John Honeywood's 'Poetical Epistle to a Young Lady, on Letter Writing' applies to letters of all kinds, much of it holds true for familiar letters in verse. Early in the poem, Honeywood explains why he thinks such advice important: 'Since letters well written give exquisite pleasure, / But mangled, as usual, offend beyond measure'.[39] A balance must be struck between the perfunctory – 'I'm in good health, thank heav'n; how is it with you?' (2) – and the laboured, as with those 'Who can talk half a day in an elegant strain, / But whatever they write seems confin'd with a chain' (9–10). For this reason, Honeywood enjoins the ease and informality of expression recommended earlier in the century by Ambrose Philips's *Spectator* essay and Newbery's *Art of Poetry on a New Plan*.[40] The 'great secret', he says, is to 'Write in just the same manner you'd speak to your friend' (15–16); but he goes on to emphasize that this still requires some art: 'For letters, though free, yet require some connection' (30). In the remainder of the poem, not altogether without patronising his addressee, he gives more mundane advice, including on spelling, layout and erasure. But his fluent, down-to-earth style and unpretentious anapestic tetrameter couplets help illustrate his precepts, as when he disarmingly concludes: 'From numbers, though artless, some good may accrue, / So with my best wishes, dear *Clara*, adieu' (69–70).

Among advisory epistles like Honeywood's, common topics include childcare and education, marriage, and choice or management of a career. While, writing from experience, Ann Yearsley offered enlightened advice 'To Mira, on the Care of her Infant', Mary Savage sought to give counsel on a subject identified in her title, 'To a School-boy at Eton. Yes and No', and Priscilla Pointon, who was fond of advisory poems, addressed two to a cousin in her early teens.[41] Addressing men at later stages of their careers, Claudero (James Wilson) contributed 'An Epistle to a Young Gentleman, Dissuading Him from Entering into Holy Orders', and Jonathan Smedley 'An Epistle to An Irish Parson, of a Small Benefice, Resolved to Live in London'; but John Straight gave ill-timed advice in 'To Mr. John Hoadly, at the Temple, Occasioned by a Translation of an Epistle of Horace, 1730', for, as Hoadly pointed out in his reply, he had already abandoned the law for the church, the better to pursue the literary interests that Straight cautioned him for favouring.[42] The first and third of these poems are in what might be called a tradition, normally masculine, of epistles to young friends. Further examples are Thomas Catesby Pagett's 'Epistle to a Young Gentleman', and, already mentioned, Alexander Nicol's 'An Epistle, or New-Year's Gift, to a Young Merchant in Perth'.[43] But perhaps the best poem of this kind is Burns's 'Epistle to a Young Friend May 1786', which is not only splendidly fluent in its control of form, tone and diction, but also, as the editors of the *Canongate Burns* point out,[44] all the more telling for its undertow of regret for the writer's own failings and their consequences. The verse form Burns chose, essentially two quatrains of ballad metre joined to make an eight-line stanza, enables him to give due weight to troublesome subjects. For example, he begins one stanza by advising his addressee to 'Luxuriantly indulge' what he calls 'weel-plac'd love' while avoiding 'th' *illicit rove*' (42, 41), and then, in the second quatrain, justifies what might otherwise seem a truism, even a self-righteous one, with a reason evidently acquired by experience:

> I waive the quantum o' the sin,
>   The hazard of concealing;
> But, Och! it hardens a' *within*,
>   And petrifies the feeling! (45–9)

The same stanza also illustrates his skill with rhyme and cadence. Especially earlier in the poem, he uses double, often humorously inventive, rhymes to lighten the impact of sober counsel, as in 'sent you'/'Memento' and 'determine'/'Sermon' (both in the first stanza), while retaining a few firmly stressed endings to avoid an impression of flippancy (as in the four lines that end the second). Here, however, the double rhyme and extra light stress of 'concealing'/'feeling', far from having any effect of comic incongruity, are unexpectedly poignant. Yet Burns does not allow this hint of remorse to dominate, ending the poem with the rueful wish: 'And may ye better reck the *rede*, / Than ever did th' *Adviser*!' It is a further brilliant stroke to close with a humorous double rhyme and light stress, especially because the word with which '*Adviser*' rhymes is 'wiser'. Very few poems manage to advise so memorably without sanctimoniousness.

Advisory epistles on marriage presented special challenges, particularly for a single woman addressing another inclined to marry or one already wed. In 'Advice to a Young Lady Lately Married', Esther Lewis sought to avoid the difficulty through self-deprecation, acknowledging her lack of experience in her closing couplet: 'I own you've ample cause to chide, / And blushing throw the pen aside'.[45] The problem with such a tactic is that it may undermine the advice. In 'An Epistle to Clemena. Occasioned by an Argument She Had Maintain'd against the Author', Elizabeth

Thomas is more assertive, not to say combative. Not only does her title indicate that she and her addressee are already at odds, but in her opening lines she risks giving offence by contrasting what she styles as Clemena's 'pettish Heats' with the 'calm *Reason*' she claims she is bringing to the question. A verse paragraph follows in which she denounces the double standard of sexual morality for men and women, and also the latter's commodification ('But *Woman*'s made a *Property* for *Life*'). Yet in the body of the poem she employs a more indirect method, presenting a cautionary tale of a young woman's neglect and ill-treatment – and, even, she suggests, sexual abuse ('*an Evil worse than Death*') – at the hands of a libertine husband who has married her for her money. The scenario is one of such unrelieved misery and brutality that it may have been more likely to alienate her addressee than persuade her, even though Thomas ends on a more comradely note, with the rueful couplet: 'Hard is that Venture where our *All* we lose; / But harder yet an honest Man to choose'.[46]

The advantage of a cautionary tale for conveying advice is that it does not reflect too directly on the addressee, leaving her free to apply it to her own position or not. Mary Leapor tried a variant of the same strategy in the longer of two poems entitled 'Mira to Octavia', in which she offers various scenarios of the possible dangers awaiting a woman in marriage, concluding them with the caution: 'Thus may *Octavia* in our Picture see, / What others are, and She must shortly be' (142–3).[47] Like Thomas, she frames these within appeals to her addressee, but she treads much more carefully, apologising for her presumption in offering advice and softening it with compliments. The main reason for such circumspection is almost certainly the inequality between Leapor's position as a servant-maid, redressed only to some extent by her literary cultivation and her wit, and that of a friend whose dowry, it seems, amounted to 'a thousand Pound' (157). Leapor finishes her poem by suggesting that Octavia will be better off unmarried, portraying in her final verse paragraph a long, happy, companionable and charitable life ending in serene and respected old age.

The fact that Leapor wrote another poem on the same subject and with the same title highlights the difficulty of conveying advice of such a kind tactfully, especially from her social position. In the other 'Mira to Octavia' the strategy is different, and so is the counsel. At 69 lines, the poem is less than two-fifths the length of its namesake, largely because Leapor omits the tableaus of unhappy wives. Instead, she relies on a lighter tone and on judicious argument, gracefully and engagingly conveyed. She is also careful both to praise her addressee – 'Fair One' (1), 'you're lovely' (13), 'I need not tell you, most ingenious Fair (23)', 'for you're mighty wise' (44) – and to depreciate herself, asking Octavia to 'pardon [her] officious

Friend' (2), styling herself as 'your Servant' (5; a conventional formula, yet one that recognizes her actual social position), and suggesting, with tongue-in-cheek disingenuousness, that she is only putting an argument 'to furnish Metre for my Song' (11). At the same time, placing herself among 'the learn'd' who 'aver / That even Beauties like the rest may err' (13–14), she wears what she knows lightly: the remark that 'outlaw'd Poets censure whom they please' (4), while self-depreciating, is also an allusion to Plato's banishment of poets from his Republic; and Richard Greene and Ann Messenger, in their notes to the poem, draw attention to the echo of Butler's *Hudibras* in lines 37–40.[48]

Leapor's main argument is that her friend should consult her long-term interests. Florio, the young man to whom Octavia is attracted, has the wit not only to amuse but deceive her – Leapor insinuates that he may be after her money – and, even if it is a love-match, neither his wit nor love will put food on the table. A much safer choice, Leapor argues, would be Dusterandus, whose name indicates his steady but unexciting qualities. The contrast in prospects she presents is stark: between reigning as 'Toast of the Village and the rural Plain' (56), with 'Peace and Plenty' on the table (58), and, 'cold and hungry' (59), making do with next to nothing. Leapor is at pains to assure her friend that wealth is no proper aim in itself; but she suggests that it is, above all, 'useful' (63), and that it will help Octavia lead a much happier life. Though she does not say so, her own experience of living on a low income surely stands behind her advice.

Yet, though Leapor's arguments are sound, she does not rely on them alone. She also seeks to win Octavia over through deft, humorous expression and versification, and it is this that makes the poem such a fine example of an advisory epistle. Here, management of tone is crucial. On the one hand, Leapor defers to her friend, and depreciates herself, in the ways already mentioned. On the other, she makes her key points forcefully, as when, allowing Florio wit, she declares: 'Enough, *Octavia*, to impose on you' (17–18), and adds: 'It only serves to gild his Vices o'er, / And teach his Malice how to wound the more' (21–2). Similarly, she ends the poem's longest verse paragraph with a telling triplet (the only such variation it has) summing up the alternative to Dusterandus: 'Or cold and hungry writhe your tired Jaws, / And dine with *Florio* upon Hips and Haws, / In troth I think there's little room to pause' (59–61). At the same time, though, she lightens the tone with comical images such as that of Florio managing, through his wit alone, to 'Adorn the Board, i'th' twinkling of an Eye, / With a hot Pasty, or a Warden Pye' (31–2), or that of errant knights, and by implication the two love-birds, having to 'sup on Grass and breakfast on the Breeze' (40). She also varies the pace cleverly to carry her addressee forward, as with two series of open couplets in lines 30–4 and 40–6; and she makes apt use of balanced line-units, especially when describing Dusterandus: 'Is yet untainted, tho' not much refin'd' (48), 'A gentle Master and a constant Friend' (52), 'His Servants' blessing and his Neighbours' praise' (54). Most of all, she sustains a dry, amused irony, as in the parenthesis 'or some Authors often deal in Lies' (35), which is clearly not to be taken straight, as she is referring to fairytale romances, and even in the apparently flattering expression 'you're mighty wise' (44), where the colloquial intensifier hints at gentle mockery. But she does not press this too far, emphasizing her love and friendship for Octavia by addressing her as 'my Dearest' in the last verse paragraph (63) and by implicitly assuring her, in the valediction already quoted, that Octavia will keep them even if she makes what Leapor believes to be the wrong decision: 'But if there's none but *Florio* that will do, / Write Ballads both, and you may thrive – Adieu' (66–7).

Richard Greene has argued that the 'Mira to Octavia' that I have just discussed predates its namesake, which, he says, 'is longer and far more detailed, suggesting that Octavia had rejected the reasoning of the earlier piece'. He couples this argument with another one, that Leapor's literary executors held back from printing her angrier poems in the first, 1748, volume of her *Poems*, reserving them for the second volume, which came out in 1751.[49] Yet it is possible that the shorter poem is the later. First, it seems unlikely that Leapor could, as he claims, have sent both poems to her friend, for similar lines appear in both.[50] Second, Greene's implication that the shorter poem is less effective – he calls it 'relatively simple in its advice'[51] – is open to question. Although the 1751 poem avoids personal reflections on its addressee, its pictures of potential husbands and married life are harsh, and Leapor may have feared that they might provoke antagonism. The 1748 poem is more gentle and much more concise, and it is more varied in tone and pace. If Leapor really was trying to write a friend out of a marriage she regarded as unsuitable, it is more likely to have made an impression. Together, the two illustrate different strategies for an advisory epistle, and it is even conceivable that both were exercises in the form, rather than intended for an actual addressee at all.

Such a suggestion may gain plausibility from Leapor's skill at writing, and varying, stock types of poem. Examples include fable, ode, pastoral, verse essay, and in 'Crumble-Hall', as is often recognized, country-house poem,[52] as well as familiar epistle. Two of her other poems, 'To Artemisia. Dr. King's Invitation to Bellvill: Imitated' and 'The Sacrifice. An Epistle to Celia', are accomplished versions of the invitation, but, as the former has been very well discussed by Karina Williamson,[53] I will

say no more of either here, but turn instead to the type of epistle, from one
man to another, that they both parody and extend. Like the poem by
William King that Leapor varies, this usually follows its source more
closely, Horace's much-imitated epistle to Torquatus.[54] King's version is
typical of the period. As Williamson argues, it not only 'uses the invitation
form to create an intimate world of male fellowship that, at the same time,
reflects on civil society at large', but also implicitly excludes others –
especially women and servants – from what she calls 'the Augustan club'.
This club, she declares, created a 'self-complacent fiction [. . .] that allows
well-educated male poets to constitute themselves as arbiters of manners
and morals by virtue of their class, gender, and classical training'.[55] Part
of the challenge presented by the imitation as a literary form, and part of
the pleasure it offers to those initiated enough to enjoy it, is, of course, the
wit with which the writer matches expressions in the original with
contemporary equivalents. The following discussion compares three
imitations of the epistle, including King's, with reference to the more
literal of the two standard verse translations of the period, paying special
attention to the kinds of knowledge required to appreciate them fully.

   All the poems are by men. King's is the earliest, first printed in 1708
and easily dated from its allusion to the British victory at Blenheim in
1704. The second, by Christopher Pitt to George Bubb Dodington, later
Lord Melcombe, was probably written a generation later.[56] Pitt had been
at Winchester College with his addressee, and, as rector of Pimperne in
Dorset from 1724, was able to enjoy the latter's hospitality at his grand
estate at Eastbury close by (*ODNB*); he mentions both places in the poem.
The third is by an anonymous Irishman. Reference to claret of 'Vintage
fifty-two', and the fact that the poem appears in the second volume of John
Duncombe's *The Works of Horace in English Verse. By Several Hands*,
first printed in 1759,[57] makes clear that it was written in the later 1750s.
Like the many other imitations in the same edition, it follows a translation
of the poem, which is the one I will cite for comparison.[58] Duncombe's,
along with most eighteenth-century versions of Horace's epistles,
including all but two of those by Philip Francis, his main competitor,[59]
renders the Latin hexameters in iambic pentameter couplets. It uses only
three lines more than Horace's 31 – a difficult feat, as Latin is more
concise than English (Francis's freer version runs to 46).

   King creates the atmosphere of a gentleman's club to which Williamson
refers partly through choice of names (*Bellvill, Freeman* and *Bellair* are
type-names evoking Restoration comedy; *Cotton* and *Winner* may refer to
actual persons), and partly by elaborating on Horace's three lines on wine,
but mostly by amplifying the easy but not exuberant camaraderie of the

original. His first line, 'If *Bellvill* can his gen'rous Soul confine', is a good example of this licence, for it renders almost nothing in the Latin; and the adjective 'gen'rous', repeated in lines 18 and 23, is, as Williamson remarks, a keyword for 'an ideal of civil conduct' and 'the Epicurean values of gentlemanly ease and recreation' at the period.[60] In several cases, however, King finds apt equivalents. Where Horace, in Duncombe's translation, assures his friend that no intimate confidences will be broken with the words ''Mongst Friends let nothing pass / The door' (26–7), King writes: 'Then for the Company I'll see it chose, / Their Emblematick Signal is the *Rose*' (35–6), referring to the expression *sub rosa*;[61] and he gets round Horace's reason for avoiding too large a company, potentially offensive to genteel ears – Duncombe renders the line: 'But in the Dog-days' Heat a Crowd offends' (32) – with a neat sidestep, 'What can you hope for better from a Crowd?' (40). But the most significant parallels that King finds for expressions in the original concern the fact that Britain was at war. His allusion to the battle of Blenheim, already mentioned, translates Horace's reference to celebrations of Caesar's birthday, but the poem also contains other military images for which there is no pretext. Where Horace challenges his friend to bring better wine – Duncombe: 'Bring yours, if better; if not, drink of mine' (6) – King throws down a gauntlet: 'I tell you with what Force I keep the Field, / And if you can exceed it, speak, I'll yield' (8–9); in the next line, referring to table furniture that merely 'shines' in Duncombe's version, he offers 'Snow-white Ensigns'; and, while Horace ends his invitation with the advice to give any importunate clients the slip, King tacks on a justification: 'A Stratagem in War is no Deceit' (44). In these ways, the epistle advertises its contemporaneity for the reader of 1708.

Christopher Pitt's version of the epistle is even freer than King's, chiefly because, with only 24 lines of tetrameter (against King's 44 of pentameter) it is considerably truncated. One of the key differences is the deference it pays its addressee. While King writes on terms of equality, Pitt begins: 'If Doddington will condescend', ends: 'And your petitioner will pray', and emphasizes the modesty of the fare he offers. This also, however, allows him to play up the warmth of his hospitality, especially in the lines 'No costly welcome, but a kind' (5), 'The master and his heart at home' (8), and 'A cellar open as his face' (9). Pitt's version works largely through self-deprecating humour, as when the line following the one just quoted promises 'A dinner shorter than his grace'. Its flattery of the addressee is adept, as when, referring to Dodington's estate, he promises 'From Eastbery – a des[s]ert – of wit' (22). But, while he omits parts of the original, including the reference to Caesar's birthday, he appreciably expands one section in a way that, as in King's version, gives it contemporaneity. This is in the six lines he devotes to the prospect of providing venison. Implying that his resources do not stretch so far, he avers that the chances of acquiring it illicitly are slim:

> Our rogues, indeed, of late, o'er-aw'd,
> By human laws, not those of God,
> No venison steal, or none they bring,
> Or send it all to master King:
> And yet, perhaps, some venturous spark
> May bring it now the nights are dark. (13–18)

The reference here is to the 'Black Act' of 1723 that converted a large number of poaching and related offences from misdemeanours to felonies. Partly for that reason, the humour is complicated. On the one hand, Pitt ironically deprecates both his own relatively limited resources and the godlessness of his social inferiors, while suggesting that they may be poaching on the sly for a tradesman ('master King' is glossed in what was probably the first printing as 'the Blandford carrier').[62] On the other hand, he not only treats airily a law that often inflicted savage penalties but also, contradicting his remark that the lower orders ignore the Commandments, applauds the enterprise of anyone willing to break them. Like King's, the poem helps illuminate the milieu and attitudes of those who wrote such epistles. As King's was often reprinted through the century, and as Pitt's seems first to have been printed as late as 1772,[63] both also suggest that those attitudes remained congenial for many readers.

The version by Duncombe's friend presents another dimension of genteel eighteenth-century male companionship, in that it is addressed by one clergyman to another, and its local allusions are either Irish or especially resonant in an Irish context. While the phrase guaranteeing the quality of the claret, '*Paul* is strictly true' (5), refers to the wine merchant Andrew Paul of Abbey Street, Dublin,[64] and 'the *Sure*' (7) is the river Suir that flows to the sea near Waterford, the rendering of Caesar's birthday as that of 'our GEORGE *the good*' (16), and the added detail of wine having the power to make even a miser charitable, would have had particular meaning for an Irish Protestant minister in a predominantly Catholic country notorious for poverty. Other distinctive additions to the original include the remark that the addressee enjoys 'better Tythes' (11); that, to attend the dinner, he will have to put by his reading – 'your favourite *Chillingworth*' (13) representing the ecclesiastic pundit whose *Works* had been most recently reprinted in Dublin in 1751;[65] and that the tablecloth 'is fair as *Lyddy*'s snowy breast' (33), presumably a reference to his own daughter or wife. Despite this compliment, the poem ends on an ungallant note, rendering Horace's advice to 'Slip from your Client through the Garden Gate' (Duncombe, 34) with the line: 'And bilk a Wife one Night, to please a Friend' (46). In this way it re-emphasizes the world of gentlemanly bonhomie that it and its whole genre inscribe.

Building on work by Patrizia Violi on the non-literary prose letter, Karina Williamson, in her discussion of the invitations by King and Leapor, calls attention to what she calls 'the special *competencies* characteristic of letter discourse'.[66] She refers in particular to the reader's need to know the original, preferably in Latin, in order to appreciate fully the writer's choice of equivalent expressions or allusions – or even to grasp the sense. The various examples of this form of competency in the three versions of Horace's epistle to Torquatus just considered are not, however, the same as in those of an ordinary letter, which are typically personal rather than literary. As Violi remarks, in a sentence quoted by Williamson, 'compared with other texts the letter personalizes its relationship with its own addressee to a maximum'.[67] For this reason, the kind of competency required by the three invitations is no different from that required by any other poem that makes much use of classical allusion, such as *The Rape of the Lock* or *Paradise Lost*. The point reinforces the argument at the start of this book that the verse epistle is more poem than letter. It also underlines the importance of distinguishing between various kinds of competency. Among these are not only the literary but the historical, as with King's allusion to Blenheim, Pitt's to the 'Black Act', or the Irish clergyman's to a now-obscure Dublin wine merchant, and also the personal, a function of Altman's 'addressee-consciousness'. The more literary the epistle, the less likely it is to contain allusions that can only be understood by the addressee and his or her relatives or friends – who '*Lyddy*' is, for example, in the poem by the Irish cleric. This is especially clear in poems not written with a view to publication in print.

Two such poems – others will be discussed later in the chapter – are an invitation from Catherine Horneck Bunbury to Oliver Goldsmith to spend the New Year at the family estate in Suffolk, and Goldsmith's reply.[68] Both are humorous, as the verse form of anapestic tetrameter couplets immediately indicates. Mrs Bunbury is well aware that she is no poet, but she does much to compensate. She begins with a triplet by way of flourish, and jokes at her need to choose an inappropriate word to make a rhyme; but she also expresses warm regard for her addressee, as when she mentions towards the end how much his 'cheerful company' is sought by his friends in London. Goldsmith's reply, 'Letter in Verse and Prose to

Mrs Bunbury', not printed till 1837, has a prose frame and five prose lines near the end, but is otherwise in the same verse form. It teases Mrs Bunbury about various supposed solecisms in her poem; and the part in verse paints a comic picture of the outcome of the card game that is one of the attractions she has promised. Goldsmith had already written two similar poems probably also preserved by the same addressee. The first, 'Verses in Reply to an Invitation to Dinner at Dr. Baker's', is in anapestic dimeter couplets – as Lonsdale points out, most likely in imitation of the postscripts in Swift's verse letter to Thomas Sheridan of 14 December 1719. The second, in anapestic tetrameter couplets, is 'The Haunch of Venison. A Poetical Epistle to Lord Clare', in which Goldsmith tells a humorous story against himself. Not intended for print publication, and both printed posthumously, the two poems would have circulated in manuscript among the poet's associates, and some of their allusions would have made sense for that circle alone.[69] They, and the exchange with Mrs Bunbury, are of special interest for the light they cast on the role played by informal verse in social relations of the period, including, on Goldsmith's part, as in some measure a kind of return for what amounted to patronage. He was indebted to friends not only for invitations to stay or to dine, but apparently to Lord Clare in particular for accommodation.[70] *Jeux d'esprit* in verse were part of his circle's entertainment, and from a famous poet they were all the more gratifying. Yet 'The Haunch of Venison' also touches uneasily on the class distinctions to which its author was especially sensitive. It does this in part by conveying a mixture of self-importance and embarrassment at the gift in his words to his visitor:

> 'Why, whose should it be?' cried I, with a flounce,
> 'I get these things often;' – but that was a bounce.
> 'Some lords, my acquaintance, that settle the nation,
> 'Are pleased to be kind – but I hate ostentation.' (41–4)

Such awkward emotions suggest that, though the man who carries off the venison is 'under-bred' (37), and the other two diners are a Scot and a Jewish hack-writer, Goldsmith is also partly to blame for his discomfiture.

Like Mary Leapor, other poets extended or subverted the conventional invitation, especially towards the end of the century. In 'The Invitation: A Jocular Poetic Epistle to a Friend, in Return for a Present of Bacon', Christopher Jones gave a lower-class twist to Goldsmith's 'Haunch of Venison', acknowledging the latter in his subtitle and using the same verse form of anapestic tetrameter couplets.[71] The joke begins with the substitution of bacon for venison, and it is compounded by the lavish praise Jones gives his present – as a poor man well might who would not always expect to see meat on his table. It then goes further. Whereas, in Goldsmith's poem, the poet does not even succeed in enjoying his present, as it is appropriated by an unwelcome acquaintance and then fails to reach the table, Jones not only reports full satisfaction but gives an invitation in return. This he accompanies with apologies for humble fare that come more convincingly from an 'uneducated journeyman wool-comber', as the subtitle to his book styles him, than from a gentleman. The welcome promised is warm and sincere, as he suggests by reducing, in the part of the poem that offers the invitation, the number of comic light endings with double rhymes. Jones takes the opportunity to reflect on social inequality by observing, before a mock-interruption from his addressee stops him: 'But kings other *nutriment* wisely have found; / They *fatten* on all their good subjects around' (31–2). But the poem is most effective as social criticism in the contrast it implies between the conviviality of the poor and the discomfort suffered by Goldsmith among better-off people in class-conscious London, both recipient and victim of patronage.

Anna Seward's 'Verses Inviting Stella to Tea on the Public Fast-Day, February, MDCCLXXXI' varies the form of the invitation still further. As Roger Lonsdale notes, 'With the American War going badly, the general fast, "To pray for a divine blessing on His Majesty's arms by sea and land", was observed in England on 21 Feb. 1781.'[72] Seward was not impressed. Adopting the Scriblerian form of iambic tetrameter couplets with occasional light endings and comic rhymes, she spends most of the poem less on inviting her friend than on ridiculing the fast-day. Her tone is ironic when she cites 'The ah's! and oh's! supremely trist' that are to go along with 'abstinence from beef and whist' (3–4), it becomes scathing in the couplet: 'Till, skipping o'er th' Atlantic rill, / We cut provincial throats at will' (7–8), and, after she has given her invitation in the first verse paragraph, her irritation takes over completely. The remaining 30 lines, more than half of the poem, are put in the mouth of 'a Patriot' (23), furious at the patent profanation of drinking, on a day of fasting in support of the war, the very beverage that had provoked it. Seward mocks such attitudes in the flatulent rhetoric in which she frames them, including mythological allusions to Até and Thyestes and portentous language such as 'libation' – a word the pretensions of which she punctures with one of her humorous rhymes. She also draws attention to the inconvenient fact that England was doing badly in the war, remarking that 'the saucy foe' – a phrase that highlights English self-confidence and condescension – has been laying 'our boasted legions low' (11–12); and her reference to Thyestes is only too apt for a civil war that did indeed cost 'Brothers', parents', children's blood' (44). Although the poem ends on a note that is deliberately absurd, the Patriot equating tea with poison, it expresses a view that is critical not only of English jingoism but also, implicitly, of the war itself. It may be significant that she did not publish it until 1791, ten years after it was written,[73] at a time when the French Revolution had taken hold and had not yet begun to deter its English well-wishers. In this way, it turns the form of the familiar verse letter, and the ladylike topic of a tea invitation, into vehicles for political satire.

As might be expected, familiar epistles accompanying gifts are usually more focused on their addressees. The gift may be humble, as when Burns sends eggs to one man or returns a newspaper to another, or cultured, as when John Sican presents Swift with a finely bound edition of Horace, or William Dunkin sends Robert Craggs Nugent a portrait of Swift in old age.[74] Common among epistles of this type are those that enclose a book, such as Robert Anderson's with Josiah Relph's *Poems*, James Delacourt's with Elizabeth Rowe's *Friendship in Death*, or Hannah More's, to a three-year-old child, with a children's book.[75] Equally frequent are those that accompany a poem or other work by the author, including at least three poems by Burns, Mary Leapor's submitting her play 'The Unhappy Father', and Joseph Mitchell's sending a pastoral.[76] The strategies of such poems vary according to their occasions, Anderson imitating Relph's favourite form for familiar verse of iambic tetrameter couplets, Dunkin following suit with the same form for Swift, and Burns often using his favourite for the same purpose of the Standard Habby. Those with more serious aims resort to pentameter couplets, as did Delacourt, Leapor and Mitchell. Sican's poem to Swift is especially adroit in that it is written as if from Horace himself, comparing his own times with those of the present and ending with a well-turned compliment.

As already mentioned, the most numerous kind of familiar epistle conveys the sort of news or information that an ordinary prose letter might. Typical examples describe life in town or country, or, more specifically, an ordinary day in either; some are written to or from relatives or friends at university; and others stem from more unusual occasions, such as Thomas Godfrey's 'Epistle to a Friend; from Fort Henry', written during military service in Pennsylvania; John Armstrong's *A Day: An Epistle to John Wilkes, of Aylesbury, Esq.*, describing the writer's experience as an army doctor on campaign in Germany; or Ann Thomas's 'To Laura, on the French Fleet Parading before Plymouth in August 1779'.[77] Even more unusual examples include two appeals for funds from imprisoned debtors, by Joseph Mitchell in 1721 or 1722 and Thomas Dermody near the end of the century, and two epistles from prison by James Montgomery following convictions for malicious libel for a poem celebrating the fall of the Bastille and a report on 'the use of the militia to fire on a riotous crowd in Sheffield'.[78] Though all these have their own interest, I will focus on characteristic examples of the more common kinds.

The first example, by Richardson Pack, illustrates many features of the form as practised by gentlemen of the period. As its amusingly lengthy and circumstantial title indicates, it is occasional verse: 'An Epistle from a Half-Pay Officer in the Country to his Friend in London, upon Reading the Address of the Two Houses, to Thank her Majesty for the Safe, Honourable and Advantageous Peace'.[79] Army officers in earlier times were placed on the half-pay list when not required for service.[80] Written after the Treaty of Utrecht ended the War of the Spanish Succession in 1713 – its dateline is 'IPSWICH *April* 1714' – Pack's poem wryly describes the impact on his social activities, diet and love life. Its iambic pentameter couplets nicely combine hints at heroic afflatus with humorous lapses into informality. Pack handles them with gusto, opening the poem with a reversed foot and a triplet, and concluding each of its four verse paragraphs with a rueful refrain (varied in the third): '*Must Heroes suffer such Disgrace as This? / O Curst Effects of* HONOURABLE PEACE!' (p. 34). The final two words of the refrain echo the phrase Parliament employed to congratulate the Queen on the treaty. Quoting the phrase in his title, Pack strikes a keynote of self-ironical humour from the start.

Despite its casual, self-deprecating air, the poem is neatly organized. The first verse paragraph outlines the stock vicissitudes of an eighteenth-century army officer's life, alternating all too quickly between prosperity and debt. Pack, who had studied law long enough to be called to the bar (*ODNB*), now regrets that he had not followed that profession or another that would have given greater security, such as the church or commerce. The remaining three verse paragraphs show respectively how half pay wrecks his social life, shortens his rations, and, most regretted of all, denies him the kind of female society he favours. Far from toasting the beauties of the season in fine wines, Pack is forced to quit the city for the provinces, a byword among people of fashion for dullness and boredom. For him, country air is anything but fresh in contrast to 'sweet *Hyde-Park*' (p. 34). Here he is obliged to find the paltriest forms of wit – 'low Conceits, and vile *Conundrums*' – amusing, and the company is even worse, ranging from 'sneaking *Parsons*' to '*Squires* – more noisy than their *Swine*'. Yet it is striking that, unlike the satirists of the period, Pack does not content himself with heaping scorn on such easy targets. The wit of the lines also consists in the rueful self-portrait of the author forced to play along through lack of alternative society. Indeed, the start of the next verse paragraph suggests through its comically rhetorical repetition – 'There was a Time – Oh! yes there was a Time' (p. 35) – that all this is tongue-in-cheek. The point of Pack's poem is not to satirize the poor conditions and pay endured by army officers, or even the emptiness of country life, but to entertain his friend Harry by making humorous and no doubt exaggerated play out of his all too humdrum plight.

The poem's predominantly comic tone is established in part by the lighthearted hyperbole and use of comic rhymes illustrated by its third verse paragraph. First, Pack pictures times of plenty, when all meals would have had several courses, beginning with soup; French delicacies, including truffles, would have figured on the menu; and mackerel might have been eaten at a time when they were not yet plentiful. From such luxuries it is a glum comedown to food ample in calories but short on flavour and subtlety: 'heavy *Dumpling*', 'nappy', or frothing, ale, and plain local cheese (p. 35). Second, the end-of-line hypermetrical light stresses and humorous rhymes ending four consecutive lines indicate again that all this is not quite serious. Pack does not really believe that he and his fellow soldiers are being punished ('Scourg'd') by Robert Harley, who had negotiated the Treaty of Utrecht and who held the 'WAND' of office as Queen Anne's chief minister. (Ironically, Harley was about to be accused of 'Treason' himself, as the proximity of the word may hint.) Nevertheless, the poem implies, that is what it feels like to be reduced to short rations. Pack brings his poem to an effective climax by showing that even this indignity palls before the snubs he has to suffer from women who had favoured him previously. Here the tone seems sharper, as he claims that women stifle their sex-drives rather than lose status, and, instead of staying true to a real if down-at-heel man, prefer a 'Lathy *Beau*' (p. 36). Yet these exaggerations stay on the humorous side of satire. The short line 'But 'tis in vain' indicates a mock-heroic register, since it burlesques the device, imitated from classical epic, sometimes used for climactic emphasis. Also, as before, Pack turns the hyperboles on himself, alleging that he has spent his 'warmest Blood' not in military but in female service, and admitting that, now he has no money to bribe feminine fondness, he is compelled to fight 'the *Jesuit's Battle*' of seductive casuistry by relying on his personal attributes alone. His rueful parenthesis '(hard Fate!)' sounds a further note of self-irony.

Much of the poem's appeal stems from the skill with which it maintains this tone of humorous suffering. Amusingly graphic in its account of the indignities of a half-pay officer's life, it lowers the tone deliberately with comically demeaning words. Neither 'heavy *Dumpling*' nor 'nappy *Ale*' (p. 35) is normally to be found in heroic company; and cheese is scarcely epic fare, especially when it fills up gastric 'Chinks'. Pack shows skill in deploying deft balance and antithesis within line-units, as in 'A while we *Glitter*, then obscurely *Dye*' (p. 34), contrasting verbs and adverbs neatly, or 'To feed their *Pride*, will even starve their *Lust*' (p. 36), juxtaposing different appetites and verbs of opposing meaning. It is in part owing to his metrical art that the tone of comic indignation is so adeptly controlled. While the poem is an enjoyable performance as well as a complaint about the ups and downs of military life, the picture it paints is lively and witty. Its publication five years after its stated date of composition points not only to straitened circumstances, but also to the chance of making money from it and other kinds of writing as the reading public developed.

Pack's epistle is characteristic in its exploitation not only of the stock eighteenth-century topic of city versus country, and the resources of the pentameter couplet, but also of the type of familiar verse written by men. It assumes attitudes and values consonant with William King's invitation to Bellvill, and all the more on account of the male homosociality of army life. But the epistle that describes an ordinary day is especially favoured by women, probably because law and social convention worked to keep them at home. Such poems often use more informal metres than Pack's pentameter couplets, usually varying them with humorous rhymes and end-of-line light stresses. Probably many more were written than have found their way into print. For example, had it not been for scholarly research, most of Anne Finch's verse in this vein would still be unknown – such as 'A Ballad to Mrs Catherine Fleming in London from Malshanger farm in Hampshire', and 'For Mrs Catherine Flemming at ye Lord Digby's at Coleshill in Warwickshire. To Coleshill Seat of Noble Pen', along with Henrietta Knight, Lady Luxborough's 'Asteria in the Country to Calydore in Town 1747–8', which also survived in manuscript.[81]

Among three familiar epistles that Jane Brereton wrote at about the same period as those by Finch and Pack, 'To Mr Thomas Griffith, at the University of Glasgow. Written in London, 1720' is of this kind.[82] She teases her friend on his progress from childhood games to university, and, though she suggests that this progress may not amount to very much – she says he needs all his logic, for example, to prove 'A foppish Coxcomb's, no Baboon' (p. 54) – it was a form of education denied to her as a woman. She goes on to imagine what Griffith may be up to in Glasgow, but she spends most of the poem describing her own life in London. As she was separated from her husband, her opportunities for amusement were limited, but, disliking fashionable social life, of which she gives a sharp vignette, she can take the air in Tuttle Fields or Millbank, or visit Westminster Abbey, and she can provide the latest news and her own opinions on foreign and domestic politics. While Brereton wrote in jaunty tetrameter couplets, with the comic rhymes common in familiar and humorous verse, Elizabeth Tollet chose heroic couplets for a parallel poem 'To my Brother at St. John's College in Cambridge', a few years later.[83] Tollet develops the theme of education with which Brereton's poem begins. Though she spends part of her first verse paragraph on her life in London, including a description of the view around her, the body of the poem consists of careful advice to an undergraduate. Like Brereton's friend, her brother is enjoying a kind of education open only to men. If she regretted her exclusion from the opportunities he can enjoy, she does not say so, but urges him all the more to exploit them. At the same time, and tellingly, she displays her own cultivation in her allusions to Cadmus, Cicero (whom she could read in Latin), Circe, Cowley and Prior. She does not press her advice too hard, as when she makes what was probably a family joke about 'Oxford' (meaning not so much the other university town but Robert Harley), and she varies her verse with several vivid metaphors and apt triplets and alexandrines. These qualities, and a compliment to Mary Villiers (Lady Lansdown) and Catherine Wyndham, make it likely that the poem was not only, like Brereton's, written for others to read as well as her addressee, but also for publication.

A generation later, Brereton's daughter Charlotte was able to publish a verse epistle of a type similar to her mother's in the *Gentleman's Magazine*.[84] Her circumstances, however, were different. Lonsdale's head-note explains that after her mother's death in 1740 she found employment 'as governess in an aristocratic Scottish family', and it was from the family's estate that the poem was written. Brereton's lively anapestic tetrameter couplets carry her through an account of a typical day from rising 'about eight' (1) till, the children put to bed, she has time to herself in which she can, for example, write. She comments humorously on various topics, including her dress, and manages several compliments to her employers – who would probably have seen the poem even if it had not been printed – and their children. Though she sustains a buoyant tone throughout, she also makes clear the impact of her new responsibilities: 'wild *Ch——ly* is grown so prudent and tame, / You hardly would know me except by my name' (49–50). An epistle in the same verse form by another young woman, Frances Macartney (later Greville), pivots on an attempt for different reasons to get the writer and her addressee to behave decorously.[85] Rather than relating a typical day, it tells how the friend's aunt tried to call her to account. Macartney renders the aunt's lecture comically, as she complains about the addressee's behaviour and cautions her about the writer: 'And of that giddy girl I beseech you take care' (30). The rest of the poem encourages her friend to ignore such advice, dismissing the aunt as an envious prude, and disregarding the gossip of matrons whose 'province is railing' while theirs is 'pleasure' (48). It is not surprising that it did not see print until long after it was written.

Susanna Blamire's 'Epistle to her Friends at Gartmore' is one of the most colourful and entertaining accounts in verse by a woman of how she spends her time.[86] Like other writers in this genre, she uses the humorous rhymes and hypermetrical end-of-line light stresses that usually flavour it, beginning with a couplet that has just such comically deliberate technical weaknesses (the rhyme is 'on ye' / 'upon ye'), and referring almost immediately afterwards to the informality of what she calls 'shortened measure' (5) – in other words, lines of four rather than five feet, apt for a familiar verse letter. Having thus depreciated what she calls her 'hobbling rhyme' (3), she describes a typical day in her life at home. The tone is comic from the start, as when she jokes about her pretence at being an early riser ('At eight I rise – a decent time! / But aunt would say 'tis oftener nine' [37–8]), and about the unlikeliness of her doing much work ('At work! quoth you;– but little's done, / Thou lik'st too well a bit of fun' [51–2]). The work to which she refers would have been needlework, one of the few manual tasks allowed to a gentlewoman.

Blamire's account of her everyday life has special interest in that much of it focuses on her relationships with people of a lower social rank. Her reference to the lunch table being laid by 'little Fan', the maidservant, leads to her reporting a dialogue as a result of which she gets permission for the maid to go to a dance in town, and then to a discussion of the ways in which people of 'different stations' (77) resemble each other. Though Blamire reveals a clear sense of social distinctions, placing herself and her addressees as 'we' and people of a lower rank as 'they', she suggests not only that the differences are more social than otherwise, but that they stem from the ways in which people of different ranks are brought up:

> They're more upon an equal par
> Than we imagine them by far.
> They love and hate – have just the same
> Feeling of pleasure and of pain;
> Only our kind of education
> Gives ours a greater elevation. (79–84)

The discussion illustrates how the familiar verse epistle may raise topics of general social interest, even though its main focus is on the everyday. Blamire follows it by describing how she helps with medical advice to the poor. This illustrates the kind of role a woman from a prosperous home might play in the countryside, especially when she was without children of her own, and again it casts light on attitudes to people of lower rank. It does this by presenting another dialogue, longer than the previous one, in which the poet prescribes medicine for a little girl's constipation, and in which the girl's mother speaks in Cumbrian dialect. The rendering of dialect – a skill Blamire displays in other poems too – is significantly not for humorous purposes, as it often was in genre pieces of the period. Though the scene has its comic side – as when the mother is too embarrassed to say what is wrong with her child ('The peer peer bairn does oft complain,– / A'd tell ye where, but I think shame' [95–6]) – the emphasis is on practical help, down-to-earth advice, and, so far as the dialect is concerned, on representing how people of the area actually spoke.

Although, in the ways described, Blamire's poem reaches beyond its immediate occasion, it also reaffirms the sense of friendship that is central to the familiar epistle. She blesses her sister's wedding nearly five years earlier for bringing into her life the friends to whom she is writing, most of all the one special companion ('my dear' [141]) to whom the letter seems especially directed.[87] And she is clearly writing to give pleasure, not just to herself but to her addressees. Despite producing enough verse to fill the collection that appeared nearly half a century after she died, and despite the printing of a few of her songs during her lifetime, she seems to have had no ambition for publication.[88] It is perhaps in part because she was not, as it were, looking over her shoulder at a potential reading public that she was able to express so convincingly the warmth and good cheer that define the familiar epistle, but that are often predicated on exclusion (of women or servants, for example) or are merely conventional. In the most important exchange of epistolary verse in the century, however, which I will discuss shortly, other factors are involved too.

Most familiar verse letters stand on their own and belong neither to a sequence nor correspondence. Though this may seem surprising, it is likely that writing of this kind was not always preserved, and that not all writers would have had the skill to produce letters in verse, or letters in verse worth preserving. Nevertheless, various poets wrote several epistles to the same addressee, among them John Bancks to John Winship, Mary Savage to 'Miss E. B.', and both Robert Burns and Alexander Wilson to a number of friends.[89] Some verse letters indicate in their titles that they answer epistles that are no longer extant, but various exchanges have survived. A few have already been mentioned, such as the three poems between Mary Barber and the Earl of Orrery, and supposedly also between Sir Charles Hanbury Williams and Mrs Bindon; Lady Mary Wortley Montagu's reply to the Countess of Hertford's overture to Sir William Hamilton; and the correspondence between Frances Seymour, Countess of Hertford, and Henrietta Louisa, Countess of Pomfret.[90] Others include Pope's 'Impromptu' and Anne Finch's witty 'The Answer', along with 'A Letter from Sr A. F. to Ardelia' and its response, Finch's 'The Agreeable', though the other halves of exchanges between Finch and her female friends do not seem to have survived.[91] There are also examples of verse letters between gentlemen in collections by John Whaley and Samuel Derrick. Whaley prints two exchanges, one an enquiry about an illness from which the poet had been suffering, along with Whaley's comic reply, the other beginning by replying to a letter from Whaley to which in turn he responds with thanks and compliments. Derrick provides two humorous invitations, from one of which I have quoted, and their replies.[92]

But the longest – and best – exchange of epistolary verse of the century is that between William Hamilton and Allan Ramsay introduced at the end of the previous chapter. It consists of six numbered poems, Hamilton's entitled 'Epistle' and Ramsay's 'Answer', all headed with place of writing and date, and one other. The first is dated 26 June, the last 2 September 1719, and the series ends with a coda from Ramsay thanking Hamilton for a barrel of herrings that he had received, according to the original title, on 19 December.[93] Hamilton was an army officer retired on half-pay who in 1706 had published a humorous poem entitled 'The Last Dying Words of Bonny Heck, a Famous Greyhound in the Shire of Fife', and in doing so had, states Allan MacLaine, inaugurated 'a new comic poetry in Scots'.[94] He wrote to compliment Ramsay on his verse, which he celebrates as outdoing his own, and to engage to meet him over 'a Bottle / Of reaming Claret' (Epistle I, 45–6) to seal friendship. His praise is cordial, generous and self-effacing, but it is also skilfully turned. The final stanza shows all these qualities, especially in its humorous rhymed signature:

> ACCEPT of this and look upon it
> With Favour, tho poor I have done it;
> Sae I conclude and end my Sonnet,
>   Who am most fully,
> While I do wear a Hat or Bonnet,
>   Yours – wanton *Willy*. (61–6)

Ramsay's response expresses his pleasure but also responds to the brio with which Hamilton had handled his chosen verse form:

MAY I be licket wi' a Bittle,	*beaten with a club*
Gin of your Numbers I think little;	*if*
Ye're never rugget, shan, nor kittle,	*untidy, feeble nor obscure*
But blyth and gabby,	*happy and fluent*
And hit the Spirit to a Title,	*tittle*
Of Standart *Habby.* (Answer I, 31–6)	

The stanza form is significant partly because it is Scottish. It consists of six lines, four of eight syllables rhyming together, and two of four syllables rhyming together, the short lines ending the stanza with a long line sandwiched between them. Its name comes from a famous comic elegy, first published about 1640, entitled 'The Life and Death of Habbie Simson, the Piper of Kilbarchan'.[95] Hamilton had revived the form for his poem on bonny Heck, and Ramsay had adopted it in three comic elegies of his own published by 1718.[96] Hamilton was repaying the compliment by writing his letter to Ramsay in the same form; but it was Ramsay who gave it the name 'Standard Habby'. It is an especially apt form for a familiar letter because, while each stanza is a suitable length for a thought or a sentence, its movement is quick and informal, the short lines at the end providing a kind of lilt or skip of often humorous gusto. As in the stanzas just quoted, hypermetrical light stresses are often added to end some or all of the lines, producing a playful double rhyme – a technical challenge in a stanza that requires the *a* rhyme to be repeated three times. The form was to be picked up later in the century by Robert Fergusson and others, above all of course Burns, especially for verse epistles.

What most distinguishes the series is the sense of open-hearted warmth that each poem expresses, all the more striking as the two appear to have known each other previously only in print. Hamilton begins his second epistle, for example, with boyish enthusiasm:

Dear RAMSAY,	
WHEN I receiv'd thy kind Epistle,	
It made me dance, and sing, and whistle;	
O sic a Fyke, and sic a Fistle	*such a commotion and*
I had about it!	*excitement*
That e'er was Knight of the *Scots* Thistle	
Sae fain, I doubted. (Epistle II, 1–6)	*so glad*

Yet none of the compliments from either man is over-egged. For his part, Hamilton displays frank delight in Ramsay's verse and disarming modesty about his own claims as a poet. Ramsay reciprocates not only by praising

Hamilton's verse but by contrasting a gentleman and 'wise judicious Lad', as he calls him, with himself as an erstwhile 'Ill bred Bog-sta[l]ker' and 'poor Scull-thacker', in comic allusion to his early life as shepherd and wigmaker (Answer II, 8, 10, 12). The homage each pays the other is the more convincing for its humour, as when Hamilton praises Ramsay's verse with a mischievous comparison: 'Thou's better at that Trade, I trow, / Than some's at preaching' (Epistle II, 23–4). Ramsay was well aware that the complimentary epistle had become a stock form – he wrote several of his own[97] – and, referring to the more unctuous examples, he adds the footnote: 'This Compliment is intirely free of the fulsome Hyperbole'.

The use of vernacular in the seven epistles is crucial not only to the campaign on the part of both poets to re-establish Scots as a literary language, but also to the expression of candour and lack of pretence. When Ramsay, at the end of his first Answer, gives his word to drink with Hamilton at Edinburgh, he declares: 'there's my Thumb' (62), and his addressee does not hold back from painting a farcical picture of himself as so blear-eyed and unsteady when finishing his second Epistle as to fall over himself: 'Upon my Bum I fairly cloited / On the cald Eard' (95–6). Carol McGuirk has argued that, 'In using a selectively Scots diction in forms such as verse-epistle, pastoral and satire, Ramsay was emulating (and extending) the work of the popular London Augustans Matthew Prior and John Gay, who had pioneered in the use of English rustic diction to spice up the "lower" literary kinds.'[98] Yet, though Ramsay clearly drew on Prior and Gay especially, the density of Scots expressions is higher in his exchanges with Hamilton – he moderates it when writing to English addressees such as John Gay and especially William Somervile[99] – and it has a different meaning from the rusticisms in English Augustan verse. Crucially, it is not mock-heroic or mock-pastoral, because it was closer than standard English to the language that the two and many of their Scots readers actually spoke; instead, it affirms their native culture and its heritage. Though Ramsay was a good self-publicist, and certainly used the exchange to promote his work, it is this that helps produce the sense of a bond between Hamilton and himself. Another of the footnotes that he added when he had the epistles printed as a series expands one of his glosses: 'An Expression used when *we* wou'd bid a Person (merrily) look brisk' (I, 127; emphasis added). It is the sense of a cultural solidarity that ignores class barriers – unlike Hamilton, Ramsay was not born a gentleman, as he gaily acknowledges – that promotes the warm camaraderie that the poems show and that helps make them such superb examples of the familiar epistle. The bond is one of male homosociality, as it is in many verse epistles of the period, but, through its lack of

deference to social privilege, it has every appearance of free and
unconstrained friendship.

It could also be argued that Ramsay, in particular, succeeds better in the
final poem of the series at naturalizing Horatian values than his English
contemporaries. First, praising Hamilton for his gentlemanly retirement
from the army, he contrasts him with a more famous soldier:

> THAT Bang'ster Billy *Caesar July*,   *brother ruffian*
> Wha at *Pharsalia* wan the Tooly,   *who won the victory*
> Had better sped, had he mair hooly   *fared;   slowly*
> Scamper'd thro' Life,
> And 'midst his Glories sheath'd his Gooly,   *large knife*
> And kiss'd his Wife. (Epistle III, 13–18)

Here, the rhymes that end with light stresses – '*July*', 'Tooly', 'hooly',
'Gooly' – amplify Ramsay's splendid irreverence, while the monosyllabic
rhymes – 'Life' and 'Wife' – make a serious point amid the humour. Then
Ramsay goes on to echo Horace in putting a case for enjoying life as it is,
and taking pleasure as you find it:

> WHEN Northern Blasts the Ocean snurl,   *ruffle*
> And gars the Heights and Hows look gurl,   *makes; hollows look bitter*
> Then left about the Bumper whirl,
> And toom the Horn,   *empty the drinking-horn*
> Grip fast the Hours which hasty hurl,
> The Morn's the Morn.
>
> THUS to *Leuconoe* sang sweet *Flaccus*,
> Wha nane e'er thought a *Gillygacus*:   *gaping fool*
> And why should we let Whimsies bawk us,   *baulk*
> When Joy's in Season,
> And thole sae aft the Spleen to whauk us   *allow so often the blues to*
> Out of our Reason?   *to beat us*
> (Epistle III, 37–48)

The dream of retirement that Horace had celebrated must have appealed
to anyone exasperated with politics and the commercialization that the
Union with England was helping to foster – even though the progress of
commerce was helping Ramsay's business as an increasingly successful
bookseller. Later epistles, some of which he did not trouble to publish,[100]
suggest that he was by no means striking an attitude. Though there is not

space to discuss them here, his 'Epistle to Robert Yarde of Devonshire, Esquire' declares: 'Believe me, Sir, the nearest Way / To Happiness, is to be gay' (II, 58, lines 49–50); and, among his unpublished poems, 'Epistle to Mr. H. S. at London Novr 1738' (III, 247–9) is a wonderfully lively performance, though he describes himself as 'plodding for Rhino, or Renown' (line 24), and 'An Epistle Wrote from Mavisbank March 1748 to a Friend in Edr.' (III, 261–4) is a tour de force in the topos of country versus city.

Familiar epistles that aim to divert or entertain their addressees are often occasionally or even intrinsically humorous, especially when they have an eye, or more, to diverting the general reader too. Robert Lloyd, who had to live by his pen after abandoning possible careers in the church or as a teacher at Westminster School, cultivated the form with special aplomb. Among the 46 original poems in English in the 1774 edition of his *Poetical Works*, no fewer than 19 are epistles, mostly in iambic tetrameter couplets, and ten of them are familiar. Probably referring both to the genre and to the verse form, Lloyd begins his 'Familiar Epistle. To a Friend who Sent the Author a Hamper of Wine' by calling his muse 'Fond of the loose familiar vein, / Which neither tires, nor cracks the brain'.[101] Not only was it a form congenial to him and his circle of male contemporaries, but it was relatively undemanding to write – a few lines later, Lloyd says his muse 'Prefers this easy down-hill road, / To dangerous leaps at five-barr'd ODE, Or starting in the Classic race / Jack-booted for an EPIC chace'. Lloyd's familiar epistles illustrate the extent to which the form lent itself to various forms of hybridity. The same poem, for example, though styled as a familiar epistle, is also to some extent discursive. Discussing not only the virtues of alcohol for poets of genius but also the dangers of servile mimicry, it runs to as many as 289 lines. At the same time, it is often humorous, as in the lines already quoted and in such remarks as: 'To POETS Wine is inspiration, / Blockheads get drunk in imitation'.[102]

Such a blend of different properties as those shown in this and other examples by Lloyd can hamper attempts to distinguish between different kinds of epistle. Nevertheless, as the familiar epistle developed in the course of the century, a distinct subtype had already emerged the chief object of which is fun. A humorous epistle may be defined as one designed primarily or exclusively to amuse. At the least it will have little or none of the ordinary content of correspondence, such as personal or other news. At its further limits – though this is not to be equated with its capacity to amuse – it is unlikely or impossible that it could have been

sent as an actual letter. Examples of this type include parodies such as
Richard Owen Cambridge's 'Elegy Written in an Empty Assembly-
Room', which travesties Pope's 'Eloisa to Abelard', and John Gay's 'To a
Young Lady with Some Lampreys', which is a brilliant spoof of a kind of
amatory poem that goes back at least to Waller.[103] While the burlesque
nature of Owen Cambridge's poem is clear – the footnote in the 1782
edition of Dodsley's *Collection* indicates that the original is so well
known as not to need quoting – closer reading is necessary to put in
question the implication that Gay actually sent his poem to the modest
virgin it pretends to address. Not only do lampreys, with their phallic
shape and supposed aphrodisiac properties, contrast jarringly with the
rose or fan of the type of epistle that he travesties, but two-fifths of the
poem consists of responses that he imagines from his addressee's maiden
aunt. The excited prurience that these display enable much of the poem's
humour, as when she refers to Rochester's poems or exclaims: 'Always in
danger of undoing, / A prawn, a shrimp may prove our ruin!' (39–40).
Here, as elsewhere, the extra end-of-line light stresses and double rhymes
further indicate the comic nature of a poem that is much more likely to
have been sent as a *jeu d'esprit* to a male companion than as an actual
verse letter, even to an unusually broad-minded young lady. The same is
probably true of William Broome's 'The Widow and Virgin Sisters, Being
a Letter to the Widow, in London', which offers humorous advice to its
addressee not to marry. Again, comic rhymes such as 'Co-ffy' / 'O! phy!',
'Commodities / Oddities' and, most ludicrously of all, *'Methusalem'* /
'use all 'em', mark the genre to which the poem belongs.[104]

   A second class of humorous epistles consists of playful pieces that did
the rounds among friends. Swift and his circle, who delighted in word
games and play with metre and rhyme, produced various examples
including 'A Letter to the Reverend Dr. Sh[erida]n', which manages 16
couplets with trisyllabic rhymes; Swift's epistle of 14 December 1719,
which is in doggerel but boasts no fewer than three postscripts, mostly in
anapestic dimeter with frequent end-of-line light stresses and comic
rhymes; 'A Letter from Dr. Sheridan to Dr. Swift', which uses the same
rhyme for its 13 anapestic lines before ending with a postscript in a
trimeter triplet; and Swift's reply, which keeps up the same rhyme for 34
lines.[105] Another specimen from the same period is Jonathan Smedley's
'Letter from the Quidnunc's at St. James's Coffee-house and the Mall,
London, to their Brethren at Lucas's Coffee-house, in Dublin', which
begins: 'Sir, having nothing else to do, / We send these empty Lines to
you', and is signed *'Dear Inquisitor, / Your, (Cumsociis,) / Most Ques-
tionful, / And Most Curious Brethren, / And humble Servants, / R, S, T, U,*

W, X, Y, Z, &c.'[106] Later in the century, and across the Atlantic, Nathaniel Evans provoked a series of humorous epistles by responding to another parody, by a female friend, of a passage from 'Eloisa to Abelard'. However, his half-joking but perhaps in part serious proposal of marriage at the end of his first rejoinder prevented these from staying quite at the level of fun, obliging his addressee to decline with playful firmness.[107] The series shows that even humorous epistles might have unexpected effects. At the same time, allusions to Swift and Stella as well as to Pope's famous epistle indicate how firmly epistolary culture was embedded.

Thirdly, there is a class of humorous epistles that, though familiar in content, are essentially hudibrastic chaff. John Smith produced three such poems early in the century, including one addressed to a friend suffering from the pox. Entitled simply 'An Epistle', it begins with perhaps the most ludicrous forced rhyme of this or any period for the title word: 'We receiv'd your sad Epistle, / In which we understand you piss ill'. The others concern his own illnesses, one describing the administration of an enema but ending with thanks for a present with which, Smith writes, 'We drank your Health at Crown / So long, till I forgot my own', and the third, which opens: 'Dear Trusty Friend, – / when you read this, / Don't think it came *ab inferis*', comically elaborating on his doctor's remedy of horse-riding and comparing himself en route to Don Quixote.[108] A generation later, Josiah Relph produced two 'burlesque' epistles that go further than Smith in mocking the form itself, though without Smith's bawdiness. The first, which is about writing with nothing to say, invokes Phoebus for help, only to fizzle out after claiming, with farcical lack of conviction, that so many ideas arrived as to 'choak the passage': 'Yes! what I fear'd is come to pass, / All my fine thoughts are stopt alass!'. The second describes his absurd attempts to amuse himself on long winter evenings, which end with tying knots in his garter until he produces one so Gordian that 'It must continue till some bully / Like Alexander draw his gully'.[109] But it took James Robertson to develop a whole doctrine out of what he called 'trifling'. Beginning 'An Epistle to a Friend. On Trifling', he seems to apologize much as Relph does: 'For want, good Sir, of something better, / I send you here a Trifling Letter'. Yet it soon becomes clear that he means the phrase literally, for the letter turns into a humorous justification of its subject – almost a discursive essay – providing a range of witty examples of why he claims: 'Trifling is a real ingredient, / And to our happiness expedient'. He ends with a fittingly cheerful flourish: 'May 6 – *the day extremely fine; / Seventeen hundred sixty-nine*'.[110]

The poems by Smith, Relph and Robertson may possibly have been sent as actual letters, though what they include of normal epistolary content varies from little to virtually nothing. More problematic, when seen as letter rather than poem, is the epistle addressed to oneself. John Hall-Stevenson's 'Epistle from John Me, Esquire, to his Excellence my Lord Self' is serio-comic, prefaced as it is by epigraphs from Juvenal and Persius (the former including the maxim 'know thyself'), yet presenting a humorous inner dialogue in the unusual form of continuous iambic tetrameters rhyming alternately. 'Me' asks, for instance: 'Who made your Lordship sour and proud? / Not I; you must give me my due: / I was, and always was allow'd, / Quite the reverse, till spoil'd by you'.[111] Such a poem turns the epistle inside out, subverting the whole idea of correspondence; and in this sense it is a type of formal parody. Another and very different example, from earlier in the century, is Isaac Hawkins Browne's to himself. By way of self-admonition, or using that as a pretext, Browne delivers a jaundiced survey of verse of the day, deploring 'this poetic itch' because he sees nothing good coming from it, and ending by debunking one of its main sources, Horace. Not only is it difficult to please, for 'Taste differs, just as men who read', but any success is fleeting: 'Peers treat their poets as their whores, / Enjoy, then turn them out of doors'. The section on Horace portrays the founder of the familiar epistle as rising 'from a bankrupt to the sum / Of human happiness – a plumb!' and as having sold out to please his master Augustus.[112] Its irony is intensified by the fact that behind the poem stands the first familiar epistle to parody itself, which is by none other than the poet Browne is lampooning. This is Epistle XX, usually known as 'To his Book', in which Horace comments by way of epilogue, part droll, part proud, on the likely fate of the work and describes himself briefly. Ramsay's free imitation catches the tone nicely: 'The future Criticks I forsee / Shall have their Notes on Notes on thee: / The wits unborn shall Beauties find / That never enter'd in my mind' (27–30).[113]

The final main class of humorous epistle is in dramatic form, and it is probably the most numerous of those printed during the century. Here the poet writes in the guise of a real or feigned correspondent, not necessarily human; for the latter reason, not all such examples are conceivable as actual messages, though they may bear, or parody, the formal properties of letters. Among humorous epistles, this type probably has the longest history, dating back at least to several poems by Rochester, such as 'Letter from Artemiza in the Towne to Chloe in the Countrey',[114] and to Alexander Radcliffe's *Ovid Travestie*, which burlesques the *Heroides* translated by Dryden and others.[115] It is more likely than other variants of the form to be employed for satire rather than humour, and for this reason satirical examples are discussed in Chapter 5. Humorous examples include Swift's 'Humble Petition of Frances Harris' and 'Mary the Cook-Maid's Letter to Dr. Sheridan', along with Pope's rather different 'Bounce to Fop. An Heroick Epistle from a Dog at Twickenham to a Dog at Court', and Robert Lloyd's 'Familiar Epistle, from the Rev. Mr. Hanbury's Horse, to the Rev. Mr. Scot'.[116] But two poems apiece by Isaac Hawkins Browne and Mary Leapor illustrate the type especially well.

Browne was skilled not only at humorous verse but writing in the style of others. *A Pipe of Tobacco*, the work for which he is now best known, presents six poems in praise of its subject in the manner of six different poets including Pope – who admired the poem – and Swift; and *The Fire Side. A Pastoral Soliloquy* hilariously adopts the voice of John Carteret, Earl of Granville, to mock his bad faith in professing a preference for retirement that his political actions belied.[117] In 'From Cælia to Cloe' and 'A Letter to Corinna from a Captain in Country Quarters', Browne plays both with the stock topic of the country's attractions versus those of the town and with the form of the familiar invitation. Cælia is a woman who lives in the country inviting her friend, who favours the town, to visit. Her letter begins with panache – 'I rural life enjoy, the town's your taste' – and goes on to wrong-foot the reader by suggesting that the pretext for the invitation is Cloe's health: she should leave town with other genteel folk now that 'the dog-star brings diseases on'.[118] The real incentive, which Cælia goes on to unfold after the first ten lines, is that all the pleasures of the town are also available in the country. For she is anything but short of amusements, even on Sundays when, she remarks, much like Swift in *An Argument Against Abolishing Christianity*, 'church serves well enough' (p. 305) because of the prospects it gives for seeing interesting company. Towards the end of the letter she crowds in the attractions thick and fast:

Is there within ten miles a troop review'd,
An auction of old goods, an interlude
By strolling players, an horse-race, or a ball?
There to be seen I have an urgent call.

Such scenes, she concludes, render the countryside 'town in miniature', so that her conventional apologies for it – 'Scenes odd as these', 'Content ev'n here' (p. 306) – become tongue-in-cheek. Browne has Cælia let slip that her pleasures disrupt the real work of the countryside as 'The labours of the plough are then forgot, / And THOMAS mounts the box in liv'ry coat' (p. 305). In this way, the poem could be said to satirize fashionable worldliness, while also registering a serious point about the spread into the countryside not only of the secular attitudes rife in the city but of amusements of all kinds. Yet, though it has the casual misogynism of much male writing of the period ('True sex, and constant to the love of change' [p. 305]), its touch is light, and the ironic tone in which Browne has Cælia write – another example is 'homely hut' (p. 304) – is sustained finely.

'A Letter to Corinna' is less decorous, as the contrast between its racy tetrameter couplets and Cælia's stylish pentameters suggests. The Captain in whose guise Browne writes is in a position similar to that actually occupied earlier in the century by Richardson Pack. Although he is not, as Pack had been, on half pay, the country quarters where he is serving bar him from his usual pleasures, especially venery. He spends the first part of his letter comically deploring his plight, as when he tells how a woman he is trying to seduce responds to his military boasts by asking 'who was slain the last review', before introducing the solution he and his friend propose: 'to keep a miss – in common' (p. 228).[119] Though he does not admit it, the implicit reason why they have to share is that they cannot afford the expenses that a mistress of the quality they want would require. He then tries to convince his addressee, outlining the reasons he supposes she will cite for refusing and going on to rebut them. Both sides of the argument give Browne further opportunities for mild satire. First, he has the Captain imagine Corinna flaunting her prospects when 'the lawyer [is] fee'd' and when Convocation is sitting (pp. 228–9). Then he has him relate the 'ills' that actually attend her, ranging from desertion by captains 'kept by quality on duty', and clients paying her little or nothing – as when 'My lord may take you to his bed, / But then he sends you back unpaid' – to imprisonment, judicial harassment or transportation (p. 229). His punchline has the double irony that characterizes Browne's work at its best: 'Then oh! to lewdness bid adieu, / And chastely live, confin'd to two'. Such indelicacy was less permissible in the 1780s than in 1758, when the poem first appeared in Dodsley's *Collection*, so in the 1782 edition it carries a solemn note from the *Biographia Britannica*, averring that it 'was designed as a strong ridicule and reproof of such kind of criminal connections', and that 'the whole must be considered as written in the character of a rakish officer, during a time of profound peace'. But the point is scarcely moral, or even satirical. It consists in the ironies of the proposal, and in the simulation, in all its witty effrontery, of the style of a licentious young officer

The humour of Mary Leapor's dramatic epistles is more at the writer's expense than Browne's. 'Strephon to Celia. A Modern Love-Letter' shows a young man attempting, with risible lack of credibility, first to flatter an heiress and then to persuade her that his proposal of marriage is in her best interests.[120] Although Leapor's work shows her keen awareness of a woman's vulnerability in marriage, Strephon's proposal is so inept and so transparently self-serving that its impact is less satirical than humorous. 'The Epistle of Deborah Dough', on the other hand, invites unpatronising amusement at the writer's simplicity.[121] Though Deborah writes just what comes into her head, with a new subject every line at the start of her letter, and though she gossips, including at the expense of Leapor herself, she is without malice or pretension. In these epistles Leapor both exploits the format of the letter and mimics not only particular styles of writing, and speaking, but also the attitudes that underlie them. Strephon, for example, opens his letter with 'Madam', offset above the line but metrically part of it, and closes melodramatically, his signature outside the line, by calling himself a 'slave' half-murdered by Celia's eyes and in danger of death if she does not favour him: 'Or else this very moment dies – / *Strephon*'. In contrast, Deborah Dough's salutation and valediction are both part of the line unit, her first line not stopping to draw breath before introducing her first topic ('Dearly beloved Cousin, These [. . .]'), but her last ending the letter affectionately: 'Your loving Cousin, / DEBORAH DOUGH'. Similarly, whereas Leapor has Strephon trot out all the Petrarchan clichés but crassly overdo them, claiming that her eyes are so bright that they scorch his forehead 'to a Cinder' (17), that her breast 'Is made of nothing else but Snow' (20), and that her cheeks are so red that it looks 'as if they bled' (23), the remarks she gives Deborah Dough are merely naïve, as with her only partly suppressed credulity about the local cunning-man, and her belief that her daughter's ability to knit a stocking and cook puddings, bacon, apples and pancakes to perfection means that she is 'better learnt' than Leapor herself (23). And while, with Strephon's letter, Leapor mimics the style of a raffish young man who seems to have profited little from his education as he reaches for lofty expressions but lapses into slang such as 'Chat' (29), 'dem' (32) and, demeaningly, 'of a Louse' (42), she lards Deborah Dough's with colourful vernacular idioms such as 'to an Hair' (26), 'thick as Plumbs in Cake' (34) and 'as I'm a Sinner' (63).

The ventriloquial ability displayed in the four epistles just discussed is one of the factors that render them more humorous than satirical. Each is a feat of impersonation by letter, and the writer's skill in adopting a particular kind of attitude and language enables much of the pleasure offered by all four. Later chapters of this book will address the two other forms of dramatic epistle: satirical, and heroic. All contributed to the rise of the dramatic monologue, but, because mimicry is central to it, the humorous type perhaps the most.

4
Discursive

A discursive epistle is a verse essay in the form, more or less, of a letter. The type goes back to Horace, whose *Art of Poetry*, addressed to the Pisos, attracted various imitations and parodies in the eighteenth century including John Byrom's 'Epistle to a Friend on the Art of English Poetry', the anonymous *Art of Preaching* and even an *Art of Wenching*.[1] Some examples advertise their discursive aims with the word 'Essay' in their titles, as does Pope's *Essay on Man*. Mary Leapor followed suit with four of her verse epistles, and so did others, ranging from Robert Craggs Nugent, in a poem first entitled *An Essay on Happiness*, and Benjamin Stillingfleet in his *Essay on Conversation*.[2] Nevertheless, most such writers maintained the guise of epistolary address required by the convention. Byrom names his addressee in his second line ('Jenkins'), as does the author of *The Art of Wenching* ('O my lamented Susan'); Pope begins with a summons at once urgent and comradely ('Awake! my St. John'), while Leapor begins one of her essay-epistles with a nod of agreement ('Nothing, dear Madam, nothing is more true'), another with a question ('Say, dearest *Stella*, why this pensive Air?').[3] Such devices can render it difficult to distinguish between discursive and familiar epistles, a problem intrinsic to the form that goes back to its originator. For, although the three poems in the second book of Horace's *Epistles* are much longer than those in the first, and so enable fuller discussion of general topics, the 20 poems in the first book often also shift from the personal and the familiar to the discursive. In his *Art of Poetry*, Horace developed a feature he had given the form to produce a new type of poem.

Some discursive epistles of the period retain only traces of epistolarity, and some not even that. For example, Thomas Warton's 'Newmarket' is included among Bell's 'Epistles Satirical and Preceptive', but has no single addressee and boasts other non-epistolary features such as an epigraph and several footnotes; while Walter Harte's *An Essay on Satire* ranks as an epistle chiefly through apostrophes to an obvious addressee, Alexander Pope.[4] Warton's poem is a satire, and generic blurrings such as these stem in part from the flexibility of the epistle as a form. Once more, however, they also go back in part to Horace, whose *Satires* were in the same metre as his *Epistles*, and who often referred to both works with the same word, *sermones* or 'conversations'.[5] Discursive poems that are only nominally or marginally epistolary may therefore invite the parallel drawn by Jay Arnold Levine, who remarks that such works pretend to belong to private correspondence in the same way that Cecily, in Wilde's *The Importance of Being Earnest*, calls her diary 'simply a very young girl's record of her own thoughts and impressions, and consequently meant for publication'.[6] Yet a verse epistle is by no means necessarily the transparent and self-serving fiction this remark suggests. Above all, writing a discursive essay in the form of a letter enables a poet to solve the problem of tone by specifying a particular addressee. As is often recognized, Pope was especially adroit in his choice of titular recipients. In the four epistles of *An Essay on Man*, he addressed Henry St John, Viscount Bolingbroke, who had led the active life in government and the meditative as a philosopher; in *Epistle to Burlington* a leading architect, patron and connoisseur; and, in a more guileful manner, his longtime friend Martha Blount in *Epistle to a Lady* – guileful in that he exploits her sex and his intimacy with her in a bid to finesse misogynistic views. The mode of address differs with the subject. As Pat Rogers puts it, in *An Essay on Man* 'Bolingbroke's function is to mitigate the loneliness of the long-distance speaker';[7] whereas the tone of *Epistle to a Lady* is more personal and informal, in keeping with the kind of light, playful conversation to which, Pope suggests, women can aspire at their best. This chapter illustrates the convention further and the various uses to which it may be put.

One of the main influences on tone, in epistles as in other poems, is versification. As a rough equivalent to the hexameters used by Horace, iambic pentameter couplets constituted the verse form of choice for the eighteenth-century discursive epistle, as for most serious poetry. About three-quarters of the discursive poems in my database of epistles from *Literature Online* are in pentameter couplets, but fewer than 10 per cent are in iambic tetrameters; only three poems are in blank verse, and John Byrom is almost alone in using stanzas. The metre in which an epistle is written, and how it is handled, has its key effect on formality. For example, the buoyant rhythms of anapestic tetrameters, often used for humorous and satirical verse in the eighteenth century, are less well suited to serious discursive aims unless the poet is either writing familiarly or

with especially frank unpretentiousness. Familiar examples include Mary
Savage's 'Letter to my Friend E. B.' and St John Honeywood's 'Poetical
Epistle to a Young Lady, on Letter Writing', both in couplets, and, in
quatrains of alternating tetrameters and trimeters rhyming alternately,
William Whitehead's 'To —— 1751', which is about contentment with a
modest position.[8] But John Byrom is unique in using anapestic tetrameter
couplets, arranged in huitaines, for most of his discursive verse. The
opening stanza of his 'Epistle to J. Bl[ac]k[bur]n, Esq; Occasioned by a
Dispute Concerning the Food of St. John, the Baptist' is a characteristic
example of his unbuttoned style:

> The Point, *Mr. Bl—k—n*, disputed upon,
> "Whether *Insects*, or *Herbs*, were the Food of *St. John*,"
> Is a singular Proof how a learned Pretence
> Can prevail with some Folks over natural Sense,
> So consistent with Herbs, as you know was allow'd;
> But the Dust that is rais'd by a critical Croud
> Has so blinded their Eyes, that plain, simple Truth
> Is obscur'd by a *Posse* of *Classics*, forsooth![9]

Such a style has the defects of its merits, nicely caught in his editor's
remark that 'Byrom's foible in literature as well as in life was – if I may
so describe it – a love of his dressing-gown rather late in the morning and
rather early at night'.[10]

Iambic tetrameter couplets are usually a notch less informal than their
anapestic cousins. Strongly influenced by the lighter verse of Matthew
Prior, including his 'Epistle to Fleetwood Shephard, Esq.', several poets
adopted them for discursive epistles from the 1730s. Among the first was
John Bancks, who, as mentioned in Chapter 2, had the chutzpah to
publish 'Love Atones for Little Crimes' as 'An Ethic Epistle', and whose
'Against Fortune: An Epistle' is a kind of poor man's *Essay on Man*; at
about the same time, Matthew Green was writing *The Spleen*, published
posthumously in 1737 and, though familiar in style, discursive in mode.[11]
Two decades further on, Robert Lloyd exploited the form for a number of
familiar epistles that become discursive, as well as for several discursive
epistles that are decidedly familiar. Examples include 'The Poet',
addressed to Charles Churchill, in which he accepts that *'Epistle* now's
your only mode'; 'Shakespeare', addressed to David Garrick, in which he
anticipates Samuel Johnson's *Preface* by debunking the doctrine of the
Unities; and, appropriately, 'On Rhyme', addressed 'to a Friend', and,
though styled as 'a Familiar Epistle', handling with wit and humour his

regular subject of the difficulties of living as a poet.[12] Because Lloyd also
wrote essay-epistles in iambic pentameter couplets, a comparison easily
shows the difference in tone that tetrameters produce. In 'The Actor.
Addressed to Bonnel Thornton, Esq.', Lloyd writes:

> Shall They, who trace the passions from their rise,
> Shew scorn her features, her own image vice?
> Who teach the mind it's proper force to scan,
> And hold the faithful mirror up to man,
> Shall their profession e'er provoke disdain,
> Who stand the foremost in the moral train,
> Who lend reflection all the grace of art,
> And strike the precept home upon the heart?[13]

Here, the verse has the pointed balance and antithesis that the form
enables, matching couplet with couplet (as within the first four lines and
the second four), line with line (as with the third and fourth, and the
seventh and eighth), and within individual lines (as in the chiastic
construction of the second line and the alliterative doublings in the fourth
and the last). It is a forceful and stylish performance, even though the use
of open couplets makes it relatively informal. In contrast, this is how
Lloyd treats the Unities in 'Shakespeare':

> When Shakespear leads the mind a dance,
> From France to England, hence to France,
> Talk not to me of time and place;
> I own I'm happy in the chace.
> Whether the drama's here or there,
> 'Tis nature, Shakespeare, every where.
> The poet's fancy can create,
> Contract, enlarge, annihilate,
> Bring past and present close together,
> In spite of distance, seas, or weather;
> And shut up in a single action,
> What cost whole years in its transaction.[14]

The tone here is breezy, even facetious, and not only because the diction
is more familiar. Lloyd maintains a lively pace by avoiding complex
constructions and, in the last four lines, by exploiting the end-of-line
hypermetrical light stresses and double rhymes that so often pepper
tetrameters. Where he uses polysyllabic words, as with 'transaction', the

effect is humorous; the chiasmus in the second line is much simpler than its pentameter counterpart; and, for the line unit or the main part of it, he favours brisk threesomes such as 'Contract, enlarge, annihilate' and 'distance, seas, or weather'. Such a style makes for easy reading; more to the point for Lloyd, it probably made for easier writing too.

Tetrameter couplets are not always as loose as Lloyd's, however. It is worth remembering that Andrew Marvell exploits the form in 'To his Coy Mistress' to turn apparent persiflage into confrontation with mortality, and eighteenth-century poets sometimes also handled them more soberly. Examples include Abel Evans, whose *Vertumnus: An Epistle to Mr. Jacob Bobart*, written in part to celebrate the end of the war of the Spanish Succession in 1713, celebrates its addressee's excellence as botanist and gardener; John Dalton, who produced two discursive epistles in the form in the 1740s; and Hannah More, whose 'The Bas Bleu; Or, Conversation', much later in the century, corrects mistaken views of the bluestockings and endorses the main function of their gatherings.[15] Others could easily be added, but a particularly interesting one is Lady Catharine Manners's 'Review of Poetry, Addressed to a Son', which, highly unusually, is in trochaic tetrameter couplets catalectic. By using the form, Manners avoids the potential pomp of the pentameter but achieves grace and concision, as in the following vignette, characteristic of how her poem works:

Sense, by studious thought refin'd,
Critic taste, with candour join'd,
Strong discernment, just and clear,
Graceful diction, truth severe,
Piety's seraphic flame
Mark enlighten'd Johnson's name.[16]

Trochaic verse is not very common in English, and rare in the epistle, though Robert Craggs Nugent uses it for his 'Epistle to Pollio, from the Hills of Howth in Ireland'.[17] Perhaps following the example of Dyer's 'Grongar Hill', Manners gains a measured, serious pace from its falling rhythms and her use of catalexis, although unlike Dyer, whose poem includes some iambic lines, she avoids these altogether.

As the example from Lloyd's 'The Actor' indicates, there is a range of formality in pentameter couplets too. This is determined largely by how far the writer uses enjambement – between couplets as well as between lines – and also by choice of rhyme-words. The same principle holds for blank verse, though few poets used it for verse epistles in the period. At one end of the spectrum, Sneyd Davies and Ann Yearsley chose it for serious purposes, as John Armstrong did for two non-epistolary poems, *The Oeconomy of Love* and *The Art of Preserving Health*.[18] The opening lines of William Hayward Roberts's 'Poetical Epistle, to Christopher Anstey, Esq; on the English Poets, Chiefly Those, Who Have Written in Blank Verse', provide an apt example:

No not in rhyme. I hate that iron chain,
Forg'd by the hand of some rude Goth, which cramps
Reluctant Genius, and with many a fold
Fast binds him to the ground.[19]

Roberts exploits enjambement and the caesura with an assurance that might have earned approval from Milton himself. On the other hand, the anonymous writer of *The Art of Wenching* resorted to mock-Miltonics, probably in imitation of Philips's *Splendid Shilling*. Blank verse, all the same, is relatively uncommon in eighteenth-century discursive epistles, along with stanzaic forms including the Standard Habby.[20]

The flexibility of the epistle form also enables wide variation in the length even of discursive epistles, as well as an almost unlimited array of possible topics. Not surprisingly, many verse essays expand to hundreds of lines – among those on which I have collected data, no fewer than 65 have more than 300 lines, and 16 have more than 500. Others show that brevity can be a virtue too, among them Thomas Odiorne's 'Poetical Epistle', which uses only 12 lines to answer the question whether true friendship can die; and Elizabeth Tollet's 'An Epistle', which runs to 43 lines that offer a post-Horatian perspective on the topics of disgust with the world and retirement.[21] These and the examples already given illustrate how discursive epistles may address almost any subject. As indicated in Chapter 1, John Bell met the challenge by adopting sub-categories for the four volumes of his anthology that he devoted to them: 'Ethic', 'Critical and Didactic', 'Descriptive and Narrative', and 'Satirical and Preceptive'. These, though, by no means cover the full range. Topics considered in discursive epistles extend from poetry itself to politics, philosophy or physiognomy; and even ethic epistles enjoy a wide remit. While their stock themes are the active life versus the contemplative, and the related binary of town versus country, they may explore, for example, 'Desire', 'Fashion', 'Nobility', 'Politeness', 'The Vanity of Human Enjoyments' or 'Virtue' itself.[22] Rather than try to represent anything like the whole span of possibilities realized in the period, this chapter focuses on epistles concerning two particular subjects: one, the nature of woman, because it was especially contentious; the other, the question of happiness, because it attracted many poets from the 1730s, when Epistle IV of Pope's *Essay on Man* first appeared, till the end of the century.

The chief means through which the discursive epistle is able to exploit epistolarity is through the relations that the poet may establish between writer (who is not necessarily the same as poet) and readers. Janet Altman, who coined the term 'epistolarity', gave it a 'working definition' as 'the use of the letter's formal properties to create meaning'.[23] In Chapter 1, I have argued that Altman's work on epistolary fiction is not often relevant to the verse epistle, except in the case of what she and Anna de Pretis call 'addressee-consciousness'.[24] A more accurate phrase might be 'addressee-relations', as the question is not whether an epistolary text shows awareness of one or more addressees, but what use it makes of the fact that, by definition, it is written to be read by them. One of the most effective resources for the discursive epistle is the opportunity to direct it to a more or less specific addressee. As I have already emphasized, for example, that opportunity enables heightened control over tone according to the nature of the addressee who is chosen.

Pope's *Epistle to a Lady*, Lady Anne Irwin's reply, 'An Epistle to Mr. Pope', and Mary Leapor's 'Essay on Woman' are all carefully directed to particular addressees.[25] Though Pope does not identify his,[26] his poem defines her as an old and intimate friend, with whom he adopts a tone of easy warmth and humour; while Irwin, taking issue with a man whom she was not in a position to address familiarly and who was the most famous poet of the day, is more formal and circumspect. Leapor, on the other hand, addresses a friend of her own sex, Bridget Freemantle, by the name she used for her, Artemisia. All these choices of addressee are strategic. For instance, as I have suggested above, Pope's choice, as he rehearses and develops prejudices of the time about women, allows him to express opinions that might, if directed generally, or even to another man, have run a greater risk of giving offence – especially to female readers. He presumes on the apparent willingness of a close female friend to accept his views, and the wit and humour of his poem are such that it is not impossible that he won it. In contrast, Leapor addresses a friend on whom she can rely not only for a sympathetic hearing but for a sense of shared exposure to the evils she depicts. She does not even name Artemisia until 19 lines into the poem – until that point it is not even clear that it is an epistle. Nor does she name or address her again, though, almost certainly, she refers to her implicitly in her modest wish for 'A Fire to warm me, and a Friend to please' (52). Yet, in a way similar to Pope's choice of addressee, Leapor's allows her a licence to express herself without reserve, even outspokenly. As both are literary epistles, designed for a wider audience, they invite their external, implicit addressees to occupy the same positions as their internal addressees. A related principle applies to Irwin's response to Pope, although, because she is challenging him, the dynamics are different. Here, the external reader is positioned as a person whose views are close to her own.

The positioning of the reader is especially complex in *Epistle to a Lady*, even leaving aside the different meanings available to those who knew or know the identity of its addressee and those who did or do not. Like many other writers of epistles since the second person singular went out of use in English, Pope is able to exploit the ambiguity of the word 'you' that does double duty instead. In the opening line of his poem, 'Nothing so true as what you once let fall', its referent, albeit unnamed, is the internal addressee, Martha Blount. But the next time the word appears, in the phrase 'You tip the wink' (33), it has acquired an extra, implicit, referent. Though it may still address his friend, the generalized context created by the naming of type-characters (Silia, Calista, Simplicius), and the following remark that 'All eyes may see' (35, 36), suggest that the external reader is being invoked too. The same applies to the various imperatives that punctuate the poem, as with 'See' (69), 'Say' (93), 'Turn then' (101), 'But grant' (199), 'Yet mark' (219) and 'See how' (243), and also to such phrases as 'Critick'd your wine, and analyz'd your meat' (81), 'But die, and she'll adore you' (139), and 'Would Cloe know if you're alive or dead?' (177). Such a double mode of address gains in complexity in two ways. First, it accommodates women who are married as well as those who, like Pope's immediate addressee, are single. This is most striking in the shift, after a warm compliment directed to his friend, from 'She, who can love a Sister's charms' (259), which would have had a special, private, meaning in light of his difficult relations with her sister Teresa, to the next line, 'Sighs for a Daughter with unwounded ear',[27] and those that immediately follow in praise of a wife who 'Charms' her husband by deferring to him (261–4), for none of these could apply to a woman styled as a 'Virgin' by an epithet a few lines before (255). Second, there are also points in the poem when the address is gender-specific, as when Pope presents a tendentious comparison between men and women:

Our bolder Talents in full light display'd,
Your Virtues open fairest in the shade.
Bred to disguise, in Public 'tis you hide;
There, none distinguish 'twixt your Shame or Pride. (201–4)

Here, the first person plural is clearly masculine, the second person plural clearly feminine, as later in the lines 'Your love of Pleasure, our desire of Rest' (274) and 'Your Taste of Follies, with our Scorn of Fools' (276). Such expressions construct Martha Blount as representative of her sex and Pope as representative for his own. Yet there is still a further twist to his use of pronouns, for he also includes his addressee in the first person plural. This is explicit in the couplet: 'Yet ne'er so sure our passion to create, / As when she touch'd the brink of all we hate' (51–2). For two reasons this is highly significant. On the one hand, Pope is aligning the immediate addressee – the unnamed Martha Blount – and, behind her, the general reader against what he presents as a typical form of objectionable femininity. On the other, through that device he does not so much invite her, and their, collusion as seek to impose it.

Should either the immediate or indirect addressee feel inclined to object to the views he presents, Pope wraps them in a kind of sugar-coating. As is often noted, he offers a justification for them at the start by quoting Martha Blount against her own sex; in addition, he addresses her as 'Dear Madam' halfway through (151) and as 'Ah Friend!' (249) before ending the epistle with affectionate, generous compliments. In these he not only commends her ability to 'raise the Thought, and touch the Heart' (250), and 'make to morrow chearful as to day' (258), but also, comparing her serenity to the moon's, her 'Virgin Modesty' (254–5); her 'Beauty' (287), playfully affecting not to know how old she is – 'I forget the year' (283); her 'Sense'; and her 'Good-humour' (292). Then, by devoting himself to her with his final word, 'a Poet' (292), he caps the whole with a brilliant variation, and intensification, of conventional epistolary valedictions. At the same time, the entire poem, with its wit, verbal dexterity and metrical skill, is offered as a winning tribute to the intelligence and discrimination both of its immediate addressee and of its wider audience. Yet it is the sharpness of the satire that necessitates such rhetorical confectionery. Although Pope may construct his friend and female readers like her as exceptions, not the less is he generalizing about their sex in a way that is demeaning. Even the bouquets he tenders do not soften the impact of what Valerie Rumbold calls 'the poem's most brutally anti-feminist couplet': 'Woman and Fool are two hard things to hit, / For true No-meaning puzzles more than Wit' (113–14).[28]

While *Epistle to a Lady* names its form in its title, it is generically a satire. Although Warburton may have tried to disguise the fact by using the umbrella title 'Moral Essays', Pope used epistolary form in the 'Epistles to Several Persons', as he called them,[29] not only for discursive but also for satirical purposes. Responding to Pope only a year after the poem was first published, Lady Anne Irwin produced not a satire but a composed and judicious counter-argument. In keeping with her considerably greater distance from her addressee, she begins by referring to him in the third person: 'No wonder, *Pope* such female triflers sees' (2). Not until 25 lines into her poem does she first address him directly ('you may enquire'), and she refrains from doing so again until appealing, in her closing lines, that he 'rescue woman' from the *'Gothick* state' (114–15) that she has described. The relations between herself as writer, her addressee and the wider readership are less complex than in his poem because he is a public figure whom the purpose of her response requires her to name. Yet they gain an extra edge from the fact that the poem invites her reader to side with her against Pope. One of the ways in which it does this is by employing the first person plural not with several possible referents, as in his poem, but with just two: herself and readers of both sexes. The appeal to men as well as women is explicit in the couplet 'Whether a crown or bawble we desire / Whether to learning or to dress aspire' (17–18) because it occurs in a paragraph that compares female ambitions systematically with male. Later in the poem, however, the first person plural represents a general reader whose views, she implies, are those that any reasonable person, not excluding Pope himself, would naturally hold. Developing her main theme that women are in a *'Gothick state'* not because of intrinsic failings but for lack of education, she claims, for example: 'As well might we expect, in winter, spring, / As land untill'd a fruitful crop shou'd bring' (43–4). Similarly, in her closing paragraph, she uses the same pronoun again when remarking that no one can now find 'such generous sentiments' as those shown by women in antiquity (105–6), and that, accordingly, 'No more can we expect our modern wives / Heroes shou'd breed, who lead such useless lives' (109–10). Because the positions with which the word 'we' associates her reader are commonsense ones, her use of the word does not have the force of imposed collusion that Pope's does.

Irwin also implies that her poem is of a different character from his. The epithet she applies to him in her third line, 'the satyrist', not only calls attention to the kind of verse on which he had chiefly been engaged since his translation of Homer, but also suggests that the poem to which she is responding is more satire than epistle. Her poem has an apt Horatian epigraph (literally, 'nor do I see how talent unrefined is any use'),[30] and it begins by half-echoing Pope's opening line in the repeated phrase 'Nothing so like' (4–5). But crucially, unlike his poem, it is a verse essay constructed as a logical argument. Its opening paragraph sets out her case succinctly: that, though 'custom' condemns women to useless lives, they do not differ essentially from men. The following two paragraphs go on first to illustrate the proposition that, while 'Women must in a narrow orbit move', 'power alike both males and females love' (23–4); and then to explain, with the line 'In education all the diff'rence lies' (33), why such great discrepancies appear to exist between the sexes. Although 'the hero' differs from 'the rural 'squire', and the well-bred lady from 'she who earns by toil her daily fare', ambition drives them all; and what separates one member of the same sex from another, and also members of different sexes from each other, is unequal opportunity (26–32). Irwin illuminates these leading ideas of her essay with metaphors of farming and mining. She then gives examples of uncultivated men – the merchant who is ignorant of agriculture, or the sailor of Aristotle – before restating her key principle: 'The whole in application is compris'd, / Reason's not reason, if not exercis'd' (63–4). In the final part of her poem, she acknowledges that the minds of many women are 'a savage waste' (80), and that too often they are 'idly busy' (82), but she attributes these faults to 'custom' (68) that urges them to depend on their physical attractions and gives them no moral or other education to know any better than to practise the arts of deception. Against this discouraging picture of contemporary abuses she sets examples from antiquity that show they are not congenital – Clelia, Lucretia, Cornelia and especially Portia – before, in her peroration, asking Pope's help in redeeming them.

In this way, Irwin's strategy in her epistle is very different from Pope's. Structurally, as the Twickenham notes document, and as Valerie Rumbold shows in detail, his poem is largely a collage of passages written earlier and for other purposes, and it lacks coherence as an argument – though he tries to pass this off by claiming that the sex it seeks to define is itself shallow and unstable. At the same time, its relation both to its immediate addressee and its other readerships are manipulative in the ways I have tried to demonstrate. Irwin replies not only with a carefully framed argument, but also with a quite different way of relating to her addressee and the general reader. Not only is her poem without the deviousness of Pope's in its invocation of a wider audience, but her flattery of her addressee at the end of the poem has a quite different tone and purpose from his. Instead of using compliments to palliate satire, as he does, she appeals to his better nature – she calls him 'generous' (118) – while praising the perspicuity about human beings that she attributes to him and his ability, in the classic Horatian formula, to 'instruct as well as please' (113). As Claudia Thomas has shown, she displays a close familiarity with his work, both in general and through specific allusions that must have been recognizable to many readers.[31] This helps give her epistle its authority; for, like Pope, she also appeals to her reader's intelligence, but more candidly, while discreetly demonstrating her own.

While Irwin's poem addressed Pope publicly, in the columns of a magazine, Mary Leapor's is more like his in addressing a friend whom it does not name. It begins abruptly by stating its topic – 'Woman' – rather as Pope buttonholes his addressee in his opening line. But the terms of the address are quite different, because Leapor does little to invoke an external reader. Not only does she refer directly to her friend just once, in a line in which she refers to herself as 'your Servant' (19), but her sole use of the first person plural is when she applies it to the sex to which she and her addressee belong. This is at the climax of her poem, in the couplet 'Tho' Nature arm'd us for the growing Ill, / With fraudful Cunning, and a headstrong Will' (57–8), where 'us' may refer not just to her friend and herself but also to an external reader who is female. The only other space that Leapor creates for an external reader is through three rhetorical questions in the second verse paragraph, beginning with 'Who would be wise, that knew *Pamphilia*'s Fate?' (21). All the questions are rhetorical because she goes on to explain what the fate of each woman is – in Pamphilia's case, that of suffering prejudice against female intelligence. For this reason, they avoid imposing on the reader in the way that Pope's epistle does. Instead, Leapor presents herself as a detached outsider, speaking her mind without presuming to speak for others. She distances herself from Pamphilia, as she did in a letter to Freemantle about the poem,[32] remarking that the evils that torment her example of female wit are 'overlook'd by *Simplicus*, and me' (38); and she also distances herself from those who seek wealth by declaring that all she requires are 'A Fire to warm me, and a Friend to please' (52). As a result, her epistle has a more private complexion than Pope's or Irwin's, even though its subject is one of manifestly public and social interest, and though she may well have hoped it would reach a wider audience.

This apparently private character corresponds to the obliqueness with which Leapor responds to Pope. Unlike Irwin, she does not reply directly but by implication. Her title not only evokes both his *Essay on Man* and his *Epistle to a Lady*, but also signals what she defines as the key issue: sex, not social rank. She does not otherwise refer to *Epistle to a Lady* at all, even though she often alludes to Pope's work in other poems, and though for part of the epistle she adopts his practice of describing typical examples, as she does elsewhere.[33] Instead, she focuses on the material conditions that determine women's lives, and that her social position gave her every reason to know well. These she identifies as financial and marital status. Her first verse paragraph gets down to business after only four lines by showing how 'Wealth' bestows personal attractions on a woman who has it: her face becomes 'plenteous' (6), because what the suitor sees in looking at it is the inviting prospect of 'blooming Acres' of productive land (8). Then, having debunked the absurdities of male love rhetoric, according to which even snow may seem dark against the whiteness of the woman's complexion and melt in distress at the comparison, she shows marriage bringing her back to earth, as Hymen 'turns the Goddess to her native Clay' (18). The second verse paragraph outlines three female destinies. Sylvia is beautiful but miserable because her husband no longer values her; Pamphilia's intelligence not only provokes dislike in other women and irritation in men, but makes her more sharply aware of her suffering; and Cordia, whose sole concern is money, lives in mean-minded squalor. Convinced that wealth has little to offer, Leapor opts in the brief verse paragraph that follows for humble contentment. Then, in her final paragraph, she sums up. Wealth is no use, because it leads to 'Avarice', like Cordia's, or 'Pride', like that of the flattered heiress (53). A woman may behave as 'A wanton Virgin' before marriage, and be attended by 'wond'ring Crouds', but after it she may find herself 'a starving Bride' who cannot speak without being 'deem'd an Idiot' (54–6). Acknowledging that women may have 'ten thousand Follies' for which to answer, Leapor suggests that what she calls their 'fraudful Cunning' and 'headstrong Will' are qualities with which Nature has 'arm'd them' against the 'growing Ill' from which they suffer (57–8). Her withering conclusion is that 'Unhappy Woman's but a Slave at large' (60) – nominally free, but effectively powerless.

   Like Irwin's epistle and unlike Pope's, Leapor's presents a reasoned argument, though compression renders it rather elliptical – she uses only 60 lines against Irwin's 120 and Pope's 292. In light especially of her status, it is surprisingly outspoken. Yet it is the epistolary convention of personal address – and also, no doubt, the fact of a genuine friendship – that grants her the privilege to define so trenchantly the evils of women's condition. Richard Greene rightly observes that 'The implied reader of Leapor's poems is, generally speaking, a female friend';[34] but the remark could be extended to say that, when she addresses a female friend directly, as in most of her verse epistles, she gains the space she needs to speak out. It is a strategy that turns disadvantage to opportunity, and one that, crucially, the tradition of the discursive epistle enables.

A selection from the many poems about happiness in the period offers a wider range of discursive strategies for comparison. Epistle IV of Pope's

Essay on Man, entitled 'Of the Nature and State of Man, With Respect to Happiness', and first printed in 1734, attracted many direct and indirect imitations, along with a few rejoinders. The imitations stretch from Nugent's *Essay on Happiness* of 1737, already mentioned, at least till the end of the century, but the topic is also treated in other types of poem, especially the non-epistolary verse essay. I will discuss a few examples of these first, in order to provide some comparisons. Because the main focus of the comparison is rhetorical and stylistic qualities, I will refer to discursive content only where it is relevant.

The dialogue, which has an even longer history than the verse epistle, is the form adopted by Robert Lucke for 'An Essay upon Happiness', one of the earliest spin-offs from Pope's Epistle IV.[35] Lucke deploys two speakers, Manly and Flutter, and, as the type-names suggest, he weights the rhetorical scales heavily in favour of the former, who has over twice as many lines as his interlocutor. Manly has the opening and closing speeches; in between, Flutter talks up various roles in which he thinks happiness can be found, dropping each one after Manly has punctured it but immediately offering another. The poem does not lack animation, especially when Manly interrupts Flutter or puts him down, and the irrepressible Flutter bounces back. Yet, because Flutter is so obviously a straw man, there is no sense of debate such as that created, for instance, by Lady Anne Irwin in her response to Pope's *Epistle to a Lady*. A key reason why the dialogue remained, in Raymond Williams's terms, a residual form, and the epistle had become a dominant one,[36] is that British culture had long shifted its character from predominantly oral to predominantly written. Although oral debates took place at the universities, and, of course, in Parliament and the law-courts, they were no longer an inherent part of everyday life as letter-writing was – and as they had been in the academies of antiquity. Not surprisingly, then, most of those who followed Pope in writing about happiness also chose epistolary form. The main alternative form for those who chose otherwise was the non-epistolary verse essay.

John Duncan's *An Essay on Happiness* was first published anonymously in 1762, and ten years later in an expanded and revised edition bearing the author's name.[37] Though it is not an epistle, Duncan mentions in the first of four prefatory letters to the second edition why he not only wrote it in verse but avoided rhyme. His reasons are that he believes 'much better Sermons in prose are often sent to the press, but not published' (p. 5) – indeed, he believes that the first edition 'would probably have met with little notice in a more solemn garb' – and that he considers rhyme to be an 'insignificant Gingle' (p. 6). However, while his blank verse is competent, and his doctrine is unexceptionable by orthodox standards of the time, the poem does little in other ways to engage its readers apart from offering the author's views on an important subject. The prefatory letters in which he responds to comments from a friend whom he had asked to give his first impressions of the work are more lively, so it is surprising that he did not write the whole poem in epistolary form. Perhaps he wished to avoid inviting direct comparisons with Pope's *Essay on Man* and its various imitations. Whether or not this is so, the result is rather cerebral, as the following verse paragraph from Book III of the second edition shows:

> Let ill success on all our steps attend;
> Our dear delights be vanish'd all; nor then
> Flies from extreme distress our well-known friend;
> High o'er the present gloom, in fancy's eye,
> Some glitt'ring form of happiness aloft
> Still waving; till our oft-eluded grasp
> Eternity at length completely fills. (146–52)

Other, contemporary, examples succeed even less. John Bland's *Genuine Happiness: A Poetical Essay* gestures towards epistolary convention in addressing, according to the subtitle, 'the Young Club at Arthur's'.[38] But this is limited almost wholly to the opening lines, which, referring to the poet's Muse, raise the question whether '*Britain's* fav'rite Sons she dare address' – a question dropped in a second, anonymously published, edition.[39] Conventionally, Bland uses iambic pentameter couplets and a relatively plain style, but, leaning heavily on abstractions such as 'DIVINEST FRIENDSHIP', 'HEALTH', 'PEACE' and 'CONTENTMENT' (second edition, p. 14), the poem too often reads as a versified treatise. Another blank verse example, Henry Meen's *Happiness: A Poetical Essay*, works slightly better as a result of pursuing its argument in part through similes (though often rather hackneyed) such as that of a 'benighted trav'ler' ambushed by a storm, or comparisons such as 'the peasant's bitter moan' with 'the monarch's Bliss'.[40] Nevertheless, though the blank verse is again quite adept, the Miltonic style does little to involve the reader directly. Even so, it does more than James Maxwell's *Happiness. A Moral Essay* and Elizabeth Birch's 'An Essay on Happiness', both in iambic pentameter couplets.[41] The quality of the former is accurately described by a general comment on Maxwell as a poet in the *ODNB*: 'He represents the terminus of the virile strain of poetry of Calvinist pietism in eighteenth-century Scotland. His work, however, rarely rises above doggerel.' The latter is pious but, though brief, regrettably diffuse.

These four examples illustrate the key limitation of the verse essay: its limited repertoire of techniques for engaging the reader. A verse epistle may, of course, fail in the same way if it does little to exploit the form's resources. A case in point is Thomas Cole's 'An Epistle on Happiness', which has no addressee at all.[42] Although Cole often seeks to involve the reader in such phrases as 'our cup' (5) and '''Tis fit we try' (16), the lack of a specific addressee deprives his poem of one of the principal assets that epistolary form has to offer, and the result is another versified essay.

Among the benefits of epistolary form are the convention of relatively plain style and considerable structural freedom. These, however, are also available to the verse essay, so the crucial advantage is the ability to direct what I am calling addressee-relations. It follows that the choice of addressee is likely to be important. One possible option is an unidentified friend, as in Charles Collington's *Happiness: An Epistle to a Friend*, and Thomas May's 'Epistle IX. On Happiness'.[43] However, while such a choice may assist the finding of a suitable style and register, it is likely to help little more if, as with the second of these examples, the references to the addressee are brief and perfunctory. Although he apostrophizes an unidentified 'you' in line 10 (p. 4), Collington does not address his friend until 25 lines into his poem, calling him 'Lorenzo' in a likely borrowing from Young's *Night Thoughts*. Instead, he uses the first and second plural pronouns quite freely, in an attempt to engage readers and assume their agreement, until he demonstrates the importance to happiness of human sympathy by citing a recent tragedy in which his friend had given aid (pp. 7–8). Such a reference lends itself to a verse epistle because it combines private and public knowledge: that of poet and addressee, but also that of general readers, as the case was widely reported.[44] Collington leaves till the final verse paragraph the information that his addressee is dead. On the one hand, this underlines the extent to which epistolary address in a discursive poem is a fiction. On the other, however, it could be read as endorsing the doctrinally conventional message that, as he puts it in the previous verse paragraph, parenthetically refining Pope's famous formula, 'WHATEVER IS (view'd in the light / Of Providence's Act and Deed) IS RIGHT' (p. 10). In such ways, Collington gives substance to an argument that otherwise risks the over-abstraction that weakens May's epistle on the same topic. This poem never rises above the level indicated by its opening couplet, with its anaemic rhyme: 'Dwells there, my friend! true happiness with man? / We know but absence from desire, or pain' (p. 121). May only addresses his unnamed friend once more, towards the end. As he indicates under his poem that it was written at the age of 18, the limited role he gives to epistolary form may betray his inexperience.

Another obvious type of addressee for a male writer in a patriarchal culture is a woman, especially a young woman, and many eighteenth-century epistles adopt the convention. Among these, the anonymous author of *Two Epistles on Happiness* addresses them, the subtitle indicates, *To a Young Lady*; and, nearly 50 years later, George Wright included in his *Lady's Miscellany* a poem in elegiac quatrains entitled 'On True Happiness, an Epistle Written to a Young Lady in the Country'.[45] The *Two Epistles* set out to deal with the difficult problem of tone in a poem of didactic morality by presuming inexperience, even naivety, in their addressee – while also flattering her both for her beauty and as the poem's 'fair Inspirer' (I, 19). So, after the first four lines, the writer asks: 'Permit the heart sincere your thoughts to move / From idle dreams of Goddesses and love, / To all the means that reason may suggest, / To make you with that blaze of beauty, blest' (I, 4–7). It is a canny, if a question-begging, appeal, as its universalizing expressions 'the heart' and 'reason' dissolve the writer's identity in a profession of general truth. But, as the detailed pages of contents for the two poems show, the argument is close and systematic; and it is illustrated by type-examples and pictorial analogies such as with a rainbow, a butterfly and a journey (I, 123–8, 243–64; II, passim). These devices are probably borrowed from Pope, whom the writer also follows by using repeated apostrophes, including not just 'But still you cry' (I, 59), anticipating an objection, and 'would you know' (I, 281), but imperatives such as 'Try' (I, 23), 'Say' (I, 37), and 'observe' (I, 77). Wright's poem is much slighter. Its design in addressing a young lady 'in the country' is to try and disabuse her of the illusion that happiness can be found in the world at all. Again, although the addressee is named 'Belinda', the message that '*True* happiness is not the growth of earth' (p. 288) is clearly for any reader, especially if she is young and female.

A more unusual example than these is *The Mistakes of Men in Search of Happiness. An Ethic Epistle, To Mrs. *******.*[46] Why it is unusual is clear from the opening couplet: 'Fair maiden once, the hope of ******'s life, / Fair woman now, and happy ******'s wife' (sig. A2), for it indicates that the anonymous author is a rejected suitor of the addressee. Unlike orthodox Christian writers on the subject, he assumes that what he calls 'certain happiness' is available in this life (p. 4), and he sets out to advise his addressee on how to achieve it, initially through the trite and, in this case, inapplicable counter-examples of miser and soldier. But, though he avoids personal recriminations, the advice he more specifically offers is deeply misogynistic, with its reference to 'your wand'ring sex' (p. 8), its remark that 'lust of pow'r, and hatred of controul, / Possess too often woman's little soul' (p. 10), its associated rebuke to Eve, and its predictable conclusion that 'A WOMAN to be happy must OBEY' (p. 11). While the writer found an appropriate addressee for such a theme, his poem fails to fulfil the expectations prompted by his title, which seems, perhaps unintentionally, to reflect his own disappointment.

Choosing an addressee against whom to argue explicitly is potentially a sounder strategy. Like Lady Anne Irwin in her response to *Epistle to a Lady*, William Ayre took on Pope himself in his *Four Ethic Epistles Opposing Some of Mr. Pope's Opinions of Man*.[47] The first two epistles appeared in 1739, but the fact that the ensemble was not published until 1753 helps indicate that it was not a personal attack on Pope, as the inclusion of the first epistle in J. V. Guerinot's collection of *Pamphlet Attacks on Alexander Pope* may seem to suggest, but an attempt to put forward dissenting views of various questions that the *Essay on Man* had treated.[48] Guerinot calls the first epistle 'very weak', and it is difficult not to apply the same judgement to the fourth. Nevertheless, it is not an utter failure. Ayre draws on the double-reference strategy characteristic of the form, for example in the line 'O thou! who never yet hadst *health* or *peace*' (p. 35), which clearly refers to Pope, but, because it does not name him, is also open to personal application by the reader. Elsewhere he paraphrases morsels of Pope's epistle and responds to them, apostrophizes 'man' (p. 37), and even addresses Pope's addressee – scoring a palpable hit in the couplet: '*Nature's* corruption, St. *John*, or thy will, / Which was it, brought to pass the *schism bill?*' (p. 40).[49] Even some of his more general remarks register genuine objections, as when he asks: 'Must one be lord of millions? – No such thing; / What proves that ever God *ordained a king?*' (p. 37), or when he observes: '*Order* was just the same, we all must own, / Before *Excisemen* or *excise* were known' (p. 38). Such rhetorical thrusts are part of the repertoire of the discursive epistle, as they are also of satire, but the knockabout nature of Ayre's is out of keeping with the politer style cultivated in most epistolary verse, especially after the 1730s.

Various other essays and epistles on happiness also appeared in the period, including 'The Regulation of the Passions, the Source of Human Happiness' and 'Life Unhappy, Because We Use it Improperly', both subtitled 'A Moral Essay' and by James Cawthorn, better known as author of *Abelard to Eloisa*.[50] Few, however, break new ground, though some, like Cawthorn's, are quite adept, and though, like those considered so far, some have their own kinds of interest. Three of the four final poems about happiness that I will discuss, however, innovate in various ways. The first of these is the poem that effectively launched the topic, Epistle IV of Pope's *Essay on Man*. Introducing the Twickenham edition, Maynard Mack observes that the poem's effect is that of 'a conversation [. . .] between cultivated men'.[51] This formula captures the tone and diction that Pope employs, and also takes account of the implicitly male reader. Much less apt, however, is Mack's remark a few pages later that 'The speaker is not Pope, but Everyman; the audience is Everyman too; and so is the subject'.[52] Instead, the poem has a number of different voices, and it seeks to position the addressee in various ways. Its wit and zest made it a very difficult act for any poet to follow, even more because of Pope's skill in exploiting the addressee-relations dimension of epistolarity. Few of his followers or opponents were able to reach anything like the subtlety with which he deploys varying modes of address.

At least six types of implicit or explicit addressee may be distinguished in the poem. The most frequent, representing human beings in general, including the poet, is identified by the first person plural, and is invoked in the opening and closing lines ('Oh HAPPINESS! our being's end and aim!', 'And all our Knowledge is, OURSELVES TO KNOW'). Next most inclusive is the second person plural, on occasion referring to specific individuals but most often to the general reader. It does not occur in this sense until line 144, 'And what rewards your Virtue, punish mine', after which it appears 13 times, including ten times in lines 194–214. Here, especially, the reader is buttonholed and potential objections are answered, as in the lines: '"What differ more (you cry) than crown and cowl?" / I'll tell you, friend! a Wise man and a Fool' (199–200). This general reader is also invoked by implication as the addressee of various questions, such as 'Where grows? – where grows it not?' (13), 'Who risk the most?' (86), or 'But who, but God, can tell us who they are?' (136), and as the object of frequent imperative verbs, such as 'Know' (77), 'Say' (85), or 'See' (99, 100, 101). Still another way of addressing the same subject is through the term 'Man' (35), or, more pointedly, with reference to the fallen human condition, 'Oh sons of earth!' (73). These expressions must also apply to the poet and his immediate addressee, Bolingbroke – though not the related phrases 'Oh blind to truth' (93), 'Weak, foolish man!' (173) and 'Oh fool!' (189), which refer to those who refuse illumination.

Along with these three more or less general modes of address go three others. One, comprising apostrophes to personifications such as happiness itself, as in the opening word, and 'Virtue' (82), is not relevant, as it is common in other types of verse. The others are more intimate than the first three. First, there are a few specific addressees: not only Boling-broke, whose role I will discuss shortly, but also 'blameless Bethel' (126),

one of Pope's oldest friends; and, by implication, the father of 'Lamented
DIGBY' (104), whose epitaph Pope had written.[53] Second, there is the
general reader again, but now as an individual through use of the second
personal singular and its cognates. No usage in this sense occurs until line
176, as if the poet is unwilling to presume on familiarity till that point.
Even after that, he uses this form of address quite sparingly, except when
he interrogates the reader for various ambitions:

> Think, and if still the things thy envy call,
> Say, would'st thou be the Man to whom they fall?
> To sigh for ribbands if thou art so silly,
> Mark how they grace Lord Umbra, or Sir Billy:
> Is yellow dirt the passion of thy life?
> Look but on Gripus, or on Gripus' wife.
> If Parts allure thee, think how Bacon shin'd,
> The wisest, brightest, meanest of mankind. (275–82)

The allusion to Bacon is ironically apt, because it is in parts of the poem
such as these that Pope redeems his pledge in 'The Design' to write such
verse as, in Bacon's words, would '*come home to Men's Business and
Bosoms*' (p. 7). It does so through direct appeals aimed to get the reader
not just to sit up and take notice, but take to heart.

All the same, the most intimate apostrophes of all are properly to the
immediate addressee, Henry St John, Viscount Bolingbroke. Pope does
not, however, overwork the convention, inviting the understanding during
most of the poem that Bolingbroke is, as it were, at his side as a kind of
chairman or sponsor. After a brief compliment early on – that happiness,
though 'fled from Monarchs, ST. JOHN! dwells with thee' (18) – he
refrains from addressing him again until line 240 ('my Lord'), but a more
significant sequence follows, beginning: 'In Parts superior what advantage
lies? / Tell (for You can) what is it to be wise?' (259–60). Not only the
initial capital indicates that it is Bolingbroke whom Pope addresses, but
also the displacement of the normal metrical stress from the fourth to the
third syllable of the line. The rest of the paragraph (261–8) also applies to
his friend, though he is not invoked directly. But it is the poem's closing
26 lines, beginning 'Come then, my Friend, my Genius, come along'
(373), that gain full value from the convention of epistolary address, as
Pope plays down his own worth and honours Bolingbroke as 'guide,
philosopher, and friend' (390). Although both the praise and the self-
deprecation are also conventional, such a tribute is appropriate for the
stated recipient of a long discursive poem at its end. In light of the help

that Pope gains from his choice of addressee in modulating the poem's tone, not to mention the tacit understanding throughout that he is addressing at least one reader who would endorse his views, it need not even be thought excessive. If such a suggestion seems contentious, it is necessary only to reread the poem with the name of its original addressee, Laelius, substituted for Bolingbroke's. Not even the aptest of allusions to Horace could make up for the loss of the personal connection and the exemplary image of his friend that it underpins. Yet it is more often readers in general that the poem addresses, in the various guises identified above. Through the challenges it poses them, not just through its brilliant imagery, versification and wit, it is constantly agile and invigorating. Its epistolarity, in the sense I have tried to illustrate, is a key part of this.

Three further examples of epistles on happiness display other ways of handling those relations. The first, by Robert Craggs Nugent, is of special interest for the later removal of its original addressee's name. First published anonymously in 1737 as *An Essay on Happiness. In an Epistle to the Right Honourable the Earl of Chesterfield*, it appeared with various revisions, including omission of the first five words of the original title, in Nugent's *Odes and Epistles* of 1739.[54] Both these editions not only name Chesterfield in the title but address him by his family name, Stanhope (1737, pp. 7, 18; 1739, pp. 63, 78). Robert Dodsley had published *Odes and Epistles*, and in 1748 the poem appeared with further revisions in the first edition of his *Collection*, remaining in all later editions and eventually finding its way into *Bell's Classical Arrangement of Fugitive Poetry*.[55] The most significant of the revisions in all the editions from 1748 is the absence of any reference to Chesterfield. However, before discussing what might be at issue in the omission of the original addressee's name, it is important to consider the types of reader-address both in the first and in the later versions of the epistle.

The versions that name Chesterfield have four main types of addressee. In order of appearance, these are the general reader, signified by the first person plural, as in the line 'But if, like them, we still must Trifles use' (pp. 58, 193); the single individual example of an unnamed 'mighty Hero' whose conquests do not allow him to sleep softly (pp. 60–61, 195); 'the Youthful and the Gay' who only seek the pleasures of the senses (pp. 61, 195); and, in three places, Chesterfield himself.[56] Like Pope, though sparingly, Nugent also addresses abstractions, though I exclude these for the reason stated above; but he uses fewer rhetorical questions and only a few imperatives to the general reader, such as 'Say', and 'Mark' (pp. 63, 196–7). Unlike Pope in Epistle I of the *Essay on Man*, he does not begin by invoking his addressee. It is, rather, the reader who is quickly brought into play through use of the first personal plural in lines 9 and 10. But Nugent does not employ the pronoun or its cognates again for nearly 100 lines, and then only twice, reserving it chiefly for a section in which he discusses the hopes, desires, disappointments and sufferings of common humanity (pp. 65–9, 198–200). Also unlike Pope, Nugent does not address subsets of the readership such as the unenlightened or, on the other hand, those with whom he has affinities. For this reason, his poem is more generous and inclusive, and also less pointedly didactic.

Nugent introduces Chesterfield without any flourish over 70 lines into the poem. It is almost as if the idea of his addressee, whom he does not immediately name, occurs to him as an example in the act of writing:

> – Then from the Croud arise
> Some Chief, in Life's full Pride maturely wise;
> Ev'n You, My Lord, with Titles, Honours grac'd,
> And higher still by native Merit plac'd. (pp. 62, 196)

He goes on to list Chesterfield's main social and personal advantages before asking: 'Say, from thy Soul, art thou sincerely blest?', and pressing the argument with some perhaps surprisingly *ad hominem* questions:

> Hast thou not quitted FLACCUS' sacred Lay,
> To talk with BAVIUS, or with FLAVIA play;
> When wasted Nature shuns the large Expence
> Of deep Attention to exalted Sense? (pp. 63, 196)

In the later version, the omission of specific reference to Chesterfield required no revision to the beginning of the section, but, at its end, the phrase 'like STANHOPE' in the earlier editions is replaced by a simple intensifier, 'how very few' (pp. 63, 196). The second occasion on which the poem addresses Chesterfield directly required no alteration at all, because it does not name him: 'Hence *Britain* throbs superior in thy Soul, / Nor idly wak'st thou for the distant *Pole*' (pp. 68, 199). In the original poem, Nugent could dispense with the name because he had given it in his title; this, of course, proved an advantage when it was removed. The third address opens the penultimate verse paragraph: 'Such, STANHOPE, are the Blessings, that attend / The *Just*, and *Good*, the *Patriot*, and the *Friend!*' (pp. 78, 205). In the revised version the first line becomes 'Such are th' immortal blessings that attend', and, because it no longer begins a new paragraph, it carries less emphasis. A further change is to a name at the end of the paragraph, for, in the line 'And, far from *Courts*, fresh bloom in COBHAM's *Grove'*, 'Curio' replaces that of the famous owner of the gardens at Stowe. The change from 'COBHAM' to 'Curio' helps identify one of the chief effects produced by removing references to Chesterfield. Both revisions depoliticize the poem, for, in the later 1730s, 'COBHAM's *Grove'* would have meant one of the main locations of the so-called Patriot Opposition of which Sir Richard Temple, Chesterfield and Nugent himself were all members.[57] In such a context, the word '*Patriot'*, in the line following Chesterfield's name, would have carried a charge that it lacks in the generalized phrasing of the revision and in altered political conditions. The poem's conclusion in its earlier form suggests an attempt to sustain Chesterfield's loyalty to the 'Patriots', for, again, its remark that '*Guilt* alone is true *Disgrace'*, and its commendation of 'glorious Exile' (pp. 78, 205), would have had a more specific meaning. The same context also helps explain the 'Truth' that the poem ends by stating, that '"Fair Virtue ever is unwisely sold"' (pp. 79, 205), for it is otherwise not easy to account for as the culminating lesson of an essay on happiness.

It seems, then, that in the earlier versions of the epistle Nugent set out both to discuss happiness and to include a political message. Because that message was only a part of the poem, it proved possible, when the political climate had changed, to eliminate it, though its vestiges remain. As a wealthy and talented man, Chesterfield was a suitable addressee, for the epistle argues that even such advantages do not provide happiness. His suitability would have reduced, however, when his health, never very strong, deteriorated in 1741 (*ODNB*). Nevertheless, the lack of a specific, appropriate addressee – Nugent could hardly have substituted a different one – weakens the poem to some extent, and in other ways too it uses personal address less effectively on the whole than the *Essay on Man*. Despite Nugent's skill with the pentameter couplet, it is less stimulating to read because it engages the reader less. Not only does it not aspire to the kind of brilliant wit and imagery that Pope's poem offers, but it refrains from challenging the general reader so often or so directly. There is, nevertheless, a sense in which these dilutions helped it appeal to its readers in Dodsley and Bell – a sense that goes along with the erasure of its original political message. For, apart from that erasure, the other effect of omitting Chesterfield's name is to produce a generalized message about political and other virtues that is in accord with the poem's attempt to express universal truths about happiness. Skilful but slightly anodyne, its rehearsal of generally uncontentious religious and moral views was well adapted to the taste of the genteel reader, the type of reader who might buy Dodsley's or Bell's collections.

The name of the addressee of another epistle by Nugent was retained when it too appeared in Dodsley. Like the poem just discussed, 'An Epistle to the Right Honourable the Lord Viscount Cornbury' had also been published previously, both independently, with the title *Political Justice. A Poem. In a Letter to the Right Hon. the Lord* ****, and in Nugent's *Odes and Epistles*. The latter provides the addressee's name, though it had been anticipated in this by a Dublin edition.[58] One reason for retaining the addressee's name in Dodsley is probably that Henry Hyde, though also a member of the 'Patriot Opposition', had been and continued to be less involved in politics than Chesterfield. Two other likely reasons are that, unlike the epistle to Chesterfield, the poem is extensively revised and considerably longer; and, even more to the point, that in both versions it addresses Cornbury only in the opening and closing lines (1736, pp. [3]–5, 23–4; 1782, II, 174–5, 192–3). Especially in its expanded form, it easily stands as a discussion of political rights and duties that can claim much more than the topical interest that gave it its initial impetus. The original title, which styles the poem not as an epistle but as a poem 'in a letter', also reflects its limited epistolarity. Though literary convention allowed it to be represented as an epistle, it exploits addresses to readers markedly less than the epistle to Chesterfield.

The next example of an epistle on happiness is another poem by Mary Leapor. Her 'Essay on Happiness'[59] invites attention because it contrasts in various ways with all the other poems on the subject discussed so far. First, it is much shorter – 114 lines compared, for instance, with the 398 of Pope's Epistle IV and the 350 of Nugent's – and this is not necessarily a drawback. Second, unlike most other examples, Pope's and Nugent's in particular, it does not obviously draw on philosophical or religious discussions of the subject. Leapor had received no extended formal education, though her editors point out that various features of her poem may be traced not only to Pope but to Juvenal.[60] Third, and crucially, the relations between writer and addressee set up by the poem are private, not public. Leapor addresses not a famous politician and philosopher, such as Bolingbroke, or a talented and wealthy aristocrat (whether named or not), but an unnamed female friend now known to have been Bridget Freemantle. This gives her epistle a different perspective from those of Pope and Nugent, that of a private person and an outsider.

Leapor addresses Freemantle directly only in her opening couplet: 'Nothing, dear Madam, nothing is more true, / Than a short Maxim much approv'd by you'. This clearly borrows from the way Pope begins *Epistle to a Lady* ('Nothing so true as what you once let fall'), but its tactic differs because it is not Leapor's aim to manipulate the remark for rhetorical purposes, as Pope does with the one he attributes to Martha Blount. What she does instead is to illustrate it, and this is striking because the maxim states a position very like the one that Pope and Nugent take many lines to reach: 'We by Experience know / Within ourselves exists our Bliss or Woe' (3–4; compare the closing couplet of Pope's Epistle IV, 'That VIRTUE only makes our Bliss below, / And all our Knowledge is, OURSELVES TO KNOW'; and, 11 lines from the end of Nugent's, 'The greatly *Virtuous* are the greatly *Blest*'). It is not, however, as if Leapor needed Pope's poem (she may not have known Nugent's), to teach her a principle that she quotes from her friend as proverbial wisdom. This, the placing of her remark suggests, is where to start in a discussion of happiness, not where to end. At the same time, the maxim brings the external reader into the poem, for the first person plural must refer not only to the poet and her friend but also to people in general. Leapor goes on to repeat the pronoun and its cognates several times, but she uses other devices as well that she had probably learned from Pope and that also seek to involve the reader, especially rhetorical questions and imperatives. Both of these, for instance, are illustrated by the line: 'Say, who can buy what never yet was sold?' (11). The structure of her epistle, too, she takes from Pope – though it resembles that of poems such as *Epistle to a Lady* more closely than that of *An Essay on Man*. It consists of an introduction of 30 lines, five exemplary cases (two male, three female), and a conclusion of 22 lines. The type-examples are Glaro, a wealthy, selfish but utterly unhappy man; Livia, whose finery makes her ill; Cloe, whose longing for appreciation in the fashionable world leaves her restless and unsatisfied; Sir Thrifty, who can never amass enough wealth; and Lavinia, who seems blessed in every respect but whose happiness would be destroyed by her husband's death. Leapor asks the reader to imagine each one – for instance, 'See *Glaro* seated on his gilded Car' (31), 'See restless *Cloe*, fond to be admir'd' (49) – and then requires the only judgement each makes possible: 'Behold him right, then envy, if you can' (40), 'Who wou'd be *Cloe* to enjoy her Charms?' (66).

It is significant that Leapor's five examples all inhabit a social world to which she was a stranger. As an outsider, she can comment with a force and succinctness lacking from most other discussions of the topic. Only five lines into the poem, for example, she can remark: 'Tho' round our Heads the Goods of Fortune roll, / Dazzle they may, but cannot chear the Soul'; and, a few lines later, she can answer the question whether wealth can buy or poverty destroy contentment with a terse 'No'. Then, having observed that contentment is 'found more frequent in a Cottage Walls', she shows that this position is not a sentimental idealization by adding:

'Her Flight from thence too often is decreed, / Then Poverty is doubly curs'd indeed' (14–16). This tough recognition of material fact gives her poem a hard edge and, consequently, its own kind of authority. It also has implications for the way she positions her reader. The word that begins the maxim she quotes from her friend, 'We', helps define it. It is not only a general position, one that she shares with the external reader as well as with her addressee, but one available to anyone prepared to observe and judge candidly. Those are the terms on which she relates to friend and external reader alike, and they have no room for complacency. For it is one thing to identify oneself, as reader, with the remark that 'We crave, we grasp, but loath the tasted Joy' (96), and another to find oneself turned upon a few lines later: 'Cease, busy Fool: Is Happiness thy Care? / Pierce thy own Breast, and thou wilt find it there' (105–6). In between, as the climax to the penultimate verse paragraph, Leapor cites a condition that was painfully her own: 'Nor Wit with Happiness can often grow, / A helpless Friend, if not an arrant Foe' (99–100). It is this kind of insight and awareness that helps justify the poem's closing imperatives and its conclusion, addressed no longer to the 'Madam' of the opening lines but to people in general: 'Then not till then, O Man, thy Heart shall know / Bliss so ador'd, but seldom found below' (111–12).

The position taken in my final example contrasts sharply not only with Leapor's but with all those yet discussed. John Gilbert Cooper published the three poems of *Epistles to the Great, from Aristippus in Retirement* in 1757, adding a fourth in 1758; the four are printed together, with various revisions including to the title, in his *Poems on Several Subjects* of 1764.[61] Three qualities in particular distinguish the four epistles. First, they unashamedly celebrate pleasure, claiming that happiness may be enjoyed in this world and that it is not necessarily fleeting. Second, they are, strictly speaking, dramatic epistles, as Gilbert Cooper underlined in the 'Advertisement' that precedes them in *Poems on Several Subjects*: 'The reader will not forget, that these four epistles were written originally under a fictitious character' (sig. A3). This is highly unusual in the genre of the discursive epistle. Third, they are in a verse form very rare in English and used for no other discursive epistle. Gilbert Cooper seems to have been the first to introduce it from France, having encountered it, the 'Advertisement' also indicates, in the work of Chapelle, Guillaume Amfrye Chaulieu, Charles-Auguste La Fare, Jean-Baptiste-Louis Gresset, Madame Des Houlières, and others. In France it is known as *vers libres*, though it is not to be confused with the even freer form of the same name developed by Laforgue and others in the later nineteenth century. The form adopted by Gilbert Cooper, mainly from Gresset's *Épitres* and from his most famous poem, which Gilbert Cooper subsequently translated, *Ver-Vert*, consists of iambic tetrameters rhyming irregularly.[62] It produces effects that perfectly suit Aristippus's message.

The source of that message, as Robin Dix points out,[63] is the *beatus ille* tradition. It is inflected, however, not just by the example of Gresset and other French poets but by the Cyrenaic school of philosophy founded by Aristippus. A quotation will illustrate both the philosophy and the verse form. Towards the end of the fourth epistle, Aristippus writes:

> Let the furr'd pedants of the schools,
> In learning's formidable show,
> Full of wise saws and bookish rules,
> The meagre dupes of misery grow,
> A lovelier doctrine I profess   5
> Than their dull science can avow;
> All that belongs to happiness,
> Their *heads* are welcome still to *know*,
> My *heart*'s contented to *possess*.
> For in soft elegance and ease,   10
> Secure of living while I live,
> Each momentary bliss I seize,
> Ere these warm faculties decay,
> The fleeting moments to deceive
> Of human life's allotted day. (pp. 46–7, line numbers added)

The lines declare Aristippus's hedonism while, through their form, . suggesting freedom from constraint. That freedom would have been more striking to an eighteenth-century reader, used to the discipline of the couplet and to relatively little enjambement. Although Gilbert Cooper uses alternating rhymes for the first ten lines – unexpectedly, however, repeating the C rhyme once and the B rhyme twice – he then mixes the pattern by introducing a new rhyme, on 'live', which he does not complete till three lines later. Similarly, he does not pause in expected places, running what initially appears to be a first quatrain into a second, and then not ending what initially appears to be a second quatrain until its fifth line. The result is an easy-going movement in harmony with Aristippus's philosophy of taking sensual and intellectual pleasure where he finds it. Gilbert Cooper also illustrates that philosophy through a simile in Epistle II: 'An osier on the stream of time, / This philosophic wanderer / Floating thro' ev'ry place and clime / Finds some peculiar blessing there' (p. 22). The position is open to the charge of complacency, though certainly no more than that of the various poets in the 'Happy Man' tradition who declare 'competence', the means to live comfortably, to be a prime requirement.[64] Pope and Leapor are among the writers of epistles on happiness who avoid that charge.

In the prefatory 'Advertisement', Gilbert Cooper claims that, in the verse form he has chosen, 'the unconfined return of the rhymes, and easiness of the diction, seem peculiarly adapted to epistolary compositions' (sig. A3). His poem, however, is a very unusual example of such writing. Not only is the writer a long-dead philosopher fancifully relocated to eighteenth-century England, and not only are the addressees of three of the four epistles unnamed, but the external reader is almost ostentatiously excluded. Epistle I, addressed to 'his Grace the Duke of ********', drops the polite forms suggested by the salutation 'my lord' (sig. A4) for a withering rejection of the kind of life his lordship leads, with all the 'wellbred insipidity' (p. 8) of 'moderniz'd gentility' (p. 11). Neither here nor in the other three epistles is the reader invoked, overtly or otherwise – there are no imperatives or rhetorical questions, let alone addresses. Instead, it is as if Aristippus writes to his friends in nonchalant detachment from any other potential reader.[65] He seems concerned to set out his way of life and its justification to them and them alone, and they appear willing recipients. Epistle II, addressed to 'Lady *******', greets her as 'Melissa' in its first line and quotes her as following much the same way of life as he (p. 19); and Epistle IV, addressed to Mark Akenside, celebrates him as a kindred soul, sharing 'our poetic heaven' (p. 42). Some early lines in Epistle III, addressed to '********* Esq.', show the peculiar reader-relations of the work clearly. The poem, entitled 'The Apology of Aristippus', begins by citing the kind of reply he might dismissively give to those who may criticize him for wasting his time, but goes on to give his real reason:

I might reply, I do no more
Than what my betters did before;
That what at first my fancy led
This idle business to pursue,
Still makes me prosecute the trade,
Because *I've nothing else to do*;
But to the candid, TOM, and you,
A better reason I could give,
To whom a better reason's due,
That in these measures I convey
My gentle precepts, how to live,
Clearer than any other way. (pp. 27–8)

He writes to his friend as a familiar – the 1757 edition is a little more formal, addressing his friend as 'Sir' (p. 36) – whom he can expect to understand him and take him seriously, caring so little for what his critics think that he will fob them off by confirming their prejudice. To the extent that he creates space for an external reader, it is through the phrase 'the candid'. Those who are prepared to give him an open-minded reading are the only readers he wants, and to them he is prepared to explain his beliefs. Similarly, the expression 'should you ask me' on the following page suggests that he feels no particular urgency to explain them, even to a friend. It is with Akenside, the addressee to the fourth epistle, that he engages most directly, referring to him in the second person singular. This, of course, confines the external reader to the margins, able only, as it were, to read over Akenside's shoulder. Indeed, the poet even attempts to exclude some classes of reader: 'the supercilious wise' / And gloomy sons of melancholy' (p. 41), along with 'any infidel [. . .] Who sneers at our poetic heav'n' (pp. 41–2). He addresses Akenside as a fellow spirit, seeking neither to argue with anyone who disagrees nor to win over the more open-minded, but only to express his way of life and his philosophy. A mark of still further detachment is the claim already cited that the poems were 'written originally under a fictitious character'.[66]

This remarkable turning inwards upon itself of epistolary convention may appear to confirm William Dowling's view that 'The Aristippus epistles represent a controlled and deliberate farewell to the epistolary audience earlier summoned into existence by Augustan poetry, a permanent valediction to the possibility of regenerating a fallen society through satire or ethical verse, and an embrace of something very like Pater's notion of the world as a dream of the solitary mind.'[67] Yet the truth is probably less dramatic. Gilbert Cooper's poem has some affinities with the kind of work commended by Edward Young in his *Conjectures on Original Composition* – first published in 1759, only two years later – as well as with that not only of his friend Akenside but William Collins, whom he also knew.[68] Nevertheless, it had little impact, and, as this book shows, poets continued to write verse epistles, including discursive epistles, till the end of the century – and even beyond. Comparing the Aristippus epistles with other poems on happiness reveals a highly distinctive mode of discourse, but one that is tailored to the philosophy it presents. Though the poems possess lyrical elements, especially in their versification and imagery, they are not lyrics; and, though Gilbert Cooper professed lack of interest in their publication,[69] they were published. In these ways they belong to a specifically eighteenth-century tradition, although, as Dowling suggests, one that was beginning to dissolve.

5
Heroic and Amatory

In his book *The Epistolary Moment*, William C. Dowling quotes Joseph Warton's remark, in *An Essay on the Writings and Genius of Pope*, that the heroic epistle invented by Ovid 'is indeed no other than a passionate soliloquy; in which, the mind gives vent to the distresses and emotions under which it labours'.[1] Dowling uses the remark in order to define the heroic epistle as a solipsistic opposite to the discursive epistle that is his main subject. He does not, however, complete Warton's sentence, which continues: 'but being directed and addressed to a particular person, it gains a degree of propriety, that the best-conducted soliloquy, in a tragedy, must ever want'. For the reason that Warton states, that the epistle is always addressed to 'a particular person', Gillian Beer, whom Dowling also quotes, is right to declare that 'these are dramatic, not lyric, poems', adding that they 'are not soliloquies. They are acts of invocation.'[2] But there is another reason, too, for calling the heroic epistle a dramatic form. As I have argued in Chapter 1, the key formal difference between it and its discursive cousin is that it is never written in the person of its author but in that of a character from history or legend. The heroic epistle is, then, not only dramatic in Warton's and Beer's sense, in that it is directed outwards to a recipient in a way that a lyric poem is not. It is also dramatic in the sense that its discourse is personated. As a result, there is always a dual expressive dynamic in the heroic epistle. On the one hand, the persona writes to a specified addressee; on the other, the author writes through persona and addressee alike to a wider audience. For this reason, too, Dowling's claim that the form is inherently solipsistic is mistaken.

The heroic epistle is also a more complex and variegated form than is usually recognized. Beginning, in Ovid's *Heroides*, as verse letters by rejected or deserted women, usually from legend, to their lovers, it first mutated when Ovid added three pairs of epistolary dialogues, all initiated by a man addressing a woman, perhaps in similar vein to replies from the men by his friend Sabinus.[3] The second change occurred in Renaissance Britain when, in *Englands Heroicall Epistles*, Michael Drayton adapted the form to English history, following the practice Ovid had already instituted of presenting epistolary exchanges between pairs of lovers. In this way Drayton displaced legend in favour of history, Ovid having included only one historical letter-writer, Sappho; and, at the same time, he used national historical contexts not only to provide tragic occasions, as in Ovid's epistles, but also for other effects including some comparable with those of Shakespeare's History plays.[4] During the Restoration and the eighteenth century, writers took up the form both as it had been inaugurated by Ovid and as modified later by Drayton. The translation to which Dryden contributed, first published in 1680, went through many editions and, in its first 30-odd years, acquired several additional poems including Pope's 'Sappho to Phaon'.[5] Shortly afterwards, however, John Oldmixon and others took up Drayton's specifically English modulation, Oldmixon publishing versions of Drayton's 24 epistles with six new ones that were entirely his own.[6] A still further application of the convention, though not a new one, was *Letters from Zilia to Aza*, a series of eight epistles adapted from Françoise de Graffigny's *Lettres d'une Péruvienne*, first published in 1753 and reprinted as 'Peruvian Letters' in Samuel Whyte's collection *The Shamrock: Or, Hibernian Cresses* in 1772.[7] This was in keeping with the vogue of Sensibility, and, as its nominal writer and all its dedicatees are female though the author was male, it also followed tradition in that, as Gillian Beer puts it, 'in the seventeenth and eighteenth centuries, it seems, heroic epistle was seen as a women's genre in its subject matter and audience, though not in its authorship'.[8] The same point is re-emphasized by a further offshoot from de Graffigny's novel, Ann Curtis's 'Zelida to Irena', in which the letter-writer addresses another woman about her betrayal, not, as in the source, a man.[9]

Two further and quite different variants sprang up in the Restoration. One was the kind of satire or burlesque invited by the heroic epistle's elevated language and erotic situation. An early example of the satirical heroic epistle is Etherege's 'Ephelia to Bajazet', mocking the Earl of Mulgrave.[10] But it was Alexander Radcliffe who, following in a tradition of classical burlesques, published the first instalment of his *Ovid Travestie* in the same year as *Ovid's Epistles*; as I shall indicate, its descendants were still going strong a century later.[11] The fourth variant does not seem to have appeared until the earlier eighteenth century, though it was anticipated by the kind of *épitre à clef* represented by 'Ephelia to Bajazet'. In this form, the heroic epistle is adapted directly and explicitly to the present. 'Epistle from Arthur Gr[a]y to Mrs M[urra]y', by Lady Mary Wortley Montagu, who also wrote two further poems of a similar kind, is one of the first and most striking examples – striking especially because it is not simply a parody.[12] Other examples, too, show how adaptable the form proved, including the several rewritings as an heroic epistle of the story of Inkle and Yarico.[13] To recapitulate, there are four main subtypes of the form: the Ovidian original, the historical variant that originated with Drayton, the satirical or parodic, and the contemporary. This chapter will focus especially on the first as the most influential, reserving the third for discussion among satirical epistles in Chapter 6; but it will also consider examples of the historical and contemporary variants, and, briefly, of the type of epistle that John Bell styled as 'Gallant'.[14]

As Karina Williamson has demonstrated, the heroic epistle often raises questions of gender. Williamson begins from the principle that, 'While the nominal writer was typically a woman, the actual author, from Ovid onwards, was normally male.'[15] Although the same point is made by many of those who have written on the form, including Gillian Beer,[16] the textual facts are more complicated. First, as already mentioned, Ovid included three letters from men in his *Heroides*; and Drayton developed the convention by distributing letters equally between women and men in *Englands Heroicall Epistles*. Second, out of the 107 eighteenth-century heroic epistles on which I have gathered details, but excluding 5 for which authorship is undetermined, 46 conform to the convention in that, though male-authored, their nominal writers are female; yet 30 others diverge from it in that both nominal and actual writers are male. These statistics are distorted to some extent by the 15 epistles from men in Oldmixon's *Amores Britannici*, yet they indicate that the nominal writers of a substantial minority of heroic epistles by men are not female, as is usually assumed. Examples include the various responses to Pope's 'Eloisa to Abelard', all but two of which are by men.[17] Where it is a man who is figured as writing an heroic epistle, he often occupies a position of dependency or victimhood equivalent to that of an abandoned or deserted woman, as Abelard does, or the enslaved Africans to be considered below. Nevertheless, the fact that not all nominal writers of heroic epistles are female suggests that the kinds of ideological work that these poems performed may have been more various than those who have tried to theorize them have allowed.[18]

All the same, Williamson's point that heroic epistles often play with gender is important. A further illustration is the fact that, among the 24 female-authored epistles in my sample of 107, the nominal writer of 12 is male. Although seven of the 12 are by the same author, Anna Seward,[19] the adoption of a male role by several female writers is still significant. Indeed, in one highly unusual female-authored epistle both the nominal writer and the addressee are male; and the same, equally unusually, is true of two male-authored heroic epistles.[20] These examples, and, conversely, the rarity of heroic epistles by one woman to another – there is only one in my sample, and it is female-authored – bear out the case argued by Williamson that gender is intrinsically important to the form.

One feature of the heroic epistle that offers much less variety is its versification. Almost all Restoration and eighteenth-century examples are in the dignified mode of iambic pentameter couplets often known as heroic couplets to denote sparing use of enjambement, especially between couplets, and a generally elevated style. This is a development of the form that Drayton had used: also iambic pentameter, but with a greater number of open couplets. It is an equivalent in English for Ovid's elegiac couplets, in which a dactylic hexameter is succeeded by an hemiepes – which, the present-day translator Daryl Hine explains, 'consists of the first part of the preceding line, repeated'.[21] Though the *Heroides* are, like nearly all classical Latin verse, unrhymed, Hine follows previous translators by using rhyming couplets for a reason stated succinctly by a fellow translator, Harold Isbell: 'In Ovid, the couplet structure is basic to the style of the poem.'[22] Virtually all writers of heroic epistles in English have done the same. In my sample of 106 there are only two partial exceptions: Lord John Hervey's 'Arisbe to Marius Junior', which is presented in Dodsley's *Collection*, though not in two other sources, in numbered iambic pentameter quatrains rhyming in couplets, and Robert Charles Dallas's 'Elegiac Epistle', a late and marginal example in elegiac quatrains.[23] A related principle, observed by all heroic epistles of the long eighteenth century, is a rhetorical style suitable for expressing impassioned feeling, though most of Drayton's successors followed him by drawing at times on a quasi-colloquial register to suggest the tone of a personal letter.

Although the heroic epistle was firmly established by the early eighteenth century, chiefly through the impact of *Ovid's Epistles*, it was Pope who gave it a new currency with 'Eloisa to Abelard'. He took his subject not from legend or political history but from the twelfth-century love affair that John Hughes's edition of the letters had recently popularized;[24] and, despite its historical source, the poem is Ovidian in that its primary concern is love. 'Eloisa to Abelard' set almost as influential an example for the heroic epistle as *An Essay on Man* was to do for the essay-epistle. One sign of this is that it began what amounts to a subgenre of replies, with, as I shall show, at least ten different poems and one 'Fragment' entitled 'Abelard to Eloisa' following in the rest of the century.

Intrinsic to the letter as a form is what Anna de Pretis, paraphrasing Janet Gurkin Altman, calls 'the "bridge/barrier" feature'.[25] As Altman puts it, 'Given the letter's function as a connector between two distant points, as a bridge between sender and receiver, the epistolary author can choose to emphasize either the distance or the bridge.'[26] Heroic epistles characteristically emphasize distance. For example, describing the situations of Ovid's heroines, Duncan F. Kennedy writes:

> Some are physically separated from their addressees by forces outside their control, such as war or its attendant politics [. . .], whilst others have been, or consider themselves, abandoned [. . .]. Others still may be physically close to the objects of their love but 'separated' from them by social convention [...], or by the consequences of its transgression.[27]

Citing Altman's 'bridge/barrier' function, Kennedy goes on to point out that Penelope, the writer of Ovid's first epistle, does not know if Ulysses will ever receive it, and that the implication of various other epistles too is that they will never reach their intended recipients. The pathos of an appeal that may never be read by its addressee is thus a potential built into the form. For this reason, and others also, Pope's choice of Eloisa and Abelard's story was exceptionally well-judged. Not only can Eloisa not be sure that Abelard will read her letter, but she responds not to him but to a letter from him to a third party; and the distance between them is a function not only of geography but also of morality and religion. These are the key factors that determine the poem's epistolarity.

For example, the reason that Eloisa does not start her letter by addressing Abelard is that he has not addressed her. She begins instead by reflecting on the feelings produced in her by the letter he has written to another, referring both to him and to herself in the third person: 'From *Abelard* it came, / And *Eloisa* yet must kiss the name' (7–8).[28] Her first apostrophes are to that name and her surroundings – the walls, rocks, and caverns in which Pope set the convent, and the shrines within it. Not until line 29 does she expressly address her former lover, and even then she focuses immediately on his name, as if direct communication is at first too fraught. She also uses the third person as a distancing device in lines 91–8, when she describes their bliss as lovers, and immediately afterwards, in lines 99–106, when she refers to his castration. Though passages such as these, and, too, lines in which Eloisa addresses herself (for example, 177–86), help account for Warton's view, already quoted, that the poem is more a soliloquy than a letter, they stem from her epistolary situation. Yet it is the second person that Pope exploits most subtly, not only for Eloisa's appeal to her former lover, but also for other effects.

First, he uses the intimate form much more often than the more distant 'you'. Eloisa addresses Abelard with the pronoun 'thou' and its cognates no fewer than 63 times, as opposed to only 7 times with 'you'. When she uses the less familiar form, it is carefully motivated: for instance, while describing their first meeting, when she did not know him (line 65, after which she shifts with similar effect to the third person), and three times as a rhyme word, giving it extra emphasis: 'Not on the Cross my eyes were fix'd, but you' (116); 'Renounce my love, my life, my self – and you' (204); and 'The phantom flies me, as unkind as you' (236). The three other occasions on which Pope has her use the pronoun to refer to Abelard also lend emphasis, one beginning a line – 'You rais'd these hallow'd walls' (133) – the other two occurring in the same line: 'Sudden you mount! you becken from the skies' (245). Yet the most interesting use of the pronoun is the first, where it does not immediately or necessarily denote Abelard at all. Line 23, 'Tho' cold like you, unmov'd, and silent grown', addresses the statues of saints around Eloisa in the convent. At the same time, it may be read as implicitly or unconsciously addressed to Abelard: distant, emasculated, and, for all that Eloisa knows, no longer willing to respond.

Second, Pope also has Eloisa invoke Abelard. As Gillian Beer remarks, '"Come" is the most important word (even, finally, the *only* important word) in heroic epistle', seeking to bridge the distance that motivates it.[29] In 'Eloisa to Abelard' it occurs 12 times, on all but one occasion at or near the start of a line; but the barriers of religion and morality mean that it can never be a simple appeal for Abelard's presence. Very soon after the first time it occurs, for instance, 'Come! with thy looks, thy words, relieve my woe' (119), Eloisa has to ask for a quite different form of contact: 'Ah no! instruct me other joys to prize' (125); and, similarly, 'Come *Abelard*' (257), 'Come, if thou dar'st' (281) and 'Come, with one glance of those deluding eyes' (283) are followed by 'No, fly me, fly me' (289) and even 'Ah come not' (291). In these ways, the word Eloisa begins by using in an attempt to summon Abelard becomes one she uses to ask him to help her renounce him. She imagines the spirits of dead nuns appealing to her to join them – 'Come, sister come' (309) – and she ends by reversing her initial invocation as she accepts the necessity of her death: 'I come, I come! prepare your roseate bow'rs' (317).

Third, as in all epistolary literature, there is the question whom else the poem addresses. Recent scholarship on the *Heroides* has proposed that, as Duncan Kennedy puts it, their destination 'cannot simply be reduced to the addressee formally identified'.[30] Other possibilities include one or more characters in the same drama – one example Kennedy cites is Hermione's mother Helen in the former's epistle to Orestes – but also people whom the actual author wishes to influence, ranging from general readers to specific individuals. Referring to the circumstances in which Ovid wrote his epistles, Kennedy quotes Patricia Rosenmeyer, who suggests: 'The *Heroides* may be read as letters from exile . . . in which Ovid pursues his fascination with the genre of letters and the subject of abandonment through literary characters'; and he goes on to remark that, in this sense, 'Ovid takes on the discursive situation and role of the heroine'.[31] Geoffrey Tillotson has argued that, in the light of Pope's correspondence, two passages in 'Eloisa to Abelard' offer evidence of specific external readers whom he may have addressed surreptitiously. One was Martha Blount, who, Tillotson speculates, was probably the subject of a conclusion that Pope discarded after Lady Mary Wortley Montagu left for Turkey; the other was Lady Mary herself.[32] The first passage is the paragraph beginning at line 73 in which Eloisa exalts a love affair over marriage. On this Tillotson comments: 'he intends Martha Blount and/or Lady Mary Wortley Montagu to be free to understand a personal invitation'.[33] The second is the role of the 'future Bard' (359) in the poem's coda, to which Pope seems to have drawn Lady Mary's attention in a letter, especially a couplet pertinent to her recent departure: 'Condemn'd whole years in absence to deplore, / And image charms he must behold no more' (361–2).[34] The issue is complicated by Pope's apparent vacillation over which of the two ladies to prefer, but it appears that at some level he addressed the epistle to either or both of them. Ellen Pollak even goes so far as to claim that 'Eloisa functions not only as a projection of Pope's desire for Lady Mary, but also – because of the analogies between the poet and Abelard – as a fantasied fulfillment of his desire that Lady Mary desire him'.[35]

David Fairer similarly suggests that the heroic epistle is 'not a means of communication but a receptacle for frustrated emotion'.[36] Whether or not his and Pollak's claims are valid, the fact that 'Eloisa to Abelard', like other heroic epistles, has more than one addressee opens other possibilities. Fairer also raises the question of the general reader's position in 'Eloisa to Abelard' – 'conscious,' he suggests, 'of eavesdropping on something intensely private and embarrassing, but also being drawn towards supplying the lack of responsiveness, the missing role of addressee'.[37] Yet, perhaps surprisingly, Pope addresses general readers too, and, not surprisingly, in much more direct ways than Martha Blount or Lady Mary. He invokes them first in the image of the 'two wandring lovers' (347) who visit the convent where Eloisa and Abelard are buried, pity them, and vow: 'Oh may we never love as these have lov'd!' (352); and then in the phrase 'some relenting eye' (355), referring to the response of any sympathetic visitor. In these implicit appeals he distils the two main elements of the poem's didactic message: not to love to excess (an appeal that any covert message to Martha Blount or Lady Mary would seem to belie), and to be open to compassion. Another way in which he seeks to include general readers is by employing, six times, the first person plural in a sense that does not refer to Eloisa and Abelard alone. The earliest occasion, 'The jealous God, when we profane his fires' (81), is in the paragraph already mentioned in which Pope has Eloisa prefer a love affair to a marriage. This is consistent with Tillotson's interpretation. But the other five are near the end, and their implications are quite different. The first is the line 'And faith, our early immortality!' (300); while the second closes the passage in which Eloisa relays what she imagines the spirits of deceased nuns saying to her: 'For God, not man, absolves our frailties here' (316). Later, addressing death, Eloisa declares: 'you only prove / What dust we doat on, when 'tis man we love' (336); and finally there is a line previously quoted, 'Oh may we never love as these have lov'd!' (352). These uses of the first person plural beg to co-opt the reader in endorsing the morally and doctrinally orthodox message that, after much struggle, Eloisa ends by presenting. As a whole, however, the poem is much less straightforward. True to its source, the three letters from Heloise in Hughes's edition, and perhaps also to Pope's own emotional and psychological situation, his heroine's repentance is not finally secure. Its message could be summarized by the title and burden of a lyric by Thomas Hardy: 'Come Not; Yet Come!';[38] and it is in this way that it exemplifies most fully and poignantly the tradition of the heroic epistle.

The key critical question that Gillian Beer raises in her superb essay on the heroic epistle is whether such poems, most often (though by no means always) written by men from a woman's position, create space for a specifically female point of view – and, if they do, to what extent. Her answer is that 'the form did function to extend the rhetorical possibilities of language for its male authors – but this extension relies upon an appeal to the authority of women, who were assumed to be naturally learned in the realms of erotic knowledge and suffering'; and that, although 'Heroic epistle takes as its pre-condition the enforced passivity of women', 'the sense of enforcement means that these are poems which sustain a constant protest against the conditions which produce the form'.[39] One way of extending this argument is to consider one of what were apparently only two responses in the same form by women to Pope's epistle – a response that is also the earliest of the series that followed through the century. Judith Cowper, later Madan, appears to have written 'Abelard to Eloisa' in 1720. As Valerie Rumbold points out, it occurs with that date, attributed to her though not in her hand, in a family album; but it did not appear in print until 1727, when it found its way under William Pattison's name into his posthumous *Poetical Works*, no doubt through the unscrupulousness of the publisher Edmund Curll.[40] After it had reappeared in *The Luscious Poet: Or, Venus's Miscellany* in 1732, the next printing I have traced is in John Whaley's *Collection of Original Poems and Translations* (1745), where it is attributed to 'a Lady'.[41] Apart from the altered attribution, this version is also significant because there are numerous variations from the text first printed as Pattison's. A somewhat corrupt version of the same text recurs in *Cupid Triumphant* in 1747, attributed to 'Mrs. C—ER', before the printing most often cited by scholars, in *Poems by Eminent Ladies* of 1755, where the poem is presented along with another one by her and where she is styled in the title to a brief introduction as 'Mrs. Madan (formerly Miss Cowper)'.[42] The complex publication history of the poem did not end here. It was not only printed, along with 'Eloisa to Abelard' and other responses, in editions of Pope's source, John Hughes's *Letters of Abelard and Heloise*, but the version published in *Poems by Eminent Ladies* reappears in the *Poetical Calendar* in 1764, assigned to Pattison. This is probably the source for that in *Bell's Classical Arrangement of Fugitive Poetry*, which has the same ascription.[43]

The reason why the poem's publication history is significant is that comparison of the two main versions – that published as Pattison's in 1727, and that published as Cowper's in 1755 – suggests that the latter revises the former. Some of the peculiarities of the version printed earlier may be explained as misreadings from manuscript. For instance, 1727 has the absurd line 'Veil'd, as in *Paraclete*'s Sea-bath'd Tow'rs' (p. 70) – absurd metrically as well as in light of the convent's location inland. The 1755 version has, instead, the phrase 'secluded Tow'rs' (p. 139). Other examples are 'whilst I the Fortune prove / Of feeble Piety, conflicting Love' (1727, p. 74), where 1755 has 'tortures' for 'Fortune' (p. 141); along with 'And thou, amazing Scene! belov'd no more' (1727, p. 76), where 'Scene' is replaced in 1755 by 'change' (p. 143). A more complex variation affects the following lines that appear in 1727:

O Eloisa! would the Fates once more
(Indulgent to thy Wish) this Form restore,

How wouldst thou from these Arms with Horror start,
To miss those Charms, familiar, to thy Heart! (p. 69)

The key differences here are that 'thy Wish' becomes 'my view', 'this
Form' becomes 'thy charms', 'these Arms' becomes 'my arms', and
'those Charms' becomes 'the form' (1755, p. 138). Because these make
sense of the passage – Abelard, his youthful looks restored, would
scarcely imagine Eloisa recoiling from him in horror – it seems likely that
the 1727 version is garbled. Other discrepancies between the two texts,
however, are not easily explained in such a way. Two striking examples
are the addition to the 1755 text of two lines describing Eloisa – ' Bright
as their beams thy eyes a mind disclose, / Whilst on thy lips gay blush'd
the fragrant rose' (p. 141) – and the substitution of the word 'destructive'
for 1727's repeated epithet in the lines: 'Let springing Grace, fair Faith
and Hope remove, / The fatal traces of voluptuous Love; / Voluptuous
Love from his soft Mansion tear' (1727, p. 71; 1755, p. 140).

The two variations just mentioned between the versions of 1727 and
1755, along with several others, are pertinent to the poem's epistolary
character and/or to Cowper's character as author. First, the extra two lines
describing Eloisa's beauty emphasize the fiction that it is a man writing to
a woman, a man still open to female charms. Second, the norms
governing the conduct and expression of unmarried young gentlewomen
of the period would have rendered the word 'voluptuous' dangerously
suggestive for anyone who knew the writer's identity. A third difference
has other implications still. In the 1727 text, the intimate second person
singular in its various forms is applied to Eloisa no fewer than 50 times,
the more formal second person plural only 13. In 1755, however, almost
half of the singular pronouns are plurals, so that the number of the former
drops to 28 while that of the latter rises to 32 (the discrepancy is the
alteration of 'thy' to 'my' in line 38 already quoted). The nature of the
differences suggests expressive intent. Until just over halfway through
both texts, both forms of the pronoun are used, though even here there is
evidence of discrimination. While line 2 of both, for instance, refers to
'thy letter', and line 7 asks: 'art thou still the same?', lines 11–12 shift to
the more distant plural form when Abelard states that he had thought
Eloisa estranged from him: 'Alas! I thought you disengag'd and free; /
And can you still, still sigh and weep for me?'. The variations begin in
line 117, 'As once to love, I sway'd your yielding mind' (1755, p. 141),
where 'your' replaces the 'thy' of 1727 (p. 73). They are most dramatic in
the poem's final 14 lines, in which 1755 replaces the singular form of
1727 with the plural a total of ten times. These differences are all the more

remarkable in comparison with 'Eloisa to Abelard', in which the woman addresses the man with the plural form only eight times in a poem that is over twice as long. The probable explanation is that they emphasize Abelard's repentance: as he renounces their love, commits himself to heaven and distances from her, so he drops the intimate form of address. At the same time, however, the different incidence of singular and plural second person pronouns in the two texts of Cowper's poem may be related to her position as writer. Valerie Rumbold and Claudia Thomas argue that the poem is limited by the social conventions that would have governed Cowper's behaviour. Rumbold finds her ending too cut-and-dried: 'There is thus no place for Pope's ambiguity in a poem whose somewhat unconvincing resolution reflects her own determination to live by rules she knows to be powerless to reduce her inner life to order.'[44] Thomas claims similarly that the unevenness she sees in Cowper's poem 'resulted inevitably from her youthful inexperience and feminine education, compounded by her reliance on Pope'.[45] However, just as Pope based his epistle on the three by Heloise in Hughes's edition, so Cowper based hers on the two by Abelard; and each reflects the way in which its half of the correspondence ends. Like Hughes's Heloise, Pope's Eloisa 'discovers some Emotions, which make it doubtful, whether Devotion had entirely triumphed over her Passion'; while Cowper follows Hughes by showing Abelard 'determin'd to put an End to so dangerous a Correspondence as that between *Heloise* and himself'.[46] Cowper, in other words, was writing according to her script in providing the ending she did – as, indeed, was Pope. Thomas is right to suggest that Abelard's description of Eloisa, 'together with Cowper's reluctance to make Abelard fully responsible, reminds us that contemporary sources trained young women to avoid seduction partly by blaming its victims', but Cowper would have found this in the source, as when Abelard declares: 'Your Looks were the beginning of my Guilt' (Letter III, p. 76). The virtually systematic use of the second person plural towards the end of the poem in its later printing works similarly. Not only does it emphasize Abelard's repentance and consequent distancing from Eloisa, but, like the difference between 'voluptuous' in the earlier printing and 'destructive' in the later, it is also more decorous, more in keeping with a poem by a young gentlewoman.

The same factor casts interesting light on Beer's formulation of the duality for women of the heroic epistle – that it simultaneously privileges and confines them. Rumbold declares that Cowper's poem reflects her 'experience of depression', and yet that, 'ironically, while Pope relished the licence of imitating a feminine sensibility, Judith, knowing its dangers from the inside, welcomed the opportunity to assert a masculine firmness'.[47] Conversely, citing the passage in which Abelard regrets the loss of his physical charms, Thomas argues that 'Cowper projects onto her male protagonist conventional feminine concern with youthful appearance'.[48] Neither critic takes Abelard's emasculation into account, though it may have made his position as lover more acceptable for a young woman to convey. More importantly, both risk essentialism, as the contradiction between the two points highlights.

But the crucial point is historical: that the heroic epistle flourished in Britain at a time when the social and cultural position of women was at issue as never before. The constant attention paid to women's role has been demonstrated extensively by scholars over the last 20 years. Among its manifestations are the feminine conduct books that, as Ellen Pollak puts it, 'became widely popular in the last decades of the seventeenth century', and 'were distinguished by an advocacy of purely passive female virtues'.[49] Another is the number of discussions elsewhere, especially in the magazines that mushroomed through the period. Pollak calls the complex of attitudes embodied by the conduct books and other sources 'the myth of passive womanhood', while Jane Spencer uses a more comprehensive term: 'a new bourgeois ideology of femininity'.[50] Other scholars have developed and complicated these concepts,[51] but the basic point is that the role of women was under constant cultural inspection.

The new ideology of femininity encouraged the heroic epistle. It did this by providing a means for male writers both to exploit a capacity attributed to women for intense, passionate feeling and, at the same time, to present its dangers and the ruin to which many believed it would lead; it also enabled opportunities for pathos in portraying suffering but in various ways sympathetic victims. The opportunity to write in a different voice, and gender, from their own also offered an enhanced expressive range to women writers, but it tended to entail greater constraints. It is partly for this reason that Cowper's poem is less complex than Pope's, especially in its epistolarity. While his relations with Martha Blount and Lady Mary Wortley Montagu helped feed the tortuous emotional and moral dynamics of 'Eloisa to Abelard', it would have been more hazardous for Cowper to address specific external readers in the same way. As a young woman, by the standards of the time she also had less authority to address the general reader. The only clear occasion when she does so is near the end, where Abelard declares: 'Behold the destin'd end of human love – / But let the sight your zeal alone improve' (165–6). Similarly, she uses the first person plural only rarely, and never in such a way as to implicate general readers; and, in her poem, invocation plays a different role from in other heroic epistles, including Pope's. If the appeal in 'Eloisa to Abelard' is 'come not, yet come', in 'Abelard to Eloisa' it is, at most, 'haste, thy lover free' (135), though even this is followed by the requirement that she be fully penitent. In this way Cowper's poem is true to its source, and she to the gender codes of her period.

The point is further clarified by comparison with treatments by male writers of the same material. First, such poets had more liberty to express sexual passion, and to refer directly to Abelard's castration as sharpening it. Richard Barford's version, for example, in one of the earliest responses, has Abelard lament his impotence no fewer than four times, using as many times either the noun or the adjective.[52] Second, most responses also have Abelard explain that his chief motive for persuading Eloisa to take the veil was jealousy – a part of the source in Hughes that reflects badly on him and that Cowper chose not to follow. Third, second person pronouns, singular and plural, tend to be used with less discrimination than in the later edition of Cowper's poem, the singular form being favoured most.[53] The same is true of the third person, which later versions generally cultivate more for dramatic effect than for its appropriateness to Abelard's changing relation to his addressee. Finally, in several of the male-authored responses the didactic message is more explicit. As David Fairer points out, in what seems to have been the first such poem Charles Beckingham 'makes his Abelard completely resistant to Eloisa's pleas'.[54] 'Fragment of an Epistle from Abelard to Eloisa', though it appears in a book with the lurid title *The Pleasures of Coition*, is neither smut nor heroic epistle but a blunt riposte to what, it appears, Beckingham saw as the sentimentality of Pope's poem. But, except for its misogynism, this is not characteristic. Barford's response, for instance, makes its expression of frustrated desire so extravagant as to call in question the subsequent profession of repentance; while James De-La-Cour's, with its prefatory appeal to 'the Ladies' (sig. [A3]), succumbs to what Beckingham had rejected as emotional self-indulgence.[55] James Cawthorn strikes a much better balance in his version, first published in 1747, which presents both Abelard's impotent desire (including fairly discreet reference to his emasculation) and his craving for penitence. A mark of this balance is that Cawthorn provides a more convincing ending than most, for he has Abelard recognize that he cannot fully repent in this life but look forward to redemption and purity in the life beyond.[56]

The versions by Cowper and Cawthorn were much reprinted, often accompanying the letters as presented by Hughes and 'Eloisa to Abelard' itself. An increasingly complex intertextual web resulted. Pope had indicated his awareness of the story's intertextuality not only in his coda, with its reference to 'some future Bard' (359), but much earlier in the poem, in a paragraph alluding to Ovidian tradition when Eloisa seeks to persuade Abelard to write to her with the words: 'Heav'n first taught letters for some wretch's aid, / Some banish'd lover, or some captive maid' (51–2). While he draws, among other sources, on Hughes as well as on Ovid, Cowper draws on his poem too; and Cawthorn alludes to Cowper as well as to several of the sources each of his predecessors had used.[57] Rousseau's *Julie: Or, The New Heloise*, first published in 1761, revived interest in the story and gave it further impetus, though it does not quite qualify as an intertext for later versions. Three of these later versions appear in successive editions of Hughes, one accredited to a 'Mr. Seymour' though the author was probably Thomas Warwick, who appears to have printed no fewer than three different versions of the poem.[58] Like Cawthorn, Warwick was a clergyman, and his versions, especially the last (that of 1785), are marked by didacticism; it is accompanied, too, by a prose account of the lives of the two lovers and is followed by notes, most quoting, without translation, the Latin of the source. Edward Jerningham's version, apparently the last by a man to appear in the century, is quite different. Much more mannered in style and sentimental in substance, it has Abelard style himself self-pityingly as 'the victim of untimely fate' and Eloisa as 'to compassion exquisitely prone' – an emotion the author evidently wished to invoke in his readers.[59] Perhaps in an attempt at greater historical authenticity, also evident in Warwick's version of 1785, Jerningham has Abelard refer only implicitly to his castration, excommunication seeming to affect him much more. But the most ingenious way of rewriting the script appears in what may have been the last 'Abelard to Eloisa' of the period, by Lady Sophia Burrell.[60] As Claudia Thomas observes, 'Lady Burrell structures her poem as if it preceded Pope's. Eloisa's statements now appear to answer Abelard's desperate questions.'[61] Burrell was not, however, able to exploit all the opportunities this move offered. Not only is the poem, as Thomas puts it, 'characteristically "ladylike"',[62] but, although it has Abelard pay tribute to Eloisa's intellect in the phrase 'thy intelligent, thy active mind', it portrays her instead in conventionally feminine guise as 'divinely fair', 'thy cheeks with blushes warm', and so on (p. 14).

The proliferation of new versions that both recycled the story and often, in such ways, gave it a new twist illustrates not only its interest for readers but also the continuing life of the heroic epistle. Abelard's castration, as well as the moral and religious taboos separating him from Eloisa, gave writers opportunities for exploiting the passion of frustrated desire that is central to the form while also allowing conventional moral assurances. The main difference between epistles from Abelard to Eloisa and canonical heroic epistles, apart from the reversed genders of writer and addressee, goes back to Judith Cowper's. They end by invoking the writer's beloved not to come to him, unless in death, but to relinquish him, so adding pathos to the already inviting mix of passion and conventional morality.

In discussing responses by women of the period to 'Eloisa to Abelard', Claudia Thomas does not limit her discussion to those from Abelard himself. This, again, draws attention to the flexibility of the form and the variety of uses to which it could be put. The examples that Thomas considers include 'Epistle to Moneses, in Imitation of Ovid', by Charlotte Ramsay (later Lennox), a rescension that, despite its subtitle, is clearly influenced by Pope's poem; Ann Curtis's 'Zelida to Irena', already mentioned; and Jael Henrietta Pye's 'Elgiva to Edwy'.[63] Generalizing about these writers, Thomas argues that,

> By placing Eloisa's cries in the mouths of virginal brides and martyred queens, they vindicated feminine passion while protecting their own reputations. Pope's poem became the vehicle through which these writers claimed 'good' women's right to love passionately. Their heroines suffered as much as any deserted mistress in the *Heroides*, but women's heroic epistles grope towards nonpejorative acknowledgment of women's sexuality.[64]

What made this possible was that although, after the 1740s, the ideology of femininity required women to be chaste in mind as well as behaviour, the Age of Sensibility allowed sexual feeling to be coded as sentiment. But Thomas's proposition is truer of the second half of the century than of the first, when the ideology of femininity was not fully established, and when Sensibility did not yet hold sway. At that time, when 'Eloisa to Abelard' had not acquired the enormous influence it was to hold for at least the last three-quarters of the century, it was the historical variant of the heroic epistle that women as well as men tended to cultivate.

A related point is that even early examples show a wish to rewrite the erotic appeal of the Ovidian form in quite different terms. For instance, Anne Finch's 'Epistle from Alexander to Hephæstion in his Sickness' is highly unusual in several ways.[65] Although clearly based on Ovidian convention, it is by a woman, and both nominal writer and addressee are male. The gender of writer and addressee license Finch to escape the normal constraints on what a gentlewoman could express, enabling her to convey passion, albeit to be read as chaste – not least because she has Alexander refer both to Hephæstion's wife and to his own in the course of the letter. At the same time, the poem displays her classical knowledge and her ability to 'imitate', in the Restoration and eighteenth-century sense, in an apt and inventive way. One of Finch's contemporaries, Elizabeth Rowe, put another slant on the heroic epistle by writing a response to a poem first published in 1684 in the first edition of Dryden's miscellany. Despite the second word its title – 'An Elegy by the Wife of St. Alexias (a Nobleman of Rome) Complaining on his Absence, He Having Left Her on his Wedding Night Unenjoy'd out of a Pious Zeal to Go Visit the *Christian Churches*' – the poem resembles an heroic epistle.[66] But Rowe turns the form round, not only by reversing the conventional genders of author, nominal writer and addressee, but also by putting divine over earthly love.[67] Without overt didacticism, the poem presents an example of steadfast obedience to God's will, guided by the principle 'Short the fatigue, eternal the reward!' (p. 152). It is a further example of how, through epistolary form, a writer can address readers beyond the poem.

Rowe turned the epistle to similar purposes in *Friendship in Death* and *Letters Moral and Entertaining*, first published together in 1733 and often reprinted throughout the century.[68] The collection contains one Ovidian imitation but as many as four stemming from Drayton. 'Penelope to Ulysses' was an appropriate choice for conveying a message of patient female fidelity, as Anne Wharton's imitation had shown.[69] Rowe's version is equally proper, though more concise. The role of loving wife imploring her husband to return required not only expression of passionate feeling but also, in this case, censure of adultery. Staying quite close to her source, Rowe has Penelope condemn 'The lustful *Phrygian*' who had caused the wars that had taken her husband away, and, 'lost to joy, and widow'd of delight' in the day, brought to 'Curse the dull lagging hours of the more tedious night' (III, 218). She also appeals to family values by citing the son whose 'soft years a parent's aid require' and the father who wishes to see his son before he dies (III, 222). All the same, in keeping with the tradition, the burden of Penelope's appeal is 'Oh! haste to me'. Different in several respects is 'Rosamond to Henry II'. Based on the first poem in *Englands Heroicall Epistles*, its writer is an adulteress who does not scruple to call herself twice, as she does in Drayton, 'prostitute' (III, 209, 211; Drayton, II, 134, line 48; 'Strumpet', 137, line 139). Rowe also follows Drayton in having Rosamond seek to palliate her offence by presenting herself as a reluctant victim of seduction, led on by a 'female fiend' (III, 209); but she departs from him (and follows another tradition) at the end of the epistle when Rosamond relates a dream in which the queen poisons her. The poem closes on a note of sinister foreboding emphasized by the final line, an alexandrine: 'This dismal omen aggravates my fears, / Before my fancy still the furious queen appears' (III, 212). In this way it invites sympathy for the sinner; and the ending is all the more effective because Rowe, unlike Drayton, provides no reply.

A generation later any woman who assumed the guise of an adulteress would risk her reputation, and the writers of Rowe's other three historical epistles, which also derive from Drayton, are morally much purer. 'Mary Queen of France to Charles Brandon Duke of Suffolk' protests against the forced marriage that had separated her from her lover, his disregard for her peace of mind while her husband was still alive, and his apparent lack of interest now she is free again. The epistle is without the racy humour of the source, in which Mary seeks to reassure Suffolk that, though Louis has taken her virginity, she is still all but untouched: 'He had indeed, but shall I tell thee what, / Beleeve me, BRANDON, he had scarcely that' (II, 264; lines 105–6). Instead, it promotes the virtues of chastity and domesticity for a quite different readership, as Mary cries: 'Defend my breast from' this perfidious love' (III, 216), and ends by declaring that she would resign her crown 'to prove / The peaceful joys of innocence and love' (III, 217). First published in Steele's *Poetical Miscellanies* of 1714, the poem is the only epistle by Rowe to appear in *Bell's Classical Arrangement*.[70] As with 'Rosamond to Henry II', Rowe provided no response; but an anonymous contributor to the *Gentleman's Magazine* obliged with an exchange matching those by Drayton and Oldmixon.[71]

Rowe's remaining two historical epistles are an exchange between Lady Jane Grey and Lord Guilford Dudley (II, 82–6). These carry different emphases, enabling her not only to put to her readers two examples of Christian fortitude and of martyrdom in the making, but also to hold up the dangers of what, as a strict Protestant, she regarded as the superstition and tyranny of Catholicism. At the same time, she has both writers wish for a retired life that has much more in common with the dreams of the eighteenth-century bourgeoisie than with those of aristocrats two centuries earlier, Dudley exclaiming: 'Inglorious in some blissful shades I'd prove, / The silent joys of unmolested love' (III, 85). Later in the century, and following convention, James Cawthorn and George Keate provided only the female half of the correspondence. Both poems bear all the hallmarks of Sensibility, preferring this to the national themes that figure in Drayton, Oldmixon and even to some extent in Rowe. Cawthorn's implicitly invites the reader along with the writer to 'Sigh to thy sighs, and weep with all thy tears' (34), while Keate's ends with the tear-jerking (or mirth-provoking) couplet: 'One last, sad, parting sigh is left for You; / The rest is Heav'n's: – a long – long – long Adieu!' (p. 45).[72] However, while Keate follows Rowe in having the *'wretched Queen'* offer the maxim that '"Content's the highest pitch of human bliss"' (p. 37), Cawthorn does so by having her rebuke what she calls the 'Mad bigotry' of Catholicism (165). But Cawthorn echoes Pope too, especially in Lady Jane's farewell to her 'Friend, father, lover, husband, saint' (184), and her speculation whether 'some bard' (211), suitably sympathetic, might write her story.

In describing the merits of 'Eloisa to Abelard', Samuel Johnson emphasized what was regarded as the poem's historical authenticity. He remarks, in his 'Life of Pope': 'The heart naturally loves truth. The adventures and misfortunes of this illustrious pair are known from undisputed history. [. . .] So new and so affecting is their story, that it supersedes invention, and imagination ranges at full liberty without straggling into scenes of fable.'[73] The same point applies, of course, to the responses, but it is especially important in helping to explain why heroic epistles drawn from British history stayed current through the century. Addison had declared in the *Spectator*: 'the short Speeches or Sentences which we often meet with in Histories, make a deeper Impression on the Mind of the Reader, than the most labour'd Strokes in a well written Tragedy. Truth and Matter of Fact sets the Person actually before us in the one, whom Fiction places at a greater distance from us in the other' (No. 397; III, 487). He went on to introduce an example, a letter by Anne Boleyn to Henry VIII before her execution that was long thought to be genuine and which he presents as such, though her most recent biographer doubts its authenticity.[74] But the reason why Addison gave such weight to impressing the reader is even more significant. He begins his essay by calling in question a principle he attributes to the Stoics, that 'they will not allow a Wise Man so much as to pity the Afflictions of another'. In a way that will influence later eighteenth-century humanitarianism, he argues instead that, 'As Love is the most delightful Passion, Pity is nothing else but Love softned by a degree of Sorrow: In short, it is a kind of pleasing Anguish, as well as generous Sympathy, that knits Mankind together, and blends them in the same common Lot' (III, 486). It is this kind of pity that, for him, the letter arouses – as, for Johnson and many other readers, did Pope's version of Eloisa's. Historical epistles, including those by Rowe, often aim at the same effect, but the most striking example of one based on the letter supposedly by Anne Boleyn produces something close to the tragic dignity of the original.

Like Shakespeare and Fletcher, for whom Anne Boleyn was still too risky a topic when they wrote *King Henry VIII*, first performed in 1613, Drayton refrained from including her as a correspondent in *Englands*

Heroicall Epistles. At the start of the eighteenth century, Oldmixon also preferred not to include her, though among the correspondents he added to Drayton's are Anne's daughter, who became Elizabeth I, and her niece, who would become Mary Queen of Scots.[75] But Addison's essay inspired at least three eighteenth-century poets to rewrite Anne's letter as an heroic epistle. For such a poem it offered a model basis: it was apparently authentic, it involves royal love and infidelity, and its political context – that of the English Reformation – was highly charged. The first is not only the best but it is also of special interest in that it is by a woman. In writing as a person of the same sex as herself, Elizabeth Tollet, like Rowe, departed from the tradition that the nominal writer of the heroic epistle is female but the actual writer is male – though in a different way from the male poets who wrote as Abelard. Partly for this reason, her poem has quite different implications from theirs and from its male-authored rivals. The earlier of these, by William Whitehead, was first published nearly 20 years after hers in 1743; the second, by Joseph Holden Pott, in 1780.[76] There is no evidence that either Whitehead or Pott knew of Tollet's poem, which had been published anonymously.[77] Instead, their versions testify to the interest of the story and to the continuing currency of the form.

Tollet had good reason to advertise her poem in her subtitle, as it is the longest and most substantial in the collection. Like Drayton, she added explanatory notes. These begin by referring to the manuscript of the supposed original letter, citing Addison's *Spectator* essay, and they are lengthy and well-informed. But the key qualities of her poem are its epistolarity, along with her command of the heroic couplet and her respect for her source. Unlike Whitehead and Pott, she has Anne address Henry exclusively in the second person plural, following not only her source, and decorum that inhibited use of the intimate form to a monarch, but also the logic of the situation, in which Anne is defined as the king's enemy and is in prison. More importantly, however, she also exploits the inherent potential of epistolary form for addressing external readers. While the epistle begins by addressing Henry, in such phrases as 'your Sov'reign Head' and 'my Liege!' (p. 85), in the fifth paragraph, the longest in the poem so far, she has Anne widen her appeal from her own position to that of women at large. 'Too well your Sex,' Anne declares, 'weak Woman knows to gain, / With fictious Vows, and a delusive Strain'; and she goes on to generalize about men, in pursuit of ambition or novelty, abandoning their wives (pp. 87, 88). Later she strikes a related note by using the first person plural: 'Unhappy Beauty! of our Woes the Spring! / Of all our Vanities the vainest Thing! / Fondly by our unthinking Sex desir'd; / The more endanger'd as the more admir'd!' (p. 92). In these ways she seeks, as in other poems of her collection, for recognition of injustices to women resulting from men's superior power, and also, sharpening conventional strictures on female vanity, from their own personal attractions.[78]

As with Hypatia, the main speaker in another of the major poems in the collection, Tollet found in Anne Boleyn a highly suitable transmitter for her own views on the position of women. But this was not the only way in which she sought to engage readers through epistolary form. In keeping with Addison's 'generous Sympathy, that knits Mankind together, and blends them in the same common Lot', she also sought to arouse pity for her subject. Initially this is by way of reproach, in the part of the poem where Anne deplores insults to her personal honour from, as she puts it,

> My own misjudging Sex, who, loth to blame
> Their own Defects, imagine mine the same;
> Or Men who triumph in a prostrate Fame.
> And scarce among the Herd of Readers, find
> One pitying Tear, to speak a gen'rous Mind. (p. 92)

The invocation of the general reader, though oblique, is unmistakable, and it recurs at the end of the poem: 'Who then shall interdicted Pity show? / Permit a Sigh to breath, a Tear to flow?' (p. 97). Although Anne addresses Henry here, and, by extension, those who have renounced her following her imprisonment, the appeal is also for the reader outside the poem and its circumstances. Elsewhere, too, she implicitly addresses the reader when she imagines death and its aftermath: 'Whither? Ah! whither must we then remove? / Where must the discontented Spirit rove? / From Pow'r, from Pleasure, all that here below / Enchants our Senses, all Mankind must go' (p. 90). Here again the first person plural invites any readers, not just Henry, to move from reflecting on Anne's mortality to their own.

Neither Whitehead's poem not Pott's does much to invoke the general reader. Instead, their versions, which follow the original letter less closely, seem rather to treat it as an opportunity for poetic pathos. Whitehead's is prefaced by a reference to his source in the *Spectator* and the hope that 'the additions he has made to it may appear natural in her unfortunate situation' (p. 82). One form that these additions take appears almost immediately, in the shape of a simile spread over four lines in which Anne compares her situation to that of a shipwrecked sailor. Unlike Tollet, who would have considered it inappropriate with respect to a woman innocent of the sexual crime with which she was charged, Whitehead also draws on 'Eloisa to Abelard'. His line 'O hear me, HENRY, husband, father, hear!' (p. 85) echoes Pope's 'Come thou, my father, brother, husband, friend!'

(153); and, more blatantly, he has Anne call on 'some pitying bard' who 'shall save from death / Our mangled fame, and teach our woes to breathe' (p. 90). The tone Whitehead gives Anne is at times bitter and resentful, unlike the steadfastness and integrity reflected by Tollet; though another of his 'additions' to the original is, inconsistently, to have Anne calmly resigned to her fate later in the poem and welcoming death: 'Thus rapt, O king, thus lab'ring to be free, / My gentlest passport still depends on thee' (p. 89). As a result, the poem is at times confused, even mawkish. It is not surprising that Whitehead's *Poems on Several Occasions* of 1754 excludes it, though it appears in his *Plays and Poems* 20 years later.

Pott's version is less clumsy and more restrained than Whitehead's, but it also looks for embellishment in figurative language that has no place in the spare style of the original letter. Among other examples, it has Anne represent the prospect of death in a four-line metaphor as a downward glance from a 'tremendous steep' (p. 53); it compares the impact of groundless rumours on a loving heart to 'feeble winds' that could never shake a mountain (p. 54); and, in another sequence of four lines, it styles her as a 'tender plant' that, rooted up, should be left to fade in peace (p. 55). But the poem's sentimentality, shown by this third example, is most explicit when Anne ends the epistle by invoking her daughter, for instance in the couplet: 'Perhaps remembrance of one once held dear / May melt your heart, and start into a tear' (p. 59). Writing at the height of the age of Sensibility, a young man such as Pott was at the time might have found it difficult to avoid such a note. But the effect, as with Whitehead's poem, is to lose the force of the original, which is distinguished by its lack of self-pity. Anne emerges as a model of the meek kind of woman patterned in conduct manuals of the period, rather than as brave and self-possessed.

Treating Tollet's poem as a response to 'Eloisa to Abelard', Claudia Thomas claims that it is to Pope's poem that Tollet's owes its structure.[79] However, although Tollet expands on the original letter, as the form of heroic epistle required, she also followed it quite closely. For example, when Anne describes her misery in the Tower, Tollet not only adapts Pope's forbidding Gothic architecture and scenery but develops part of Anne's valediction, 'From my doleful Prison in the *Tower*' (*Spectator*, No. 397; III, 489). At the same time, she uses the opportunity to evoke the various tragic events that have taken place there, including the murders of Henry VI, Edward V and the young princes (p. 81); and, too, she reflects her own experience of the place in which she had spent most of her life and in which she was probably still living when she wrote the poem (*ODNB*). Parts of the poem in which she draws fairly directly on the letter include Anne's declarations that she had never sought to be raised to her position, and that she had never taken it for granted; her denial of any offence, along with her suspicion that the charge against her stemmed from Henry's love for Jane Seymour; her demand for a fair trial in open court; and her appeal for her daughter and those charged with her to be spared. Unlike Whitehead and Pott, she uses no extended metaphors but relies instead on the force of well-chosen words tightly ranged in compact couplets. Examples include Anne's request at the start of the poem: 'Permit one Object to disturb the Scene, / An injur'd Lover and a captive Queen' (p. 85), with the pointed balance of its second line; striking use of the caesura, as in 'Said I my Henry? I the King design'd' (p. 89); and apt chiasmus, as in 'To move Compassion, or Belief to win' (p. 86). Perhaps following the translators of *Ovid's Epistles*, she varies the pace with occasional triplets, but for dramatic effect rather than poetic ostentation. The first example in the poem, with the unexpected caesura in the first line of a new paragraph and its unexpected run-on lines, shows this well: 'Irresolute I sit; alike 'tis vain / Or to suppress my Sorrows, or complain / Of Woes that Language never can contain' (p. 85). In all, Tollet's single heroic epistle is one of the most interesting and impressive of the century.

From the historical heroic epistle and, as noted above, its satirical cousin,[80] it was a short step to poems in the same form about people and events in the present. Thomas Tickell helped develop this variant with 'An Epistle from a Lady in England, to a Gentleman at Avignon', first printed in 1717 and a subtle piece of advocacy for the Hanoverians.[81] On the one hand, the poem clearly stems from the heroic epistle in its form, its style and its culminating appeal: 'O return to me!' (p. 77); it also follows the convention of male author, female writer and erring male addressee. On the other hand, it refers equally clearly to contemporary events and to political and moral choices that would have exercised many of its readers: should those who supported the Stuarts – sympathizers at home, as well as exiles with the Pretender in Avignon – now accept Hanoverian rule? Yet the poem is not a satire. Samuel Johnson came close to catching its tone in observing that 'it expresses contempt without coarseness, and superiority without insolence'.[82] By writing in the guise of a woman sympathetic to the Jacobite cause, Tickell is able to convey criticism of the Pretender that is all the more telling because it appears unpartisan and delivered in a spirit more of sorrow than of anger. Though couched in terms of domestic affection, the appeal is politically skilful as the lady urges her husband to accept the inevitable: 'The fate of James with pitying eyes I view, / And wish my homage were not Brunswick's due' (p. 75).

The tradition that the addresser of an heroic epistle should be female made the form especially hospitable to pleas for sympathy. An example that hovers between public and private, though in a different way from Tickell's poem, is Noel Broxholme's 'Letter from a Lady to her Husband Abroad', printed in 1728. According to a manuscript note in a copy cited by David Foxon, the lady was the daughter of John Hollings and she had been abandoned by Edward Walpole, second son of Sir Robert.[83] This made the poem inherently political, though its primary motive appears to be that of seeking justice for a woman who has been wronged. The poem appeals to its external readers in such lines as: 'Each lover speak, to aid a lover's sighs, / To save a wife, let every woman rise', and seeks the fullest publicity: 'Wide as the world my history be known' (p. 197). But it also implies a political position, as when the lady, describing herself as 'Born in the boasted Land of Liberty', declares: 'For me no shield the cobweb Laws appear, / I feel by proof that Tyranny is here'. The poem is part of the intense pamphleteering that lasted for much of Walpole's period in office, and most later examples of its genre avoid political partisanship. A case in point is George Woodward's 'Letter from a Lady to her Husband in Spain, in her Last Sickness', which, like Tollet's 'Anne Boleyn to King Henry VIII', and the Yarico to Inkle poems to be considered shortly, derives from a paper in the *Spectator*.[84] Woodward follows his source quite closely, and he tailors it not only to the sensibility of his readers but also to their religious and moral views, as when the lady describes marriage as 'A State, which some the Curse of Heav'n believe, / A State which, rightly held, the greatest Joys can give'; and when, reflecting on God's will and the need to accept it, but the need for consolation too, she uses the first person plural to include general readers as well as writer and addressee (p. 63). A similar poem, printed over 40 years later, is the anonymous but male-authored 'To Colonel R—s', also from a dying wife to a husband on service abroad.[85]

Another pioneer of the new variant was Lady Mary Wortley Montagu, but the only example of the three she wrote that was published in her lifetime did not see print until 1747, though all would have circulated in manuscript.[86] One such poem, 'Miss Cooper to ——', is about an acquaintance who happens to have been the author of the first 'Abelard to Eloisa'. According to Valerie Rumbold, the poem reflects Montagu's jealousy, literary and physical, complicated further by Judith Cowper's friendship with Pope.[87] Yet, in keeping with the tradition of heroic epistle, most of it centres on a woman's sufferings from a capricious lover, so that he rather than she, along with the kind of masculinity he represents, seems its target. This way of reading the poem gains support from the fact that Montagu transferred six lines from the poem to 'Epistle from Mrs. Y[onge] to her Husband',[88] which expresses fully deserved contempt for the well-known libertine William Yonge who, while legally separated from his wife, had detected her in a love affair and cashed in by recovering damages from her lover, divorcing her and remarrying to advantage. As Isobel Grundy remarks, 'Epistle from Mrs. Y[onge]' not only attacks the sexual double standard but 'broadens out from this particular case to general advocacy for ill-used wives'.[89] Both epistles are adroit Ovidian adaptations, unusual in that their author was a woman too.

But the first of the three poems to be written, 'Epistle from Arthur G[ra]y to Mrs M[urra]y', is the most striking. Here, Montagu crosses boundaries not only of sex and rank to write in the voice of a footman convicted of the attempted rape of his mistress, but boundaries of genre too. In part the poem is another Ovidian epistle, though the author is a woman and the rejected lover a man; in part it is also a satire. Its obvious satirical targets are the upper-class men who, like William Yonge, 'make Love a Trade' and enjoy their lovers' beauties 'in a Strumpet's Arms' (44, 55). But Grundy suggests that the rape charge may have been brought to cover up an affair between Griselda Murray and Gilbert Burnet, that Gray may have aimed to catch the couple in bed, and that Montagu may have known all this. If so, Grundy argues, 'She was not sympathizing with the proletarian lover, but mocking him as an improbable fiction; she did not blame a rape victim but mocked and goaded a false claimant to chastity.'[90] Yet, though it is difficult, perhaps impossible, to recover all the ideological assumptions from which the poem would have been written, it is also difficult not to find in it some sympathy with the writer's frustrated passion as he urges his addressee to 'Turn from those Triflers that make Love a Trade' and assures her: 'This is true Passion in my Eyes you see, / They cannot, no, they cannot, love like me' (44–6). The mockery of 'a false claimant to chastity' is clear; but, as Gray was probably under sentence of death when the poem was written (he was later reprieved), his image of Griselda Murray seeing him 'waver in the Wind' on the scaffold (91) is also not easy to take lightly.

Even if they had been printed in the 1720s, the three versions of heroic epistle by Montagu were probably too unconventional to invite imitation. Instead, those that proved influential were several stemming from the story of Yarico and Inkle. Frances Seymour, Countess of Hertford, seems to have been the first to adapt as an heroic epistle Steele's account of the Amerind princess who saved a young Englishman's life and was bearing his child when he sold her into slavery. The poem follows her 'Story of Inkle and Yarico', also in verse; the two were first printed anonymously, probably in 1725.[91] Having already told the story, Hertford was free to spend most of the epistle on Yarico's appeal, which she directs to religious and moral ends: held back from suicide by what she has been taught by a Christian priest, Yarico warns Inkle that he is risking his soul through perjury. William Pattison also tried his hand at converting the story to an epistle, but he left only a fragment of 22 lines when he died suddenly in 1727.[92] It is clear, however, both from the fragment and from his comments, reprinted in a prefatory memoir, on his project for a new translation of Ovid's epistles, that his aim was pathos in the manner of 'Eloisa to Abelard' (pp. 47–8). The same purpose animates a version printed anonymously in 1736 and attributed on dubious grounds to Edward Moore, for its dedicatory verses, addressed to Arabella Saintloe, imagine a 'Virgin' weeping over it 'While tenderly she pleads the Negro's Cause, / And melts in soft Compassion at her Woes' (p. ii).[93] Its author distinguishes carefully between the second person singular and plural, Yarico addressing her betrayer in the plural form but quoting him addressing her, deceitfully, in the intimate singular. The appeal to the general reader is mainly implicit, except when, in an obvious echo of 'Eloisa to Abelard', Yarico predicts how 'People, unborn, shall my sad Tale relate, / And curse your Cruelty, and weep my Fate' (p. 8). As in the version of the story in the *Spectator*, where it is told as an example of male inconstancy to outdo the story of the widow of Ephesus, the emphasis is not on the evils of slavery but on perfidy and ingratitude. Edward Jerningham's attempt, first published in 1766, is quite different. Influenced at the time by Rousseau and Voltaire (*ODNB*), he makes it an attack on 'Christian' avarice and deceit, repeating the epithet several times, as well as on men's cruelty to women: 'Deluded Sex! the Dupes of Man decreed, / We, splendid Victims, at his Altar bleed' (p. 9).[94]

Although Jerningham has Yarico refer to slavery, especially that part of Steele's embellishment to the original story that presents her bearing a child as increasing her value as a commodity, his poem has little interest either in the institution or in the racism that it both promoted and helped to aggravate. His Yarico is a noble savage, reflected in the fact that he makes her not an Amerind – even less, as in the 1736 dedication, a 'Negro' – but a Nubian. Wylie Sypher captures the contradictions in his remark that this Yarico is 'a "Nubian" maiden who dwells in a pseudo-African, pseudo-American world and behaves much like a Roman vestal virgin'.[95] An earlier pair of poems, published by William Dodd in 1749 and based on recent events, draws on the same convention but tells a more reassuring story.[96] 'The African Prince, Now in England, to Zara, at his Father's Court' has its writer captured and enslaved but released when his

vendor dies and his royal rank is revealed. As with Oroonoko, in the play
adapted by Thomas Southerne from Aphra Behn's narrative and recalled
in the poem when the Prince mentions being shocked by a performance
(p. 123),[97] royalty tells. Dodd has the Prince rehearse the familiar conflict
of 'love and duty' (p. 118), echo 'Eloisa to Abelard' in describing his
farewell to his wife ('I caught thy fleeting soul, and gave thee mine', p.
118), and emphasize the key epistolary fact, distance from writer to
addressee: 'Between us still unmeasur'd oceans roll' (p. 123). Yet, though
the poem seeks to portray some of the miseries of slavery, it also has the
Prince celebrate 'Freedom's happy shore' (p. 122), 'long to tell' her about
the 'prodigies' he sees all around him (pp. 122, 123), and end by pleading
that he survive the return voyage for missionary purposes: 'to evangelize
my race' (p. 124). Not surprisingly, the response is less euphoric. The
chief appeal in 'Zara, at the Court of Anamaboe. To the African Prince,
When in England' is that defined by Gillian Beer as central to the
tradition: 'Once more, O come!' (p. 131). Indeed, a few lines later Dodd
gives Zara a wonderful remark that could stand as epigraph to the entire
form: 'My hand still writes, and writing prompts desire'.

    While it was one thing to invite sympathy for a 'royal slave', in the
phrase of Behn's subtitle, it was quite another in the case of enslaved
black people in general. As Wylie Sypher remarks, Dodd has the Prince
follow Oroonoko in expressing contempt for slaves not of royal rank, and,
after an outcome very different from that in Behn, seem to assume that,
'by the release of one royal slave, justice has been done'.[98] Thomas Day
and John Bicknell took a much less complacent view in 'The Dying
Negro', first published in 1773, often reprinted and a leading text in the
Abolitionist movement.[99] The poem, most of which was written by Day,
is again based on actual events. Although it emerges that the writer is of
high rank in his own land, Day does not have him disparage his fellow
slaves, and the word 'Negro' in the title aligns him with them. Instead he
attacks the 'pallid Christians' (p. 133) – a phrase in which the adjective
has a moral as well as a corporal sense – who condone the horrors and
injustices of slavery. His epistle is addressed to his fiancée, a white servant
in the same house whom he had been prevented from marrying when it
had been discovered that he had had himself christened for the purpose.[100]
It therefore overturns taboos of rank as well as of race. Furthermore, not
only does it rebuke the 'pallid tyrants' whose 'softer frames a feeble soul
conceal' (p. 142), but, following the idea of the noble savage and the ideas
of Rousseau, to whom the second edition was dedicated,[101] it honours
'Man's majestic race' in his African form (p. 137). Day also added ethno-
graphical notes to the second edition, but it is the tone of 'The Dying

Negro' that distinguishes it most from other poems of its genre. Unlike many heroic epistles, it does not appeal to his lover to join him – or rather, it does so only to recant almost immediately in case she might persuade him not to take his own life. Its dominant emotions are anger and revenge as the writer calls on the 'Christian God' (p. 146) to curse his captors, and looks forward to Africans conquering Europe to create a juster world.

In a less ambiguous way than is typical of the dramatic monologue, which it almost certainly helped to inspire, the heroic epistle almost always invites sympathy for its subject. The history of the form shows the range of its subjects widening, as was happening in tragedy: first from figures chiefly of myth or legend, as in Ovid, then to the kings, queens and their consorts of Drayton, and finally, in the eighteenth century, to private persons and those – albeit usually royal – of another race. Edward Lovibond's 'Julia's Printed Letter to Lord ——' is an heroic epistle from a seduced and abandoned 'village maid' (p. 89).[102] According to its editor, John Nichols, the poem was first published in the *St. James's Chronicle*,[103] and its aim must in part have been to expose the seducer's conduct. Opening with the address 'insulting Lord!', Lovibond has the woman state her intention to tell her story 'in public characters' (p. 87) and her wish to 'blaze' the man 'to a nation's view' (p. 88), though she decides to 'hide the traitor's name' because she is still in love with him. As so often in the century, it is an appeal on behalf of injured innocence, and it is frequently effective, as when one of its paragraphs ends: 'coward man, to woman brave, / Insults the virtue he was born to save' (p. 91).

Unconventional in a different manner, yet all too familiar in another, are two poems by men written in the persons of men denouncing women who have betrayed them. Thomas Pearson's 'Epistle to a Lady. In the Character of her Husband' rehearses a stock narrative of wifely adultery, predicting that she will be betrayed in turn and sink to prostitution, but ending by offering forgiveness.[104] John Gerrard's 'Epistle from an Unfortunate Gentleman' is an address by a dying man to the 'relentless nymph' who has disdained him, also ending with forgiveness, but not before foreseeing her grief and self-recriminations.[105] Both poems illustrate the impact of Sensibility as a cultural movement – a movement that gave new impetus to the heroic epistle – and also a kind of turn against it. Rather like men claiming disadvantage from feminism in recent times, they accuse the sex that the culture of Sensibility, not to mention the heroic epistle, usually privileges. Yet, at the same time, they are further examples of how poets continued to return to the form and adapt it to different ends.

Although this chapter centres chiefly on the heroic epistle, eighteenth-century letter-writing culture also encouraged epistolary poems between lovers, especially in the earlier part of the period. Amatory epistles from men often follow the familiar *carpe diem* conventions, though there are interesting exceptions. It was less open to women to write poems of such a kind, particularly once the ideology of femininity had taken full hold. However, a series of female-authored love letters, certainly not intended for publication, found its way into the *Barbados Gazette* and later into *Caribbeana*, the two-volume compilation extracted from it.[106] The probable author, Martha Fowke, later Sansom, also wrote other amatory verse. A second type of love poem, quite often found in women's writing, refuses an overture from a man. Two other subtypes consist, first, of poems that, though not themselves amatory, comment on love in interesting ways; and, second, poems that are, in one of the title words for Volume VI of *Bell's Classical Arrangement of Fugitive Poetry*, 'gallant'.[107] This section will illustrate briefly each of these four kinds.

John Hervey's 'A Love Letter' is a good example of a *carpe diem* poem in epistolary mode by a male author.[108] Though it is not paragraphed, the argument unfolds in three clearly defined stages. In the opening 20 lines, the writer sets out his aim of persuading his addressee to consummate their love, the means he may employ, and the motives that may sway her either way. As in much verse of its genre – Marvell's 'To his Coy Mistress' is an obvious example – he combines gentle cajolery with a barely concealed threat of coercion. On the one hand, for instance, he claims he is resorting to 'argument' because 'intercession from a lover' has failed (p. 114), though this also carries the tacit reproach that she has proved unreasonably unresponsive. On the other hand, while his opening sentence, framed as a question ('What can I say to fix thy wav'ring mind [. . .]?'), implies an appeal to her judgement, this is covertly denied by the verb 'force' in the second line. He goes on to suggest that her refusal may stem from cooling love on her part, to represent her choice in terms not of 'inclination' and 'prudence' but 'prudence' and 'heart', and to imply that her choice should also be favoured by 'Gratitude', summarizing his opening case in a flagrant example of persuasive definition: ''Tis virtue to indulge, 'tis wisdom to improve'. This carefully balanced alexandrine neatly concludes the first section and, at the same time, introduces the second, in which he offers the usual *carpe diem* arguments. Though conventional, these are also skilfully turned, as with his use of expressive enjambement in the remark: 'Not ev'n thy charms can bribe the ruthless hand / Of rigid time' (p. 115), and his portrayal of the effects of time on himself too. The latter twist to the convention also has a malicious undertow when he points out the risks he claims she is running: 'cold esteem' may 'succeed to warm desire', or he may fall ill: 'If pain should pall my taste to all thy charms, / Or Death himself should tear me from thy arms'. Towards the end of the poem's second and main part, he distils the traditional plea into the couplet: 'Come then, my love, nor trust the future day, / Live whilst we can, be happy whilst we may', reinforcing it with the poem's only triplet (p. 116).

But the final lines are the most interesting, not least because they help demonstrate the poem's epistolarity. Literary love-letters require ingenious solutions to the problem discussed in Chapter 3 of the external reader's competency,[109] because much that is written by one lover to another may be meaningful to the two alone. Part of that competency is knowledge of the appropriate conventions. This enables readers to appreciate the finesse with which the poem is written, the conventions renewed. Some amatory epistles go no further, but Hervey's poem also employs another device in the closing 18 lines. Here, the poet recalls a night he spent with his beloved in passionate but chaste intimacy as she 'By turns reprov'd [him], and by turns caress'd'. In doing so he reminds her of the strength of their mutual desire and re-emphasizes how non-consummation is affecting him: 'My senses ach, I can no word command'. For the external reader, the effect is to convey a memory of deep closeness, shared by two lovers alone, and so to suggest that the relationship presented was real, that the conventions the poem follows are not merely conventions. Whether or not Hervey refers to an actual relationship there is probably no way of telling, although, in what may have been the poem's first printing, it is addressed 'To ─────'.[110] But the question is beside the point. As a literary epistle, the poem gives apparently personal, private, details that yet remain comprehensible to an external reader. Providing that impression of intimacy, Hervey gives just enough information for such a reader to grasp, from the position almost of voyeur, what for the writer was at stake. In this way the poem's literary nature becomes manifest.

Not all male-authored love poems, however, aim at seduction. Another example in Dodsley's *Collection*, 'An Epistle to a Lady', the author of which remains unknown,[111] could be termed a farewell to love following rejection. Like Hervey's poem, this one too cites circumstances that should be, or appear to be, fully comprehensible only to the addressee. It also falls into three sections, though, unlike Hervey's, it is paragraphed. The opening 20 lines define the writer's position, bereft of his beloved; the main body, the next 35 lines, explain why he has no choice but to let her go; while the final 17 lines further describe his feelings as, having lost his 'only paradise below', he can only 'dread the prospect of succeeding woe'

(p. 209). It is the middle section of the poem that is most interesting from an epistolary point of view, for, by referring to the reasons why the writer has to accept the loss of his beloved, it both engages the external reader and suggests that the situation from which the epistle was written was real, as it may conceivably have been. The cause, it transpires, was 'Scandal' (p. 208) that the writer is not in a position to refute: 'Condemn'd to suffer, but deny'd redress', for a reason that does him credit: 'Too delicate to injure what I love' (pp. 208, 209). Another point of interest about the poem is that the idea of love it expresses is very different from that in Hervey's. The writer claims his passion is 'chaste', 'By reason prompted', and declares: 'In vain I sought a friendship free from fault, / Where sex and beauty were alike forgot' (p. 208). This could be seen as part of an attempt to exculpate himself, but the poem also succeeds in expressing desperate misery, as in its first line – 'When the heart akes with anguish, pines with grief' (p. 207) – and a later couplet: 'So my torn heart must all the sorrows prove / That torture constancy, or sadden love' (p. 209). Again unlike Hervey, who uses the second person singular throughout his poem, this writer emphasizes the distance that now separates him from his addressee by confining himself to the formal plural.

Especially in the eighteenth century, love-letters in verse by women are much rarer than those by men. Martha Fowke, who also wrote the woman's half of *Epistles of Clio and Strephon*, co-authored with William Bond,[112] provides a fair proportion of the exceptions. I have discussed some of these in *A Letter to my Love*, but two cast intriguing light on her amatory epistles. The first, 'To Lady E— H—',[113] does not appear epistolary at first, and it is anything but amatory, but the phrase 'this letter in the press' near the end (72) suggests that it is one of those epistles sent not through the post but through print – so ensuring that the external reader has a grandstand view from the start. Fowke's addressee may have been Eliza Haywood, who had attacked her in print several times; though Haywood was by no means, in the style of the title, a 'Lady', that may have been part of the satirical sting. The poem begins by conceding that its addressee has won, and won by exploiting skills that Fowke has taught her. At the same time, however, Fowke boasts that she invented one of the methods Haywood is now using: 'Did I not the art discover / How, in verse, to hunt a lover?' (13–14). This allows her to celebrate 'the Female Poet' (26) who can make fools of men, and even to link herself with her enemy: 'We're a sort of midnight witches, / Men are our obedient switches' (35). As a result, the poem's tone becomes increasingly scornful, an effect amplified by Fowke's use of singsong trochaic tetrameter couplets with ludicrous extra syllables to complete some of the lines: 'wand-a'/'hand-a' (19–20), 'fret-a'/'coquet-a' (33–4).[114] Not only men but the addressee too are the targets of her scorn, the poem ending by complimenting itself: 'Which, for wit, deserves a name-a / In the brazen book of fame-a' (73–4).

'To Lady E— H—' is an extraordinary if distinctly unappealing poem. If Fowke's boasts are true, though, they suggest that she was adept at using verse to ensnare lovers. A possible example of such a poem is 'To Cleon's Eyes', first printed six years previously.[115] Again, at first reading the poem may not appear epistolary, but it is in effect a love letter. Its message is paradoxical. On the face of it, the poem says: 'Your eyes tell me you love me, and I like that because they are more truthful than words, whether spoken or written'. Covertly, however, it is a very clever invitation, a come-on, indicating that she knows the addressee is attracted to her, and that she reciprocates the attraction, while remaining apparently demure because she is telling him not to put it into words. This is one way in which a woman might, just, get round the taboos against a woman expressing attraction to a man to whom she is not married, and it produces a poem centred on an interesting idea – 'there is poetry in eyes' (14) – that conveys both tender feeling and subtly veiled eroticism, as in the sounds, rhythm and imagery of the closing lines, the last two lengthened:

> Or if kind souls must sound at all,
> Slow be the words and gently fall;
> As winds that whisper, and with tremblings move
> The newborn blossoms of the infant grove. (31–4)

Here, the erotic invitation is framed all the more skilfully as a concession: 'if we must talk, let us talk very softly'.

There are two further paradoxes in 'To Cleon's Eyes'. First, the poem's mode of address is oblique, for it is not addressed 'To Cleon'. Instead, the title suggests that, true to its central principle, it prefers ocular to verbal communication. Second, despite the same principle, it is, precisely, a communication not only in words but in writing. This raises the question how far the poem is playing with the notions it is elaborating, and so too a further question, one that applies to other amatory verse of the period by women: how far it is to be read as autobiographical. A case in point is *Clio*, Fowke's autobiography-cum-apologia-cum-extended-love-letter that she addressed in 1723 to Aaron Hill, not intended for publication and printed only 19 years later, after Hill's death.[116] Like the poems printed in the *Barbados Gazette*, the work gives every impression of passionate, even abject, devotion to its addressee, yet the boasts about ensnaring lovers in verse in 'To Lady E— H—' open that devotion to question.

Either Fowke was not as much in control in her love affairs as that poem pretends, or it was part of her ploy to pretend to be out of control. Whatever the truth of the matter, which will probably never be known, she was a very subtle and interesting writer of amatory epistles.

In *The Family, Sex and Marriage in England 1500–1800*, Lawrence Stone considers the marital story of Mary Granville, later Pendarves, later still Delany, and remarks: 'The case of Mrs Pendarves shows how in the eighteenth century even an upper-class girl, if married against her will to an obviously incompatible husband, was constantly subjected to invitations to adultery by married and unmarried men of her own social status.'[117] Several poems by women of the period not only confirm the point but suggest that in some cases not even a compatible husband was a barrier. Among these are verse epistles by Sarah Fyge Egerton and Lady Mary Wortley Montagu that rebuff men for sexual harassment. Both begin dramatically, as if all but incredulous of sexual propositions to them from married men: 'What is't you mean, that I am thus approached?' (Fyge Egerton, 'The Repulse to Alcander'), and 'Is it to me, this sad lamenting strain?' (Wortley Montagu, 'An Answer to a Love-Letter in Verse').[118] Fyge Egerton goes on to tell how she has tried to make sense of her addressee's behaviour and insists she has done nothing to encourage him, while, at the same time, drawing attention to the constraints on a woman's behaviour. Her poem ends by emphasizing how Alcander is attacking not only her virtue but her reputation – either by false boasts on his own account (49–50), or through gossip spread by others (51–4). Wortley Montagu is more aggressive, widening her attack very quickly from the addressee, who is only recently married, to men in general – 'How vile is man!' (7). She goes further than Fyge Egerton with the charge 'In sport you break the heart, and rend the fame' (16), but follows it up with the statement that, having fallen in love once and been hurt, she is impervious to future assaults. Wortley Montagu ends by wishing a broken heart on her harasser as a taste of his own medicine, and rounds the poem off with a powerful simile of rakes who have played highwaymen for fun, in order to enjoy the torment of their victims, being brought to justice.

Both these poems raise special questions about the reader's position, and the author's. Like Hervey's epistle and 'An Epistle to a Lady', they provide enough information for an external reader both to understand what is at issue and to believe that they were actual communications sent to real addressees. But several different positions are open for the reader to occupy. Reading as a woman, it is easier to assume the writer's role than if reading as a man, not only because the writer is female but also because the behaviour of men is under attack. The result in the one case might be to extend or confirm views, or experience, of men; in the other it would be more uncomfortable. Reading as a man, the position offered is that of the male addressee, which would be still more uncomfortable; whereas, reading as a woman, the addressee's position might offer a sense of his likely humiliation almost at first hand. These various alternatives illustrate how potent a means epistolary verse can be for raising such questions. But another complication is the relation between author and letter-writer. It is most often assumed that both poems, and others like them, are autobiographical; and supporting evidence is sometimes given where it is available.[119] Yet the assumption is not always a necessary one. Thomas Hardy remarks in the prefaces to three of his collections that, in the words of one of them, 'The pieces are in a large degree dramatic or personative in conception; and this even when they are not obviously so.'[120] While, in the case of some of these poems, his aim was probably to distance himself from biographically sensitive material, it is conceivable that, even if not 'dramatic or personative in conception', poems such as the two just considered developed in that direction. Irrespective of how directly they refer to events that had actually taken place, their effect is to dramatize critical situations, in this case for a woman, and so all the better to expose abuses that were all but taken for granted.

Some verse epistles by women, however, are based on verifiable facts. Among them are Fyge Egerton's 'To One Who Said I Must Not Love' and Mehetabel Wright's 'Address to her Husband'.[121] Both stem from unhappy marriages, and both are startlingly angry. Fyge Egerton demands the passion of love as her birthright, however painful or dangerous its impact. She declares that she cannot help loving even though, it turns out, loving is a sin as far as she is concerned because she is married – to a man she does not love. The poem implies that she has fallen in love with someone who either does not or cannot reciprocate, leading her to try not only flirtation but marriage as alternatives. As Warren Chernaik suggests, the poem probably refers to her second marriage, to Thomas Egerton, at a time when she was still in love with Henry Pierce.[122] The poem is frank and vehement, opening with a series of dramatic similes, and using other graphic images such as 'fettered soul' (15) and 'double slave' (16). It states the case for a woman trapped in an unhappy marriage with uncompromising directness. Wright's poem differs in several respects. First, it specifies her addressee. However, though it may indeed have been given or sent to her husband, it was probably meant to be read by members of her family as well. Second, Wright chafes less against marriage, as Fyge Egerton does, despite her protests against it elsewhere,[123] than what she claims is her addressee's failure to honour his role as husband. Third, the poem is remarkable for its change of tone: quiet and temperate at first, it increasingly expresses anger and defiance. After line 52, when Wright has described herself as wearing 'an endless smile' for her husband, her tone and attitude alter decisively. It is as if, having described how hard she has tried to please him and defer to him, she feels she has the right to challenge his failure to reciprocate – indeed, she positively lets rip in attacking his friends and the kind of entertainment he enjoys with them. A poem that set out as an attempt to plead with her husband thus ends as an ultimatum to him to change his ways: 'Soft as I am, I'll make thee see / I will not brook contempt from thee!' (73–4).

A further difference between Wright's poem and Fyge Egerton's is that Wright did not necessarily intend hers to be printed. This does not, however, affect the various positions that the external reader may occupy; that epistolary principle still applies. Another difference still is that, unlike Wortley Montagu's poem, and the two by Fyge Egerton, Wright's uses iambic tetrameter rather than pentameter couplets. Although tetrameters are much more common in light verse, and also in amatory verse that, like Fowke's 'To Cleon's Eyes', sets out to pay court, Wright obtains force and directness from the shorter line. But perhaps most striking of all is that none of the four examples by Fyge Egerton, Wortley Montagu and Wright appears to borrow in any significant way from the heroic epistle, despite the fact that it was the contemporary form that dealt with the predicament of suffering, vulnerable women. This may suggest that they saw it as a masculine domain and that other kinds of response from women to oppression were required. The point is made by Jane Barker in a sardonic poem from the late seventeenth century addressed to Ovid's heroines that begins: 'Bright Shees, what Glories had your Names acquir'd, / Had you consum'd those whom your Beauties fir'd, / Had laugh'd to see them burn, and so retir'd'.[124]

Iambic tetrameter couplets were also often chosen for the many poems, male-authored by definition, that *Bell's Classical Arrangement* termed 'gallant'. Originating in the later seventeenth century, the number of these that appear in collections such as those by Dodsley, Pearch and Nichols, as well as Bell, indicates their appeal to readers of the period. There is no space here to explore the reasons for their popularity, though it probably grew from the rise of politeness and refinement as key social and cultural values in that long process by which the bourgeoisie took over styles of conduct from the aristocracy in order to enhance its legitimacy.[125] In the gallant as opposed to the amatory epistle, the emphasis is more on skilful compliments to the addressee than tenders of love, and the fact that the epistle is intended to be read by others as well as the addressee is more marked. Three examples already mentioned are those between Sir Charles Hanbury Williams and, purportedly, Mrs Bindon, the first two of which are, unusually, in anapestic metre suggesting humorous play.[126] Another is George Canning's 'Birth-Day Offering to a Young Lady. From her Lover', which begins by reflecting wryly on the fact that he is eleven years older but goes on to consider the effect of future years on them both, ending with a compliment that epitomizes bourgeois gallantry: 'Still in my heart she'll hold her throne, / Still in my eyes be twenty-one'.[127]

Many poems of the gallant type accompany a gift, so enabling them not only to suggest discrimination on the part of the writer, depending on its nature, but also to provide a topic around which to build compliments. Among the examples in Bell, gifts include 'a Bough of an Orange Tree' (enabling the compliment: 'See the young fruit thy power confess, / And love their own Bermudas less'), 'a Present of Shells and Stones Designed for *a Grotto*' ('How sweet, how charming, will appear this Grot, / When by your art to full perfection brought!'), and 'a Book of Morality, Entitled *Visions*' ('For nature now triumphantly can shew / A living instance of those rules in You').[128] Other examples build their compliments on one of the addressee's special qualities or talents, such as 'To a Lady, in Answer to a Letter Written in a Very Fine Hand' ('Throughout the finish'd piece we see display'd / Th' exactest image of the lovely maid'), 'To Miss Charlotte Collins, of Winchester, on Her Drawing the Judgment of Paris' ('Why copy then what Fiction drew, / When Nature holds herself to view!') and 'To a Young Lady, on Seeing Her Dance' ('May you, thro' life's perplexing maze, / Direct your steps with equal praise').[129] The last of these poems represents a variant of the form in which compliment is turned to morality – again, of course, for the external reader's benefit as well as that of the addressee. One of the best examples of this type, also included by Bell, is Samuel Johnson's 'To a Young Lady, on Her Playing upon the Harpsichord, in a Room Hung with Some Flower-Pieces of her own Painting', which Howard Weinbrot calls 'a splendid poem advising "Stella" how to navigate in the shoals of sexual attraction'.[130] While the circumstantial title specifies its addressee and occasion closely, the moral application is clearly not only for her but for any other reader.

Bell's 'epistles gallant' are intermingled with 'epistles panegyrical', the object of which is also to compliment. The difference is that the complimentary epistle proper has little or, much more often, no amatory element. For this reason, and to provide a contrast with the satirical epistle, it is considered in the next and final chapter.

6
Satirical and Complimentary

Just as satire is one of the most important genres of eighteenth-century verse, so it provides one of the commonest modes for verse epistles in the period. Complimentary verse is now much less well known, but in its day it was widely practised and it also often took epistolary form. Though it may seem odd to couple the two in the same chapter, in different ways they further help define the culture of the eighteenth-century verse epistle. In one sense, they are two sides of the same coin, for, as Abigail Williams remarks, 'To put it in the crudest terms, those who supported the political establishment tend to write panegyrics, verse eulogies on affairs of state or public figures, while those who opposed it wrote poetic satires criticizing the regime and mocking its supporters.'[1] Indeed, as branches of epideictic rhetoric, the function of which is to praise or blame, panegyric and satire are closely related.[2] Like examples of these genres in other literary forms, satirical and complimentary epistles share the same duality.

But there also deeper ways in which satirical and complimentary epistles are related. In particular, as David Fairer argues, it is misleading to assume that, somewhere around the middle of the century, there occurred a shift '"from Satire to Sensibility"': 'Between 1700 and 1800, these modes, with their subjective and objective emphases, existed side by side.'[3] In much the same way, the complimentary epistle coexisted throughout the century with the satirical. Introducing a survey of the period, Pat Rogers offered an alternative view of the same paradox by juxtaposing an older with a newer way of characterizing it: George Saintsbury's 'place of Rest and Refreshment', and the emphasis given by Martin Price to 'dialectical excess'.[4] As Rogers observes, 'There is undoubtedly a superficial calm about much eighteenth-century writing; a well-bred air of self-possession and decent restraint', while, nevertheless, 'strong currents of feeling often stream beneath this apparently untroubled surface'.[5] A society of increasing refinement and politeness was at the same time a polity of conflicting interests. This chapter considers the contrasting epistolary forms that reflect and embody such reciprocities. In *Satire: A Critical Reintroduction*, Dustin Griffin notes: 'Whether or not satire and epistle can be distinguished in Horace (and in Pope) is a question that continues to vex and divide critics.'[6] As Griffin shows, the formal mixture that characterizes much satire helps explain the dilemma. While the term was often derived falsely from the Greek *satyros*, meaning a horse- or goat-like creature, it in fact stems from the Latin *satura lanx*, or full dish, meaning a mixture.[7] Griffin argues that formal as well as verbal play is an essential though often neglected element in many satires, and this illustrates the genre's tendency to transgress all kinds of decorum, including generic boundaries. Pope's *Epistle to Dr. Arbuthnot* is a case in point, as it is more dialogue than letter. Similarly, in the Index he added to the 1721 edition of his *Poems*, Allan Ramsay placed 'The Rise and Fall of Stocks' not under 'Epistolary' but 'Satyrick', even though he included the word 'Epistle' in its subtitle.[8] There is much other evidence of satire's mixed nature. For instance, although iambic pentameter couplets are the preferred metre for formal verse satire, among the epistolary poems on which I have collected data fewer than half of the 168 that could be classed as satirical are in that form. The rest are in a range of metres that, for the eighteenth century, is profuse: 28 in iambic tetrameter couplets, 24 in anapestic tetrameter couplets, 11 in irregular forms, 8 in the 'Song to David' stanza, 7 in quatrains, and 4 in other stanzaic units, including 2 in Standard Habby. Blank verse is a notable exception, though it was often used for parodic or mock-heroic purposes in non-epistolary verse, and though there is a marginal satirical example in Thomas Warton's 'Epistle, from Thomas Hearn, Antiquary, to the Author of the Companion to the Oxford Guide'.[9] These figures are influenced, of course, by assumptions about how an epistolary verse satire might be defined – assumptions that allow, for example, the inclusion of the 19 poems in Christopher Anstey's *New Bath Guide* and *An Election Ball*, 14 of which are in anapestic measure,[10] and also the verse of Peter Pindar (John Wolcot) and Anthony Pasquin (John Williams), which is often formally diverse. Nevertheless, they are part of the evidence for the mixed and miscellaneous nature of satire, in eighteenth-century epistolary verse as elsewhere.

Two other parts of that evidence are the elastic length of epistolary satire in the period and the generic transgressions outlined above that so often complicate its definition. A verse satire is as long as a piece of string, whether in letter form or not, and epistolary examples range from Christopher Jones's 'To an Injudicious Critic, Who Assumed the Name of

Cato Censor', at 20 lines, to John Wolcot's *Brother Peter to Brother Tom. An Expostulatory Epistle*, which runs to over 800.[11] Satire, too, always feels free to tackle any subject, whether its target is an individual, a social or cultural practice, an institution, or a whole society. For this and other reasons, it constitutionally crosses, flouts or blatantly overturns generic boundaries. Examples to be considered in the course of the following discussion will include versions of the heroic epistle, the verse essay and the complimentary poem. And, although Lady Mary Wortley Montagu is one of the few eighteenth-century women to have produced epistolary verse satire, her work illustrates its transgressive tendencies very well. As mentioned in Chapter 5, 'Epistle from Arthur G[ra]y' is both an Ovidian epistle, though its author is female and its nominal writer male, and, on more than one level, a satire; while, to give another example, 'P[ope] to Bolingbroke' is a witty send-up of the complimentary epistle,[12] further illustrating the point made at the start of this chapter: polite and offensive often rubbed shoulders in the period.

Given that both satire and epistle are inherently such mixed forms, it might seem impossible to resolve the problem of definition cited by Griffin. A possible solution, however, is to focus on what is specifically epistolary in a particular verse satire; and Janet Altman's concept of 'addressee-consciousness'[13] again provides a way forward. Crucially, it enables two kinds of distinction: first, between various modes of relation between writer and readers (whether addressed explicitly or not); second, between varying degrees of epistolarity in satirical writing.

The primary difference in relations between writer and reader(s) hinges on whether the one addresses the other(s) in his or her own guise or in a guise that is assumed. This is not to imply that, in poems addressed as from the biographical author, the writer may be equated with that author, for almost any literary expression – satirical more than most – to some extent requires playing a role. Nevertheless, there is still a large and easily identifiable difference between, for instance, Pope's role as addresser in his *Epistle to Burlington* and the role that the brash Whig loyalist Nicholas Amhurst plays in *A Congratulatory Epistle from his Holiness the Pope to the Reverend Dr. Snape*.[14] A large number of eighteenth-century satirical epistles are, to use the term introduced in Chapter 1, dramatic in this sense. But, to begin with those addressed as from the author, rather than from some other real or invented figure, the next set of distinctions is between various types of addressee. The two main types require that the addressee be specified, a function usually performed by the title. In one case he or she can be relied on to support the poet's position; in the other, he or she is the satirical butt. These opposite kinds of addressee may be termed sympathizer and adversary. Examples of sympathetic addressees in satirical epistles, mostly identified in their titles, include all four in Pope's *Epistles to Several Persons*; Pope himself in various satires, including Young's *Two Epistles to Mr. Pope* and Paul Whitehead's *The State Dunces*; George, Lord Ramsay, in Allan Ramsay's 'The Rise and Fall of Stocks'; and the Reverend Dr. Mann in the poem addressed to him by Henry Jones.[15] Such epistles often name as the addressee a figure not only sympathetic to the writer but prestigious in some way – like three of Pope's addressees, all well-known and titled, in *Epistles to Several Persons*, or Pope himself in the epistles addressed to him by Young and Whitehead. By doing so they create a comfortable space for the external reader, who is invited to identify with the values both of the writer and of the person addressed. The potential importance of such a space is difficult to overstate. If it is constructed skilfully, it increases the prospect that the external reader will endorse the views that the epistle expresses.

It goes without saying that the dynamics of satirical epistles addressed by the writer in his or her own person to an adversary are very different. This type is also common in the eighteenth century, though, more often than the first type, it is complicated by anonymity. Where the identity of the writer is stated, as in Welsted's *Of Dulness and Scandal. Occasion'd by the Character of Lord Timon*, or in Churchill's *Epistle to William Hogarth*,[16] orientation for the reader may be easier. Where it is not, the writer may instead define a position that invites sympathy, support or collusion on the part of the external reader, as Akenside does through the role of outraged patriot in his *Epistle to Curio*, or William Combe in his various epistles ridiculing public figures.[17] Otherwise, there is a greater risk of alienating a reader who has not already taken sides, as with *Verses Address'd to the Imitator of the First Satire of the Second Book of Horace*, now seen as probably the joint work of Lady Mary Wortley Montagu and Lord Hervey.[18] Even then, however, much will depend on the extent to which the external reader is prepared to accept the satirist's viewpoint. In such epistles to adversaries, it is unlikely that the external reader will want to occupy the same position as the addressee. He or she is much more likely to prefer siding with the writer – for obvious reasons, invariably the response encouraged – or standing on the touchline as an interested if not necessarily impartial observer. Taking the writer's side allows vicarious indignation, provided always that, in the view of readers, he or she does not go too far; while the touchline offers different kinds of satisfaction, ranging from critical detachment to *Schadenfreude*.

Two other kinds of reader-relation may be offered by epistles addressed as from the author rather than another figure. Instead of specifying a particular addressee, the first type invokes a general reader. Such a reader is usually assumed to be sympathetic; he or she will normally also either possess one or more special competencies or be in need of instruction. Epistles that adopt versions of this strategy include James Bramston's 'The Art of Politicks', and two by the Warton brothers: 'Fashion' (Joseph), and 'Newmarket' (Thomas).[19] Secondly, the author may address a fictional figure represented by a type-name. Though not a common ploy, this is appropriate for an epistle conveying general advice or for use by a writer who prefers to avoid giving offence. Mary Leapor uses it in 'Advice to Myrtillo', a kind of streetwise *Art of Poetry* in which the tongue-in-cheek counsel is aimed to produce maximum monetary advantage.[20]

Epistles in which the author plays a role not his or her own provide different ways of defining relations between writer and readers. The two main positions in such epistles may be termed butt and stand-in – the former, obviously, being the satirical target, the latter the position from which that target is attacked. Various permutations are then possible: butt to butt, as with Lady Mary Wortley Montagu's 'P[ope] to Bolingbroke', or the anonymous *The Golden Age*, supposedly addressed by Erasmus Darwin to Thomas Beddoes; stand-in to butt (Jonathan Smedley's 'Cloe to Mr. Tickell, Occasioned by his Avignon-Letter'); butt to stand-in (William Preston's *Seventeen Hundred and Seventy-Seven; Or, a Picture of the Manners and Character of the Age. In an Epistle from a Lady of Quality, in England, to Omiah, at Otaheite*); and stand-in to stand-in (the anonymous *Historic Epistle, from Omiah, to the Queen of Otaheite; Being his Remarks on the English Nation*).[21] The writer may also assume, ironically, a stock attitude for purposes of satirizing it, rather than the role of a particular butt. In such cases the address is to a general reader who has the (limited) competency needed to appreciate the joke. An especially good example is the boorish guise that James Bramston adopted for *The Man of Taste*, epitomized by its principle that 'True Taste to me is by this touchstone known, / That's always best that's nearest to my own' (p. 312), and its conclusion: 'This is true Taste, and whoso likes it not / Is blockhead, coxcomb, puppy, fool, and sot' (p. 326).[22] Such an epistle all but requires the reader to take up a position close to the author's in order to enjoy, and avoid endorsing, the nominal writer's self-exposed stupidity and prejudice. It is a highly effective form of persuasion.

Limits on space preclude detailed illustration of the whole range of strategies I have outlined. However, discussion of a few examples may help put some flesh on these dry analytical categories, and bring out more fully what kinds, and degrees, of epistolarity they enable. To take two poems less well known than those by Pope (or indeed Bramston), Allan Ramsay's 'The Rise and Fall of Stocks' and Henry Jones's 'To the Reverend Dr. Mann' are epistolary satires that deploy an identifiable writer and a named, sympathetic addressee in quite different ways. Ramsay's poem is a satire on the bursting of the South Sea Bubble. Addressed 'to the Right Honourable my Lord *Ramsay*, now in *Paris*', it was published in 1721, apparently both as a pamphlet and in the first volume of the author's *Poems*.[23] The addressee was the eldest son of the Earl of Dalhousie – whom, Ramsay's modern editors explain, the poet regarded as the chief of his clan.[24] As he would have been about 20 when the poem was written, he would probably have been finishing his education on the Continent in the manner of aristocrats of the period. He was, then, a prestigious addressee but one to whom, on account of his youth, Ramsay might presume to offer advice. Even more to the point, his absence authorized the giving of news – probably also with an eye, his editors suggest, to the virtually simultaneous collapse of John Law's Mississippi System in France.[25] If Ramsay intended such an allusion, he chose not to make it explicit, possibly because Law was also a Scot.

The poem begins with a respectful 'MY LORD', outside the verse line, and its second paragraph opens deferentially with an 'Allow me then' and a 'with your Leave' (9, 13).[26] It ends with equal courtesy, but also with a perhaps unexpected warmth and informality: 'God grant your Lordship Joy and Health, / Lang Days of Rowth of real Wealth; / Safe to the Land of Cakes Heav'n send ye, / And frae cross Accidents defend ye' (193–6). The salutation and valediction frame Ramsay's comments on the crisis, which range from rueful to acerbic, and are in Hudibrastics as lively as his colloquial Scots. In the body of the poem, however, he addresses Lord Ramsay directly only when imagining the prospects had there been no crash: 'O wow, my Lord, these had been Days / Which might have claimed your Poet's lays' (135–6). Elsewhere, he uses the first person plural in a way that offers to include other readers as well – and, more important still, not just Scots. On the one hand, the poem is full not only of Scottish expressions but idioms that might not have been meaningful to those from south of the Border. For instance, while 'Land of Cakes', for Scotland, is an example that the context explains, the word 'Rowth' in the previous line, meaning 'plenty', is not so easily understood. On the other hand, Ramsay went out of his way to make the poem accessible to those without knowledge of Scots. Not only did he provide footnotes for words or phrases that might need explanation, but, from the first, he included in collections of his *Poems* a full Glossary.[27] The poem's intended readership might therefore be described as extending outwards from Lord Ramsay to fellow Scots and then to fellow Britons. For example, when he refers to his addressee leaving '*Lothian* and the *Edge-well* Tree' (12), the allusion to a family tradition requires a note that even Scottish readers may have welcomed, but they would not have needed telling that '*John a Groat's House*' (16) is, as another note puts it, 'The Northmost House in *Scotland*'. The latter reference is especially significant because it occurs in a couplet that makes it unmistakable that Ramsay is addressing not just a Scottish but a British catastrophe: 'Since Poortith o'er ilk Head does hover / Frae *John a Groat's* House, South to *Dover*'.

Ramsay also uses the first person plural to convey a sense not only of collective suffering but collective responsibility. The suffering is clear from the start, when he portrays 'our poor bambouzl'd Nation, / Biting her Nails, her Knuckles wringing, / Her Cheek sae blae, her Lip sae hinging' (4–5); but so too, from early on, is the fact that people have no one but themselves to blame: 'We madly at our ain Expences, / Stock-job'd away our Cash and Senses' (21–2). The latter remark tacitly includes Ramsay too, like another one later in the poem when he comments: 'We thought that Dealer's Stock an ill ane, / That was not wordy haf a Million' (123–4). But Ramsay also brings himself into the poem more directly. First, he illustrates the impact of the crash on himself as on others by referring to its impact on his plans to publish his collection: 'O had this Golden Age but lasted, / And no sae soon been broke and blasted, / There is a Person well I ken / Might wi' the best gane right far ben' (127–8). The effect is to personalize both epistle, as an address from a citizen affected by the crisis to a senior member of his clan, and satire, half-angry from hurt and vexation, half-rueful because aware of error. Second, Ramsay mentions his earlier satire on the Bubble, *Wealth, Or, the Woody* (164–5), in which, he declares: 'Rapt into future Months, I sa' / The rich Aerial *Babel* fa''' (167–8). Yet, in pointing out that he had foreseen the crisis and warned against it, he avoids self-righteousness or recriminations, and, in the final part of the poem that follows, he looks forward to 'a sweeter Scene' (175) of justice and prosperity when '*Britons* shall smile at Follies past' (192). This willingness to look on the bright side, and to accept some of the responsibility for the crash, is uncharacteristic of satire, yet it gives the poem the kind of buoyancy and self-confidence that might help its readers to move on. It is as if Ramsay is discussing family troubles – he twice uses extended similes from children's games (23–32, 89–96) – but with an open heart as well as a critical eye. He brings to satire the warmth of a familiar epistle, and, it may be argued, the satire is all the more effective for it.

Henry Jones's poem is much more formal, though its full title is familiar enough: 'To the Reverend Dr. Mann, Occasioned by the Author's Asking Him for a Subject to Write on, and His Saying He Could Think of None'.[28] His motive stated, Jones launches straight into his theme, seeking to drive his reader into responding with a string of questions beginning: 'Is ev'ry moral Subject found so trite? / Hath wholsome Satire nothing new to write?' (1–2). Because he does not salute his addressee at the start, the external reader is invoked immediately, and indeed he makes little reference to the clergyman to whom the poem is inscribed until near the end. The reason for this is probably that, unlike Ramsay, who could assume that his Scottish readers, at least, would know his identity, and probably also that of his addressee, Jones could not. As William Christmas points out, his status as artisan and Irishman made him doubly marginal, and his prefatory 'Advertisement' plays down any claim on his part 'to the Rank of a Poet', adding that 'It will be needless, perhaps, to declare, that he has had no Assistance from Learning.'[29] Similarly, his addressee, a clergyman whose first significant preferment, as Archdeacon of Dublin, did not occur until 1757, eight years after the poem was first published, is likely to have been little known outside Ireland's capital.[30] All the same, Mann was an appropriate addressee for an epistle that seeks to 'Inlist a Poet on Religion's Side' (20). Jones can welcome him as a 'Friend' who can help him expose the neglect and abuse of the Christianity that his satirical targets profess, as when he begins his attack: 'Say first, Why rolls the Force of Fashion's Tide / So smoothly swift against Religion's Side?' (51–2). He can also cite Mann as a positive example, a 'rev'rend Patriot' (155) who was also, apparently, an historian and a poet (156, 157), ending by celebrating him as 'so bright a Guide, so good a Friend' (186). Even so, he borrows a supporter, 'thy lov'd Lelius', from him, asking: 'And give me leave, for once, to call him mine' (179–180), presumably because he had no one else in an appropriate social position to call upon.[31]

The fact that Mann is only an implicit addressee for much of the poem tends to encourage the external reader to stand in for him. This happens in a different way from in Ramsay's epistle, where the appeal, through the first person plural, is also to a collective knowledge. Here, it is instead the external reader who is invited to respond to the poem's insistent opening questions. At one point Jones even creates an interlocutor in order to put an expected objection so that he may answer it:

'But why such Wealth and Grandeur? Why so great?
'Like Lords attended, and like Kings they eat.'
This more betrays the Rancour of your Will,

> You'd have the Clergy barefoot Beggars still, [. . .]
> The Wealth they have was by the State bestow'd;
> Or rather paid them as a Debt it ow'd. (129–36)

This interrogative manner is much closer to the style of Pope's satirical epistles than to that of Ramsay's, confirming Eric Rothstein's remark, quoted by Christmas, that several of the poems in the same collection 'make one think of both Pope and Johnson'.[32] Like Pope, Jones cites satirical examples with type-names from Juvenal – 'Smart *Virro*' and '*Sporus*' (95–102, 103) – but also celebrates models (in this case clerical) from past and present: Hugh Boulter, Archbishop of Armagh, George Berkeley, Bishop of Cloyne and philosopher, and Henry Maule, Bishop of Meath.[33] Christmas argues that Jones wrote 'the sort of verse epistles that recall an earlier age because they are addressed to specific audiences and exhibit a strong sense of historical topicality', but that he did so not for stylistic reasons but 'because they allow him to discuss current social issues and to maintain a political stance in his writing'.[34] There may also have been some opportunism in this, though the only sense in which Christmas applies the word concerns Jones's adroitness in exploiting fashionable poetic conventions.[35] As an outsider trying to establish a career as a poet, Jones may have deferred to expediency more than Christmas allows, especially as he was invoking Protestant clerics in a country in which, unlike in England, Catholicism was the majority religion. All the same, the ways in which he employs the conventions of the satirical epistle both help illustrate standard practice and cast light on how his particular position led him to modify it.

Adversarial satirical epistles also construct various forms of addressee- and reader-relations. At one extreme there is downright obloquy, as in Wortley Montagu and Hervey's *Verses Address'd to the Imitator of the First Satire of the Second Book of Horace*, which mocks Pope's physical appearance ('our own Species in Burlesque' [13]), his character and status ('Hard as thy Heart, and as thy Birth obscure' [20]), and his satire ('You, only coarsely rail, or darkly sneer' [28]), threatens him with beating ('Sure 'tis as fair to beat who cannot fight, / As 'tis to libel those who cannot write' [62–3]), and ends by cursing him: 'But as thou hate'st, be hated by Mankind, / And with the Emblem of thy crooked Mind, / Mark'd on thy Back, like *Cain*, by God's own Hand; / Wander like him, accursed through the Land' (110–11).[36] David Fairer points out how cleverly, and cruelly, the epistle isolates its addressee the more to expose him: 'The spotlight is on him alone, cut off from his accustomed social context of readers and friends'; and Isobel Grundy rightly calls it 'the most outrageous as well as the most poetically forceful of all the attacks on Pope'.[37] Yet, as Grundy also mentions, eighteenth-century print culture provided powerful means of counter-attack, for James McLaverty has shown that a version of the poem may have been printed at Pope's instigation in order to justify satire he had already published and to license satire to come.[38] Whatever the truth of the matter, this type of epistle is likely to polarize the responses of readers not directly or indirectly addressed, and all the more if the author's identity is known – part of McLaverty's case turns on the epistle's ascription: 'By a Lady'.[39] From an external position it may, in the heated and often intemperate print culture of its period, have been possible to appreciate the wit amidst the abuse. But, while readers hostile to Pope may have found the engineer well hoist with his own petard, sympathizers will have found it a disgusting libel.

An alternative method to that of the author(s) of *Verses* is to ridicule rather than thrash. This is the strategy of William Mason's *Heroic Epistle to Sir William Chambers*, according to the *ODNB* entry on its author 'one of the best-selling poems of the eighteenth century', and to a lesser extent of its sequel, *An Heroic Postscript*.[40] Mason's main weapon is mock-heroic afflatus, so he begins the first poem by hailing his addressee with a title bestowed in Sweden but risibly inflated for Britons: 'Knight of the Polar Star!' If, in the remark quoted by Pope, 'Praise undeserv'd is satire in disguise',[41] exaggerating the one heightens the other, as when Mason defers to 'the gracious ear / Of him, whom we and all the world admit, / Patron of science, taste, and wit' (15–16). The satire is on Chambers's precepts and practice as a prestigious designer of gardens, especially in the Chinese style that he had advocated in his *Dissertation on Oriental Gardening* (1772),[42] but much of it is oblique. Though Mason addresses Chambers with obvious scorn when he asks to be taught 'Like thee to scorn Dame Nature's simple fence; / Leap each Ha Ha of truth and common sense' (11–12),[43] more often he mocks him at second hand by poking fun at his supporters or his patron George III, or by parodying his treatise. He disposes of the philosopher David Hume, for example, in a few lines of which 'The fattest Hog of Epicurus' stye' (24) is the most pungent, and he paints a picture of a chaotic festival supposedly based on Chinese traditions in which anything is permitted, including to triumphant Jews: 'They seize, they bind, they circumcise C[harle]s F[o]x' (132). Mason quotes from Chambers at length in elaborate notes, but he also alludes to the best-known champions of the aesthetic principles that he accuses his addressee of transgressing, quoting Pope with calculated anti-climax in the line '"A work to wonder at, perhaps a" Kew' (70).[44] These tactics to some extent displace the attack from Chambers to other representatives, for Mason, of cultural perversion – including the King. In doing so they, along with his handling of mock-heroic idiom, discourage the response that the satire is vindictive or personal. Not only does Mason seek to enlist the external reader in such ironic phrases as 'we and all the world', already quoted, 'as we feel' (42), and 'Brentford with London's charms will we adorn' (111), but he could rely on widespread dislike for many of his targets, not excepting the King himself. Although he took pains to preserve his anonymity, his epistolary and satirical tactics also helped insulate him from the opprobrium to which lampoons are liable, and to which Wortley Montagu was exposed not only by the very different tactics of *Verses* but by the imputation that she was the writer.

An alternative form of anonymity is the adoption of a different name and identity from one's own. As mentioned above, the satirical dramatic epistle originated in the Restoration.[45] After enjoying renewed favour in the early part of the eighteenth century,[46] it came back into its own in the 1760s, perhaps partly in reaction to Churchill's satires, which are nothing if not direct.[47] Martin S. Day has demonstrated the extensive influence, stretching well into the nineteenth century, not only of Mason's *Heroic Epistle* but of a quite different work first published in 1766, Christopher Anstey's *New Bath Guide*.[48] As the *Guide* specializes in humorous ridicule rather than full-blown satire, preserving his anonymity was less important to Anstey than for Mason with the *Heroic Epistle* and its successors. Nevertheless, except briefly in the Epilogue that he added to the original book soon after its first publication,[49] he did not write in his own voice. Instead, he channels his commentary on Bath life and the fashions and fads of the period through three fictional visitors writing home. Ten letters of the original 15 are from 'Mr. S[imkin] B[lu]n[de]r[hea]d' to his mother in Northumberland, nine of them arranged in two continuous sequences, one of five letters and the other of four. All are almost wholly in anapestic tetrameter couplets. Three are from 'J[enny] W[il]d[ai]r' to 'Lady Eliz. M[o]d[ele]ss' in the same county, and the remaining one is from Simkin's sister Prudence to the same addressee. These are in various verse forms, sometimes in the same letter, but the main ones are iambic quatrains that alternate rhyming tetrameters and trimeters, iambic tetrameter couplets and trochaic tetrameter couplets. In the first edition, neither addressee is given a reply but has the role simply, in William Ray's phrase, of 'post-box', though Anstey later added a letter to Jenny from Lady Elizabeth.[50] Anstey uses his main character, Simkin, both as butt – the name means a fool (*OED*) – and as naïve exposer of the follies and vices of others. The reader is therefore invited to occupy the position of confidant(e) but also of amused and superior onlooker as Simkin's naïvety leads him into errors and troubles. Though Jenny's commentary is more alert, so placing her closer to the reader, she also functions as a vehicle for parody of the sentimental ode, Prudence for broad satire on religious enthusiasm.

The New Bath Guide is unlike most epistolary verse of the period in that it is also a connected narrative, but, partly because the addressees are mostly inert, Anstey does little to exploit the possibilities this enables. Though some of the sequels and imitations registered by Day also have a narrative element, the *Guide* probably exercised greater influence in encouraging other satirical dramatic epistles, in this case also parodying Ovid's. A series that appeared in the wake of John Hawkesworth's account of the voyages to the Pacific of 1764–71, first published in 1773,⁵¹ provides several examples. Hawkesworth had made liberal use of journals not only by commanders including Captain Cook but detailed records and descriptions by Joseph Banks, a wealthy, enlightened and free-living botanist who, like several of his companions, had apparently enjoyed liaisons with Tahitian women.⁵² Not surprisingly, the story attracted much prurient interest. As Banks's biographer points out, referring to Daniel Solander, one of the naturalists on the *Endeavour*, 'the satirists in London had their field days for many years to come, their sources hard to identify but surely to be found in the joviality of club conversations from Solander's evident hobby of polite pornography'.⁵³

First in the field, and with no hesitation, was John Scott (later Scott-Waring) with *An Epistle from Oberea, Queen of Otaheite, to Joseph Banks, Esq.*, which he followed a few months later with *A Second Letter from Oberea*, on the pretext that the first had received no reply.⁵⁴ Scott made it clear in copious notes that he was adapting not only Hawkesworth but Ovid's *Oenone to Paris*, and he also included spoof information. A reply of sorts, however, there had been, for between these squibs had appeared the anonymous *Epistle from Mr. Banks, Voyager, Monster-Hunter, and Amoroso, to Oberea, Queen of Otaheite*,⁵⁵ effectively a parody of a parody, with its trumping of the subtitle of Scott's first epistle: his *Translated by T. Q. Z. Esq. Professor of the Otaheite Language in Dublin* becomes *Transfused by A. B. C. Esq. Second Professor of the Otaheite, and Every Other Unknown Tongue*. In the two mock-epistles by Scott, both nominal writer and her addressee are satirical butts. For example, they are made to look ridiculous when Scott, adapting an incident in Hawkesworth, has Oberea remembering how Opano – the Tahitian pronunciation of Banks – cried out: 'Some thief has stol'n my breeches from my head' and she dressed him with her petticoat (p. 9). But Scott has Hawkesworth in his sights too, as when he insists, alleging motives of authenticity, on rendering an especially lubricious episode as 'a piece of justice due to that *great man*' (p. 11, note). The cod-response pushes the farce further by mocking the actual writer, still then anonymous, too – for example, by providing extracts from his first epistle, rather than any classical source, in notes.

All three of these satirical responses to Hawkesworth touch, briefly and opportunistically, on the corruption of upper-class British life and on the evils – especially diseases – that the explorers brought with them.[56] Later responses develop such themes. For instance, John Courtenay's *Poetical Epistle (Moral and Philosophical) from an Officer at Otaheite to Lady Gr[os]v[e]n[o]r* uses the Grosvenor scandal both to satirize aristocratic sexual excess at home and to present luridly imagined erotic episodes abroad;[57] and two epistles in which the famous Tahitian visitor Omai is, respectively, writer and addressee take the first of these themes further. The anonymous *Historic Epistle, from Omiah, to the Queen of Otaheite; Being his Remarks on the English Nation* satirizes Britain in Enlightenment terms from the viewpoint of a putative noble savage, contrasting what it represents as a state of uncorrupted nature with its cultured British perversion.[58] The other poem, *Seventeen Hundred and Seventy-Seven*, subtitled *A Poetical Epistle from a Lady of Quality*, focuses more on the perversion. Its author, William Preston, claimed 16 years after its initial publication that, arriving in London as a young man, he had been led 'to compare those vices, which are forced up and reared, as one may say, in a hot-bed, and are the result of art, study, and refinement, with those, which are the spontaneous growth of an indulgent soil and climate', though he also admitted that he had fallen short of his aims.[59]

But the furthest that any writer carried such an attitude also has its limits. As Shef Rogers shows, Gerald Fitzgerald's *The Injured Islanders, or the Influence of Art upon the Happiness of Nature* presents 'a countervailing account' both to Hawkesworth and to the epistolary satires by attempting a more scholarly approach and by seeking to reclaim 'the format employed by Oberea's satiric detractors' – the heroic epistle. On the one hand, Rogers argues, 'Oberea deplores the effects of European visitations, which introduced fatal diseases, as well as the iron tools that led to civil bloodshed and her loss of power'. On the other, to quote Rogers again, these laments 'succeed only in provoking a typically British emotional response in accord with the tenets of sensibility', one that does no more than sustain the status quo.[60] Yet Fitzgerald's poem – which is by no means satirical – nevertheless casts light on its facetious predecessors, and it offers a different position for the reader. It does not invite derision for Tahitian culture or even for Banks, Hawkesworth, and others. Neither, like the satirical epistles, does it depict bawdy or sub-pornographic episodes for presumably gentleman's-club consumers while flattering their knowledge of the classics. Instead, its approach discourages frivolous responses; and, crucially, because it is addressed to a fellow Englishman, Samuel Wallis, who is not a satirical target, it enables a more critical perspective, even if, as Rogers contends, it falls short.

The multiple reader-positions available to the dramatic epistle – ranging from advocate, through various vantage points for outsiders, to butt – give it great expressive potential. Even though, unlike Wortley Montagu in the 1720s, the writers of the satirical epistles just discussed failed to exploit that potential to the full, the form offered richer formal resources than its opposite, which is the epistle addressed to the general reader alone. Yet the critical question is always how well the chosen form is used, and James Bramston's 'The Art of Politicks' employs the latter strategy with special skill. Unlike Horace's *Art of Poetry*, which the poem explicitly imitates, it has no named addressee. Instead, its primary addressee, implied rather than stated, is anyone wishing to follow a career in Parliament. Such a reader is invoked in the couplet: 'Thy task be this, young knight, and hear my song, / What politics to every age belong' (p. 289).[61] Significantly, this is the only occasion when Bramston uses the second person singular. Much of the poem takes the form of advice to such an aspirant, just as Horace advises an aspiring poet. It is non-partisan, and at its centre is the injunction to be consistent: 'But you, from whate'er side you take your name, / Like Anna's motto, always be the same' (p. 278). Yet the poem also invokes other readers and other addressees. At its most general, the implied readership could be defined as the socially privileged and classically educated men who made up what Karina Williamson calls 'the Augustan club'.[62] Such men are hailed in the first term of address in the poem, 'Sirs' (p. 277), and their collusion is sought through occasional use of the first person plural: 'We take a different turn at twenty-six, / And lofty thoughts on some lord's daughter fix' (p. 291). A classical education is part of the competency needed to appreciate the wit with which Bramston translates Horace's advice into another language, culture and subject, for, as often with such imitations, passages from the original Latin are provided, without translation, in footnotes. At times, though, Bramston addresses subsets of this readership, such as 'ye judges learned in the law' (p. 295), or 'Lack-learning knights' (p. 307), and even people more or less outside it, as with 'Ye weekly writers of seditious news' (p. 279), or, in allusion to an event that had taken place over 25 years before the poem was printed, 'ye petitioners of Kent' (p. 284). He also identifies his own position as that of a sober expositor with no axe to grind: 'Too low in life to be a justice I, / And for a constable, thank God, too high: / Was never in a plot, my brain's not hurt; / I politics to poetry convert' (p. 300). The result is to present a kind of simulated dialogue between men of substance and sense, energized by occasional rhetorical questions and injunctions: 'Can men their inward faculties controul? / Is not the tongue an index to the soul? / Laugh not in time of service to your God, / Nor bully, when in custody o' th' rod' (p. 285).

There are other ways of handling the same strategy of an unnamed reader. For example, Joseph Warton begins and ends 'Fashion: A Satire' by addressing an unnamed reader, but calls on him only indirectly in the body of poem through such means as deixis – 'Yon purblind, poking peer' (p. 284), questions – 'Why loves not HIPPIA rank obscenity?' (p. 285), and injunctions – 'Mark well his feather'd hat, his gilt cockade' (p. 286).[63] He also seeks to enlist the external reader by using the first person plural, as when he exclaims: 'How fondly partial are our judgments grown, / We deem all manners odious but our own!' (p. 290). As well as the reader, Warton apostrophizes France and Fashion itself (pp. 286–7, 288), though he relies for most of the poem on Pope's portrait-gallery method. But, although he pays relatively little direct attention to his addressee, he ends the poem by refining his role in an interesting way. At the start, he addresses someone reluctant to accept his argument: 'Yes, yes, my friend, disguise it as you will, / To right or wrong 'tis Fashion guides us still' (p. 284). Similarly, he plays the role of instructor in the passage beginning: 'Ask you, why whores live more belov'd than wives' (p. 289). The poem ends, however, with a reversal, positioning the addressee as someone who is above it all and who should enlighten the writer: 'O teach me, friend, to know wise NATURE's rules, / And laugh, like you, at FASHION's hoodwink'd fools' (p. 290). In this manner, Warton has it both ways, constructing a reader who needs satirical instruction and who yet turns out to occupy a higher moral standpoint, that of Horatian retirement. Though few actual readers could have been described, like his addressee, as 'to woods remov'd from modish sin', despising 'the distant world's hoarse, busy din' (p. 290), that was an ideal widely accepted in the period, and citing it is an effective means of providing the closure that is often difficult to achieve in satire.[64]

It is also possible to position unnamed addressees as the object of the satire. Unlike his brother's epistle, Thomas Warton's 'Newmarket' is primarily addressed not to a sympathetic reader but to the racing and gambling fraternity that it attacks. The poem uses similar rhetorical devices, such as deictic injunctions and questions. Examples are 'Of each

vain youth, say, what's the darling joy?' (p. 47), and 'Behold the youth'
(p. 48).[65] These, clearly, are addressed to a general reader. Yet the principal
addressees are such figures as 'ye leisure-loving Squires' (p. 48), 'Ye rival
Youths' (p. 49), 'brave youths' (p. 52), and people in general who attend
horse-races, as in the phrase 'Thy sages' or when Warton exclaims: 'See,
like a routed host, with headlong pace, / Thy Members pour amid the
mingling race!' (p. 51). The position from which Warton speaks is that of
right-thinking advocate of the public good. This he seeks to establish by
apostrophizing Britain (pp. 51, 54), by frequently echoing Pope, and by
invoking Greece as both model and, in her decline, warning (pp. 54–5).
His tone suggests that he probably did not expect devotees of Newmarket
to read his poem. Instead, he aims to rouse the reader against them.

The poems by Bramston and the Warton brothers employ a strategy
with apparently less potential epistolarity than that of the dramatic form
adopted by the satirists of Hawkesworth, Banks and the Tahitians. Yet,
when the two groups of epistles are compared, it is the former that
exploits epistolary form to greater effect. The matter is not merely one of
rhetorical choices, for, as scholars of the period usually argue, much post-
Augustan satire lacks force because it has lost touch with generally
accepted principles.[66] Many satirical epistles written after roughly mid-
century confirm that view, though it should also be recognized that the
collapse of such social and moral consensus as had existed brought gains
in other, often non-satirical, ways by allowing more scope for discordant
or previously marginalized voices. That is not a topic that needs exploring
here, even if there were room to do so. Instead, though the changes that
took place in writing of the period are plainly not just questions of form,
comparison of various kinds of satirical verse epistle helps show what is
at stake in different formal choices and their fulfilment. In this respect,
Altman's concept of addressee-consciousness enables discrimination not
only between the potential advantages of different epistolary forms, but
also between the extent to which those advantages are realized.

One purpose self-evidently served by the satirical epistles about the
English in Tahiti was to make money. To judge by the five extant editions
claimed of Scott's first effort, in that case at least the enterprise was
successful.[67] A less obvious motive may have been to attract patronage, in
much the same way as young men such as John Donne sought it with
witty poems in the English Renaissance.[68] This may conceivably have
been part of Preston's purpose, perhaps also part of Courtenay's, although
he was already receiving patronage from George Townshend (*ODNB*). It

was more likely one of Scott's objectives, for, when he wrote his two epistles, he was serving in the Bengal army, and, a few years later, he was to become aide-de-camp and subsequently political agent to Warren Hastings (*ODNB*). In another example of the connections between satire and sentiment mentioned at the start of this chapter, the complimentary epistle was often used for the same purpose.

In Chapter 1, I have argued that the complimentary epistle developed, chiefly through Dryden, from the tradition of commendatory verses.[69] If this account has any substance, it has several implications. First, this type of epistle is almost wholly a phenomenon of the long eighteenth century. As distinct from commendatory verses, which were written to preface the books of others, and panegyrics, which are not necessarily epistolary, the complimentary epistle did not exist before the 1680s, and it died out soon after the nineteenth century began. Second, in keeping with its source, its initial function was to praise the work of a colleague – usually but not always another writer. Dryden's various poems to other poets and dramatists, such as 'To my Dear Friend Mr Congreve', are complemented, for example, by a poem to an artist, 'To Sir Godfrey Kneller'.[70] Third, however, although this variant remains one of the most common in the history of the form, continuing till the early nineteenth century, the complimentary epistle rapidly developed new offshoots. In particular, poets quickly realized that, like panegyrics and dedications, the new type of epistle could be exploited to solicit patronage. From this further applications developed, especially when its use to court potential or actual patrons began to wear thin. Instead of seeking money, preferment or other material favours, poets could bid for kudos or other forms of recognition; or they could cultivate complimentary verse as an established genre that might have exchange-value with booksellers or editors of magazines.

The range of the complimentary epistle makes it one of the most difficult kinds of epistolary verse to classify. Not only could it celebrate various kinds of occasion, but, as pointed out in Chapter 1, it is often a formal hybrid. Indeed, most types of epistle, especially the familiar and the discursive, may include compliments – though not usually, for obvious reasons, the heroic. Still, despite this pliability, a few generalizations may be offered. First, the verse form most often used for complimentary epistles is iambic pentameter couplets. Among the more than 300 such poems on which I have gathered details, some of which are marginal examples in the category of hybrids just mentioned, a little over 70 percent are in that form. This is not surprising, given that heroic couplets were the form most often used in the period for serious verse. But, when used for complimentary epistles, heroic couplets heighten a risk inherent in this type of poem, as the pomp and ceremony that they tend to encourage all too easily appears insincere. Probably for this reason, some poets resorted to the more familiar tetrameter couplet, a form that makes up just over 17 percent of my sample. The remainder of the sample is made up of small numbers of poems in various forms, including different kinds of stanza – among them the Standard Habby. Because of their humorous associations, anapestic tetrameter couplets are an unusual choice for complimentary poems, though there are a few examples; and blank verse, which is even rarer, is only used for very specific reasons, as in Adam Ottley's manuscript poem to John Philips, in tribute to its addressee's use of the form.[71] Only two other generalizations may be ventured, though both are all but self-evident. Complimentary poems are rarely very short, though few make excessive demands on their hearers; and, it almost goes without saying, they are hardly ever anonymous. Most of the following discussion focuses on examples of some of the main types. The aim is partly to explore how they work, but also to show that, though critics often disparage the form, it includes some fine examples.

In *Literary Patronage in England, 1650–1800*, Dustin Griffin shows that the patronage system was a 'pervasive feature of eighteenth-century culture' that 'took many forms', and that, though it was resisted as well as exploited, even in the latter part of the period it was far from defunct.[72] Attracting patronage – whether in the form of cash, preferment or various kinds of non-material capital – is perhaps the most evident function of the complimentary epistle. Griffin's study provides examples of successful pursuit of each of these rewards. Remuneration in cash is illustrated by Joseph Mitchell, who, according to Griffin, apparently earned 'some £500 over the years' for epistles to Walpole; and the acquiring and sustaining of another form of capital by Pope, who, though writing few complimentary epistles, employed dedications to other epistolary verse to 'reaffirm' and 'advertise' his 'connection with the patronage class'.[73] The earlier career of Edward Young, who, Griffin shows, later turned his back on the patronage system, is an especially interesting example. Not only, Griffin argues, did Young court both of the leading political interests, Tories with *An Epistle to the Right Honourable George Lord Lansdown* and Whigs with *On the Late Queen's Death, and his Majesty's Accession to the Throne*, addressed to Addison, but his seven satires first entitled *The Universal Passion* and later collected as *The Love of Fame* were all but one addressed to people of influence, while 'Satire the Last', addressed to Walpole, led to his appointment as chaplain to the Princess of Wales as well as to a pension of £200 a year.[74] The *Love of Fame* poems are, indeed, not only satirical but complimentary – another surprising link between the two forms – as David Fairer demonstrates in his discussion of a passage from the third satire, addressed to George Bubb Dodington.[75] At the same time as bidding for patronage, complimentary epistles could also play a civic role by demonstrating political support. Examples include not only the early poems by Young just mentioned, but also Laurence Eusden's *Letter to Mr. Addison, on the King's Accession to the Throne* and two poems from the same period by Ambrose Philips: *An Epistle to the Right Honourable Charles Lord Halifax, One of the Lords Justices Appointed by His Majesty,* and *An Epistle to the Honourable James Craggs, Esq., Secretary at War: At Hampton-Court.*[76]

The use of the complimentary epistle to seek non-material capital is especially revealing, even though other kinds of poem could also serve the same purpose. Griffin uses Pierre Bourdieu's term 'symbolic capital' to denote one of the rewards that the patron might expect for sponsoring a writer,[77] and the related term 'social capital' may be applied to the non-material gains that might flow the other way. This Bourdieu defines as

> the aggregate of the actual or potential resources which are linked to possession of a durable network of more or less institutionalized relationships of mutual acquaintance and recognition – or, in other words, to membership in a group – which provides each of its members with the backing of the collectively-owned capital, a 'credential' which entitles them to credit, in the various sense of the word.[78]

Richard Savage illustrates how a poet could bid both for material and social returns. Perpetually without cash, he exploited the complimentary epistle repeatedly, so much so that his *Volunteer Laureat* poems became routine performances. As Griffin indicates, he gained a present of 20 guineas for an epistle to Walpole in 1733, and the second *Volunteer Laureat* brought a pension of £50 a year until the Queen's death in 1737.[79] But Savage cultivated the form for social purposes too. As a member of the circle around Aaron Hill, he took part in exchanges of complimentary poems that, while tending to give the impression of a mutual admiration society, not only commended the talents and abilities of its members to others, but sought to confer on them a certain prestige.[80] In Bourdieu's terms, this constitutes a form of social capital, and Joseph Mitchell emulated Savage by writing epistles not only to Walpole but to the painters Hogarth, Dandridge and Lambert.[81] The practice was still current much later in the century. William Hayley not only addressed epistles on painting to George Romney, on history to Edward Gibbon and on epic poetry to William Mason, but also celebrated the career of Admiral Augustus Keppel, congratulating him on his acquittal in his highly unpopular court-martial following the Battle of Ushant.[82] Like Mitchell's series on painting, Hayley's series on the same subject, on history and on epic poetry are discursive as well as complimentary epistles, and part of their aim was probably to attract kudos. Anna Seward, who addressed a complimentary epistle to Hayley before she fell out with him, inscribed others to various people, including two to Romney, one of which thanks him for presenting her picture to her father. As this example suggests, however, her motives may have been more disinterested than Hayley's, especially as most of the addressees of her complimentary epistles were not widely known.[83]

To consider an example in more detail, Ambrose Philips's *Epistle to the Honourable James Craggs*, already mentioned, is fairly representative of the type that tacitly seeks patronage while expressing political support.[84] Philips flatters his addressee both overtly – 'O *Craggs*, for Candour known!' (3) – and indirectly, emphasizing how busy his addressee is and how entitled, therefore, to share his hours of leisure with 'cheerful Friends' (2), while half-apologizing for sending him 'a Long Epistle, though in Rhyme' (6). His own stance, as this piece of self-deprecation suggests, is modest. He calls his verse 'artless' (11), claims: ''tis my Heart that dictates, not the Muse' (12), and contrasts his role, as a humble state official, with the grander pursuits of his addressee: 'You to the healthful Chace attend the King, / And hear the Forrest with the Hunstmen ring: / While in the dusty Town We rule the State, / And from *Gazettes* determine *England*'s Fate' (129–32). He also maintains the fiction of a private letter by professing that his aim is to 'ease the Burden of a Loyal Mind' (8), disclosing 'secret Transports' (9) to an addressee who, he suggests, is doing him a favour by attending. Such 'Transports' are anything but secret, of course, in a letter written to be printed and circulated, and it soon becomes clear that Craggs is not the only reader Philips has in mind, or even the most important. First, it is to the Crown that he attributes his inspiration – his heart, he says, 'at the name of BRUNSWICK fires' (13). Second, he claims that only Craggs's heart 'with stronger Raptures beats' than his own 'For GEORGE's Glory and the publick Weal' (18, 16). Third, and crucially, the body of the poem – well over 100 lines out of 157 – is devoted not to his addressee but to the King. He ends this long section by declaring: 'Secure, on *GEORGE*'s Councils I rely, / Give up my Cares, and *Britain*'s Foes defy' (137–8), sure that, when it comes to enemies, the King always 'Defeats their Plots, and over-rules th'Event' (143). Effective closure can be as difficult to achieve in a complimentary epistle as in a satire. Philips manages it here by claiming that celebrating the King is an endless task to which he is 'Unequal' (150): 'Divided in my Choice, from Praise to Praise / I rove, bewilder'd in the pleasing Maze' (146–7), and by presenting a kind of poetic posy to his addressee in the form of an extended simile. The simile compares his own activity as poet with that of a bee skimming 'o'er hundred Flowers for one she spoils' and 'soon o'erburden'd with the fragrant Weight' (155, 156). This both embellishes the points he has just made, and allows him to seek respite by ending the poem: 'Homeward she flies, and flags beneath her Freight' (157).

It is difficult to deny the skill of Philips's poem, not only in its covert appeal to others underneath its address to Craggs but also in its rhetorical artifice and its verbal and metrical proficiency. Not all writers of complimentary epistles were so adept, among them Patrick Delany in his *Epistle to his Excellency John Lord Carteret*.[85] Delany's poem differs from Philips's in that it is a request for further patronage rather than a statement of political support in which the appeal for patronage is tacit. It begins in the expected manner with fulsome praise and self-deprecation. Carteret is the 'wise, and learned Ruler of our Ile' whose 'generous Soul' occasionally condescends 'T'Instruct or entertain' the 'humble' poet (1, 3, 4). The latter, moreover, sits by 'abash'd and mute' at the 'Wit' and 'Genius' his addressee displays in conversation – qualities that do not prevent him from closing 'with kind Enquiries of my State' (17, 12, 19). Delany makes these enquiries explicit enough to provide a peg for the rest of the poem. He introduces the ploy cautiously with the remark: 'SUPPOSE at such a Time, I took the Freedom / To speak these Truths, as plainly as you read 'em' (25–6), and with two provisos: that Carteret will have a chance to reply, and that, if he wishes, Lady Carteret will have the final say. He then has the temerity to stage a dialogue between himself and his patron in which he expresses gratitude for what Carteret has given him but complains that it is insufficient, while Carteret's replies at first allow him to detail his supposed grievances and then endorse one of his proposals for relieving them. The poem ends with another devious artifice. Having contrasted his condition with that of his addressee – 'Then how unblest am I! how blest are you' (85) – Delany has Carteret ask him to state what he wants. To this Delany responds with a deference that most of his epistle belies: 'My Lord, I challenge nothing as my Due, / Nor is it fit I should prescribe to You' (90–1), only to do precisely that in the last two lines: '"My Lord, I'd wish – to *pay the Debts I owe*, – / "I'd wish besides – to *build*, and to *bestow*"' (94–5), in other words, not only to clear his debts and expand his estate but to have the means of giving charity to others.

The fact that Delany had his epistle printed 'in a sumptuous folio'[86] and circulated makes his audacity all the more startling. To publish such a poem was to appeal to readers as well as addressee. He presumably hoped to impress them with what he evidently regarded as the strength of his case and the wit with which he had expressed it; perhaps he also wished to shame Carteret into greater generosity. Thanks to bitter experience, Swift had a keen idea of what was at issue. First, he rebuked his friend in 'An Epistle upon an Epistle', advising him: 'Be Modest: nor Address your Betters / With Begging, Vain, Familiar Letters' (p. 479).[87] Then, in *A Libel on D[octor] D[elany], and a Certain Great Lord*, he rounded on Carteret too, and the whole chain of patronage. As Griffin puts it, the latter poem's joke 'is not on the client Delany, but on his would-be patron, Carteret, and ultimately on *his* masters, Walpole and the King himself'.[88]

Delany's attempt to obtain further patronage, and Swift's ripostes, cast light not only on the system of patronage but on how difficult, by 1730, it had become to write epistles soliciting money or preferment. Mitchell had already responded, in his epistles to Walpole, by substituting conventional compliments with tongue-in-cheek humour, and others were to follow suit. Among these was Henry Fielding in 'To the Right Honourable Sir Robert Walpole', which he claimed to have been 'Written in the Year 1730' when it was printed in his *Miscellanies* in 1743.[89] Fielding trimmed the iambic pentameter couplets that were the stock in trade of complimentary verse to tetrameters, as Mitchell was to do in his 1735 epistle to Walpole[90] – though he did not go so far as Swift, who, in 'An Epistle upon an Epistle', had reduced Delany's pentameter couplets to Hudibrastics. The gambit on which the poem turns is that its writer is 'a greater Man' than his addressee. Fielding seeks to prove the contention with a number of witty false syllogisms: if status is shown by dining late, not dining at all is more prestigious still; if by the number of people at one's door, the debtor besieged by creditors every day except Sunday is most in demand; if by unapproachability, then a person seen only at his window stands highest (in both senses). This he caps with the conclusion: 'If with my Greatness you're offended, / The Fault is easily amended. / For I'll come down, with wond'rous Ease, / Into whatever Place you please' (43–6) – a suggestion repeated in the poem's closing appeal for 'a – *Sinecure*' (60). As Donald Thomas points out, 'The reference to a sinecure was omitted when the poem was reprinted in a shorter and revised version by the *Gentleman's Magazine* in 1738'.[91] But, although Thomas adds that 'the tone of the letter in its original form suggests that the writer, as much as the recipient, is the object of the humour', Thomas Lockwood is surely right to remark that the request is put 'half-jokingly, but only half-jokingly.[92] Fielding's irony allows the epistle to be taken both ways: both as a jest, offered to Walpole and others for their amusement, and as an invitation for bounty.

As Ronald Paulson says, he was 'leaving open the hope of rewards from the Great Man'.[93]

But the best example of this humorous type of complimentary epistle is probably William Dunkin's *Epistle to the Right Honourable James Lord Visct. Charlemont*. Masquerading as a dedication, it eclipses the work it is intended to introduce, his *Translation of the Sixth Satire of the Second Book of Horace*, not only on the title page but in the facts that it has line numbers, unlike the translation, and that it is almost twice as long.[94] In an often quoted phrase, Swift described Dunkin as 'a Gentleman of much Wit, and the best English as well as Latin poet in this Kingdom [Ireland]',[95] and, as far as Dunkin's English verse is concerned, the poem bears him out. The dedicatee was James Caulfeild (1728–99), fourth Viscount Charlemont, later Earl of Charlemont. A youth of 15 or 16, as Charlemont would have been at the time the poem was written, is not an obvious dedicatee for a complimentary epistle, even though from a noble and wealthy family. Part of the poem's art is to imply its aptness to addressee and occasion alike.

The reason Dunkin's epistle is such an outstanding example of epistolary compliment is that it brings off the apparently impossible double feat of satirizing the form and yet paying its addressee convincing tribute. It is a long poem, and it may be divided into three parts. First, Dunkin states the problems inherent in writing complimentary verse. Not only does it affirm the obvious – poets persist with it to seek patronage 'Although they mean to say no more / Than what their Lordships knew before' (9–10) – but its praise is always absurdly exaggerated. Second, he introduces a dialogue with 'a Poet by Profession' (147) who rebukes him for traducing his fellow rhymesters. This allows him not only to continue his attack on complimentary verse – 'I deal in Satire over much, / And are not all your Praises such?' (169–70), but to mock contemporary publishing practices, including the timing of publications – 'The Maggots of Poetic Sperm, / Like other Insects, have their Term' (185–6), the gullibility of the public who 'never look / Beyond the Surface' (203–4), and the irrelevance of critics: 'Yet still your Patron shall admire / The Flights of your heroic Fire' (221–2). Reassured, Dunkin returns to trawling through possible models for inspiration, only to fall asleep over the verse of Sir Richard Blackmore, a byword among the Scriblerians for soporific bombast. This ushers in the third section, a dialogue with Momus, 'God of Criticks, and Detraction' (235), who takes the opposite tack from the fellow poet by trying to talk him out of his aim and into a more useful one. Although Momus has some good arguments – for example: 'In Poetry no Medium lies; / You sink of Course, unless you rise' (293–4), this interlocutor Dunkin more than

matches, albeit at times self-demeaningly: 'If Rhiming be an Itch, and catching, / Permit the Benefit of Scratching' (301–2). Conceding such points, and advising Dunkin to pursue his original intention of finding a suitable dedicatee for his translation, Momus yet objects to all the poet's suggestions – including, of course, Charlemont himself. This gives Dunkin his opportunity to compliment them, his addressee most of all.

The poem's strategy is, then, ingenious. Not only does Dunkin expose the artifice and insincerity common in complimentary verse, but he avoids it himself with his jaunty tetrameters – Hudibrastics in the true sense, for the rhymes are usually witty rather than merely forced or crude[96] – as well as any kind of direct praise. Although the poem has a specific addressee, he also renders it highly readable to others, not least the various 'old-fashion'd Men of Honour' (378) whom he compliments on the way. These include Robert Jocelyn, Lord Chancellor of Ireland, recently created Baron Newport (*ODNB*), who 'from an Oratorio flies, / To listen to the Widow's Cries' (365–6), along with William Stewart, third Viscount Mountjoy, and Charles Moore, second Baron Tullamore, against whom Momus objects: 'Why, Man alive, they pay their Debts' (376).[97] Dunkin also makes it clear that in translating Horace he has no wish to rival Swift, who had published several Horatian imitations.[98] He finally introduces his addressee obliquely – 'You know a certain hopeful Youth' (384) – upon which Momus spends 66 lines emphasizing his unsuitability, but in terms that are wholly favourable. Not only does Charlemont spend his time with the classics instead of 'At Ombre, Whist, Basset, Quadrille' (390), but he thinks it no indignity 'To take a Curate [presumably Dunkin himself] by the hand' (422); he knows no more 'Of Dress, or Fashions, than a Hermit' (424); and, when he makes the Grand Tour, he will bring back descriptions of landscapes and antiquities instead of 'Love-Intrigues' (434). Such satire is praise in disguise, yet Dunkin has Momus cap it: 'Abstemious in the Midst of Plenty, / What must he prove at Five-and-Twenty?' (443–4). Dunkin then closes the epistle briefly by telling how his dream ended and by putting a simple question to his addressee: 'I wak'd my Lord: Now let me see, / Convince me, who this Lord shall be' (455–6).

The occasion of Dunkin's poem further brings out its skill. According to James Kelly's biographical article on Charlemont, 'the young nobleman's discovery of "cards and late hours" caused "all thoughts of the university" to be put aside'; instead, he would make the Grand Tour with his tutor (*ODNB*, citing the family papers). Dunkin not only refers to this plan, in the passage cited above, but indicates that, before leaving, Charlemont was to study in the school at which he was a teacher, St Michael-le-Pole in Dublin (*ODNB*, Dunkin), and also to Edward Murphy, the tutor who was to accompany Charlemont. Indeed, he compliments Murphy too by commenting on his ability to explain the jokes in Lucian (399–402). As Dunkin's poem was printed in 1744, but Charlemont did not set out with Murphy until 1746, this further tuition was evidently a determined attempt to ensure that the young man leave properly prepared and without habits of dissipation. It is likely that the poem was part of the family's strategy, especially as it presents an image of its addressee that he might wish to emulate. Dunkin's closing line-and-a half deftly suggests this, for it asks him to match up to the picture of him given ('Convince me') and, quite literally, become it ('who this Lord shall be'). It is also probable that the praise-in-disguise was not without grounds, for, after nine years in Europe, Charlemont returned to lead a distinguished career as a patriotic politician and man of letters, a man whom Kelly calls 'learned, principled, and honourable'.

The epistle to Charlemont illustrates again the connections between satire and compliment, but Dunkin also showed that he could write formal complimentary verse in, for example, 'An Epistle to the Earl of C[hesterfiel]d'.[99] To heighten the tribute, he wrote it both in Latin and English – printed side by side, as with some of his other poems, a few in Greek as well as Latin, in his posthumous *Poetical Works* – and, while maintaining all due respect to his patron, without obsequiousness. What is more, the poem seeks aid not for himself but for a friend, 'A--m--r', perhaps the James Armour who, along with Dunkin, was a subscriber in 1749 to Henry Jones's *Poems on Several Occasions*.[100] Surprisingly, Dunkin's epistle to Charlemont appears neither in *Poetical Works* nor in the *Select Poetical Works* that preceded it, though both include a prose epistle to Chesterfield as well as the poem in Latin and English.[101] The editors of two recent and excellent anthologies of eighteenth-century Irish verse have pointed out Dunkin as a poet who demands to be better known.[102] His epistle to Charlemont confirms how much he deserves rescuing from obscurity.

The wit of Swift, Fielding and Dunkin, among others, failed to inhibit unctuous complimentary verse, as various poems from the 1730s till near the end of the century demonstrate. It would be easy to multiply examples, as, among others, Samuel Boyse, Thomas Cooke and James Woodhouse wrote several each.[103] As late as 1784, for instance, Elizabeth Ryves does not disdain the stock trope of disclaiming flattery while laying it on thick in her *Epistle to the Right Honourable Lord John Cavendish*, as when she exclaims, after some encomiastic lines: 'Such, CAVENDISH, art thou; nor dares my lyre / At the full harvest of thy praise aspire, / Let Envy's

blackening tongue accuse the rhyme / Of Adulation, while I scorn the crime' (73–6).[104] However, the complimentary epistle also took other and often more appealing forms. One is the epistle accompanying a gift, discussed briefly in Chapter 3;[105] two others are poems between poets, and poems celebrating special occasions. Among instances of the second type, William Somervile addressed complimentary epistles to Pope, James Thomson and others, and exchanged them with Allan Ramsay; while, near the end of the century, Burns both addressed and received several.[106] Ramsay's 'Epistle to Mr. John Gay, Author of the Shepherd's Week, on Hearing her Grace Dutchess of Queensberry Commend Some of his Poems' is an especially fine and attractive example.

Ramsay's poem shows an unusual form of addressee-consciousness, particularly in complimentary epistles, because it implies no other reader than its addressee and his patron. More than that, it addresses Gay as a poet in the genre for which he was most famous, pastoral, and it honours him by using the Scots language and verse form – the Standard Habby – in which Hamilton and Ramsay had complimented each other several years before. This is significant, because Ramsay tended to use standard English and more conventional stanza forms in verse to Englishmen; and this is his only poem to an Englishman in the Standard Habby. It means not only that he addresses Gay fully as poet to poet, but that he can draw on the associations of his own language and culture with pastoral. The poem also expresses a kind of joyous affection from its opening lines, addressing Gay as composing his *Pastorals* while walking swiftly over open country – 'Dear Lad, wha linkan o'er the Lee, / Sang *Blowzalind* and *Bowzybee*' (1–2), to its unaffected valediction: 'Nae mair at present I've to say, / But am your Friend' (107–8).[107] In between, Ramsay tells his friend's Fortune – 'Now, lend thy Lug, and tent me, *GAY*, / Thy Fate appears like Flow'rs in *May*' (13–14); both praises his verse and stresses that his praise is not lightly given; compliments him on the beauty and taste of his patron – 'But bide ye Boy, the main's to say, / *Clarinda* bright as rising day' (43–4); and encourages him to keep writing: 'EXALT thy Voice, that all around, / May echo back the lovely Sound' (79–80). The several stanzas he devotes to the poem's occasion, Gay's patronage by the Duchess of Queensberry, also express solidarity between one poet who had struggled to make his way and another, as well as pleasure in Gay's success. Before he closes, Ramsay declares his longing to visit London, implicitly so that he can meet his friend, and his consolation in the meantime amidst 'the Gowans, Broom and Trees, / The Crystal Burn and Westlin Breez' of his own land (97–8), so reaffirming the pastoral link between the two. The poem is one of the most exhilarating and delightful

of epistles from one poet to another, not excepting those between Hamilton and Ramsay, and from Burns to John Lapraik and David Sillar.[108]

English poets writing in the same vein are less demonstratively warm. Instead, they show how fully, by mid-century, a code of easy politeness had spread through their culture. Two typically urbane examples are William Whitehead's epistles congratulating David Garrick on obtaining the patent of Drury Lane in 1747 and Benjamin Hoadly on the success in the same year of his comedy *The Suspicious Husband*.[109] Like Dunkin, Whitehead filtered his compliments partly through mouthpieces in both poems. Most of 'To Mr. Garrick' consists of a dialogue between Thalia, muse of comedy, and Melpomene, muse of tragedy, both speaking in the style of ladies of fashion. The touch is light, but the tribute clear, as when Melpomene hails the actor 'whose all-expressive powers / Can reach the heights that SHAKESPEARE soars' (p. 263), or Thalia appeals to him to join Hannah Pritchard 'in [her] behalf, / And teach an audience when to laugh' (p. 265). Whitehead ends the poem, however, in his own voice, blending praise with injunction – 'A nation's taste depends on you; / – Perhaps a nation's virtue too' (p. 265) – and advice: 'Nor e'er descend from reason's laws / To court what you command, applause' (p. 266). The poem does not stand comparison with Johnson's prologue on the same occasion, but its aim was different, and it succeeds not only in complimenting Garrick without flattery but also in expressing serious theatrical purpose.

Whitehead used the same unpretentious form of tetrameter couplets for 'Nature to Dr. Hoadly, on his Comedy of the Suspicious Husband' and for two humorous poems to his friends, the Wrights of Romely Hall near Eckington in Derbyshire, with whom, according to his memoirist, 'he spent several of his college vacations'.[110] Unlike 'To Mr. Garrick', all three poems are wholly in dramatic form. As its title implies, the poem to Hoadly is in the voice of Nature pretending to reprove him for borrowing 'Pæon's sacred name' (p. 266) – alluding to his addressee's other career as a doctor – in order to represent human behaviour so convincingly. The device also allows Whitehead to compliment Garrick, who played Ranger, the male lead, and it is wittily sustained, as when 'Nature' presents beaux and ladies asking: 'What does he mean? Is this a play? / We see such people every day' (p. 267). 'An Epistle from a Grove in Derbyshire to a Grove in Surrey' and its 'Answer' are equally adept, offering a humorous epithalamium between them. Having begun with the claim that 'root-bound trees, like distant creatures, / Can only correspond by letters' (p. 75), the Derbyshire grove ends by asking her sister to help persuade the master to marry, an act that would ensure her own future: 'Avert that fate

[her] fear foresees, / And, for his children, save his trees?' (p. 79).[111]
Whitehead gives the Surrey grove town-manners and diction. She begins
by apologizing for her delay in replying – 'Dear grove, I ask ten thousand
pardons, / Sure I'm the most absurd of gardens!' (p. 80) – patronizes her
country sister, and finally discusses the marriage that has now been
celebrated. This, again, is a device enabling compliment without unction,
and Whitehead takes full advantage by exploiting the blasé airs of the
town lady: 'I don't know what you'll say at Romely, / We really think the
woman comely; / Has some good qualities beside / They say, but she's as
yet a bride' (p. 82). The owners of both estates are praised in the same
way: 'Our masters, all the world allow, / Are honest men as times go now'
(p. 83); but the underlying standard is that of the countryside where
Whitehead's friends lived, and which he also praises obliquely: 'A lie
perhaps in Derbyshire / May be as strange as truth is here' (p. 82).

These epistles by Whitehead were all, so to speak, one-way traffic,
though the poet benefited from the hospitality, at least, of the Wrights.
When, however, he rather unexpectedly became Poet Laureate in 1757, his
close friend Richard Owen Cambridge returned a compliment Whitehead
had paid him some years earlier. Both poems display the same urbane wit
as Whitehead's to Garrick, Hoadly, and his friends in Derbyshire, but they
also carry an understated affection. Whitehead's begins: 'Dear Cambridge,
teach your friend the art / You use to gain the Muse's heart' (p. 118), and
goes on to compliment his friend on his fluency in composition despite a
very busy life: 'But you, reversing every rule / Of ancient or of modern
school, / Nor hurt by noise, nor cramp'd by rhymes, / Can all things do,
and at all times' (p. 119).[112] Praising Cambridge as a kind of eighteenth-
century Renaissance man, capable of all things, Whitehead celebrates
most 'that unexhausted vein, / That quick conception without pain, / That
something, for no words can show it, / Which without leisure makes a
poet', and ends by declaring: 'I'll write like you, or write no more' (p.
121). The poem's affection, though never direct, consists in the lively
energy and dexterity of its tribute, all the more telling, in this context, for
the lightness with which it is expressed. Cambridge shows an even lighter
touch in his epistle of congratulation, with its at first banteringly casual
but then forthright opening couplet: ''Tis so – though we're surprised to
hear it: / The laurel is bestow'd on merit' (p. 337).[113] But his main
response is ironic commiseration on the libels that Whitehead will now
suffer; for, he says, comparing literary bile with political, 'each Aonian
politician / (Whose element is opposition), / Will shew how greatly they
surpass us / In gall and wormwood at Parnassus'. In the second part of the
poem, the compliment becomes even droller as Cambridge points out that

a poet laureate is likely to be esteemed only when dead, before drawing back to reassure his friend that he does not want to lose him yet. He ends with the only approach to encomium that the poem contains, calling on Whitehead to teach 'How free-born bards should strike the strings, / And how a Briton write to kings' (p. 339), referring not only to the role of laureat but also to the 'democratic state' (p. 337) that gives freedom to abuse as well as praise.

Cambridge's poem manages an adroit solution to the problem of how to congratulate without any kind of effusiveness. At the same time, though, it is very much of its period in its easy, refined wit; and it is also characteristic of a culture in which direct expression of fondness might be suspect. Not all English complimentary poems were so restrained, as a final example will show. George Farewell's 'To the Archdeacon' is both a New Year's gift and an apology for not being present to offer it in person. It begins by ruefully acknowledging that his absence will be no surprise: 'Under the sun is nothing new? / Nothing, if Solomon says true. / Archdeacon, you'll excuse me then / If I today should not be seen' (1–4).[114] Soon, however, Farewell expresses unqualified feeling: 'But lo! sir, compliments apart, / My muse shall greet you from her heart' (9–10), and he goes on not only to praise his addressee warmly – 'he, whose riches are bestowed / In constant offices of good' (21–2) – but to wish him well in a way that is subtle and inventive. Instead of calling for him to prosper – 'A wish of wealth for such a man / Would be superfluous and vain' (27–8) – he asks for a long life, and, envisaging the payment of 'the only debt' that will ever be asked of his addressee, he pitches this appeal in a quite different verbal and emotional key from the rest of the poem:

> Whilst your white locks will seem to be
> But blossoms of the mystic tree
> Of life eternal, which shall spread
> Up to the sky its glorious head:
> Where none but youthful years attend;
> And now farewell, my heavenly friend. (37–42)

It is a moving close to a poem that might otherwise be considered slight.

Farewell's poem is an appropriate one with which to end this book, as it distils some of the main features that define the best eighteenth-century British epistolary verse. It is occasional and unostentatious, but it also gives every appearance of being heartfelt; and these qualities, along with the quiet accomplishment of its versification, movement and phrasing, are wholly in keeping with a form that originated with the familiar letter.

Appendix 1: Verse Epistles in Dryden's Miscellany, Dodsley's and Pearch's Collections, and Lonsdale's Anthologies

References are in the order in which poems are mentioned in Chapter 2, or otherwise to that of original pagination. Those to Dryden's miscellany are to the edition of 1716, those to Dodsley's to that of 1782, and those to Pearch's to that of 1783, followed in the latter two cases, where applicable, by references to Bell's Classical Arrangement of Fugitive Poetry.

1 Dryden's Miscellany Poems

A Presumably counted by Havens ('epistle' or 'letter' in title)

1 Thomas Otway, 'Epistle from Mr. Otway, to Mr. Duke', I, 73–6
2 Unattributed, 'A Letter to a Friend', I, 77–8
3 Unidentified ('J. P.'), 'A Letter from J. P. to Colonel H. Occasion'd by the Colonel's Two Late Letters', II, 195–7
4 Matthew Prior, 'A Letter to Sir Fleetwood Shepherd. By Mr. Pryor', II, 263–8
5 John Dryden, 'A Letter from Mr. Dryden to Sir George Etheridge', II, 281–3
6 George Etherege, Sir, 'Sir George Etheridge's Second Letter to the Lord Middleton', II, 284–5
7 Francis Knapp, 'An Epistle to Mr. B—. By Mr. Fr. Knapp, of Magdalen College in Oxford', IV, 73–6
8 Joseph Addison, 'A Letter from Italy, to the Right Honourable Charles Lord Halifax. [. . .] By Mr. Joseph Addison', V, 1–6
9 Charles Hopkins, 'An Epistle from Mr. Charles Hopkins to Mr. Yalden in Oxon', V, 51–3
10 Unidentified, 'A Familiar Epistle to Mr. Julian, Secretary of the Muses. By Mr. Dryden' (false attribution), V, 359–61

B Other epistolary

1 George Etherege, Sir, 'Sir George Etheridge to the Earl of Middleton', II, 279–81
2 Unattributed, 'On her Majesty's Grant of Woodstock-Park, &c. to his Grace the Duke of Marlborough. In a Letter to Signior Verrio at Hampton-Court', VI, 246–8
3 Thomas Yalden, 'To Mr. Congreve. An Epistolary Ode. Occasioned by his late Play. From Mr. Yalden', III, 128–30
4 Unattributed, 'Invitation into the Country. In Imitation of the XXXIVth

Epig. of Catullus', III, 64–5
5   Behn, Aphra (unattributed), 'Bajazet to Gloriana', II, 80–2
6   Charles Hopkins, 'To C. C. Esq; by Mr. Charles Hopkins', III, 168–9
7   ——, 'To Antony Hammond, Esq; by Mr. Charles Hopkins', IV, 24–5
8   ——, 'To Walter Moyle, Esq; by Mr. Charles Hopkins', IV, 63–5
9   Joseph Addison, 'An Account of the Greatest English Poets. To Mr. H. S. April 3, 1694. By Mr. Jo. Addison', IV, 288–92
10 Unidentified ('J. P.'), 'The Eighteenth Epistle of the First Book of Horace', II, 241–7
11 Unattributed, 'Some Verses Sent by a Friend to One Who Twice Ventur'd his Carcase in Marriage', II, 180–1
12 John Mennis, Sir, 'To Parson Weeks. An Invitation to London', VI, 365–7

C   Also epistolary

1   Unattributed, 'To a Lady, Sent Her with Mr. Granvill's Play, Call'd Heroic Love', V, 145
2   Samuel Garth, 'To the Lady Louisa Lenos; with Ovid's Epistles', VI, 145–6
3   Thomas Tickell, 'To a Lady, with the Description of the Phoenix', VI, 186
4   ——, 'To a Lady; with a Present of Flowers', VI, 191–2
5   Unattributed, 'To a Lady; to Whom the Author Sent a Book of his Composing', VI, 221–2
6   William Worts, 'Presenting a Father's Advice to his Daughter', VI, 245
7   William Harrison, 'To Mrs. M. M. with a Bough of an Orange-Tree', VI, 283
8   Thomas Brown, 'To the Lords Assembled in Council: The Petition of Tho. Brown', II, 191–2

2   Dodsley's Collection of Poems by Several Hands

A   **Presumably counted by Havens ('epistle' or 'letter' in title)**

1   Thomas Tickell, 'An Epistle from a Lady in England, to a Gentleman at Avignon', I, 69–7
2   Mary Wortley Montagu, Lady, 'An Epistle to Lord Bathurst', I, 119–22 (Bell, II, 9–12)
3   Matthew Green, 'The Spleen. An Epistle to Mr. Cuthbert Jackson', I, 127–58 (Bell, II, 134–63)
4   William Melmoth, 'Of Active and Retired Life. An Epistle to H. C. Esq;', I, 216–27 (Bell, I, 9–19)
5   George, Baron Lyttelton (unattributed), 'An Epistle to Mr. Pope. From Rome, 1730', II, 40–2
6   Robert Craggs Nugent, Earl Nugent (unattributed), 'An Epistle to the Right Honourable the Lord Viscount Cornbury', II, 174–93 (Bell, I, 85–105)
7   ——, 'An Epistle ['Thro' the wild maze of life's still varying plan']', II,

193–206 (Bell, I, 106–19)

8   Robert Craggs Nugent, Earl Nugent (unattributed), 'An Epistle to a Lady', II, 206–13 (Bell, I, 123–30)

9   ——, 'An Epistle to Mr. Pope', II, 213–15 (Bell, I, 120–2)

10   ——, 'Epistle to Pollio, from the Hills of Howth in Ireland', II, 215–18 (Bell, II, 27–9)

11   Thomas Seward (unattributed), 'The Female Right to Literature, in a Letter to a Young Lady from Florence', II, 309–15 (Bell, VI, 17–23)

12   William Whitehead, 'The Danger of Writing Verse. An Epistle', II, 249–59 (Bell, III, 57–67)

13   Joseph Spence (unattributed), 'An Epistle from a Swiss Officer to his Friend at Rome', III, 60–3 (Bell, III, 160–2)

14   Edward Rolle (unattributed), 'Life Burthensome, Because We Know Not How to Use It. An Epistle', III, 64–6 (Bell, I, 20–2)

15   ——, 'The Duty of Employing one's Self. An Epistle', III, 67–70 (Bell, 23–6)

16   ——, 'On Scribbling against Genius. An Epistle', III, 70–3 (Bell, III, 53–6)

17   Horace Walpole (unattributed), 'An Epistle from Florence. To Thomas Ashton, Esq; Tutor to the Earl of Plymouth', III, 78–93 (Bell, I, 48–62)

18   ——, 'The Beauties. An Epistle to Mr. Eckardt the Painter', III, 94–100 (Bell, III, 133–8)

19   Soame Jenyns, 'An Epistle from S. J. Esq; in the Country, to the Right Hon. the Lord Lovelace in Town', III, 133–40 (Bell, II, 1–8)

20   ——, 'To a Lady, in Answer to a Letter Wrote in a Very Fine Hand', III, 150–2 (Bell, VI, 37–9)

21   Unidentified, 'An Epistle to a Lady', III, 207–9

22   William Collins, 'An Epistle Address'd to Sir Thomas Hanmer, on his Edition of Shakespear's Works', IV, 70–7

23   John Hervey, Baron of Ickworth, Epistles in the Manner of Ovid. 'Monimia to Philocles', IV, 86–93 (Bell, VI, 79–86)

24   ——, 'Flora to Pompey', IV, 94–8 (Bell, VI, 69–73)

25   ——, 'Arisbe to Marius Junior. From Fontenelle', IV, 99–105 (Bell, VII, 63–8)

26   ——, 'Roxana to Usbeck. From Les Lettres Persanes', IV, 106–10 (Bell, VII, 74–8)

27   John Hervey, Baron of Ickworth, 'A Love Letter', IV, 114–16

28   Mary Wortley Montagu, Lady, 'An Answer to a Love-Letter', IV, 207–8

29   Henry Fielding, 'A Letter to Sir Robert Walpole. By Henry Fielding, Esq;', V, 126–7

30   Stephen Clay [unattributed], 'An Epistle from the Elector of Bavaria to the French King, after the Battle of Ramilies', V, 128–140

31   Henry St. John, Lord Viscount Bolingbroke, 'Epistle from Henry St. John Lord Viscount Bolingbroke to Miss Lucy Atkins', VI, 289–90

32   John Gilbert Cooper, ['An Epistle from the King of Prussia, to Monsieur Voltaire. 1757'], VI, 307–9 (Bell, I, 157–9)

33 Isaac Hawkins Browne, 'A Letter to Corinna from a Captain in Country
    Quarters', V, 226–9 (Bell, II, 63–6)
34 Thomas Lisle, 'Letter from Smyrna to his Sisters at Crux-Easton, 1733', VI,
    182–8 (Bell, II, 88–93)
35 ——, 'Part of a Letter to my Sisters at Crux-Easton, Written from Cairo in
    Egypt, August 1734', VI, 188–9 (Bell, II, 94–6)
36 ——, 'Letter from Marseilles to my Sisters at Crux-Easton, May 1735', VI,
    190–3 (Bell, II, 97–100)
37 Edward, Littleton, 'A Letter from Cambridge to Master Henry Archer, a
    young Gentleman at Eton School', VI, 316–20 (Bell, II, 58–62)

B   Presumably also counted by Havens as epistolary

1   John Hoadly, 'To the Rev. Mr. J. Straight, 1731', V, 267–70 (Bell, II, 76–9)
2   John Straight, 'Answer to the Foregoing', V, 270–2 (Bell, II, 80–2)
3   Lewis Thomas, 'Captain Lewis Thomas, of Battereau's Regiment, in the Isle
    of Skie, to Captain Price, at Fort Augustus', V, 258–62 (Bell, 67–70)
4   George Lyttelton, Baron Lyttelton, 'To the Reverend Dr. Ayscough at
    Oxford. Written from Paris in the Year 1728', II, 28–34
5   ——, 'To Mr. Poyntz, Ambassador at the Congress of Soissons, in the Year
    1728. Written at Paris', II, 35–8
6   John Straight, 'To Mr. John Hoadly, at the Temple, Occasioned by a
    Translation of an Epistle of Horace', 1730', V, 262–7 (Bell, II, 71–5)
7   Isaac Hawkins Browne, 'From Cælia to Cloe', II, 304–6 (Bell, II, 30–1)
8   James Bramston, 'The Man of Taste. Occasion'd by an Epistle of Mr. Pope's
    on that Subject', I, 312–26 (Bell, V, 64–75)

C   Also epistolary

1   Soame Jenyns, 'An Essay on Virtue. To the Honourable Philip Yorke, Esq;',
    III, 182–9 (Bell, I, 1–8)
2   John Hervey, Baron of Ickworth, 'To the Same [i.e., Stephen Fox]. From
    Hampton-Court, 1731', III, 197–204 (Bell, I, 77–84)
3   John Brown, 'Honour. A Poem', III, 295–309 (Bell, I, 27–37)
4   Benjamin Stillingfleet, 'An Essay on Conversation', I, 327–51 (Bell, V,
    118–41)
5   John Brown, 'An Essay on Satire, Occasioned by the Death of Mr. Pope', III,
    327–52 (Bell, V, 1–21)
6   Sneyd Davies, 'To the Worthy, Humane, Generous, Reverend, and Noble,
    Mr. Frederick Cornwallis', VI, 153–6 (Bell, I, 140–4),
7   ——, 'To his Friend and Neighbour Dr. Thomas Taylor', VI, 157–63 (Bell,
    I, 145–51)
8   ——, 'To Charles Pratt, Esq;', VI, 286–8 (Bell, I, 152–4)
9   Charles Hanbury Williams, Sir, 'To Mrs. Bindon at Bath', V, 168 (Bell, VI,
    134–5)
10 Bindon, Mrs. (dubious attribution), 'Mrs. Bindon's Answer', V, 169 (Bell,

VI, 136)

11 Charles Hanbury Williams, Sir, 'Sir Charles's Reply', V, 169–170 (Bell, VI, 137)

12 James Hammond, 'Elegy to Miss Dashwood. In the Manner of Ovid', IV, 80–2

13 Mary Wortley Montagu, Lady (attributed to Lord Hervey), 'Answer to the Foregoing Lines', IV, 83–5

14 Frances Thynne Seymour, Countess of Hertford (attributed to Lady Mary Wortley Montague), 'Lady Mary Wortley Montague, to Sir William Yonge', VI, 246–7

15 Mary Wortley Montagu, Lady (attributed to Lord Hervey), 'Sir William Yonge's Answer', VI, 247

16 John Sican, 'Verses Sent to Dean Swift on his Birth-day, with Pine's Horace Finely Bound', IV, 203–5 (Bell, VI, 29–31)

17 Soame Jenyns, 'To the Right Hon. the Lady Margaret Cavendish Harley, Presented with a Collection of Poems', III, 144–5 (Bell, VI, 32–3)

18 ——, 'To a Lady, Sent with a Present of Shells and Stones Design'd for a Grotto', III, 148–50 (Bell, VI, 34–6)

19 Edward Rolle (unattributed), 'To a Young Lady, with Fontenelle's Plurality of Worlds', III, 241–3 (Bell, VI, 47–9)

20 George Bubb Dodington, later Lord Melcombe, 'To the Right Hon. Sir Robert Walpole', VI, 143–9

21 Edmund Waller, 'Verses to Dr. George Rogers, on His Taking the Degree of Doctor in Physic at Padua, in the Year 1664', IV, 117–18

22 Stephen Clay, 'To the Duke of Marlborough', V, 140–2 (Bell, VI, 108–10)

23 Richard Owen Cambridge, 'To Mr. Whitehead, on His Being Made Poet Laureat', VI, 337–9 (Bell, VI, 77–9)

24 William Whitehead, 'To Mr. Garrick', II, 262–6

25 ——, 'Nature to Dr. Hoadly, on his Comedy of the Suspicious Husband', II, 266–7 (Bell, VI, 85–6)

26 George Lyttelton, Baron Lyttelton, 'To my Lord Hervey in the Year 1730. From Worcestershire', II, 43–5

27 Soame Jenyns, 'To a Lady in Town, Soon after her Leaving the Country', III, 140–3

28 Joseph Warton, 'Fashion: A Satire', III, 284–90 (Bell, VI, 56–63)

29 James Bramston, 'The Art of Politicks, in Imitation of Horace's Art of Poetry', I, 276–311 (Bell, V, 97–117)

30 John Hervey, Baron of Ickworth, 'To Mr. Fox, Written at Florence. In Imitation of Horace, Ode IV. Book 2', III, 194–6 (Bell, I, 74–6)

31 George Lyttelton, Baron Lyttelton, 'Advice to a Lady', II, 46–51

32 Richard Owen Cambridge, 'An Elegy Written in an Empty Assembly-Room', VI, 330–4

D   Marginally epistolary

1   Philip Dormer Stanhope, Earl of Chesterfield (unattributed), 'Advice to a Lady in Autumn', I, 359–60 (Bell, II, 36–7)

2   Richard Berenger, 'To Mr. Garrick, on His Erecting a Temple and Statue to Shakespeare', VI, 296–8 (Bell, V, 87–9)

3   Charles Parrott, 'To a Lady on a Landscape of her Drawing', VI, 149–51 (Bell, VI, 40–2)

4   Sir James Marriott, 'To a Lady Making a Pin-basket', IV, 304–5 (Bell, VI, 153–5)

5   Thomas Tickell, 'On the Prospect of Peace, A Poem. To the Lord Privy-Seal', I, 3–25

6   ——, 'To the Right Honourable the Earl of Warwick, &c. On the Death of Mr. Addison', I, 25–30

7   ——, 'To Sir Godfrey Kneller, at his Country Seat', I, 39–41

8   Mary Wortley Montagu, Lady, 'In Answer to a Lady Who Advised Retirement', IV, 209

3   Pearch's Collection of Poems by Several Hands

A   Designated as 'epistle'

1   John Dalton, 'Epistle to the Right Hon. Lord Viscount Beauchamp', I, 60–70 (Bell, I, 63–73)

2   ——, 'Epistle to the Right Hon., the Countess of Hertford, (Afterwards Dutchess of Somerset) at Percy-Lodge', I, 71–81 (Bell, II, 108–18)

3   William Melmoth, 'Epistle to Sappho', II, 151–2 (Bell, I, 131–2)

4   John Dyer, 'An Epistle to a Friend in Town', I, 175–6

5   Unattributed [Antony Alsop], 'Epistle to the Rev. Sir John Dolben', II, 294–7 (Bell, II, 17–20)

6   Mark Akenside, 'An Epistle to Curio', III, 36–49

7   George Canning, 'Epistle from Lord William Russel, to Lord William Cavendish', III, 190–205 (Bell, VII, 46–62)

8   John Scott, 'Winter Prospects in the Country. An Epistle to a Friend in London, 1756', IV, 108–10

9   William Whitehead, 'On Nobility: An Epistle. To the Earl of ——', IV, 237–45 (Bell, I, 38–47)

10   Thomas Pearson, 'An Epistle to a Lady. Written in the Year MDCCLXVI. In the Character of her Husband', IV, 259–63

11   John Gerrard, 'An Epistle. From an Unfortunate Gentleman to a Young Lady', IV, 317–22

12   James Cawthorn, 'Abelard to Eloisa', I, 1–13 (Bell, VII, 104–16)

13   William Dodd, 'The African Prince, Now in England, to Zara at his Father's Court', IV, 222–30 (Bell, VII, 117–24)

14   ——, 'Zara. At the Court of Anamaboe, to the African Prince When in

England', IV, 230–6 (Bell, VII, 125–32)

B   Also epistolary

1   James Cawthorn, 'To Miss ——, of Horsemanden, in Kent, with the foregoing epistle', I, 14–15 (Bell, VII, 161, in endnotes)
2   John Dalton, 'A Descriptive Poem: Addressed to Two Ladies, at their Return from Viewing the Mines Near Whitehaven', I, 39–59 (Bell, IV, 47–59)
3   ——, 'Some Thoughts on Building and Planting. To Sir James Lowther, Bart. of Lowther Hall', I, 82–5 (Bell, III, 157–9)
4   George Bubb Dodington, Lord Melcombe, 'Verses Sent by Lord Melcombe to Dr. Young, Not Long before his Lordship's Death', I, 327–8
5   Unattributed [George Villiers, Duke of Buckingham], 'To a Lady, with a Pair of Gloves on Valentine's Day', II, 301 (Bell, VI, 156)
6   Unidentified [false attribution to Samuel Johnson), 'To Myrtillis. The New-Year's Offering', III, 251–3 (Bell, VI, 53–6)
7   George Keate, 'To a Lady, Going to Bathe in the Sea', III, 271–3 (Bell, II, 127–8)
8   John Duncombe, 'The Feminead: Or Female Genius', IV, 176–91 (Bell, VI, 1–16)
9   George Canning, 'A Birth-Day Offering to a Young Lady. From her Lover', III, 205–9 (Bell, VI, 170–4)
10   Samuel Johnson, 'To Miss ——. on her Playing upon the Harpsichord in a Room Hung with Some Flower-Pieces of her own Painting', III, 249–50 (Bell, VI, 57–8)

3   Lonsdale's New Oxford Book of Eighteenth-Century Verse

A   Designated as 'epistle'

1   Mary Collier, from *The Woman's Labour. An Epistle to Mr. Stephen Duck*, pp. 325–6
2   Robert Dodsley, 'An Epistle to my Friend J. B.', pp. 261–3
3   William Dunkin, from 'An Epistle to R[o]b[er]t N[u]g[en]t, Esq. With a Picture of Doctor Swift [in Old Age]', pp. 341–2
4   Thomas Gilbert, from *A View of the Town. In an Epistle to a Friend*, p. 283
5   Matthew Green, from *The Spleen. An Epistle to Mr. C— J—*, pp. 287–90
6   Mary Leapor, 'An Epistle to a Lady', pp. 411–12
7   Robert Lloyd, from 'Shakespeare, an Epistle to David Garrick, Esq.', pp. 473–4
8   ——, 'A Familiar Epistle to J. B.', pp. 474–5
9   Thomas Maurice, from 'An Epistle to the Right Hon. James Fox', pp. 697–8
10   Richardson Pack, 'An Epistle from a Half-Pay Officer in the Country', pp. 111–12

11   Alexander Pope, 'Epistle to Miss Blount, on Her Leaving the Town, after the Coronation', pp. 99–100
12   ——, from *An Epistle to Richard Boyle, Earl of Burlington*, pp. 234–6
13   ——, *An Epistle from Mr. Pope to Dr. Arbuthnot*, pp. 239–48
14   ——, *Epistle to a Lady: Of the Characters of Women*, pp. 248–54

B   Designated as 'letter'

1   Joseph Addison, 'A Letter from Italy, to the Right Honourable Charles Lord Halifax', pp. 41–4
2   John Ellis, 'Sarah Hazard's Love Letter', pp. 412–14
3   Matthew Prior, 'A Letter to the Honourable Lady Miss Margaret Cavendish-Holles-Harley', p. 60

C   Also epistolary

1   Anonymous, 'To a Lady, with a Present of a Fan', p. 759
2   —— ('J. T.'), 'A Sea-Chaplain's Petition to the Lieutenants', pp. 480–2
3   ——, from *The Art of Wenching*, pp. 299–300
4   John Armstrong, from *The Oeconomy of Love. A Poetical Essay*, pp. 293–4
5   ——, from *The Art of Preserving Health*, pp. 294–6
6   James Cawthorn, from 'Of Taste. An Essay', pp. 494–6
7   William Diaper, from *Brent, a Poem. To Thomas Palmer, Esq.*, pp. 82–3
8   John Dyer, 'To Clio. From Rome', pp. 166–7
9   John Byrom, 'To Henry Wright of Mobberley, Esq. On Buying the Picture of F[ather] Malebranche', pp. 207–9
10   George Farewell, 'To the Archdeacon', pp. 268–9
11   John Gay, 'To a Young Lady with Some Lampreys', pp. 127–8
12   Oliver Goldsmith, from *The Traveller, or A Prospect of Society*, pp. 521–2
13   Samuel Henley, 'Verses Addressed to a Friend, Just Leaving a Favourite Retirement, Previous to Settling Abroad. Written in the Close of Winter', pp. 662–5
14   Charles Morris, 'Addressed to Lady ****, Who Asked What the Passion of Love Was?', pp. 734–6
15   Thomas Morris, '[Sapphics: At the Mohawk-Castle, Canada. To Lieutenant Montgomery]', pp. 498–500
16   Ambrose Phillips, 'A Winter-Piece. To the Earl of Dorset', pp. 84–5
17   Alexander Pope, from *An Essay on Man*, pp. 236–8
18   William Somervile, 'Hudibras and Milton Reconciled. To Sir Adolphus Oughton', pp. 204–5
19   Jonathan Swift, 'The Humble Petition of Frances Harris', pp. 9–11
20   Leonard Welsted, 'The Invitation', pp. 147–8
21   Gilbert White, 'The Naturalist's Summer-Evening Walk. To Thomas Pennant, Esq.', pp. 563–4
22   Ann Yearsley, 'To Mr.****, an Unlettered Poet, on Genius Unimproved', pp. 727–8

D   Marginally epistolary

1   Anna Laetitia Barbauld, 'To Mr. [S. T.] C[olerid]ge', pp. 817–18
2   William Parsons, 'To a Friend in Love During the Riots', pp. 810–11
3   Matthew Prior, 'A Better Answer to Cloe Jealous', pp. 56–7
4   Philip Dormer Stanhope, Earl of Chesterfield, 'Advice to a Young Lady', pp. 276–7
5   John Smith, 'A Solitary Canto to Chloris the Disdainful', pp. 104–5
6   John Thelwall, from 'Lines Written at Bridgwater, 27 July 1797 [To S. T. Coleridge]', pp. 814–15
7   Horace Walpole, Earl of Orford, 'To Lady [Anne Fitzpatrick], When about Five Years Old', pp. 587–8
8   Edward Thompson, 'To Emma, Extempore. Hyaena, off Gambia, June 4, 1779', p. 668

E   Doubtfully epistolary

1   Robert Craggs Nugent, Earl Nugent, 'To Clarissa', pp. 423–5
2   Alexander Pope, 'To Mr. Gay, Who Wrote Him a Congratulatory Letter on the Finishing his House', pp. 102–3

4   Lonsdale's Eighteenth-Century Women Poets: An Oxford Anthology

A   Designated as 'epistle'

1   Anonymous ('Eliza' [Day]), from 'A Tour to the Glaciers of Savoy. An Epistle to John Waller, Esq.', pp. 496–9
2   Susanna Blamire, 'Epistle to her Friends at Gartmore', pp. 279–83
3   Charlotte Brereton, 'To Miss A[nn]a M[ari]a Tra[ver]s. An Epistle from Scotland', pp. 188–90
4   Jane Brereton, from 'Epistle to Mrs Anne Griffiths. Written from London, in 1718', p. 80
5   Susanna Centlivre, from 'An Epistle to the King of Sweden, from a Lady of Great Britain', pp. 75–6
6   Mary Collier, from *The Woman's Labour. An Epistle to Mr. Stephen Duck*, pp. 172–3
7   Maria and Harriet Falconar, 'A Prefatory Epistle [to the Reviewers]', p. 452
8   Anne Ingram, Viscountess Irwin, from 'An Epistle to Mr. Pope. Occasioned by his *Characters of Women*', pp. 150–1
9   Mary Jones, 'An Epistle to Lady Bower', pp. 156–60
10   ——, 'Epistle from Fern Hill', pp. 163–5
11   Mary Leapor, from 'An Epistle to Artemisia', pp. 204–6
12   ——, 'The Epistle of Deborah Dough', pp. 209–10
13   ——, 'An Epistle to a Lady', pp. 215–17
14   Mary Wortley Montagu, Lady, 'Epistle [to Lord Bathurst]', pp. 63–5

Notes

Preface

1   William C. Dowling, *The Epistolary Moment: The Poetics of the Eighteenth-Century Verse Epistle* (Princeton: Princeton University Press, 1991); see pp. 17–18 above.

2   *An Epistle to the Right Honourable James Lord Visct. Charlemont. With a Translation of the Sixth Satire of the Second Book of Horace* (Dublin: by and for George Faulkner, 1744), discussed on pp. 190–2 above.

1. Definition

1   *Fiction and Diction*, trans. by Catherine Porter (Ithaca, NY, and London: Cornell University Press, 1993), pp. 1–29.

2   See, e.g., Lady Mary Wortley Montagu's verse letter to Lord Hervey, considered on pp. 24–6 above.

3   *Horace: Satires, Epistles, and Ars Poetica*, Loeb Classical Library, ed. with trans. by H. Rushton Fairclough, rev. edn (London: William Heinemann; Cambridge, MA: Harvard University Press, 1929), pp. 442–89. For a less literal translation, also with the Latin text, see *The Epistles of Horace*, trans. by David Ferry (New York: Farrar, Straus and Giroux, 2001), pp. 150–85.

4   'Voice, Gender, and the Augustan Verse Epistle', in *Presenting Gender: Changing Sex in Early-Modern Culture*, ed. by Chris Mounsey (Lewisburg, PA: Bucknell University Press; London: Associated University Presses, 2001), pp. 76–93 (p. 79).

5   'Voice, Gender, and the Augustan Verse Epistle', pp. 77, 78.

6   *Poems on Several Occasions. With Anne Boleyn to King Henry VIII. An Epistle* (London: for John Clarke, 1724), pp. 16–17, 72–84.

7   *Poems on Several Occasions*, pp. 21–2; repr. in *Eighteenth-Century Women Poets: An Oxford Anthology*, ed. by Roger Lonsdale (Oxford and New York: Oxford University Press, 1989), pp. 96–8.

8   'To Dr. James Sherard, M. D. On the Hortus Elthamensis', 'To Mr. Handell', 'To Mrs. Rokeby, Junior, at Arthingworth', in *Poems on Several Occasions. With Anne Boleyn to King Henry VIII. An Epistle* (London: for John Clarke, 1755), pp. 130–1, 136–7, 138.

9   *Poems on Several Occasions* (London: C. Rivington, 1734; properly 1735); *The Description of Bath, A Poem. [. . .] To Which are Added, Several Poems by the Same Author*, 4th edn (London: for James Leake, 1738); *Poems on Various Subjects and Occasions*, 2 vols (London: for C. Parker, 1777). On

epistolary verse by Tollet and Barber, see also pp. 55–6 above; for the correct year of publication for Barber's *Poems*, see A. C. Elias, Jr., 'Editing Minor Writers: The Case of Laetitia Pilkington and Mary Barber', in *1650–1850: Ideas, Aesthetics, and Inquiries in the Early Modern Era*, III, ed. by Kevin L. Cope (New York: AMS Press), 129–47 (pp. 136–7).

10 *Poems on Several Occasions*, ed. by James Nichols (London: Simpkin, Marshall, 1862), 'An Epistle to my Lord Oxford. 1732' (pp. 487–90), and two poems entitled 'An Epistle to my Lord Oxford' (pp. 494–7, 501–3); 'An Epistle to my Lord Orrery' (pp. 594–7); 'Whigs and Tories: In Four Poetical Epistles' (pp. 524–33); 'A Poetical Epistle to my Brother Charles' (pp. 132–5); 'To Miss Martha Wesley. An Epistle' (pp. 559–61); 'An Epistle to Me' (pp. 577–8); 'A Familiar Epistle to a Friend' (pp. 201–4).

11 'A Letter to a Friend Who Came to Thank Me for His Having Got Preferment' (pp. 465–7), 'A Letter to Mr. Kilner on his Marriage' (pp. 471–2), 'A Letter from a Guardian to a Young Lady' (pp. 118–24), 'Neck or Nothing; A Consolatory Letter from Mr. Dunton to Mr. C—ll, on His Being Toss'd in a Blanket' (pp. 304–11), 'A Letter from a Gentleman at Avignon to his Mistress Here: In Answer to "A Letter from a Lady" by Mr. Tickell' (pp. 589–94). The squib on Curll was first published in 1716, Tickell's poem in 1717.

12 These include eight poems congratulating male friends on their marriage, and other occasional verse including 'To a Young Gentleman, on his Recovery from a Fit of Sickness' (pp. 154–5), 'To James Oglethorpe, Esq.' (pp. 428–31), and 'To W. Colman, Esq., 1735' (pp. 655–6).

13 London: by B. Motte for Charles Harper, 1700.

14 *The Poems of John Byrom*, ed. by Adophus William Ward, 3 vols (Manchester: Charles E. Simms for the Chetham Society), 'An Epistle to a Friend, Occasioned by a Sermon Intituled "The False Claims to Martyrdom Consider'd"' (I, 332–57); 'An Epistle to J. Bl—k—n, Esq., Occasioned by a Dispute Concerning the Food of St. John the Baptist' (I, 477–82); 'An Epistle to a Gentleman of the Temple' (II, 138–66); 'Familiar Epistles to a Friend, upon a Sermon Entitled the Office and Operations of the Holy Spirit, by the Rev. Mr. Warburton' (II, 249–73, divided into six 'Letters'); 'Four Epistles to the Rev. Mr. L—, Late Vicar of Bowdon, upon the Miracle at the Feast of Pentecost' (II, 282–304).

15 'Three Epistles to G. Lloyd, Esq; on the Following Passage in Homer' (I, 483–500); 'An Epistle to a Friend, Proposing a Correction in the Following Passage' (I, 502–7); 'An Epistle from the Author to his Sister' (II, 107–10); 'An Epistle to a Friend on the Art of English Poetry' (I, 394–410).

16 'A Poetical Version of a Letter from the Earl of Essex to the Earl of Southampton' (II, 345–53); 'A Poetical Version of a Letter from Jacob Behmen to a Friend' (II, 358–69); 'An Answer to the Following Letter, Requesting the Author's Solution of a Rebus, Commonly Ascribed to Lord Chesterfield' (I, 558–66).

17 'Tunbridgiale, Being a Description of Tunbridge, in a Letter to a Friend at London' (I, 10–18); 'A Letter to R. L., Esq.' (I, 30–4); 'A Letter to R. L.,

Esq., on His Departure from London' (I, 38–46); 'A Full and True Account of an Horrid and Barbarous Robbery, Committed on Epping Forest upon the Body of the Cambridge Coach. In a Letter to M. F., Esq.' (I, 62–73).

18 'A Letter to a Lady, Occasioned by Her Desiring the Author to Revise and Polish the Poems of Bishop Ken' (II, 114–26); 'Remarks on a Pamphlet Entitled Epistles to the Great, from Aristippus in Retirement in a Letter to Dr. S—' (I, 448–58); 'On the Patron of England; In a Letter to Lord Willoughby, President of the Antiquarian Society' (I, 465–76); 'A Letter to a Friend, upon the Meaning of St. Paul's Expression of "Speaking with Tongues"' (II, 305–13). The first lines quoted are from 'On the Patron of England', and 'A Letter to a Friend'; 'A Letter to a Lady' begins with the words, 'Your Book again, with Thanks!'.

19 'An Epistle to a Gentleman of the Temple' (II, 144), Epistle I of 'Four Epistles to the Rev. Mr. L—' (II, 284), Epistle IV of the same (II, 299), 'An Epistle to J. Bl—k—n, Esq.' (I, 477). Contrast 'Dear *Peter*' for the two verse letters addressed to 'R. L., Esq.' and for 'Tunbridgiale' (I, 32, 38, 10); and 'Dear *Martin Folkes*, dear Scholar, Brother, Friend' for 'A Full and True Account of an Horrid and Barbarous Robbery' (I, 64).

20 *Poems*, II, 130–4, 167–97. Ward's headnote to the latter mentions a copy bound up with 'Epistle to a Gentleman of the Temple', suggesting that the two are of the same kind.

21 London: by H. Hills, 1709, repr. in *The Miscellaneous Works of Joseph Addison*, ed. by A. C. Guthkelch (London: G. Bell and Sons, 1914), pp. 51–62; London: for Jacob Tonson, 1714; London: for A. Dodd and E. Nutt, 1729, repr. in *The Complete Works of William Congreve*, 4 vols, ed. by Montague Summers (London: Nonesuch Press, 1923), IV, 177–8.

22 'Voice, Gender, and the Augustan Verse Epistle', pp. 77–8; *The Spectator*, ed. by Donald F. Bond, 5 vols (Oxford: Clarendon Press, 1965), V, 112–13 (no. 618, 10 November 1714).

23 Jay Arnold Levine cites Thomas Lodge's *A Fig for Momus* (1595) as 'The first clear and elaborate introduction of the verse epistle to English readers', but claims that the seven epistles that Lodge includes, all by himself, 'are presented so rhetorically as to *deny* the epistolary mode of the form rather than fulfill it'. See 'The Status of the Verse Epistle before Pope', *Studies in Philology*, 59 (1962), 658–84 (p. 658).

24 2 vols, London: for J. Newbery, I, 116–28. The earlier version is *The Art of Poetry Made Easy [. . .] Being the Seventh Volume of the Circle of the Sciences* (London: for J. Newbery, 1746). For details, see S[ydney] Roscoe, *John Newbery and his Successors 1740–1814: A Bibliography* (Wormley, Herts: Five Owls Press, 1973).

25 *The Poems of Gray, Collins, and Goldsmith*, ed. by Roger Lonsdale (London and Harlow: Longmans, Green, 1969), p. 627.

26 Lyttelton's epistle was first printed in 1730 (London: for J. Roberts), repr. in *A Collection of Poems by Several Hands* (London: for J. Dodsley, 1782), II, 40–42; Pope's in the first volume of his *Works* (London: by W. Bowyer, for

Jacob Tonson and Bernard Lintot, 1717), pp. 373–5, repr. in *The Poems of Alexander Pope*, Twickenham Edition, 11 vols (London: Methuen; New Haven, CT: Yale University Press, 1939–69), VI, *Minor Poems*, ed. by Norman Ault and John Butt, 2nd edn (1964), 124–7.

27 First printed in *The Tatler*, no. 12, 7 May 1709 (ed. by Donald F. Bond, 3 vols [Oxford: Clarendon Press, 1987], pp. 109–111); repr. in *The New Oxford Book of Eighteenth-Century Verse*, ed. by Roger Lonsdale (Oxford: Oxford University Press, 1984), pp. 84–5.

28 2 vols (London: for L. Gilliver), II, 64–6; first printed in *Works* (London [The Hague?]: by T[homas] J[ohnson], 1720), pp. 97–9; repr. in Twickenham edn, VI, 202–7.

29 2 vols (London: by T. Aris for the author, 1738), I, xx, iii, xvii–xviii. The second edition lists 'the several Species' under five headings on its title page, styling the epistles as 'Ethic, Amorous, and Familiar' (London: for James Hodges, 1739).

30 London: by Will. Stansby.

31 *Ben Jonson: The Complete Poems*, ed. by George Parfitt (Harmondsworth: Penguin Books, 1975), p. 19.

32 2 vols, London: for Jacob Tonson and Bernard Lintot. The items in vol. I are 'Rural Sports', 'The Fan', 'The Shepherd's Week', 'Trivia', and 'The What D'Ye Call It'.

33 Edinburgh: Mr. Thomas Ruddiman, for the Author, pp. 399–400, repr. in *The Works of Allan Ramsay*, 6 vols: 1 and 2 ed. by Burns Martin and John W. Oliver, 3–6 by Alexander M. Kinghorn and Alexander Law, Scottish Text Society, 3rd ser., 19–20, 29; 4th ser., 6–8 (Edinburgh and London: William Blackwood & Sons, 1945–74), I, 264–5.

34 See, e.g., Allan H. MacLaine, *Allan Ramsay* (Boston: Twayne Publishers, 1985), especially pp. 5–6, 8, 10, 21–4, 59–60, 78–9, 133, 134–9.

35 *Poems by Allan Ramsay. Volume II* (Edinburgh: Mr. Thomas Ruddiman, for the Author, 1728), pp. xi–xii.

36 *The Poems of Allan Ramsay. A New Edition*, 2 vols (London: by A. Strahan, for T. Cadell Jun. and W. Davies).

37 London: by W. Bowyer for Jacob Tonson and Bernard Lintot.

38 London: for L. Gilliver.

39 *The Works of Alexander Pope Esq*, 9 vols (London: for J. Knapton, H. Lintot, J. and R. Tonson, and S. Draper).

40 *Original Poems, by John Dryden, Esq.* Nine years later, the Foulis brothers began a series of poets that had reached 48 volumes in 1776. See Thomas F. Bonnell, 'Patchwork and Piracy: John Bell's "Connected System of Biography" and the Use of Johnson's *Prefaces*', *Studies in Bibliography*, 48 (1995), 194–229 (p. 229, n. 36).

41 *The Poems of John Dryden*, 5 vols, ed. by Paul Hammond and David Hopkins (London and New York: Longman, 1995–2005), I (1995), x.

42 *The Comedies, Tragedies, and Operas Written by John Dryden*, 2 vols (London: for Jacob Tonson, Thomas Bennet, and Richard Wellington);

Dramatic Works (London: Jacob Tonson).

43 London: for J. and R. Tonson.

44 *The Poets of Great Britain Complete from Chaucer to Churchill*, 109 vols (Edinburgh: Apollo Press, by the Martins, 1776–82).

45 Thomas F. Bonnell, 'John Bell's *Poets of Great Britain*: The "Little Trifling Edition" Revisited', *Modern Philology*, 85 (1987), 128–52 (p. 134).

46 *The Poetical Works of Matthew Prior*, in *Poets of Great Britain*, vols 47–9, but printed 15th–17th in the series (Bonnell, p. 131).

47 *Poets of Great Britain*, vols 35 (1779), 51 (1779), 74–5 (1780).

48 For Sonnleithner and Hoerling, 1783–86, 'Index of the various Poems, distinguishing the classes, to which they belong', VI, unpaginated back matter.

49 *The Poetical Works of William Congreve* (London: for C. Cooke, [1796]).

50 *Poems on Several Occasions* (London: by E. Hodson, 1796).

51 John Cunningham, *Poems, Chiefly Pastoral* (London: for the author, 1766), pp. 195–6; *Choice of [. . .] the Most Eminent English Poets*, VI, 203–4; *Poets of Great Britain*, 108, *The Poetical Works of John Cunningham* (1781), pp. 161–2.

52 'Contents', *Poetical Works of William Congreve*; John Dryden, *The Satires of Decimus Junius Juvenalis [. . .] Together with the Satires of Aulus Persius Flaccus* (London: for Jacob Tonson, 1692 [1693]), sig. A4^{r-v}.

53 18 vols (London: by John Bell, 1789–94; vols 17–18 by and for James Cawthorn, 1796, 1797). Details of first publication of the poems mentioned are given only where the context requires it.

54 Authors to whom poems are falsely attributed are Samuel Johnson ('To Myrtilis', author unknown), William Pattison ('Abelard to Eloisa', a common misattribution at the period; the poem is actually by Judith Cowper, later Madan), and Richard Savage ('Dennis to Mr. Thomson', actually by John Duick); those to whom poems are dubiously attributed are Mrs Bindon ('Mrs. Bindon's Reply', perhaps by Sir Charles Hanbury Williams); Alexander Pope ('To His Grace the Duke of Argyll', 'To the Author of a Panegyric on Mrs. Grace Butler'); and 'Mr. Webster' ('The Stage', probably by Francis Reynardson). For the false attributions to Johnson and Savage see, respectively, *The Poems of Samuel Johnson*, ed. by David Nicol Smith and Edward L. McAdam, 2nd edn, rev. by J. D. Fleeman (Oxford: Clarendon Press, 1974), p. 465, and C. Lennart Carlson, *The First Magazine: A History of the Gentleman's Magazine* (Providence, RI: Brown University Press, 1938), p. 251. For the dubious attributions to Mrs Bindon, Pope and Webster, see *A Collection of Poems by Several Hands*, ed. by Michael F. Suarez, SJ, 6 vols (London: Routledge/Thoemmes Press, 1997), I, 125; *The Poems of Alexander Pope*, Twickenham Edition, 11 vols (London: Methuen, 1938–68), VII, *Minor Poems*, ed. by Norman Ault and John Butt, 422, 458; and David Foxon's bibliographical note (Foxon R176).

55 The eight authors represented by more than three poems are John Dalton (4), Sneyd Davies (4), John Duncombe (4), Lord Hervey (6), Soame Jenyns (5), Samuel Johnson (5, but including the falsely attributed poem identifed in the

previous note), Robert Craggs Nugent (8), and Edward Rolle (4).

56 Dodsley's *Collection* first appeared in two volumes in 1748 and was successively expanded to six volumes by 1758; further editions with minor changes continued till 1782. See Michael F. Suarez, SJ, 'The Formation, Transmission, and Reception of Dodsley's *Collection of Poems by Several Hands*', in his edition of the *Collection* cited in note 54 above, I, 1–119.

57 8 vols (London: by and for J. Nichols, 1780–2); *Supplements to Dodsley's Collection of Poems*, Oxford Bibliographical Society Occasional Publication No. 15 (Oxford: Oxford Bibliographical Society, 1980), p. vii. Forster's remark that Bell's material came 'particularly from the "Supplements"' is somewhat misleading for the seven volumes devoted to the verse epistle, as almost 40 percent are traceable from Dodsley's *Collection*. Excluding multiple representations in the case of a few poems, 33 had appeared in Nichols, 24 in the *Poetical Calendar*, 20 in one or more of the editions of Pearch, 16 in the *New Foundling Hospital for Wit*, 1 in one of the editions by Mendez, and 2 in Dryden's miscellany. Of the remaining 13, 1 first appeared in Dodsley's *Museum* in 1747, 1 probably comes from the *European Magazine*, and 11 I have not been able to trace in collections.

58 The Irish writers are James Dalacourt, Oliver Goldsmith, Robert Craggs Nugent, Thomas Parnell, John Sican and Richard Steele; the Scot, William Julius Mickle. The Scottish verse epistle flourished before Burns in the work of writers such as Allan Ramsay and Robert Fergusson. Though the collection was published a little too early to have included Burns, it would almost certainly have omitted his most characteristic epistles because it never ventures beyond standard English.

59 *New Oxford Book of Eighteenth-Century Verse*, p. xxxvi; see also Lonsdale's *Eighteenth-Century Women Poets*, p. xlii.

60 Lady Mary Wortley Montagu, 'To Lord Bathurst' (II, 9–12); Miss Courtenay, 'To Miss Anne Conolly. May, 1753' (II, 32–5); Elizabeth Carter, 'To a Friend, Occasioned by an Ode Written by Mrs. Cath. Philips' (VI, 50–2); The Honorable Miss Yorke, 'To the Lady Marchioness Grey' (VI, 141–2); and Judith Cowper (later Madan), 'Abelard to Eloisa'. For the false attribution of 'Abelard to Eloisa', and for the possible male authorship of 'Mrs. Bindon's Answer', see note 54 above.

61 See *The Epistolary Moment* and pp. 17–18 above.

62 *A Poetical Epistle to Sir Joshua Reynolds* (London: for Fielding and Walker).

63 Here Bell was very up to date, as White's book had only been published in December 1788. See Gilbert White, *The Natural History of Selborne*, ed. by Roger Mabey (Harmondsworth: Penguin Books, 1977), pp. xxiv, xxvii.

64 William Melmoth, 'Of Active and Retired Life. To Henry Coventry' (I, 9–19); Edward Rolle, 'Life Burthensome, Because We Know Not How to Use It' (I, 20–2); John Dalton, 'To the Lord Viscount Beauchamp' (I, 63–73).

65 *The Monthly Review; or, Literary Journal*, 81 (1789), 456.

66 *Epistolary Moment*, p. 21.

67 *Epistolary Moment*, p. 9.

68 'Voice, Gender, and the Augustan Verse Epistle', pp. 78–9.
69 *Epistolary Moment*, p. 12 and passim.
70 *Epistolary Spaces: English Letter Writing from the Foundation of the Post Office to Richardson's Clarissa* (Aldershot, Hants, and Burlington, VT: Ashgate, 2003), p. 9, citing Robert Adams Day, *Told in Letters: Epistolary Fiction before Richardson* (Ann Arbor: University of Michigan Press, 1966).
71 *Epistolary Spaces*, p. 53; 'Voice, Gender, and the Augustan Verse Epistle', p. 76.
72 *Epistolary Bodies: Gender and Genre in the Eighteenth-Century Republic of Letters* (Stanford, CA: Stanford University Press, 1996), pp. 2, 11, citing *The Structural Transformation of the Public Sphere: An Enquiry into a Category of Bourgeois Society*, trans. by Thomas Burger and Frederick Lawrence (Cambridge, MA: MIT Press, 1989; first published in German, 1962).
73 *English Poetry of the Eighteenth Century, 1700–1789* (Harlow and London: Pearson Education, 2003), p. 60; 'Between Manuscript and Print' is the title of Fairer's first chapter.
74 See *English Poetry of the Eighteenth Century*, pp. 3–4. Satirical epistles are obvious examples.
75 *Women, Fire, and Dangerous Things: What Categories Reveal about the Mind* (Chicago: University of Chicago Press, 1987), p. 16. I am grateful to Neal Swettenham for calling Lakoff's work to my attention and for giving me a pre-publication draft of his essay 'Categories and Catcalls: Cognitive Dissonance in *The Playboy of the Western World*', in *Performance and Cognition: Theatre Studies and the Cognitive Turn*, ed. by Bruce A. McConachie and F. Elizabeth Hart (New York: Routledge, 2006), pp. 207–22, which summarizes key parts of it.
76 The five are anapestic tetrameter couplets (7 examples), blank verse (4), iambic pentameter couplets (104), iambic tetrameter couplets (63), and trochaic tetrameter couplets (2).
77 For discussion of the Standard Habby, see p. 94 above.
78 Philip Hobsbaum identifies Joseph Warton's 'The Dying Indian' (1755) as the first true example of the form in 'The Rise of the Dramatic Monologue', *Hudson Review*, 28 (1975), 227–45. See further the discussion in Chapter 5 above. The earliest use of the term 'dramatic epistle' I have come across is by Isobel Grundy in 'Ovid and Eighteenth-Century Divorce: An Unpublished Poem by Lady Mary Wortley Montagu', *Review of English Studies*, 23 (1972), 417–28 (p. 422), discussing 'Epistle from Mrs. Y[onge] to her Husband'. The poem is collected in Lady Mary Wortley Montagu, *Essays and Poems, and Simplicity, a Comedy*, ed. by Robert Halsband and Isobel Grundy (Oxford: Clarendon Press, 1977, 1993), pp. 230–2.
79 'To Their Excellencies the Lords Justice of Ireland. The Humble Petition of Frances Harris', and 'Mary the Cook-Maid's Letter to Dr. Sheridan', in *The Poems of Jonathan Swift*, ed. by Harold Williams, 2nd edn, 3 vols (Oxford: Clarendon Press, 1958), I, 68–73, III, 985–7; 'P[ope] to Bolingbroke', in *Essays and Poems*, pp. 279–84.

80 *Epistolary Moment*, pp. 7–13, 31–2, 35–6, 60–1, 81.
81 *Epistolarity: Approaches to a Form* (Columbus: Ohio State University Press, 1982), p. 189.
82 *Epistolarity*, p. 206.
83 *Epistolarity*, p. 112, n. 2; 'Epistolary Discourse' is the title of her Chapter 4.
84 'The Weight of the Reader' is the title of Altman's Chapter 3; for 'addressee-consciousness', see p. 111.
85 *'Epistolarity' in the First Book of Horace's Epistles*, Gorgias Dissertations: Classics, I (Piscataway, NJ: Gorgias Press, 2002).
86 London: for J. Dodsley, 1766; London: for H. D. Symonds and T. Bellamy, 1796.
87 *'Epistolarity' in the First Book of Horace's Epistles*, p. 27.
88 *The Complete Letters of Lady Mary Wortley Montagu*, ed. by Robert Halsband, 3 vols (Oxford: Clarendon Press, 1965–7), II, 98–9.
89 Mary, Lady Chudleigh, *Poems on Several Occasions* (London: by W. B. for Bernard Lintott), pp. 22–5; repr. in *The Poems and Prose of Mary, Lady Chudleigh*, ed. by Margaret J. M. Ezell (New York and Oxford: Oxford University Press, 1993), pp. 67–9.
90 *Women, Authorship and Literary Culture, 1690–1740* (Houndmills, Basingstoke, and New York: Palgrave Macmillan, 2003), p. 53.
91 'To Almystrea', 'To Eugenia', 'To the Learn'd and Ingenious Dr. Musgrave of Exeter', *Poems and Prose*, pp. 66–7, 74–5, 120–3; *Poetical Recreations* (London: for Benjamin Crayle, 1688), pp. 65–9, 70–72. Epistles by Barker in iambic pentameter couplets include 'To Mr. G. P. my Adopted Brother; On the Nigh Approach of his Nuptials' (pp. 11–12), 'To my Honoured Friend, Mr. E. S—t' (pp. 40–2), 'To my Brother, Whilst He Was in France' (pp. 46–7), and 'To my Dear Cousin Mrs. M. T. after the Death of her Husband and Son' (pp. 59–61); but 'To my Adopted Brother, Mr. G. P. on My Frequent Writing to Him' (pp. 95–6) is in iambic tetrameter couplets ending with a pentameter couplet.
92 London: by R. E. for Jacob Tonson, pp. 343–8, praising *The Old Bachelor*.
93 IX, 235–6, signed 'Q. A.'; Philadelphia: John Dunlap, 1772, pp. 9–11; Florence: printed in the Stamperia Bonducciana, pp. 19–21. Later still, Thomas Dermody calls his 'Tam to Rab' an 'Odaic Epistle', in *Poems, Consisting of Essays, Lyric, Elegiac, &c.* (Dublin: J. Jones, 1792), pp. 53–4; necessarily, as a poem addressed to Burns, this is in Standard Habby form.
94 Yalden's poem is an irregular ode in numbered stanzas; that by 'Q. A.' in ballad metre (quatrains of alternating iambic tetrameter and trimeter, only the trimeter lines rhyming); Evans's in three numbered sections of iambic tetrameters rhyming alternately, but including 12 lines of trochaic tetrameter couplets; and Merry's in sixaines of iambic tetrameter rhyming *aabccb*.
95 E.g., the epistle to Julius Florus (I, iii) names friends and topics likely to be known only to a small group but also points a general moral ('Such is the study that each of us ought to pursue', p. 21); the invitation to Torquatus (I, v) also raises general themes ('What's money for, if it isn't put to use?', p.

25); that to Tiberius (I, ix) asks patronage for a friend but also presents a model of how to make such a request; and the equally specific object of the epistle to Vinius Asina (I, xiii), to look after the books he is taking for Horace to Augustus, itself gives the poem a public dimension; while the final epistle in Book I, 'To His Book', provides the clearest possible evidence of the artificial nature of the whole series (translations from Ferry, *Epistles of Horace*). The three epistles in Book II, which include *Ars Poetica*, are longer than any of those in Book I and are much closer to verse essays.

96 I am grateful to Adam Rounce for encouraging me to compare Akenside's *Epistle to Curio* with his 'Ode to Curio'.

97 See *The Poetical Works of Mark Akenside*, ed. by Robin Dix (Cranbury, NJ, and London: Associated University Presses, 1996), p. 64.

98 *The Lives of the Most Eminent English Poets*, 4 vols, ed. by Roger Lonsdale (Oxford: Clarendon Press), IV, 175.

99 *Epistolary Moment*, pp. 122, 123, 124.

100 'Akenside's Political Muse', in *Mark Akenside: A Reassessment*, ed. by Robin Dix (Cranbury, NJ, and London: Associated University Presses, 2000), pp. 19–50 (pp. 43, 28).

101 *Poetical Works*, p. 64.

102 Ignoring changes in accidentals and punctuation, lines unaltered in wording are 48/16, 63/25, 70/29, 108/46, 133–4/58–9, 139/62, 147/68, 161–2/75–6, 164/79, 167/81, 171/82, 208/99, 240/104, 274/112, 286–8/127–9, 296/124, 304/119; lines in which a single word is changed are 1/1, 3/2, 52/19, 104/44, 116/49, 124/54, 127/55, 163/78, 172/84, 177/88, 210/100, 238/103, 301/115, 303/118. References before the oblique are to the epistle, after to the ode.

103 References before the oblique are to the ode, after to the epistle.

104 London: for R. Dodsley, 1739.

105 'To the Country Gentlemen of England. MDCCLVIII', and 'To the Authors of Memoirs of the House of Brandenburgh: MDCCLI'.

106 I am grateful to David Fairer for calling my attention to the fact that Coleridge's Dejection Ode originated from a verse letter.

107 See *The Collected Works of Samuel Taylor Coleridge*, 16 vols (Princeton, NJ: Princeton University Press; London: Routledge & Kegan Paul, 1969–2002), XVI, *Poetical Works*, ed. by J. C. C. Mays (2001), 677–9, 695–7, 861–4.

108 *Poetical Works*, 696.

109 'Ode to Sara, Written at Shurton Bars, near Bridgewater, in Answer to a Letter from Bristol', *Poetical Works*, 235–40; 'The Silver Thimble. The Production of a Young Lady, Addressed to the *Author of the Poems* Alluded to in the Preceding Epistle', *Poetical Works*, 243–6; despite the title, Coleridge wrote almost all of the poem. Around the same time, he also drafted parts of an epistle that survive only as 'Fragments of an Epistle to Thomas Poole'; see *Poetical Works*, 246–7.

110 'Verse Letter to Miss Isabella Addison and Miss Joanna Hutchinson'; 'To Mr Amphlett' (*Poetical Works*, 659–62, 855–6).

111 'Commendatory Verses: The Rise of the Art of Puffing', *Studies in Bibliography*, 19 (1966), 1-15 (p. 1).

112 See p. 23 above.

113 See, e.g., Clay Hunt, 'The Elizabethan Background of Neo-Classic Polite Verse', *ELH*, 8 (1941), 273-304 (pp. 273-85); Patricia Thomson, 'Donne and the Poetry of Patronage: The *Verse Letters*', in *John Donne: Essays in Celebration*, ed. by A. J. Smith (London: Methuen, 1972), pp. 308-23; Margaret Maurer, 'John Donne's Verse Letters', *Modern Language Quarterly*, 37 (1976), 234-59.

114 *The Poems of John Dryden*, I, 9, 10, 73. Line references are given in parentheses; subsequent references include volume and page numbers.

115 For the details of the verse letter to Etherege, see *Poems of John Dryden*, III, 19-21. The presentation piece is entitled 'To the Lady Castlemaine, upon Her Encouraging his First Play', the prologue 'To the Dutchess of York, on her Return from Scotland in the Year 1682'. See *Poems*, I, 80-3; II, 35-7.

2. Frequency

1 'Status of the Verse Epistle before Pope', p. 658, citing Raymond D. Havens, 'Changing Taste in the Eighteenth Century: A Study of Dryden's and Dodsley's Miscellanies', *PMLA*, 44 (1929), 501-36, and Calvin D. Yost, Jr., *The Poetry of the Gentleman's Magazine: A Study in Eighteenth-Century Literary Taste* (Philadelphia: University of Pennsylvania, 1936), p. 103.

2 See Arthur Sherbo, 'Dryden as a Cambridge Editor', *Studies in Bibliography*, 38 (1985), 251-61, and Stuart Gillespie, 'The Early Years of the Dryden-Tonson Partnership: The Background to their Composite Translations and Miscellanies of the 1680s', *Restoration*, 12 (1988), 10-19. I am grateful to Stuart Gillespie for sending me marked-up photocopies of the contents pages of the various editions of each volume of Dryden's miscellany, prepared for the forthcoming edition by himself and David Hopkins.

3 See 'The Formation, Transmission, and Reception of Robert Dodsley's *Collection of Poems by Several Hands*', in *A Collection of Poems by Several Hands*, ed. by Michael F. Suarez, I, 1-119. As there were very few omissions or additions of material between the first complete edition of 1758 and that of 1782, the latter is the one generally cited in this book.

4 'Changing Taste in the Eighteenth Century', 532.

5 'Changing Taste in the Eighteenth Century', 507, 507 n. 13.

6 *Miscellany Poems*, 6 vols (London: for Jacob Tonson).

7 'Sir George Etheridge to the Earl of Middleton', *Miscellany Poems*, II, 279-81 (Poem 1 in Appendix 1, section 1B).

8 As some of these and also other examples show, a poem designated as 'by' rather 'from' a particular writer may also be epistolary.

9 *Miscellany Poems*, II, 241, 180.

10 Examples include 'To Cælia. By Mr. Duke', I, 96-7; 'To Mr. Riley,

Drawing Mr. Waller's Picture. By Mr. T. Rymer', I, 267; 'To the Right Honourable Charles, Earl of Dorset and Middlesex, &c. By Mr. Charles Hopkins', III, 165–6; 'To Mr. Dryden. By Mr. Jo. Addison', III, 245–56; 'To his Perjur'd Mistress. From Horace. [. . .] By Mr. T. Yalden', IV, 60–2; 'To Doctor Gibbons. By Mr Charles Hopkins', V, 48–9; 'To Myra. By the Same Hand [George Granville, Lord Lansdowne]', V, 115–18; 'To My Friend, Mr. Pope, on his Pastorals. By Mr. Wycherley', VI, 115–16; and 'To Chloe Mask'd', VI, 222–3.

11 Samuel Garth, 'To the Lady Louisa Lenos; with Ovid's Epistles' (VI, 145–6).

12 Nothing of substance is known about 'Mrs. Bindon'; as mentioned above (p. 214, n. 54), Suarez suggests that the poem attributed to her may be by Sir Charles (Dodsley's *Collection*, I, 125, 224).

13 *Collection*, IV, 83–5 (attributed to Lord Hervey); VI, 247 (attributed to Sir William Yonge); to compound the latter misidentification, the man to whom the Countess addressed her love letter was William Hamilton. Suarez explains the misidentifications in both pairs of poems in *Collection*, I, 161, 185–6, 225–6; see also Isobel Grundy, *Lady Mary Wortley Montagu* (Oxford: Oxford University Press, 1999), pp. 307–8, 581.

14 Hammond was best known for his *Love Elegies*, first published in 1742 and, according to Suarez, mostly 'close translations of Tibullus' (*Collection*, I, 161).

15 *An Epistle to the Right Honourable Sir Robert Walpole* (London: for J. Walthoe, 1726).

16 London: for R. Dodsley, 1742.

17 'Be plain in Dress and sober in Diet; / In short my Dearee, kiss me, and be quiet' (quoted by Grundy, *Lady Mary Wortley Montagu*, p. 308).

18 *Miscellany Poems*, I, 15–18; II, 387–96; IV, 369–95; VI, 3–24, 409–20.

19 *Collection*, II, 1–17; II, 229–30; II, 293–301; IV, 373–82; V, 288–94; IV, 365–9; V, 40–5; IV, 370–2; VI, 43–8; II, 243–8; V, 305–8. Not included as separate items are the components of multi-part poems such as John Gilbert Cooper's *Estimate of Life* (III, 223–33), or Benjamin Hoadly's *The Trophy* (III, 264–74).

20 'Epistle to R. D. from T. O.', and 'A Letter to a Friend' (*Miscellany Poems* [London: for Jacob Tonson, 1684], pp. 218–24, 225–7); *Sylvæ* (London: for Jacob Tonson, 1702), pp. 223–32.

21 Appendix 1, section 1D, poems 2–7.

22 'Bajazet to Gloriana', 'Some Verses Sent by a Friend to One Who Twice Ventur'd his Carcase in Marriage', 'A Letter from J. P. to Colonel H.', 'A Familiar Epistle to Mr. Julian', 'To Parson Weeks. An Invitation to London'. 'Bajazet to Gloriana' is a slightly longer version of Aphra Behn's 'Ovid to Julia. A Letter'. See *The Works of Aphra Behn*, ed. by Janet Todd, 7 vols (London: William Pickering, 1992–6), I, *Poetry* (1992), 182–4, 412–13, 469–70.

23 See Suarez, 'Formation, Transmission, and Reception', pp. 11–12.

24 See Suarez, 'Formation, Transmission, and Reception', pp. 83–4, 75–8. On the supplements, see Harold Forster, *Supplements to Dodsley's Collection*.

25 *Poetry of the Gentleman's Magazine*.

26 See Carlson, *First Magazine*; Anthony D. Barker, 'Edward Cave, Samuel Johnson and the *Gentleman's Magazine*', DPhil thesis, University of Oxford, 1981. I am grateful to Dr Barker for permission to cite his thesis.

27 Carlson suggests that 'Cave's *nom de plume* seems to have been intended to suggest that he would provide fare for readers in both city and country' (p. 3, n. 25). At the period, 'Urban' would also have connoted business, and 'sylvanus' retirement and culture.

28 *Poetry of the Gentleman's Magazine*, p. 19.

29 *Poetry of the Gentleman's Magazine*, p. 25.

30 *Poetry of the Gentleman's Magazine*, p. 103.

31 *Gentleman's Magazine*, III (1733), 95, 147, 206, 434.

32 See *Eighteenth-Century English Labouring-Class Poets*, 3 vols, ed. by John Goodridge, William Christmas, Bridget Keenan, and Tim Burke (London: Pickering & Chatto, 2003), I (1700–1740), ed. by William Christmas, 231.

33 Examples are Robert Dodsley, *A Muse in Livery* (1732); Mary Masters, *Poems on Several Occasions* (1733); Jean Adam, *Miscellany Poems* (1734); Robert Tatersal, *The Bricklayer's Miscellany* (1734); Mary Barber, *Poems on Several Occasions* (1735); Stephen Duck, *Poems on Several Occasions* (1736). See F. J. G. Robinson and P. J. Wallis, *Book Subscription Lists: A Revised Guide* (Newcastle upon Tyne: Harold Hill and Son, for the Book Subscription List Project, 1975); and P. J. and R. Wallis, *Book Subscription Lists: Extended Supplement to the Revised Guide* (Newcastle upon Tyne: Project for Historical Biobibliography, 1996).

34 *Gentleman's Magazine*, III, 40.

35 *Gentleman's Magazine*, III, 151; *Poems on Several Occasions*, pp. 158–60.

36 '*Mrs. B-rb-r, to Mrs. C--s--r, at Bath*', *Gentleman's Magazine*, I (1731), 23, which is also complimentary. A revised version appears in Barber's *Poems on Several Occasions*, pp. 156–7.

37 See pp. 29–31 above.

38 *Gentleman's Magazine*, III, 152.

39 London: for Jacob Tonson, 1722; London: for L. Gilliver, 1734; *Miscellaneous Poems and Translations* (London: for Samuel Chapman, 1726), pp. 126–8; see further *The Poetical Works of Richard Savage*, ed. by Clarence Tracy (Cambridge: Cambridge University Press, 1962), pp. 59–60, 215–18.

40 See p. 15 above.

41 See *First Magazine*, p. 251. According to Tracy in *Poetical Works of Richard Savage*, p. 182, the attribution to Savage is an inference from remarks in the anonymous *Life of Mr. John Dennis* (1734). Tracy indicates that the poem was published in the *Daily Journal* for 22 December 1733 and reprinted in the *Grub-Street Journal* on 27 December, but does not mention publication in the *Gentleman's*. The title in Tracy's copy text, the *Grub-Street Journal*, is longer and more circumstantial than that in the *Gentleman's*; Tracy oddly

calls the poem 'Epigram on John Dennis' and leaves its authorship undetermined. The poem was reprinted with extensive changes in Vol. IV of Dodsley's *Collection*, first published in 1755, and it was probably from this or a later edition that it found its way into *Bell's Classical Arrangement*, where it appears among the 'Epistles Panegyrical and Gallant' (VI, 105). In the 1782 annotated edition of the *Collection* it appears in IV, 326, with a note on Dennis and the source for the attribution to Savage cited by Carlson. Michael F. Suarez indicates that the attribution to Savage is not certain, but does not mention Carlson. See his edition of the *Collection*, I, 202.

42   *Gentleman's Magazine*, III, 40, 322. The anonymous poem appears among five in Mary Barber's *Poems* assigned to her son Constantine, pp. 246–55 (p. 252), spelling out the recipient's name as Frances-Arabella Kelly. Barber had addressed two of her own poems to the same person (pp. 151–4).

43   The only two examples before 1750 are 'Charles Brandon, Duke of Suffolk, to Mary Queen of France', XII (August and September 1742), 439, 489; and 'Mary, Dowager Queen of France, to Charles Brandon, Duke of Suffolk', XIII (February and March 1743), 99–100, 153.

44   See 'Cave, Johnson and the *Gentleman's*', pp. 118–40. Barker gives evidence that Cave's employment with the Post Office began in 1721 and lasted until 1745 (pp. 5, 135). Cave continued to edit the *Gentleman's* until his death in 1754; Barker suggests that his influence in the Post Office was such that he may still have been able to exploit it for distributing his magazine even after retirement (pp. 135–8).

45   *Gentleman's Magazine*, VI, 745. Introducing an extract from the poem in *Eighteenth-Century Women Poets*, Roger Lonsdale suggests it was 'Perhaps first printed in a newspaper' (p. 150). It is discussed below on pp. 110–16.

46   *Gentleman's Magazine*, III, 431–2.

47   *Gentleman's Magazine*, IV, 508. Barker notes that the poem was 'written in such indelicate terms that some thought Cave was the author', and suggests that it 'was essentially a puff for the poetry competition' ('Cave, Johnson and the *Gentleman's*', p. 59). A further seven poems by 'Fidelia' followed.

48   *Gentleman's Magazine*, V, 677; VI, 49, 159; repr. in Jane Brereton, *Poems on Several Occasions* (London: by Edward Cave, 1744), pp. 278–80, 289–94, 298–303.

49   'Cave, Johnson and the *Gentleman's*', pp. 60–3, 61. An Advertisement in Brereton's *Poems* recounts Beach's deception, mentioning his suicide (though not its motive), and referring to Brereton's unsigned letter of May 1737 in the *Gentleman's*, p. 310. In this she mentions several recent suicides, including that of a close friend who was evidently Beach. The *Gentleman's* reprinted an account of Beach's death from the *Daily Post* and *Evening Post* on the first page of its Historical Chronicle for June 1737 (VII, [377]).

50   *Gentleman's Magazine*, III, 209; 209–10; 264; VIII, 319, 370–1.

51   Carlson says: 'It lacks intellectual vigor; it is quite without individualized expression or original talent' (p. 197); Yost is less harsh, referring to 'a definite loss of individualism both in invention and in execution', but also to

'a certain external finish and a completeness of proportion' (p. 139).

52 See 'Formation, Transmission, and Reception', especially pp. 5–6, 14–15, 18–19, 33–69.

53 Carlson, *First Magazine*, and Barker, 'Cave, Johnson and the *Gentleman's*', make clear that Cave did a lot of the editorial work himself, later aided especially by Johnson, John Hawkesworth and Thomas Birch, and later still by two literary clubs (Barker, pp. 238–67).

54 See Appendix 2, which details the methods I have used for constructing and analysing my database of verse epistles taken from *Literature Online*.

55 Poems in Dryden's miscellany including one or more of the keywords are in Appendix 1, section 1: A1–10, B2–3, B10.

56 Poems in Dodsley's *Collection* including one or more of the keywords are in Appendix 1, section 1: A1–37, B6, B8.

57 Only a few women writers are represented in Dryden's miscellany, among them Aphra Behn, Elizabeth Rowe and Anne Finch; of the 130 authors counted by Suarez in Dodsley's *Collection* ('Formation, Transmission, and Reception', p. 91), only 19 are female, accounting for 29 of the 586 poems. As the selection in *Literature Online* is based largely on the *New Cambridge Bibliography of English Literature*, it does not take full account of women's verse recovered more recently by Roger Lonsdale and others.

58 *Eighteenth-Century Women Poets*, pp. xliv–xlv.

59 *Pope to Burney, 1714–1779: Scriblerians to Bluestockings* (Houndmills, Basingstoke, and New York: Palgrave Macmillan, 2003), p. 107. I am grateful to Stuart Gillespie for drawing these remarks to my attention.

60 For details, see Appendix 1, section 3; for *Eighteenth-Century Women Poets*, section 4.

61 London: for T. Jauncy. Considerations of space preclude itemization for this and subsequent collections discussed in the chapter.

62 See Grundy, *Lady Mary Wortley Montagu*, pp. 159, 197–8.

63 'To Walter Moyle, Esq; by Mr. Charles Hopkins. In the Year 1609' [sic], pp. 140–3 (*Miscellany Poems*, IV, 63–5); 'To Anthony Hammond, Esq; by Mr. Charles Hopkins. In the Year 1694', pp. 144–6 (*Miscellany Poems*, IV, 24–5). The second edition of *The Annual Miscellany* became Volume IV of *Miscellany Poems*, but has different pagination.

64 *A Miscellany of Poems by Several Hands* (Oxford: by Leon. Lichfield, 1731).

65 On Husbands's collection, see R. S. Crane, 'An Early Eighteenth-Century Enthusiast for Primitive Poetry: John Husbands', *Modern Language Notes*, 37 (1922), 27–36. On the social groupings of poets represented in Hammond's *Miscellany*, see Prescott, *Women, Authorship and Literary Culture*, pp. 28–9.

66 London: for H. Clements; *Restoration and Eighteenth-Century Poetry, 1660–1780* (London and Boston: Routledge & Kegan Paul, 1981), p. 190.

67 London: for Benj. Motte, 1731; York: by C. Ward and R. Chandler, 1740.

68 *Poems. By* ***** (London: for R. Dodsley). I have not counted Latin originals printed before imitations.

69 See *The Poems of Alexander Pope*, Twickenham Edition, VI, *Minor Poems*, ed. by Norman Ault and John Butt (1964), 24–9, 107–10, 366–71. The total number of Pope's epistolary poems approaches 40.

70 'Advertisement', *Works*, I, x.

71 'Edward Young', in *Eighteenth-Century British Poets, First Series*, ed. by John Sitter, *Dictionary of Literary Biography* (Detroit: Bruccoli Clark Layman, 1990), 95: 353–63 (p. 358).

72 *The Poetical Works of the Reverend Edward Young*, 2 vols (London: for Messrs Curll, Tonson, Walthoe, Hitch, Gilliver, Browne, Jackson, Corbett, Lintot and Pemberton); *ODNB. Night Thoughts* was not to begin publication till the following year.

73 *English Poetry of the Eighteenth Century*, pp. 60–1.

74 London: for Charles Bathurst.

75 *Miscellany Poems, on Several Occasions: Written by a Lady* (London: for John Barber).

76 *The Poems of Anne, Countess of Winchilsea* (Chicago: University of Chicago Press, 1903; repr. New York: AMS Press, 1974). Subsequent references are to this edition except where otherwise indicated.

77 *The Anne Finch Wellesley Manuscript Poems: A Critical Edition*, ed. by Barbara McGovern and Charles H. Hinnant (Athens and London: University of Georgia Press, 1998), p. xliii. As the editors point out, 'A noncritical edition of the Wellesley poems, not available for purchase, was privately printed in Florence, Italy, in 1989 by Jean M. Ellis D'Alessandro' (p. xxxix).

78 *Wellesley Manuscript Poems*, pp. xviii–xxiii, xxxi–xxxix (p. xxxi).

79 *The Poetry of Anne Finch: An Essay in Interpretation* (Newark: University of Delaware Press; London: Associated University Presses, 1994), p. 19.

80 The only clear examples are 'A Poem for the Birth-Day of the Right Honble the Lady Catharine Tufton', pp. 79–81; 'To Mr. F. Now Earl of W.', pp. 20–3; and 'A Letter to the Same Person', pp. 23–4. Other poems of private origin, such as 'The Following Lines Occasion'd by the Marriage of Edward Herbert Esquire, and Mrs. Elizabeth Herbert' (p. 55), and 'On the Death of the Honourable Mr. James Thynne' (pp. 56–9), have a public dimension through their subjects; while 'Friendship between Ephelia and Ardelia' (p. 46), like 'A Pastoral Dialogue between Two Shepherdesses' (pp. 144–7), could be read as a pastoral.

81 'Classical and Biblical Models: The Female Poetic Tradition', in *Women and Poetry 1660–1750*, ed. by Sarah Prescott and David E. Shuttleton (Houndmills, Basingstoke and New York: Palgrave Macmillan, 2003), pp. 183–202 (p. 188).

82 Work she had printed includes a paper in the *Spectator*, probably her essay on inoculation, and *The Nonsense of Common Sense*; to what extent, if any, she was responsible for printing *Verses Address'd to the Imitator of the First Satire of the Second Book of Horace* remains controversial. See Grundy, *Lady Mary Wortley Montagu*, pp. 71–2, 217–18, 371–8, 338–40, 518.

83 'Classical and Biblical Models', p. 188.

84 *Complete Letters of Lady Mary Wortley Montagu*, II, 98–9, 74–5, 238–9.

85 *Essays and Poems and Simplicity, A Comedy*; see pp. 24–6 above.

86 Examples are 'To the Right Honourable the Countess of Hartford, with her Volume of Poems' (*Poems*, p. 61), 'To the Countess of Hertford on her Lord's Birthday' (BL Add ms. 4457, cited in Barbara McGovern, *Anne Finch and Her Poetry: A Critical Biography* [Athens and London: University of Georgia Press, 1992], p. 115), and 'To the Right Honourable Frances Countess of Hartford Who Engaged Mr Eusden to Write upon a Wood Enjoining Him to Mention No Tree but the Aspin and No Flower but the King-cup' (*Anne Finch Wellesley Manuscript Poems*, pp. 31–6).

87 *Correspondence between Frances, Countess · of Hartford, (Afterwards Duchess of Somerset,) and Henrietta Louisa, Countess of Pomfret, between the Years 1738 and 1741*, 3 vols (London: for Richard Phillips, 1805; 2nd edn, 1806).

88 *Epistolary Spaces*, pp. 119, 123–8, 131.

89 *Correspondence*, I, 114–15, 119, 189–93, 205–7, 225–9, 292–6; II, 53–4, 73–5, 87–8, 137, 169, 183–5, 186, 197–201, 253, 255–8 (attributed); I, 272, 273; II, 117, 160, 189–90; III, 291 (unattributed). For the poem possibly by Hertford see II, 189–90.

90 *Correspondence*, I, 93, 146, 188, 221, 235; II, 37; III, 241, 243, 261–3, 279 (attributed); I, 93, 109, 181; II, 117, 171 (unattributed). For the fragments possibly by Pomfret, see I, 109, 181.

91 *Correspondence*, II, 259–62, 139–51; I, 306–8; III, 69–71. As Karina Williamson remarks in an interesting brief discussion of the correspondence, Hertford's epistle is 'seamlessly embedded [. . .] within the frame of a prose letter'. See 'Voice, Gender, and the Augustan Verse Epistle', p. 81.

92 *Correspondence*, I, 307–8; this part, by Hertford, is included by Lonsdale in *Eighteenth-Century Women Poets*, pp. 109–10.

93 *Poems on Several Occasions. With Anne Boleyn to King Henry VIII. An Epistle* (London: for John Clarke), pp. 16–17, 21–2, 72–84.

94 See p. 57 below.

95 *Poems on Several Occasions. With Anne Boleyn to King Henry VIII. An Epistle* (London: for John Clarke, 1755), pp. 130–1, 136–7, 138.

96 'Written in the Conclusion of a Letter to Mr. Tickell', 'The Prodigy. A Letter to a Friend in the Country', 'A Letter Written for my Daughter, to a Lady', 'The Conclusion of a Letter to the Rev. Mr. C--', 'A Letter to a Friend, on Occasion of Libels Written against Him', 'A Letter for my Son to One of his Schoolfellows', 'A Letter Written for my Son to a Young Gentleman', 'A Letter Written from London to Mrs. Strangeways Horner', 'To the Right Honourable the Lady Kilmorey, with a Letter', 'To Mrs. Strangeways Horner, with a Letter from my Son', in *Poems on Several Occasions*, pp. 6, 22–7, 55–6, 58–62, 67–9, 78–9, 128–30, 149–50, 169, 189–93.

97 *Women, Authorship and Literary Culture*, pp. 95–9 (p. 99).

98 *Poems on Several Occasions*, p. xvi.

99 London: for William Hinchliffe; London: for W. Hinchliffe, with false

William Aikman' (I, 225–6).

133   E.g., 'To Dr John Theophilus Desaguliers, on Presenting Him with my Book' (IV, 259), 'To Mr. Jo. Kerr of King's College, Aberdeen' (III, 158), 'To my Unknown Corospondent in Irland' (sic; III, 197–8).

134   See, e.g., 'Epistle to John Wardlaw' (III, 238–40), 'Epistle to Mr. H. S. at London Novr 1738' (III, 247–9), and several epistles to and from Sir Alexander and Lady Dick (III, 256–9, 270–1; VI, 158–9).

135   Examples include Adam Ottley, 'In a Letter to Mr J. Philips in Christ Church Oxon', printed from a manuscript in the National Library of Wales by Juan Christian Pellicer in *John Philips (1676–1709): Life, Works, and Reception* (Oslo: Unipub AS, 2002), pp. 342–5; and a verse letter by John Theophilus Desaguliers to John Thurloe Brace in Bodleian Mss Add B105. I am grateful to Juan Christian Pellicer and Audrey Carpenter respectively for calling these epistles to my attention.

3.   Familiar and Humorous

1   For brief discussion of the discursive epistle, see pp. 13–14 above; for detailed discussion, Chapter 4.

2   For details of the database, see p. 45 above and Appendix 2.

3   Discursive verse letters from abroad include Addison's 'Letter from Italy' and Goldsmith's 'The Traveller', mentioned above (pp. 7, 14), and Horace Walpole's 'Epistle from Florence. To Thomas Ashton Esq; Tutor to the Earl of Plymouth', in Dodsley's *Collection* (III, 78–93), which also includes 'The Spleen' (I, 127–58).

4   *Miscellany Poems on Several Subjects* (London: for Tho. Combes, 1722), p. 99; Samuel Whyte, *The Shamrock: Or, Hibernian Cresses* (Dublin: by R. Marchbank, 1772), pp. 285–303. Whyte's 'Prefatory Epistle' states: 'This Volume is the production of different hands' (p. iv), and the poem is unlikely to be by him because it is footnoted as written from Kent in 1761 (p. 258) and he was running his academy in Dublin from 1758 (*ODNB*).

5   See *The Poems of Sir George Etherege*, ed. by James Thorpe (Princeton, NJ: Princeton University Press, 1963), pp. 35–53; *Miscellany Poems*, II, 279–85, 263–8; *Poems of John Dryden*, III, 19–27; *The Literary Works of Matthew Prior*, ed. by H. Bunker Wright and Monroe K. Spears, 2 vols (Oxford: Clarendon Press, 1959), I, 85–91. The Etherege exchanges are discussed by James How in *Epistolary Spaces*, Chapter 2.

6   *Miscellany Poems*, III, 168–9; IV, 24–5, 63–5; V, 51–3; I, 73–6; IV, 73–6.

7   The 'Song to David' stanza consists of six iambic lines rhyming *aabccb*, the *a* and *c* lines tetrameter, the *b* lines trimeter. Though it takes its name from Christopher Smart's poem of 1763, it was in much earlier use, including in Chaucer's 'Sir Thopas'.

8   *Bell's Classical Arrangement of Fugitive Poetry*, II, 129–31; *Works*, pp. 69–71.

9 *Nature Without Art: Or, Nature's Progress in Poetry* (Edinburgh: by P. Matthie, 1739), pp. 82–4, 87–9. In his *Poems on Several Subjects, Both Comical and Serious* (Dundee: for the author and James Stark, 1766), which omits the first poem to Ramsay, the second poem ends 'A. Nicol' (p. 58).

10 The Cherry and Slae stanza, so called after the poem of that title by Alexander Montgomerie (1597), consists of 14 lines of iambic verse in the pattern *a4a4b3c4c4b3d4e3d4e3f(2)g2f(2)g3*, where letters refer to rhymes and numbers to length of line, and parentheses indicate a double rhyme. An example is given on p. 73 above.

11 *Poems on Several Subjects*, pp. 59–60, 276–8.

12 *A Miscellany of Poems* (Glasgow: by Robert Foulis, 1747), pp. 40–3; Samuel Derrick, *A Collection of Original Poems* (London: for the author, 1755), pp. 137–8; Dodsley's *Collection*, V, 258–62.

13 *Familiar Epistles between W-- H-- and A-- R--* [Edinburgh: n. p., 1719?], pp. 25–8; *Poems* (Edinburgh: for the author, 1720), pp. 197–200; the 1721 edition omits the valediction.

14 'Epistle to John Wardlaw', *Works*, III, 238–40, and '[To Saunders Wood]', III, 318–19; 'An Epistle to James Clerk, Esq. of Pennycuik', III, 271–4; 'An Epistle Wrote from Mavisbank March 1748 to a Friend in Edr.', III, 261–4. The notes to 'Epistle to John Wardlaw' in *Works* provide a humorously circumstantial subscription from the first printing, in 1797 (VI, 151). Of two poems to Lady Dick, one begins with the date and 'Madam', and ends 'From your Ladyships / Most humble servt, / A. R.', the other with 'Madam' and ends with the comic valediction 'M[adam,] Y[our] L[adyship's] H[umble] S[ervant] / A. R. / Ed^r the last day of the year / 1746' (III, 256–9; VI, 154).

15 'An Epistle, from Mr D—— L—— Schoolmaster at Kinnaird [. . .]', *Poems on Several Subjects*, pp. 101–2.

16 Charlotte Brereton, 'To Miss A[nn]a M[ari]a Tra[ver]s. An Epistle from Scotland', *Gentleman's Magazine*, 12 (1742), 103; repr. in Lonsdale, *Eighteenth-Century Women Poets*, pp. 188–90 ('And that still I continue with affection so fervent, / Your friend most sincere, and true humble servant'; Relph, 'Epistle to Mr. C----r at P--rth', *Miscellany of Poems*, p. 55 ('At bottom protestation fervent; / Then close and send it to your servant'); Burns, 'Epistle to J. Lapraik: An Old Scotch Bard, April 1, 1785' ('Who am, most fervent, / While I can either sing, or whissle, / Your friend and servant'), and 'To Alexander Findlater. Ellisland, Saturday Morning' ('I am, most fervent, / Or may I die upon a whittle! / Your Friend and Servant—'), in *The Canongate Burns*, ed. by Andrew Noble and Patrick Scott Hogg (Edinburgh: Canongate Books, 2001), pp. 133–6, 962–3; Robert Anderson, 'Epistle I. To Robert Burns', *Poems on Various Subjects* (Carlisle: by J. Mitchell, for the author, 1798), pp. 69–78; repr. in *Eighteenth-Century English Labouring-Class Poets*, III, 310–15. Less adeptly, Lewis Thomas rhymes 'servant' with 'observant' (Dodsley's *Collection*, V, 262).

17 'Answer III', *Works*, I, 131–4; 'From London to Cambridge. An Epistle to Mr. Roche', *Poetical Works* (London: for E. Curll, [1727]), pp. 188–90; 'A

Letter to a Lady in London', *Poems Moral and Entertaining [. . .]* (Bath: by
S. Hazard, 1789), pp. 298–300, extract in *Eighteenth-Century Women Poets*,
pp. 233–4; 'Answer to Mr J. S.'s Epistle', *The Poems of Robert Fergusson*,
ed. by Matthew P. McDiarmid, 2 vols, Scottish Text Society, 3rd ser., 21, 24
(Edinburgh and London: William Blackwood & Sons, 1956), II, 71–4.

18 'The Following Letter by the Author, to her Brother E. P. at Lichfield, after
her Arrival at Chester', 'The Following Epistle to a Young Lady, Who Greatly
Complained to the Author of her Long Silence', and 'An Epistle to a Friend',
in *Poems on Several Occasions*, pp. 13–15, 80–82* [pagination error], pp.
81–2, and 'To Miss Seward, on Being Honour'd with Hearing Her Read her
Louisa, at the Palace, Litchfield', in *Poems by Mrs. Pickering*, pp. 16–18;
'Letter to my Friend E. B.', in *Poems on Various Subjects and Occasions*, 2
vols (London: for C. Parker), I, 19–25.

19 'Letter to Miss E. B. at Bath', *Poems on Various Subjects and Occasions*, I,
10–16, repr. in *Eighteenth-Century Women Poets*, pp. 346–8.

20 *The London-Spy Compleat* (London: by J. How, 1703), X, 223–8.

21 Twickenham edn, VII, *Minor Poems*, 24–8; *Poems upon Several Occasions*
(London: for H. Clements, 1713), pp. 55–9; *Bell's Classical Arrangement*,
II, 17–20; *Collection of Original Poems*, pp. 86–8; *Bell's Classical
Arrangement*, II, 101–7.

22 *Works*, pp. 93–5; 'Mira to Octavia', pp. 142–4, repr. in *Eighteenth-Century
Women Poets*, pp. 200–2. The two poems so entitled are discussed on pp.
77–9 above.

23 *Works*, pp. 125–7; pp. 59–61, repr. in *Eighteenth-Century Women Poets*, pp.
197–8; pp. 186–8, repr. in *Eighteenth-Century Women Poets*, pp. 209–10.

24 For example, 'Epistle to John Ranken, Enclosing Some Poems', 'Epistle to
Captain William Logan at Park. 30th October, 1786' and 'To Alexander
Findlater. Ellisland, Saturday Morning' include the salutation in the opening
line but have a separate signature; 'To William Stewart' seems alone in
having a separate prose salutation and valediction (*Canongate Burns*, pp.
148–50, 641–3, 962–3, 712–13).

25 *Canongate Burns*, pp. 141–6, 568–70, 606–7. It will be noticed that the first
two of these examples are in the Standard Habby stanza, the third in the
Cherry and Slae; and that Burns often included the date in his titles.

26 'Epistle I', *Works of Allan Ramsay*, I, 118; 'An Epistle, or New-Year's Gift'
and 'Mr Smith's Answer', *Poems on Several Subjects*, pp. 278, 124; 'To
William Simson, Ochiltree, May 1785' and 'To Collector Mitchell', *Canongate Burns*, pp. 144–6, 876; *Poems on Several Occasions*, p. 130; *Poems of
John Byrom*, I, 46; *Poems on Several Occasions*, p. 216. Evan Lloyd's
Epistle to David Garrick, Esq. (London: for the author, 1773) is a discursive
epistle that unusually has a postscript (pp. 23–4).

27 *Classical Arrangement*, pp. 17, 18, 19–20.

28 Written according to its subscription in March 1725/6, it was apparently not
printed until 1775, when it appeared in Pearch's *Collection* (II, 296–8; 1783
edn, II, 294–7).

29 *Miscellaneous Works*, II, 127–33; first version (*Poems on Several Occasions*, pp. 124–8) repr. in *Eighteenth-Century English Labouring-Class Poets*, I, 208–11.

30 *Miscellaneous Works*, II, 134–41 (p. 140).

31 *An Epistle to D[aniel] B[raithwaite] from T[homas] P[earson]* (London: J. Nichols and Son, n.d.). The poem is superscribed '*Calcutta, Dec. 26th*, 1761'.

32 According to Simon May of the British Library, for whose help I am grateful, it was probably printed between 1802 and 1805. This is likely to have been in tribute to Pearson, who had died in 1781, coinciding with a memoir that appeared in the *European Magazine* in April 1804 (45: 243). Braithwaite had been one of the proprietors of the *Magazine*, which Isaac Reed edited, and it is to Reed, who had been a close friend of Pearson, that Arthur Sherbo attributes the memoir in 'Isaac Reed and the *European Magazine*', *Studies in Bibliography*, 37 (1984), 210–27 (pp. 219–20).

33 *Mary Leapor*, pp. 80–1.

34 *Works*, pp. 222–3.

35 *The Poems and Literary Prose of Alexander Wilson*, 2 vols, ed. by Alexander B. Grosart (Paisley: Alex. Garner, 1876), II, 98–102 (p. 102). Marginal notes are from Grosart's Glossary.

36 *Canongate Burns*, pp. 725–6; marginal notes are the editors'.

37 The concept of 'addressee-consciousness' is introduced on p. 23 above.

38 *Epistle to a Friend Concerning Poetry*, p. 5.

39 *Poems* (New York: by T. and J. Swords, 1801), pp. 80–3.

40 See pp. 6–7 above.

41 *The Rural Lyre* (London: for G. G. and J. Robinson, 1796), pp. 113–24, extract in *Eighteenth-Century Women Poets*, pp. 398–9; *Poems on Various Subjects and Occasions*, II, 69–75, repr. in *Eighteenth-Century Women Poets*, pp. 349–51; *Poems on Several Occasions*, 36–7, 69–70 (both 'to her Cousin Miss H. B. of Chester').

42 *Miscellanies in Prose and Verse, on Several Occasions*, 4th edn (Edinburgh: for the author, 1771), pp. 90–1; *Poems on Several Occasions* (London: by S. Richardson, for the author, 1721), pp. 133–6; Dodsley's *Collection*, V, 262–7. Hoadly's reply, 'To the Rev. Mr. J. Straight' (V, 267–70) elicited an 'Answer to the Foregoing, 1731' (V, 270–2), in which Straight sought to justify himself.

43 *Miscellanies in Prose and Verse* (London: n.p., 1741), pp. 351–3; *Poems on Several Subjects*, pp. 276–8.

44 *Canongate Burns*, pp. 118–22.

45 *Poems Moral and Entertaining*, pp. 83–7, repr. in *Eighteenth-Century Women Poets*, pp. 230–2. Lonsdale notes that the poem appeared in the *Gentleman's Magazine*, 22 (1752), 234–5.

46 *Miscellany Poems on Several Subjects*, pp. 174–9, repr. in *Eighteenth-Century Women Poets*, pp. 34–6 (lines 5, 6, 14, 97, 102–3).

47 *Works*, pp. 202–6.

48 *Works*, pp. 142–4, repr. in *Eighteenth-Century Women Poets*, pp. 200–2.

49 *Mary Leapor: A Study in Eighteenth-Century Women's Poetry* (Oxford: Clarendon Press, 1993), pp. 61, 153.

50 Compare 'Your wond'ring Servant has been lately told, / That you, despising Settlements and Gold, / Resolve to take *Philander*, poor and gay, / To Have and Hold, for Ever and for Aye' (1751, 4–7) with 'Thus we begin – your Servant has been told, / That you (despising Settlements and Gold) / Determine *Florio* witty, young and gay, / To have and hold for ever and for ay' (1748, 5–8); 'But out-law'd Poets scorn the beaten Rules' (1751, 14) with 'But out-law'd Poets censure whom they please' (1748, 4); ''Tis true, this Case will not *Octavia* fit; / For ev'n his Foes allow *Philander* Wit' (1751, 47–8) with 'No such is *Florio*, he has Wit – 'tis true, / Enough, *Octavia*, to impose on you' (1748, 17–18).

51 *Mary Leapor*, p. 61.

52 See especially Valerie Rumbold, 'The Alienated Insider: Mary Leapor in *Crumble Hall*', *British Journal for Eighteenth-Century Studies*, 19 (1996), 63–76, and David Fairer, 'Mary Leapor: "Crumble-Hall"', in *A Companion to Eighteenth-Century Poetry*, ed. by Christine Gerrard (Malden, MA, and Oxford: Blackwell Publishing, 2006). Greene considers discussions of the poem up to 2001 in *Works*, pp. xxxi–xxxiii.

53 *Works*, pp. 61–2, 125–7; 'Voice, Gender, and the Augustan Verse Epistle', pp. 82–7; King's poem was first printed in his *The Art of Cookery, in Imitation of Horace's Art of Poetry* (London: for Bernard Lintott, [1708]), pp. 15–17.

54 Examples date back to the sixteenth century. A well-known variant is Ben Jonson's 'Inviting a Friend to Supper', which, though based on Martial, takes some hints from Horace. See *Complete English Poems*, pp. 70–1, 498. An example in Lonsdale's *New Oxford Book of Eighteenth-Century Verse* is Leonard Welsted, 'The Invitation', pp. 147–8.

55 'Voice, Gender, and the Augustan Verse Epistle', pp. 83, 86.

56 It was apparently first printed in 1772 in *Letters, by Several Eminent Persons Deceased. Including the Correspondence of John Hughes*, 2 vols [ed. by John Duncombe], (London: for J. Johnson, 1772), I, 52–3; repr. in Nichols's *Select Collection*, IV, 310–11, and in *Bell's Classical Arrangement*, II, 21–2.

57 2 vols (London: for R. and J. Dodsley; vol. 1, 1757), 356–8 (p. 356).

58 *Works of Horace in English Verse*, IV, 353–7.

59 *The Epistles and Art of Poetry of Horace*, 4 vols (London: for A. Millar, 1746), IV, 44–9. Christopher Smart chose tetrameters for Horace's epistles on the ground that that was the proper form for English familiar verse. See his Preface to *The Works of Horace, Translated into Verse*, 4 vols (London: for W. Flexney; Mess. Johnson and Co., and T. Caslon, 1767), I, xi.

60 'Voice, Gender, and the Augustan Verse Epistle', p. 83.

61 E.g., *The British Apollo*, [2 vols?], 3rd edn (London: for John Isted and Richard King, 1718), states: 'the Rose was an Emblem of Old, / Whose Leaves, by their Closeness, taught Secrets to hold' (I, 735). See also *OED*.

62 *Letters, by Several Eminent Persons Deceased*, II, 53.

63 King's appears, e.g., in Pope's *Miscellaneous Poems and Translations by Several Hands*, 3rd edn, 2 vols (London: for Bernard Lintot, 1720), II, 1–3; in the first edition of Dodsley's *Collection* (1748; I, 248–50); and, as well as in the various editions of King's *Works*, as late as *A Collection of Scarce, Curious, and Valuable Pieces* (Edinburgh: for T. Ruddiman, 1785), pp. 143–4. The earliest printing of Pitt's poem I have traced is the one cited in *Letters, by Several Eminent Persons Deceased*.

64 Peter Wilson (comp.), *Wilson's Dublin Directory, for the Year 1766* (Dublin: for Peter Wilson, 1766), p. 45.

65 *The Works of William Chillingworth* (London: by M. Clark for A. and J. Churchill, 1704); repr. 2 vols (Dublin: for William Brien, 1752).

66 'Voice, Gender, and the Augustan Verse Epistle', p. 83.

67 'Letters', in *Discourse and Literature*, ed. by Teun A. Van Dijk (Amsterdam/ Philadelphia: John Benjamins, 1985), pp. 149–67 (p. 159); Williamson, p. 80.

68 *Poems of Gray, Collins, and Goldsmith*, pp. 735–40.

69 See *Poems of Gray, Collins, and Goldsmith*, pp. 660–3, citing *Poems of Jonathan Swift*, III, 1014–15; pp. 696–704.

70 *Poems of Gray, Collins, and Goldsmith*, p. 696.

71 *The Miscellaneous Poetic Attempts of C. Jones, an Uneducated Journeyman Wool-comber* (Exeter: for the author, 1782), pp. 10–13; repr. in *Eighteenth-Century English Labouring-Class Poets*, II, 314–16.

72 *Eighteenth-Century Women Poets*, pp. 314–15, 530.

73 Lonsdale notes that it was first published in the *Gentleman's Magazine*, 61 (1791), ii, 1140 (*Eighteenth-Century Women Poets*, p. 530).

74 'To Alexander Findlater. Ellisland, Saturday Morning', 'To Captain Riddell on Returning a Newspaper. Ellisland, Monday Even', *Canongate Burns*, pp. 962–3, 748–9; 'Verses Sent to Dean Swift on his Birth-day, with Pine's Horace Finely Bound', Dodsley's *Collection*, IV, 203–5; 'An Epistle to R[o]b[er]t N[u]g[en]t, Esquire. With a Picture of Doctor Swift', *Poetical Works*, 2 vols (London: for W. Nicoll, 1774), II, 169–74 (extract in *New Oxford Book of Eighteenth-Century Verse*, pp. 341–2).

75 'Epistle VII. To a Young Lady, with a Copy of Relph's Poems', *Poems on Various Subjects* (Carlisle: by J. Mitchell for the author, 1798), pp. 104–6; 'To a Lady. With Mrs. Rowe's Letters from the Dead to the Living, Stiled Friendship in Death', *Poems by the Revd. James De-La-Cour* (Cork: by Thomas White, 1778), pp. 87–9; 'An Heroic Epistle. To Miss Sally Horne, (Aged Three Years)', *Works*, 11 vols (London: for T. Cadell, 1830), I, 355–62.

76 'Epistle to John Ranken, Enclosing Some Poems', 'To The Rev. John M'Math, Inclosing a Copy of Holy Willie's Prayer. Sept. 17, 1785', 'To Miss Ferrier. With a Copy of *Elegy on the Death of Sir James Hunter Blair*', *Canongate Burns*, 148–50, 570–3, 666–7; 'To a Gentleman with a Manuscript Play', *Works*, pp. 146–8; 'A Familiar Epistle, To Major Richardson Pack, with the Following Pastoral', *Poems on Several Occasions*, 2 vols (London: for Harmen Noorthouck, 1732), I, 177–8.

77 *Juvenile Poems on Various Subjects* (Philadelphia: by Henry Miller, 1765),

pp. 20–1; London: for A. Millar, 1761; *Poems, on Various Subjects* (Plymouth: by M. Haydon and Son, 1784), pp. 4–7, repr. in *Eighteenth-Century Women Poets*, pp. 361–3.

78 'To ********* *******, Esq;' (probably Jonathan Blenman), *Caribbeana*, 2 vols (London: for T. Osborne and others, 1741), I, 54–5; 'An Epistle Nugatory, or, (as some write it,) Newgate-ry', *Poems, Consisting of Essays, Lyric, Elegiac, &c.* (Dublin: by J. Jones, 1792), pp. 47–9; *Prison Amusements, and Other Trifles [. . .]. By Paul Positive* (London: for J. Johnson, 1797), pp. 42–72; *ODNB*. Mitchell's poem is dated '*Jan.* 2, 1721', but it is unclear whether the year is in New Style, as in Scots usage, or Old, as in English. See *A Letter to my Love: Love Poems by Women First Published in the Barbados Gazette, 1731–1737*, ed. by Bill Overton (Newark, NJ: University of Delaware Press; London: Associated University Presses, 2001), p. 31.

79 *Miscellanies in Verse and Prose* (London: for E. Curll, 1719 [1718]), pp. 33–6, the text cited here; repr. in *New Oxford Book of Eighteenth-Century Verse*, pp. 111–12.

80 See Corelli Barnett, *Britain and her Army, 1509–1970: A Military, Political and Social Survey* (London: Allen Lane, 1970), p. 138.

81 *Anne Finch Wellesley Manuscript Poems*, pp. 56–9, repr. in *Eighteenth-Century Women Poets*, pp. 23–5; MS Harleian 7316, text available from http://www.jimandellen.org/finch/finchtexts.html; *Shenstone's Miscellany 1759–1763*, ed. by Ian A. Gordon (Oxford: Clarendon Press, 1952), pp. 30–4, repr. in *British Women Poets 1660–1800: An Anthology*, ed. by Joyce Fullard (Troy, NY: Whitston Publishing, 1990), pp. 72–4.

82 *Poems on Several Occasions*, pp. 53–62.

83 *Poems on Several Occasions* (1724), pp. 21–2; repr. in *Eighteenth-Century Women Poets*, pp. 96–9. Discussion of this and the following three poems is indebted to Lonsdale's edition; quotations are from the first printings, with line numbers from Lonsdale.

84 'To Miss A[nn]a M[ari]a Tra[ver]s. An Epistle from Scotland', 12 (1742), 103; repr. in *Eighteenth-Century Women Poets*, pp. 188–90.

85 'Miss F[an]ny M[acar]t[ne]y to Miss P[egg]y B[ank]s', *Gentleman's Magazine*, 54 (1784), i, 123–4; repr. in *Eighteenth-Century Women Poets*, pp. 191–2.

86 *The Poetical Works of Miss Susanna Blamire*, [ed. by Henry Lonsdale and Patrick Maxwell] (Edinburgh: John Menzies, 1842; repr. London and New York: Woodstock Books, 1994), pp. 153–8; repr. in *Eighteenth-Century Women Poets*, pp. 279–83.

87 Christopher Hugh Maycock gives the details in *A Passionate Poet: Susanna Blamire* (Penzance: Hypatia Publications, 2003), pp. 34–5, adjusting the year of composition to 1773, a year later than suggested by Lonsdale.

88 Lonsdale refers to the printing of some of Blamire's songs, and, citing Henry Lonsdale's account of the manuscripts, describes them as 'often written on the backs of old letters or recipes' (*Eighteenth-Century Women Poets*, p. 279). Jonathan Wordsworth remarks that, as 'Blamire could afford to write

for pleasure', she 'could choose whether or not to publish – and seems not to have been interested' (Introduction to the Woodstock Facsimile, [p. 5]).

89 'To Mr. John Winship at Greenwich, Excuse for not Coming to See Him', *The Weaver's Miscellany* (London: by the author, 1730), p. 24; repr. in *Eighteenth-Century English Labouring-Class Poets*, I, 204–5; 'To Mr. J. W. A Very Elegant Epistle', 'A Very Critical and Moral Epistle, to the Same', *Poems on Several Occasions* (London: for the author, 1733), pp. 107–10, 111–20; 'Letter to Miss E. B. at Bath', 'Letter to my Friend E. B.', *Poems on Various Subjects and Occasions*, I, 10–16, 19–25, II, 4–12; to Davie and to J. Lapraik (*Canongate Burns*, pp. 133–6, 137–40, 568–70, 97–101, 321–2); to James Dobie, William Mitchell, James Kennedy and Andrew Clark (*Poems and Miscellaneous Prose*, II, 79–84, 91–102, 229–31, 102–4, 250–3, 105–7).

90 See above, pp. 41–2, 34, 35, 54–5.

91 Twickenham Edition, VI, *Minor Poems*, 120–2; *Anne Finch Wellesley Manuscript Poems*, pp. 10–12; McGovern and Hinnant mention friends and connections with whom Finch corresponded on pp. xxxi–xxxxii.

92 *Collection of Poems* (1732), pp. 134–41, 164–70; *Collection of Original Poems*, pp. 86–9, 135–8; p. 69 above.

93 *Works*, I, 115–37; for the date of the coda, which is in a different stanza form, see VI, 39.

94 *Allan Ramsay*, p. 5.

95 See Helen Damico, 'Sources of Stanza Forms Used by Burns', *Studies in Scottish Literature*, 12 (1975), 207–19 (pp. 208–11).

96 MacLaine, *Allan Ramsay*, pp. 4–5, 8.

97 E.g., Ramsay exchanged complimentary poems with Josiah Burchett (*Works*, I, 112–14) and William Somervile (II, 178–89), and addressed them to the Earl of Dalhousie (I, 217–19) and William Aikman (I, 225–6).

98 'Augustan Influences on Allan Ramsay', *Studies in Scottish Literature*, 16 (1981), 97–109 (p. 98).

99 *Works*, II, 109–12, 186–9; his first poem to Somervile (II, 178–81) is in standard English.

100 A manuscript biography, thought to be by Ramsay's son, quotes him as saying, sometime after his retirement in 1738, '*That he was more inclined, if it were in his power, to recall much of what he had already given; and that if half his printed works were burnt, the other half, like the Sybill's books, would become more valuable by it*' (*Works*, IV, 74). The remark suggests both modesty about his output and humorous mischief.

101 *Poetical Works*, 2 volumes (London: for T. Evans, 1774), II, 119. Lloyd also acknowledges a key debt by remarking that his addressee has the same name as Prior's in 'Epistle to Fleetwood Shephard' (II, 119–20).

102 *Poetical Works*, II, 128.

103 Dodsley's *Collection*, VI, 330–4; *John Gay: Poetry and Prose*, 2 vols, ed. by Vinton A. Dearing and Charles E. Beckwith (Oxford: Clarendon Press, 1974), I, 247–9, repr. in *New Oxford Book of Eighteenth-Century Verse*, pp.

127–8; Dearing and Beckwith note the derivation from Waller (II, 595).

104   *Poems on Several Occasions* (London: by J. Roberts, 1739), pp. 201–5.

105   *The Poems of Jonathan Swift*, 2nd edn, 3 vols (Oxford: Clarendon Press, 1958), III, 987–9, 1012–15, 1016, 1017–18.

106   *Gulliveriana* (London: for J. Roberts, 1728), pp. 94–100.

107   *Poems on Several Occasions* (Philadelphia: by John Dunlap, 1772), pp. 149–57 (pp. 152, 154).

108   *Poems on Several Occasions*, pp. 241–4, 55–9, 116–20.

109   *Miscellany of Poems*, pp. 19–21, 22–3.

110   *Poems on Several Occasions* (London: for T. Davies, G. Robinson, and T. Cadell, 1773), pp. 54–9.

111   *The Works of John Hall-Stevenson*, 3 vols (London: by J. Nichols for J. Debrett and T. Beckett, 1795), II, 224–32 (p. 228).

112   *Bell's Classical Arrangement*, II, 44–8 (pp. 44, 45, 47). Browne irreverently quotes Horace against himself in the line 'Yet still an aukward dirty Pig' (p. 47), which translates the closing phrase of Epistle IV, To Albius Tibullus.

113   *Works*, I, 245–6.

114   *The Works of John Wilmot, Earl of Rochester*, ed. by Harold Love (Oxford: Oxford University Press, 1999), pp. 63–70; Karina Williamson discusses this and another example by Rochester in 'Voice, Gender, and the Augustan Verse Epistle', pp. 87–91.

115   The first edition came out soon after *Ovid's Epistles, Translated by Several Hands* (both London: for Jacob Tonson, 1680); a second, expanded, edition followed in 1681, also from Tonson.

116   *Poems of Jonathan Swift*, I, 68–73, repr. in *New Oxford Book of Eighteenth-Century Verse*, pp. 9–11; III, 985–7; Twickenham Edition, VI, *Minor Poems*, 366–71; *Poetical Works*, II, 54–62.

117   Dodsley's *Collection*, II, 293–301 (first printed London: for L. Gilliver, 1736); London: for Henry Carpenter, 1746, repr. in *New Oxford Book of Eighteenth-Century Verse*, pp. 403–4.

118   Dodsley's *Collection*, II, 304–6.

119   Dodsley's *Collection*, V, 226–9.

120   *Works*, pp. 59–61.

121   *Works*, pp. 186–8.

4.   Discursive

1   *Poems of John Byrom*, I, 395–410; London: for R. Dodsley, [1738], sometimes attributed to George Smalridge; Dublin: George Faulkner, 1737 (extract in *New Oxford Book of Eighteenth-Century Verse*, pp. 299–300).

2   'Essay on Happiness', 'Essay on Hope', 'Essay on Friendship', 'Essay on Woman', *Works*, pp. 33–6, 36–9, 44–7, 184–6; *An Essay on Happiness. In an Epistle to the Right Honourable the Earl of Chesterfield* (London: for J. Walthoe, 1737; repr. as 'An Epistle' in Dodsley's *Collection*, 1782 edn, II,

193–206, and in *Bell's Classical Arrangement of Fugitive Poetry*, I, 106–9); London: for L. Gilliver and J. Clarke, 1737 (repr. in Bell, V, 118–41).

3 Twickenham edn, III.i, *An Essay on Man*, ed. by Maynard Mack (1950), p. 11; *Works*, pp. 33, 95.

4 *Bell's Classical Arrangement*, V, 47–55; London: for Lawton Gilliver, 1730. Another *Essay on Satire*, by John Brown (London: for R. Dodsley, 1745; repr. in Dodsley's *Collection*, III, 327–52, and in Bell, V, 1–21), principally addresses Warburton, though it also apostrophizes Pope at the end.

5 See Anna de Pretis, *"Epistolarity" in the First Book of Horace's Epistles*, pp. 19, 37.

6 'Status of the Verse Epistle before Pope', 678.

7 *An Introduction to Pope* (London: Methuen, 1975), p. 64.

8 *Poems on Various Subjects and Occasions*, I, 19–25; *Poems*, 80–3 (discussed on pp. 74–5 above); *Poems on Several Occasions* (London: for R. and J. Dodsley, 1754), pp. 141–4.

9 *Miscellaneous Poems*, 2 vols (Manchester: by J. Harrop, 1773), I, 281–5 (pp. 281–2); *Poems of John Byrom*, I, 477–8.

10 *Poems of John Byrom*, I, xix.

11 *Miscellaneous Works*, I, 202–14; II, 194–200 (on both, see p. 59 above); London: by A. Dodd; often reprinted, including in all editions of Dodsley's *Collection* from the second (1782 edn, I, 127–58) and in Bell (II, 134–63).

12 *Poetical Works*, II, 17–32 (p. 17); I, 77–83; II, 105–18.

13 *Poetical Works*, I, 21.

14 *Poetical Works*, I, 78–9.

15 Oxford: by L[eonard] L[ichfield] for Stephen Fletcher, 1713; *A Descriptive Poem, Addressed to Two Ladies, at their Return from Viewing the Mines near Whitehaven. To Which Are Added, Some Thoughts on Building and Planting, to Sir James Lowther* (London: for J. and J. Rivington, and R. and J. Dodsley, 1755), repr. in *Bell's Classical Arrangement*, IV, 47–59, III, 157–9; *Florio: A Tale, for Fine Gentlemen and Fine Ladies: And, the Bas Bleu; Or, Conversation* (London: for T. Cadell, 1786).

16 *Review of Poetry, Ancient and Modern* (London: for J. Booth, 1799), p. 28.

17 Dodsley's *Collection*, II, 215–18; it first appeared in the second edn, 1748; Bell, II, 27–9.

18 'To the Worthy, Humane, Generous, Reverend, and Noble, Frederick Cornwallis' and 'To his Friend and Neighbour Dr. Thomas Taylor, 1744', in Dodsley's *Collection*, VI, 153–56, 157–63 (Bell, I, 140–4, 145–51); 'Night. To Stella', *Poems on Several Occasions* (London: for T. Cadell, 1785), pp. 1–15, and 'To Mr. ****, an Unlettered Poet, on Genius Unimproved', *Poems on Various Subjects* (London: for the author, 1787), pp. 77–82, repr. in *Eighteenth-Century English Labouring Class Poets*, III, 90–2; London: for T. Cooper, 1736; London: for A. Millar, 1744.

19 *Poems by Dr. Roberts of Eton College* (London: for J. Wilkie, 1774), pp. 101–14 (p. 101).

20 Byrom's anapestic tetrameter huitaines are an exception; for a discursive

epistle in Standard Habby form, see John Learmont, 'The Petition of the Journeymen Gardeners of Scotland', *Poems Pastoral, Satirical, Tragic, and Comic* (Edinburgh: for the author, by Alexander Chapman and Company, 1791), pp. 176–85; repr. in *Eighteenth-Century English Labouring Class Poets*, III, 205–10. Learmont's epistle is influenced by the example of Burns, some of whose familiar epistles are also to some extent discursive.

21 *The Progress of Refinement* (Boston: by Young and Etheridge, 1792), p. 166; *Poems on Several Occasions*, 1724 edn, pp. 16–17.

22 Mary Jones, *Miscellanies in Prose and Verse* (Oxford: for Messrs Dodsley, Clements and Frederick, 1750), pp. 26–35; Joseph Warton, *Fashion: An Epistolary Satire to a Friend* (London: for R. Dodsley, 1742; repr. in Dodsley's *Collection*, III, 284–90); John Dalton, *An Epistle to a Young Nobleman from his Praeceptor* (London: for Lawton Gilliver and Robert Dodsley, 1736; repr. in Bell, I, 63–73), and William Whitehead, *On Nobility: An Epistle to the Right Honble. the Earl of* ****** (London: for R. Dodsley, 1744; repr. in Bell, I, 38–47); James Miller, *Of Politeness. An Epistle to the Right Honourable William Stanhope*, 2nd edn (London: for L. Gilliver and J. Clark, 1738); James Cawthorn, *Poems* (London: by W. Woodfall, 1771), pp. 172–87; Soame Jenyns, *Poems* (London: for R. Dodsley, 1752), pp. 45–54; repr. in Dodsley, III, 182–9, and Bell, I, 1–8.

23 *Epistolarity*, p. 4.

24 See pp. 23–4 above.

25 Twickenham edn, III, ii, *Epistles to Several Persons*, ed. by F. W. Bateson, 2nd edn (1961), 46–74; *Gentleman's Magazine*, 6 (1736), 745, repr. in the text cited here, *British Women Poets 1660–1800*, pp. 303–5, and, as two extracts, in *Eighteenth-Century Women Poets*, pp. 150–1; *Works*, pp. 184–6, and *Eighteenth-Century Women Poets*, pp. 207–8.

26 See *Epistles to Several Persons*, pp. 46–7.

27 For discussion of Pope's relations with both sisters, see Valerie Rumbold, *Women's Place in Pope's World* (Cambridge: Cambridge University Press, 1989), pp. 253–63; Bateson notes that Pope substituted the word 'Daughter' (260) for the 'Sister' of early editions (*Epistles to Several Persons*, p. 71), apparently because, as Rumbold explains, it 'pointed too clearly to his early attachment to Teresa' (*Women's Place in Pope's World*, p. 278).

28 *Women's Place in Pope's World*, p. 270. The remark is, indeed, not so much anti-feminist as directly misogynistic.

29 See 'Introduction', *Epistles to Several Persons*, pp. xiv–xv.

30 'Ars Poetica, or Epistle to the Pisos', in *Horace: Satires, Epistles, Ars Poetica*, p. 484 (line 410); my translation.

31 *Alexander Pope and his Eighteenth-Century Women Readers* (Carbondale and Edwardsville: Southern Illinois University Press, 1994), pp. 146–50.

32 *Works*, p. 299.

33 See Greene, *Mary Leapor*, pp. 76–81, and Thomas, *Alexander Pope and his Eighteenth-Century Women Readers*, pp. 152–7, 199–204, 232–4.

34 *Mary Leapor*, p. 77.

35 *A Miscellany of New Poems, on Several Occasions* (London: by Edward Cave, 1736), pp. 1–7.
36 *Marxism and Literature* (Oxford: Oxford University Press, 1977), pp. 121–7; summarized in *Culture* (Glasgow: Fontana Paperbacks, 1981), pp. 203–5.
37 London, for R. and J. Dodsley; London, for T. Cadell. References are to the second edition.
38 London: for J. Townsend, 1759.
39 *Genuine Happiness* (1759), p. 2; Edinburgh: n.p., 1767, p. 2.
40 London: by T. and J. W. Pasham, for J. Johnson and Co., Mr. Dodsley, and Mr. White, 1766, pp. 3–4, 5.
41 Paisley: by John Neilson for the author, 1786; *Poems on Various Subjects* (Manchester: by C. Wheeler and Son, 1800), pp. 19–20.
42 *The Life of Hubert* (London: for the author, by Samson Low, 1795), pp. 49–59.
43 Cambridge: by J. Bentham, 1763; *Poems on Various Subjects* (Henley: by and for the author, [1790?]), pp. 122–4. Collington was Professor of Anatomy at the University of Cambridge.
44 See *Annual Register*, 1762 (London: for R. and J. Dodsley, 1763), 67–8; Royal Society, *Philosophical Transactions*, 52 (London: for L. Davis and C. Reymers, 1763), 523–33; *Gentleman's Magazine*, 33 (1763), 493–4.
45 London: for Edward Easton, bookseller, in Salisbury, 1754; London: for Chapman and Co., 1793, pp. 188–9.
46 London: for R. and J. Dodsley, 1761.
47 London: for Samuel Paterson, 1753.
48 *Truth. A Counterpart to Mr. Pope's Essay on Man. Epistle the First*, and *Truth. [. . .] Epistle the Second* (London: for the author, 1739), confirming the claims on the title pages to the first two epistles that they were first published in that year; *Pamphlet Attacks on Alexander Pope, 1711–1744: A Descriptive Bibliography* (London: Methuen, 1969), pp. 277–8. Ayre also published *Memoirs of the Life and Writings of Alexander Pope, Esq;*, 2 vols (London: for the author, 1745), which ends by calling its subject 'THE GREATEST POET' of all periods in English (II, 389). His response to the *Essay* is discussed briefly by A. D. Nuttall in *Pope's Essay on Man* (London: George Allen & Unwin, 1984), p. 179, but doubts have been raised as to his identity and even his existence. See Pat Rogers, *The Alexander Pope Encyclopedia* (Westport, CT, and London: Greenwood Press, 2004), p. 16.
49 The reference is to a bill of 1714, supported by Bolingbroke, that sought to abolish dissenting academies (*ODNB*).
50 *Poems*, pp. 81–92, 172–87; Cawthorn's *Abelard to Eloisa* is discussed briefly on pp. 145–6 above.
51 III, i, *An Essay on Man*, ed. by Maynard Mack, 1950, p. lxxiii.
52 *Essay on Man*, p. lxxvii.
53 See *Essay on Man*, pp. 140, 138.
54 London: for J. Walthoe; second edn (London: for R. Dodsley), pp. 57–79; the revisions include the addition of six new lines.

55 The title in all editions of the *Collection* is simply 'An Epistle' (1748 edn, II, 175–89); 'Epistle XII', *Bell's Classical Arrangement*, I, 106–19.

56 Quotations are from *Odes and Epistles* unless indicated otherwise, followed by page references to the text in Dodsley (1782 edn, II, 193–206). The text in Claud Nugent, *Memoirs of Robert, Earl Nugent, with Letters, Poems, and Appendices* (London: William Heinemann, 1898), pp. 153–61), reprints that in Dodsley, and the memoir contains nothing relevant to the poem.

57 See Christine Gerrard, *The Patriot Opposition to Walpole: Politics, Poetry, and Myth, 1725–1742* (Oxford: Clarendon Press, 1994).

58 London: for J. Walthoe, 1736; *Odes and Epistles*, pp. [31]–56; by Geo. Faulkner, 1737).

59 *Works*, pp. 33–6.

60 *Works*, p. 317–18.

61 London, for R. and J. Dodsley; *The Call of Aristippus. Epistle IV. To Mark Akenside, M. D.* (London, for R. and J. Dodsley); 'Epistles to his Friends in Town, from Aristippus in Retirement', *Poems on Several Subjects* (London, for R. and J. Dodsley), sig. A–p. 47. All were published anonymously, like much of Gilbert Cooper's work, though *Poems* is accredited to 'the Author of the Life of Socrates', which had gone through several editions since its first in 1749. All references are to *Poems* unless indicated otherwise.

62 I am grateful for advice on French versification from Peter Cogman and Derek Connon.

63 'John Gilbert Cooper: A Poet in Search of his Metier and Meter', *The Age of Johnson*, 13 (2002), 255–81 (pp. 270–1).

64 See Maren-Sofie Røstvig, *The Happy Man: Studies in the Metamorphoses of a Classical Ideal*, 2 vols, 2nd edn (Oslo: Universitetsvorslag; New York: Humanities Press, 1971), II (1700–1760), especially 143–61.

65 Among its various other revisions, the 1764 edition styles the addressees of the first two epistles differently. In the 1757 edition they were 'the Right Honourable the Earl of ********', and 'the Honourable Mrs. *****'. Presumably either their status had changed or, for some reason, Gilbert Cooper substituted different addressees.

66 Dix notes that 'Aristippus was more than a pseudonym for Gilbert Cooper', pointing out that he used the name on his bookplates ('John Gilbert Cooper', p. 270), yet the fact that after 1755 the poet lived mostly in London (*ODNB*) is at odds with his persona's appeal to an ideal of rural retirement.

67 *Epistolary Moment*, p. 161.

68 See Dix, 'John Gilbert Cooper', pp. 267–8, 278 (n. 27).

69 The 'Editor's Preface' to *Poems* states that Gilbert Cooper was 'prevailed upon' to permit the collection, and quotes him as saying that 'he wrote most of them, when he was very young, for his own amusement', and that he 'was very little sollicitous what would be the fate of them for the future'. Yet, as Dix remarks, the fact that most of the reprinted poems had been revised suggests a continuing authorial ambition ('John Gilbert Cooper', p. 275).

5. Heroic and Amatory

1 *Epistolary Moment*, p. 27; London: for M. Cooper, 1756, p. 286.
2 '"Our Unnatural No-voice": The Heroic Epistle, Pope, and Women's Gothic', in *Modern Essays on Eighteenth-Century Literature*, ed. by Leopold Damrosch, Jr. (New York and Oxford: Oxford University Press, 1988), pp. 379–411 (p. 389).
3 See Duncan F. Kennedy, 'Epistolarity: the *Heroides*', in *The Cambridge Companion to Ovid*, ed. by Philip Hardie (Cambridge: Cambridge University Press, 2002), pp. 217–32 (p. 218).
4 See Richard F. Hardin, 'Convention and Design in Drayton's *Heroicall Epistles*', *PMLA*, 83 (1968), 35–41; *The Works of Michael Drayton*, ed. by J. William Hebel, Kathleen Tillotson and Bernard Newdigate, 5 vols (Oxford: Basil Blackwell for the Shakespeare Head Press, 1931–41), II, [129]–308.
5 *Ovid's Epistles, Translated by Several Hands* (London: for Jacob Tonson). 'Sappho to Phaon' arrived in the eighth edition in 1712.
6 *Amores Britannici* (London: for J. Nutt, 1703). Oldmixon also translated Ovid's 'Deianira to Hercules', which, like 'Sappho to Phaon', first appeared in the 1712 edition of *Ovid's Epistles*, preceding the original anonymous version.
7 Dublin: by and for Henry Saunders; Dublin: by R. Marchbank, 1772, pp. 377–414. A manuscript note to the Dedication in the Bodleian Library copy of the 1753 edition assigns the poems to 'Col. Beaver, who was killed in America in the War that began in 1755'. There is an account of the death of Lieutenant-Colonel Beaver in *The Annual Register* for 1760 (London: for R. and J. Dodsley, 1761), pp. 104–5.
8 '"Our Unnatural No-voice"', p. 399.
9 Ann Curtis (née Kemble, later Hatton), *Poems on Miscellaneous Subjects* (London: for the author, 1783), pp. [30]–35.
10 *The Poems of Sir George Etherege*, ed. by James Thorpe (Princeton, NJ: Princeton University Press, 1963), pp. 9–10.
11 London: for Jacob Tonson; see pp. 179–81 above.
12 *Essays and Poems*, pp. 221–4; see also 'Miss Cooper to ——', pp. 227–30, and 'Epistle from Mrs. Y[onge] to her Husband', pp. 230–2. 'Epistle from Arthur G[ra]y' is discussed above, p. 156.
13 Several examples are discussed above, pp. 156–7. Versions of the story are edited by Frank Felsenstein in *English Trader, Indian Maid: Representing Gender, Race, and Slavery in the New World: An Inkle and Yarico Reader* (Baltimore, MD, and London: The Johns Hopkins University Press, 1999).
14 The title of Volume VI of *Bell's Classical Arrangement of Fugitive Poetry* is 'Epistles Panegyrical and Gallant'.
15 'Voice, Gender, and the Augustan Verse Epistle', p. 78.
16 '"Our Unnatural No-voice"', pp. 384, 385. As Williamson notes (p. 78), Beer does not discuss any heroic epistles actually written by women.
17 The exceptions are by Judith Cowper (later Madan) and Lady Sophia Burrell.

Cowper's, apparently the first such response, was written by 1720 and first published as William Pattison's in his *Poetical Works* (London: for H. Curll, [1727]), pp. 67–77; it was not accredited to her until much later. Burrell's appears in her *Poems on Several Occasions* (London: for S. Paterson, 1747), pp. 73–80. See, respectively, pp. 141–5 and 146 above.

18 See, e.g., Linda Kauffman, *Discourses of Desire: Gender, Genre, and Epistolary Fiction* (Ithaca, NY: Cornell University Press, 1986); Martin Wechselblatt, 'Gender and Race in Yarico's Epistles to Inkle: Voicing the Feminine/Slave', *Studies in Eighteenth-Century Culture*, 19 (1989), 197–223.

19 These are the seven epistles, all by Evander, in 'Love Elegies and Epistles', a series that also contains eight elegies, all but two of which are by Evander. The series is reprinted in *Bluestocking Feminism: Writings of the Bluestocking Circle, 1738–1785*, 6 vols (London: Pickering & Chatto: 1999), ed. by Gary Kelly and others, vol. 4, *Anna Seward*, ed. by Jennifer Kelly, pp. 1–22.

20 Anne Finch, 'Epistle from Alexander to Hephæstion in his Sickness', *Poems*, ed. by Myra Reynolds, pp. 139–41; Daniel Hayes, 'An Epistle from the Celebrated Abbé de Rance to a Friend', in *The Annual Register [. . .] for the Year 1766* (London: for J. Dodsley, 1767), pp. 232–40 (2nd p. seq.); repr. in *The Works in Verse of Daniel Hayes* (London: n. p., 1769), pp. 135–52; George Canning, *An Epistle from Lord William Russel, to William Lord Cavendish* (Newcastle: n. p., 1775), repr. in *Bell's Classical Arrangement*, VII, 46–62.

21 *Ovid's Heroines: A Verse Translation of the Heroides* (New Haven, CT, and London: Yale University Press, 1991), p. xiv.

22 Ovid, *Heroides*, trans. by Harold Isbell (London and New York: Penguin Books, 1990), p. xix.

23 *Collection of Poems by Several Hands*, 1782 edn, IV, 99–105, though the poem is set out in heroic couplets in *Bell's Classical Arrangement*, VII, 63–8, and in *Amatory Pieces* ([Ludlow]: by George Nicholson, 1799), pp. 28–32; *Miscellaneous Writings* (London: for T. N. Longman, 1797), pp. [73]–7, addressed by Petrarch to Laura.

24 *Letters of Abelard and Heloise*, 3rd edn, corrected (London: for J. Watts, 1718; first published 1713). Cecilia A. Feilla calls the 1713 printing 'The first stand-alone edition of the letters in English', pointing out that Hughes translated not from the original Latin but from a 'patchwork collection' by François Nicolas DuBois of various French publications appearing between 1687 and 1695, two of the letters in which were 'pure invention'; and that no definitive English translation of the complete correspondence was published until Joseph Berington's of 1787. See 'From "Sainted Maid" to "Wife in all her Grandeur": Translations of Heloise, 1687–1817', *Eighteenth-Century Life*, 28 (2004), 1–16 (pp. 3, 2).

25 *"Epistolarity" in the First Book of Horace's Epistles*, p. 99.

26 *Epistolarity*, p. 13.

27 'Epistolarity: the *Heroides*', p. 221.

28 Twickenham edn, II, *The Rape of the Lock and Other Poems*, ed. by Geoffrey

Tillotson, 3rd edn (1962), 291–349.

29 "'Our Unnatural No-voice'", p. 386. Beer adds: 'The secondary sexual sense of the word in English remains always secondary.'

30 'Epistolarity: the *Heroides*', p. 221.

31 'Epistolarity: the *Heroides*', pp. 229, 230.

32 *The Rape of the Lock and Other Poems*, pp. 311–13.

33 *The Rape of the Lock and Other Poems*, p. 325.

34 *The Rape of the Lock and Other Poems*, pp. 312, 348.

35 *The Poetics of Sexual Myth: Gender and Ideology in the Verse of Swift and Pope* (Chicago and London: University of Chicago Press, 1985), p. 185.

36 *English Poetry of the Eighteenth Century*, p. 72.

37 *English Poetry of the Eighteenth Century*, p. 73.

38 *Thomas Hardy: The Complete Poems*, ed. by James Gibson (London: Macmillan, 1976), pp. 709–10.

39 "'Our Unnatural No-voice'", p. 397.

40 *Women's Place in Pope's World*, p. 146, n. 33. As the date of the family album is unknown, it is impossible to establish which text came first.

41 London: for T. Dormer, pp. 57–64; London: for the author, pp. 297–306.

42 London: by J. Jefferies, pp. [155]–160, mispaginated for [161]–166; also London: for M. Hope, same p. nos; 2 vols [comp. by George Colman the elder and Bonnell Thornton], (London: for R. Baldwin), II, 137–51 (p. [136]). Unless indicated otherwise, references here are to the 1755 text, reprinted by Joyce Fullard in *British Women Poets 1660–1800*, pp. 103–7.

43 *Letters of Abelard and Heloise* (Dublin: for J. Williams, 1769) is the first edition I have been able to trace that includes Cowper's poem; *Poetical Calendar*, 12 vols [comp. by Francis Fawkes, and William Woty], (London: by Dryden Leach for J. Coote, 1763–4), II, 27–33; Bell, VII, 97–103.

44 *Women's Place in Pope's World*, p. 147; see also Rumbold's 'The Poetic Career of Judith Cowper: An Exemplary Failure?', in *Pope, Swift, and Women Writers*, ed. by Donald C. Mell (Newark, NJ: University of Delaware Press; London: Associated University Presses, 1996), pp. 48–66 (p. 65).

45 *Alexander Pope and his Eighteenth-Century Women Readers*, p. 134.

46 *Letters of Abelard and Heloise* (3rd edn, 1718), summaries for Letters V and VI, pp. [96], [105].

47 *Women's Place in Pope's World*, p. 146.

48 *Alexander Pope and his Eighteenth-Century Women Readers*, p. 133.

49 *Poetics of Sexual Myth*, p. 2. See also *Eighteenth-Century Women: An Anthology*, ed. by Bridget Hill (London: Unwin Hyman, 1984), and *Women in the Eighteenth Century: Constructions of Femininity*, ed. by Vivien Jones (London and New York: Routledge, 1990).

50 *Poetics of Sexual Myth*, p. 3; *The Rise of the Woman Novelist: From Aphra Behn to Jane Austen* (Oxford and New York: Basil Blackwell, 1986), p. 15.

51 See, e.g., Mary Poovey, *The Proper Lady and the Woman Writer: Ideology as Style in the Works of Mary Wollstonecraft, Mary Shelley, and Jane Austen* (Chicago and London: University of Chicago Press, 1985); Janet Todd, *The*

Sign of Angellica: Women, Writing and Fiction 1660–1800 (London: Virago Press, 1989); Harriet Guest, 'Eighteenth-Century Femininity: "A Supposed Sexual Character"', in *Women and Literature in Britain*, ed. by Vivien Jones (Cambridge: Cambridge University Press, 2000), pp. 46–68.

52 *Abelard to Eloisa* (London: by J. Bettenham, 1725), pp. 2, 3, 6, 16.

53 In the 326 lines of the 1771 edition of his poem, James Cawthorn has Abelard address Eloisa with 'thou' and its cognates 58 times, 'you' only once. Writers less careful in this respect, including Barford, Warwick and Birch, shift between the singular and plural forms for no apparent reason, For details of the poems by Warwick and Birch, see note 58 below.

54 *English Poetry of the Eighteenth Century*, p. 74; *The Pleasures of Coition* (London: for E. Curll, 1721), pp. 47–50.

55 *Abelard to Eloisa* (Dublin: by S. Powell, for Abraham Bradley, 1730).

56 London: for M. Cooper, 1747; repr. with minor revisions in *Poems*, pp. 56–74.

57 For example, Cawthorn's 'Some pious friend' (1771 edn, 313) combines Pope's 'two wandring lovers' and 'some future Bard'; while his line 'Lean abstinence, wan grief, low-thoughted care' (1771 edn, 123) recalls Cowper's 'Lean Abstinence, pale Grief, and haggard Care' (1728 edn, p. 69).

58 An edition of Hughes's *Letters* probably first printed in 1777 (London: for B. Law and others) adds to Pope's epistle and Cowper's one by 'an unknown Hand'; one of 1781 adds Cawthorn's (London: for T. Lowndes and others); and one of 1787 adds two more, one by Samuel Birch, the other attributed to 'Mr. Seymour' (London: for W. Lowndes and others). The poem attributed to Seymour is substantially the same as that by Thomas Warwick, 'Abelard to Eloisa. Written in the Year 1777', in *Abelard to Eloisa, Leonora to Tasso, Ovid to Julia, Spring and Other Poems*, 4th edn (London: n.p., [1785?]), pp. [1]–17, which revises the anonymously published *Abelard to Eloisa: A Poetic Epistle. Newly Attempted* (London: for J. Bew, 1782). The version in Warwick's *Abelard to Eloisa. An Epistle. To Which Are Prefixed, Sonnets* (Bath: for R. Cruttwell, 1783), pp. [5]–23 (2nd p. seq.), is a different poem, though there are a few similarities with the 1782 version, but his *Abelard to Eloisa. An Epistle. With a New Account of their Lives* (Bath: by R. Cruttwell, 1785) has nothing in common with his earlier versions.

59 *Abelard to Eloisa: A Poem* (London: for J. Robson, 1792), p. 14; *Poems*, 2 vols (London: for J. Robson, 1796), II, 88.

60 *Poems*, 2 vols (London: by J. Cooper, 1793), I, 12–17.

61 *Alexander Pope and his Eighteenth-Century Women Readers*, p. 186; *Poems*, 2 vols (London: by J. Cooper, 1793), I, 12–17.

62 *Alexander Pope and his Eighteenth-Century Women Readers*, p. 187.

63 *Alexander Pope and his Eighteenth-Century Women Readers*, pp. 174–93; 'Epistle to Moneses', *Poems on Several Occasions*, pp. 73–80; 'Elgiva to Edwy', *Poems* (London: for J. Walter, 1772), pp. 87–95.

64 *Alexander Pope and his Eighteenth-Century Women Readers*, p. 180.

65 *Poems*, ed. by Myra Reynolds, pp. 139–41.

66 *Miscellany Poems*, 1716 edn, I, 78–82.

67 'An Epistle from Alexias', *Miscellaneous Works in Prose and Verse*, 2 vols (London: for R. Hett and R. Dodsley, 1739), I, 150–3.

68 London: for T. Worrall; New York: Garland, 1972 (facsimile reprint). This edition paginates its three parts separately.

69 *Ovid's Epistles, Translated by Several Hands*, 8th edn (London: for Jacob Tonson, 1712), pp. 160–9.

70 London: Jacob Tonson, 1714, pp. 72–80; Bell, VII, 26–31; oddly, the poem is unattributed, though it had been printed as Rowe's since at least 1733.

71 XII (1742), 439, 489; XIII (1743), 99–100.

72 *Poems*, pp. 97–109; Bell, VII, 32–45, first printed as *An Epistle from Lady Jane Gray to Lord Guilford Dudley* (London: for R. and J. Dodsley, 1762).

73 *The Lives of the Most Eminent English Poets*, ed. by Roger Lonsdale, 4 vols (Oxford: Clarendon Press, 2006), IV, 72.

74 See Eric Ives, *The Life and Death of Anne Boleyn* (Oxford and Malden, MA: Blackwell, 2004), p. 58.

75 *Amores Britannici*, Part 2 (paginated separately), pp. 93–126.

76 *Ann Boleyn to Henry the Eighth. An Epistle* (London: for R. Dodsley), repr. in *Plays and Poems*, 2 vols (London: by J. Dodsley, 1774), II, 81–90, the text cited here; *Poems* (London: for T. Beckett, 1780). The first edition of Whitehead's poem cites the Cotton Library MS rather than the *Spectator*.

77 First printed in her *Poems on Several Occasions* of 1724, pp. 72–84; a revised version, 41 lines shorter, appears in the second edition (London: for John Clarke, 1755; for T. Lownds, [1756?]), the latter of which is the text cited. All editions are subtitled *With Anne Boleyn to King Henry VIII. An Epistle*.

78 See 'Apollo and Daphne', 'From Virgil', 'Hypatia' and 'On a Death's Head', 1724 edn, pp. [3]–7, 56–7, 61–5, 54–5; [1756?] edn, pp. [3]–8, 60, 65–75, 58–9.

79 *Alexander Pope and his Eighteenth-Century Women Readers*, p. 175.

80 See pp. 134–5 above.

81 London: for J. Tonson; repr. in Dodsley's *Collection*, I, 69–77 (1782 edn), the text cited here.

82 *Lives of the Poets*, III, 114.

83 London: for J. Roberts; Foxon B541; repr. in *A Select Collection of Poems*, 8 vols (London: by and for J. Nichols, 1780–2), VII (1781), 196–203, the text cited here.

84 *Poems on Several Occasions* (Oxford: Clarendon Printing-House, 1730); *Spectator*, II, 301–2 (no. 204, pp. 299–302).

85 *A Collection of Poems in Four Volumes* (London: for G. Pearch, 1770), III, 41–3. The poem appears only in the 1770 edition of Pearch's collection.

86 'Epistle from Arthur G[ra]y to Mrs M[urra]y', *Essays and Poems*, pp. 221–4; first printed in *Six Town Eclogues* (London: for M. Cooper), pp. 39–43.

87 *Essays and Poems*, pp. 227–30; *Women's Place in Pope's World*, p. 149.

88 *Essays and Poems*, pp. 229n, 232.

89 *Lady Mary Wortley Montagu*, p. 240.

90 *Lady Mary Wortley Montagu*, p. 230.
91 *A New Miscellany: Being a Collection of Pieces of Poetry* (London: for T. Warner, [1725?]), pp. 32–41, repr. as *The Story of Inkle and Yarrico* (London: for J. Cooper, 1738). Both poems are edited by Frank Felsenstein in *English Trader, Indian Maid*, pp. 89–98, the text cited here.
92 *Poetical Works*, pp. 53–4.
93 *Yarico to Inkle: An Epistle* (London: for Lawton Gilliver).
94 *Yarico to Inkle: An Epistle* (London: for J. Dodsley).
95 *Guinea's Captive Kings: British Anti-Slavery Literature of the XVIIIth Century* (Chapel Hill: University of North Carolina Press, 1942; repr. New York: Octagon Books, 1969), p. 129, qtd by Felsenstein in *English Trader, Indian Maid*, p. 17.
96 No copy of the first edition of *The African Prince* appears to survive, though a few copies of the responding poem do. Both were reprinted in the second edition (London: for Mr. Waller and Mr. Ward, 1755); in Dodd's *Poems* (London: by Dryden Leach for the author, 1767); in Pearch's *Collection of Poems in Four Volumes* (London: for G. Pearch, 1770, 1775; for J. Dodsley, 1783), vol. IV, and in *Bell's Classical Arrangement*, VII, 117–32; references are to the text in Bell except where stated otherwise. The anonymous *The Royal African: Or, Memoirs of the Young Prince of Annamaboe* (London: for W. Reeve, G. Woodfall and J. Barnes, [1749]) is a prose account of the story.
97 This is based on an event reported in the *London Magazine*, 18 (1749), 94; the report is reprinted in Aphra Behn, *Oroonoko*, Bedford Cultural Edition, ed. by Catherine Gallagher (Houndmills, Basingstoke, and London: Macmillan; Bedford/St. Martin's Press: Boston, MA, 2000), pp. 445–7.
98 'The African Prince in London', *Journal of the History of Ideas*, 2 (1941), 237–47 (p. 243); extract repr. in Aphra Behn, *Oroonoko*, ed. by Joanna Lipking (New York: W. W. Norton, 1997), pp. 156–7 (p. 157).
99 *The Dying Negro, A Poetical Epistle* (London: for W. Flexney, 1773); repr. in *Bell's Classical Arrangement*, VII, 133–49, the text cited here.
100 This is stated in the 'Advertisement' preceding the poem in most editions.
101 London: for W. Flexney, 1774, pp. [ii]–viii; repr. in Bell, VII, 164–73.
102 *Poems on Several Occasions* (London: for J. Dodsley, 1785), pp. 19–35; repr. in Bell, VII, 87–96, the text cited here.
103 *Select Collection*, VI, 163n.
104 *A Collection of Poems in Four Volumes* (London: for J. Dodsley, 1783), IV, 259–63.
105 *Poems* (London: for the author, 1769), pp. 62–70; repr. in *Collection of Poems in Four Volumes*, IV, 317–22, the text cited here. Both editions have the footnote: 'Occasioned by a catastrophe well known in the West'. Gerrard was a curate in Devon; see Harold Forster, *Supplements to Dodsley's Collection of Poems*, pp. 102–3.
106 See *A Letter to my Love: Love Poems by Women First Published in the Barbados Gazette, 1731–1737*. Phyllis J. Guskin has argued that the poems are all by Martha Fowke, a view virtually confirmed at least for most of

them by Christine Gerrard. See, respectively, '"Not Originally Intended for the Press": Martha Fowke Sansom's Poems in the *Barbados Gazette*', *Eighteenth-Century Studies*, 34 (2000), 61–91; *Aaron Hill: The Muses' Projector, 1685–1750* (Oxford: Oxford University Press, 2003), pp. 91–2.

107   The volume's title is 'Epistles Panegyrical and Gallant'.

108   Dodsley's *Collection* (1782 edn), IV, 114–116; it first appeared in the *Collection* in 1755 (IV, 110–12), and, because it appears in other anthologies, it must have become well known. See, e.g., D. Burgess, *The Entertainer; Or, Youth's Delightful Preceptor* (Berwick: by R. Taylor, 1759), pp. 291–3; *A Select Collection of Modern Poems from the Best Authors* (Edinburgh: n.p., 1759), pp. 58–60 (in first p. seq.); *A Poetical Dictionary* [ed. by S. Derrick], 4 vols (London: for J. Newbery and others, 1761), IV, 212–13 (extract of lines 21–34 under 'Vicissitude', attributed to 'Oldfield'; Anne Oldfield, the actress, seems unlikely to have been writer or addressee).

109   See pp. 82–3 above.

110   *London Magazine*, 19 (1750), 89, 'Written by the late Lord Hervey'.

111   1782 edn, III, 207–9. Listed among 'Unidentified Poems' in Michael F. Suarez's facsimile edition, VI, 413–14, the poem first appeared in the second edition of Dodsley (1748; III, 193–6). Though it occurs in *Poems Written Occasionally by the Late John Winstanley*, 2 vols (Dublin: by S. Powell, for the editor, vol. 2, 1751), pp. 218–21, the book's subtitle indicates that Winstanley's poems are 'interspers'd with many others, by several ingenious hands', and few of the poems in it are easily attributed.

112   London: for J. Hooke, F. Gyles, and W. Boreham; a few of the epistles are in prose. The series is also of interest because the epistles are dramatic – the two authors are not to be identified directly with the two letter-writers.

113   *Miscellaneous Poems and Translations* (often known as 'Savage's *Miscellany*'), pp. 182–6; repr. in *Eighteenth-Century Women's Verse*, pp. 88–9, the text cited here.

114   Fowke probably had in mind Henry Carey's *Namby Pamby: Or, a Panegyrick on the New Versification Address'd to A----- P----* ([Dublin: n. p., 1725]), a parody of odes to children by Ambrose Philips that gave him the nickname 'Namby-Pamby'. Both deliberately overdo the singsong effect produced by Philips's practice of making some lines fully trochaic rather than catalectic. David Foxon cites *To the Honourable Miss Carteret* (Dublin: by George Grierson, [1725]; Foxon P221) as 'the classic example' of the odes that Carey mocked; others include 'A Supplication for Miss Carteret, in the Small-Pox' and 'To Miss Georgina, Youngest Daughter of the Lord Carteret', first printed in *The Following Poems, Writ[t]en by Mr. P[hillip]s* (Dublin: by George Faulkner, 1725).

115   *A New Miscellany of Original Poems* (London: for T. Jauncy, 1720), pp. 264–6; repr. in *Eighteenth-Century Women's Verse*, p. 87, the text cited here.

116   *Clio: Or, a Secret History of the Life and Amours of the Late Celebrated Mrs. S---n---m* (London: for M. Cooper, 1752); *Clio: The Autobiography of Martha Fowke Sansom (1689–1736)*, ed. by Phyllis J. Guskin (Newark, NJ:

University of Delaware Press; London: Associated University Presses, 1997).

117 London: Weidenfeld and Nicolson, 1977, p. 532; for the full account, see pp. 309–13.

118 *Poems on Several Occasions* (London: for J. Nutt, [1703]), pp. 25–7; *Essays and Poems*, pp. 244–6; repr. in *Eighteenth-Century Women Poets*, the text cited here, pp. 27–8 (p. 27), 65–6 (p. 65). Halsband and Grundy note that Wortley Montagu's poem was not printed until 1750.

119 See, e.g., in the case of the poem just discussed, Grundy, *Lady Mary Wortley Montagu*, pp. 243–4.

120 *Complete Poems*, p. 6; see also pp. 84, 190.

121 *Poems on Several Occasions*, pp. 42–3; Adam Clarke, *Memoirs of the Wesley Family* (London: by J. and T. Clarke, 1823), pp. 491–3; repr. in *Eighteenth-Century Women Poets*, pp. 29–30, 111–13, the text cited here.

122 *Sexual Freedom in Restoration Literature*, p. 131.

123 See especially 'Wedlock. A Satire', *Eighteenth-Century Women Poets*, p. 80.

124 'To Ovid's Heroines in his Epistles', *Poetical Recreations*, pp. 28–9.

125 See, e.g., Terry Eagleton, *The Rape of Clarissa: Writing, Sexuality and Class Struggle in Samuel Richardson* (Oxford: Basil Blackwell, 1982), pp. 13–15; Vivien Jones, 'Introduction', Harriet Guest, 'Eighteenth-Century Femininity: "A Supposed Sexual Character"', Ros Ballaster, 'Women and the Rise of the Novel: Sexual Prescripts', in *Women and Literature in Britain 1700–1800*, pp. 1–13, 47, 200–1; E. J. Clery, *The Feminization Debate in Eighteenth-Century England: Literature, Commerce and Luxury* (Houndmills, Basingstoke, and New York: Palgrave Macmillan, 2004).

126 *Classical Arrangement*, VI, 134–7; p. 214, n. 54 above.

127 *Classical Arrangement*, VI, 170–4 (p. 174).

128 *Classical Arrangement*, VI, 157–8 (p. 157; William Harrison); 34–6 (p. 35; Soame Jenyns); 147–8 (p. 148; anonymous).

129 *Classical Arrangement*, VI, 37–9 (p. 37; Soame Jenyns); 45–6 (p. 46; unattributed, but ascribed to R. G. R. Fusee in *An Asylum for Fugitives*, 2 vols [London; for J. Almon, 1776–9], II, 80, and *New Foundling Hospital for Wit*, 6 vols [London; for J. Debrett, 1784], VI, 117); 164–5 (p. 164; Peter Pinnell).

130 *Classical Arrangement*, VI, 57–8; 'Johnson's Poetry', in *The Cambridge Companion to Samuel Johnson*, ed. by Greg Clingham (Cambridge: Cambridge University Press, 1997), pp. 34–50 (p. 37).

6. Satirical and Complimentary

1 'Whig and Tory Poetics', in *Companion to Eighteenth-Century Poetry*, pp. 444–57 (p. 446).

2 See Jon Thomas Rowland, *Faint Praise and Civil Leer: The 'Decline' of Eighteenth-Century Panegyric* (Newark, NJ: University of Delaware Press; London and Toronto, Associated University Presses, 1994), especially pp. 1–2, 18–19, 52, 83–4, 145.

3 *English Poetry of the Eighteenth Century*, p. 75.
4 *The Augustan Vision* (London: Weidenfeld and Nicolson, 1974), pp. 1–2, citing the subtitle of Saintsbury's *The Peace of the Augustans* (London: G. Bell and Sons, 1916), and Price, *To the Palace of Wisdom: Studies in Order and Energy from Dryden to Blake* (New York: Anchor Books, 1964).
5 *Augustan Vision*, p. 2.
6 Lexington: University Press of Kentucky, 1994, p. 200, n. 9, à propos of Horace's distribution of 'his satiric work over several forms – satires, epistles, and epodes' (p. 9).
7 *Satire: A Critical Reintroduction*, passim, especially Chapter 3; on *satura*, see, e.g., pp. 5, 6; *OED*.
8 *Poems*, pp. 275, 400; *Works of Allan Ramsay*, I, 177, 264–5.
9 *Poems on Several Subjects* (London: for G. G. J. and J. Robinson, 1791), pp. 177–8; first printed in *The Oxford Sausage* (London: for J. Fletcher and Co., 1764), pp. 27–8, a self-ironical squib against his own satire on guidebooks to Oxford, *A Companion to the Guide* (London: for H. Payne, [1760?]).
10 *New Bath Guide* ([London etc: for J. Dodsley and others], 1766), ed. by Gavin Turner (Bristol: Broadcast Books, 1994), the edition cited here; *An Election Ball*, 2nd edn (Bath: for the author by S. Hazard, 1776).
11 *Miscellaneous Poetic Attempts of C. Jones*, p. 67; repr. in *Eighteenth-Century English Labouring-Class Poets*, II, 323–4; London: for G. Kearsley, 1788.
12 *Essays and Poems*, pp. 279–84.
13 See pp. 23–4, 100, 119 above.
14 Twickenham edition, III: ii, *Epistles to Several Persons*, 127–56; London: for E. Curll, 1718.
15 London: for Lawton Gilliver, 1730; London: for W. Dickenson, 1733; Edinburgh: for the author, 1721; 'To the Reverend Dr. Mann', *Poems on Several Occasions* (London: for R. Dodsley and W. Owen, 1749), pp. 73–82.
16 London: for T. Cooper, 1732; London: for the author, 1763.
17 *Epistle to Curio* is discussed above, pp. 26–8; for examples of lampoons by Combe, see *An Heroic Epistle to the Right Honourable the Lord Craven* (London: for John Wheble, 1775); *An Heroic Epistle to an Unfortunate Monarch* (London: n.p., [1778]); *An Heroic Epistle to Sir James Wright* (London: for J. Bew, 1779).
18 See *Lady Mary Wortley Montagu: Essays and Poems*, pp. 265–70; James McLaverty, *Pope, Print and Meaning* (Oxford: Oxford University Press, 2001), pp. 176–82.
19 London: for Lawton Gilliver, 1729; with the subtitle *An Epistolary Satire to a Friend* (London: for R. Dodsley, 1742); London: for J. Newbery, 1751. References are, respectively, to Dodsley's *Collection* (1782 edn), I, 276–311, III, 284–90, and *Bell's Classical Arrangement*, V, 47–55.
20 *Works*, pp. 93–5.
21 *Essays and Poems*, pp. 279–84; London: for F. and C. Rivington, and Oxford: for J. Cooke, 1794: see Donald F. Reiman's Introduction to the facsimile

reprint (New York and London: Garland Publishing, 1978), pp. viii–ix; *Poems on Several Occasions* (London: for S. Richardson, 1721), pp. 81–5; London: for T. Evans, 1777; London: for T. Evans, 1775.

22 London: by J. Wright for Lawton Gilliver, 1733; repr. Dodsley's *Collection* (1782 edn), I, 312–26, the text cited here.

23 Edinburgh: for the author. Foxon notes: 'Copies were issued in late states of Ramsay's *Poems*, 1720 [. . .]. Subsequently reprinted without title-page for later issues of that collection', but points out that the poem 'is signed and dated 25 March 1721' (Foxon R87).

24 *Works*, VI, 45.

25 *Works*, VI, 45.

26 *Works*, I, 176–82.

27 *Poems* (1720), pp. 365–82; *Works*, I, 247–63.

28 *Poems on Several Occasions* (London: for R. Dodsley and W. Owen, 1749), pp. 73–82; repr. in *Eighteenth-Century English Labouring-Class Poets*, II, 13–17, the text cited here.

29 *Lab'ring Muses*, pp. 146, 137–8; *Eighteenth-Century English Labouring-Class Poets*, II, 9.

30 The note about Isaac Mann in *Eighteenth-Century English Labouring-Class Poets* is mistaken in stating that he became Archbishop of Dublin in 1757, though more accurate about his preferment as Bishop of Cork (actually Cork and Ross) in 1772 (II, 390).

31 Jones may have found the name in the early editions of Pope's *Essay on Man* (it was later replaced by Bolingbroke's). The Twickenham notes (III: i, 11) derive it from Horace, though Cicero's *De Amicitia*, in which Gaius Laelius is the main speaker in a dialogue about friendship, is another possible source.

32 *Restoration and Eighteenth-Century Poetry 1660–1780*, p. 214; *Lab'ring Muses*, p. 133.

33 Henry Maule, to whom Jones refers as 'mitred *Maul*', and 'Bishop of Meath' in a footnote, is so listed in *The Court and City Register for the Year 1746* (London: for R. Amey and others, 1746), p. 183; the note in *Eighteenth-Century English Labouring-Class Poets*, p. 390, referring to an earlier bishop of Meath called Jones is incorrect.

34 *Lab'ring Muses*, pp. 145, 146.

35 *Lab'ring Muses*, p. 153.

36 *Essays and Poems*, pp. 265–70.

37 *English Poetry of the Eighteenth Century*, pp. 64–5 (p. 64); *Lady Mary Wortley Montagu*, p. 338.

38 '"Of Which Being Publick the Publick Judge": Pope and the Publication of *Verses Address'd to the Imitator of Horace*', *Studies in Bibliography*, 51 (1998), 183–204; *Pope, Print and Meaning*, pp. 176–82.

39 See '"Of Which Being Publick the Publick Judge"', especially pp. 186–94; *Pope, Print and Meaning*, p. 180.

40 London: for J. Almon, 1773 (the text cited here); London: for J. Almon, 1774. Both poems are included in *Bell's Classical Arrangement*, V, 86–91

[mispaginated 81], 92–6, which completes names of individuals satirized by replacing the original asterisks. Martin S. Day shows how popular the poem was by tracing the history of its many imitations in 'The Influence of Mason's *Heroic Epistle*', *Modern Language Quarterly*, 14 (1953), 235–52.

41 *The First Epistle of the Second Book of Horace, Imitated*, in Twickenham edition, IV, *Imitations of Horace*, ed. by John Butt (2nd edn, 1953), line 413, quoting the anonymous poem 'The Celebrated Beauties', in Dryden's miscellany, VI (1709 edn), [p. 514] (1716 edn, p. 229).

42 London: by W. Griffin. See further Stephen Bending, 'A Natural Revolution? Garden Politics in Eighteenth-Century England', in *Refiguring Revolutions: Aesthetics and Politics from the English Revolution to the Romantic Revolution*, ed. by Kevin Sharpe and Steven N. Zwicker (Berkeley, Los Angeles and London: University of California Press, 1998), pp. 241–66, especially pp. 250–6.

43 Day notes: 'Chambers had objected to the Ha Ha, or ditch, to restrict animals to a specific area' ('Influence of Mason's *Heroic Epistle*', p. 237, n. 8).

44 The allusion is to Pope's *Epistle to Burlington*: 'A Work to wonder at – perhaps a STOW' (Twickenham edn, *Epistles to Several Persons*, III: ii, 143).

45 See pp. 134–5 above.

46 Examples include Samuel Wesley, *Neck or Nothing: A Consolatory Letter from Mr. D[u]nt[o]n to Mr. C[u]rll upon his Being Tossed in a Blanket* ([London]: n. p., 1716); Nicholas Amhurst, *A Congratulatory Epistle from his Holiness the Pope to the Reverend Dr. Snape*; Jonathan Smedley, 'Cloe to Mr. Tickell, Occasioned by his Avignon-Letter', in *Poems on Several Occasions* (London: for S. Richardson, 1721), pp. 81–5; and various poems by Lady Mary Wortley Montagu, including 'P[ope] to Bolingbroke' (not printed till 1803; *Essays and Poems*, pp. 279–84).

47 Thomas Lockwood points out that Churchill 'became famous, and liked becoming famous, as "The Bruiser"' (*Post-Augustan Satire: Charles Churchill and Satirical Poetry, 1750–1800* [Seattle and London: University of Washington Press, 1979]), p. 142.

48 'The Influence of Mason's *Heroic Epistle*'; 'Anstey and Anapestic Satire in the Late Eighteenth Century', *ELH: A Journal of English Literary History*, 15 (1948), 122–46.

49 See Section 3 of Turner's Introduction to his edition (pp. 33–9); Turner indicates that Anstey's authorship of the guide was known 'certainly by the beginning of 1768 and very likely as early as June 1766' (p. 33).

50 *Story and History: Narrative Authority and Social Identity in the Eighteenth-Century French and English Novel* (Cambridge, MA, and Oxford: Basil Blackwell, 1990), p. 347, n. 5; Turner, pp. 35–6.

51 *An Account of the Voyages Undertaken by the Order of his Present Majesty for Making Discoveries in the Southern Hemisphere*, 3 vols (London: for W. Strahan and T. Cadell).

52 See *ODNB*, or, for fuller details, Harold B. Carter, *Sir Joseph Banks, 1743–1820* (London: British Museum [Natural History], 1988).

53 *Sir Joseph Banks*, p. 82.
54 London: J. Almon, 1774; London: by T. J. Carnegy for E. Johnson [1774].
    The Introduction to the first epistle is subscribed '*Dublin, Sept. 20th*, 1773'
    (p. 4), though the date is probably as fictitious as the address.
55 [London]: n. p., [1773], with fictitious imprint 'Batavia, for Jacobus Opano'.
56 See *Epistle from Oberea*, p. 12; *Second Letter from Oberea*, p. 15; *Epistle
    from Mr. Banks*, p. 14.
57 London: for T. Evans, 1774. For the Grosvenor scandal, see Bill Overton,
    Fictions of Female Adultery, 1684–1890: Theories and Circumtexts (Hound-
    mills, Basingstoke, and New York: Palgrave Macmillan, 2002), pp. 127–9.
58 London: for T. Evans, 1775.
59 London: for T. Evans, 1777; *Poetical Works*, 2 vols (Dublin: for the author
    by Graisberry & Campbell, 1793), I, [64].
60 London: for J. Murray, 1779; 'Composing Conscience: *The Injured Islanders*
    (1779) and English Sensibility', *The Eighteenth Century*, 38 (1997), 259–65
    (pp. 261, 263, 263–4).
61 Dodsley's *Collection* (1782 edn), I, 276–311.
62 'Voice, Gender, and the Augustan Verse Epistle', p. 86.
63 Dodsley's *Collection* (1782 edn), III, 284–90.
64 See Griffin, *Satire: A Critical Reintroduction*, Chapter 4, 'Satiric Closure'.
65 *Bell's Classical Arrangement*, V, 47–55.
66 See, e.g., Lockwood, *Post-Augustan Satire*; Dowling, *Epistolary Moment*;
    and, for a recent statement with respect to Churchill, one of its main
    examples, Brean Hammond, 'Verse Satire', in *Companion to Eighteenth-
    Century Poetry*, pp. 369–85 (p. 383).
67 All were published in 1774 by J. Almon.
68 See especially Arthur Marotti, *John Donne, Coterie Poet* (Madison:
    University of Wisconsin Press, 1986); George Parfitt, *John Donne: A
    Literary Life* (Houndmills, Basingstoke, and London: Macmillan, 1989).
69 See pp. 29–31 above.
70 *Poems of John Dryden*, IV, 326–34, 342–55.
71 See p. 228, n. 135, above.
72 Cambridge and New York: Cambridge University Press, 1996, p. 5; for a
    summary of the book's argument, see pp. 10–11.
73 *Literary Patronage in England*, pp. 53, 127.
74 *Literary Patronage in England*, pp. 155–6, 156–7.
75 *English Poetry of the Eighteenth Century*, pp. 60–1.
76 London: for J. Tonson, 1714; London: for J. Tonson, 1714; London: for
    Jacob Tonson, 1717.
77 *Literary Patronage in England*, pp. 16, 25, 26.
78 'Forms of Capital', trans. by Richard Nice, in *Handbook of Theory and
    Research for the Sociology of Education*, ed. by John G. Richardson (New
    York and London: Greenwood Press, 1986), pp. 241–58 (pp. 248–9); repr. in
    Education: Culture, Economy, Society, ed. by A. H. Halsey, Hugh Lauder,
    Philip Brown, and Amy Stuart Wells (Oxford and New York: Oxford Univer-

sity Press, 1997), pp. 47–58 (p. 51). Stephen Baron, John Field and Tom Schuller, eds of *Social Capital: Critical Perspectives* (Oxford and New York: Oxford University Press, 2000), review the development of the concept and analyse its utility in 'Social Capital: A Review and Critique', pp. 1–38.

79 *Literary Patronage in England*, p. 173.

80 There are various examples in *Miscellaneous Poems and Translations* (London: for Samuel Chapman, 1726), itself produced for Savage's benefit. See further Christine Gerrard, *Aaron Hill: The Muses' Projector*, pp. 96–9.

81 See, e.g., *The Sine-Cure. A Poetical Petition to the Right Honourable Robert Walpole, Esq;* (London: n. p., 1725), *The Promotion, and the Alternative: Two Poetical Petitions to the Right Honourable Sir Robert Walpole* (Westminster: by A. Campbell, for J. Millan, 1726), *A Familiar Epistle to the Right Honourable Sir Robert Walpole; Concerning Poets, Poverty, Promises, Places, &c.* (London: for Alexander Cruden, 1735); *Three Poetical Epistles to Mr. Hogarth, Mr. Dandridge, and Mr. Lambert, Masters in the Art of Painting* (London: for John Watts, 1731).

82 *A Poetical Epistle to an Eminent Painter* (London: for T. Payne and Son, J. Dodsley, and Robson and Co., 1778), *An Essay on History; in Three Epistles to Edward Gibbon, Esq.* (London: for J. Dodsley, 1780), *An Essay on Epic Poetry; in Five Epistles to the Revd. Mr. Mason* (London: for J. Dodsley, 1780), *Epistle to Admiral Keppel* (London: for Fielding and Walker, 1779). Unusually, the first editions of *Poetical Epistle to an Eminent Painter* and *Epistle to Admiral Keppel* were anonymous.

83 'Epistle to William Hayley, Esq.', 'Epistle to Mr Romney, Being Presented by Him with a Picture of William Hayley, Esq.', 'Epistle to George Romney, Esq. on His Having Presented the Author's Picture to her Father, May 1788', *Poetical Works*, ed. by Walter Scott, 3 vols (Edinburgh: by James Ballantyne and Co. for John Ballantyne and Co.; London: Hurst, Rees and Orme, 1810), II, 144–9, 124–9, 345–7. See also 'Epistle to the Rev. Dr William Bagshot Stevens, of Repton, Derbyshire, Written in 1783' (II, 165–71); 'Epistle to Nathaniel Lister, Esq. of Lichfield, on Having Read his Verses in Manuscript, Written December 1786' (II, 333–44); 'Epistle to F. C. R. Mundy, Esq. of Marketon, Derbyshire. – Written 1794' (II, 199–206).

84 The text cited is that of *The Poems of Ambrose Philips*, ed. by M. G. Segar, Percy Reprints, no. 14 (Oxford: Basil Blackwell, 1937), pp. 97–101.

85 Dublin, by George Grierson, [1729]; repr. in *The Poems of Jonathan Swift*, ed. by Harold Williams, 3 vols (Oxford: Clarendon Press, 1937), II, 471–4, the text cited here.

86 *Jonathan Swift: The Complete Poems*, ed. by Pat Rogers (Harmondsworth and New York: Penguin Books, 1983), p. 806.

87 Dublin: n. p., 1730; *Poems of Jonathan Swift*, II, 475–9, the text cited here.

88 [Dublin]: n. p., 1730; *Literary Patronage in England*, p. 119.

89 *Miscellanies by Henry Fielding, Esq*, 3 vols, Welseyan Edition of the Works of Henry Fielding, I, ed. by Henry Knight Miller (Oxford: Clarendon Press, 1972), 56–8.

90 *A Familiar Epistle to the Right Honourable Sir Robert Walpole; Concerning Poets, Poverty, Promises, Places, &c.*

91 *Henry Fielding* (London: Weidenfeld and Nicolson, 1990), p. 125. For the version in the *Gentleman's* see *Miscellanies*, I, 249–50, and, for discussion, III, ed. by Hugh Amory with introduction and commentary by Bertrand A. Goldgar (Oxford: Clarendon Press, 1997), 206 and note.

92 'Fielding and the Licensing Act', *Huntington Library Quarterly*, 50 (1987), 379–93 (p. 385).

93 *The Life of Henry Fielding: A Critical Biography* (Malden, MA, and Oxford: Blackwell Publishing, 2000), p. 57.

94 *An Epistle to the Right Honourable James Lord Visct. Charlemont. With a Translation of the Sixth Satire of the Second Book of Horace* (Dublin: by and for George Faulkner, 1744). The epistle occupies pp. 3–25 and has 456 lines, the translation pp. 29–44 and has 240.

95 *The Correspondence of Jonathan Swift*, ed. by Harold Williams, 5 vols, 2nd edn (Oxford: Clarendon Press, 1965), V (1737–1745), 86, qtd by Andrew Carpenter in his edition of *Verse in English from Eighteenth-Century Ireland* (Cork: Cork University Press, 1998), p. 207.

96 See Alvin Snider, 'Hudibrastic', *Restoration: Studies in English Literary Culture, 1660–1700*, 12 (1988), 1–9. Snider's remark that Samuel Butler's rhymes show a 'penchant for bringing dissimilarities into concatenation and revealing heretofore unrecognized correspondences' (p. 6) could be extended to Dunkin's – for example, 'hopes' / 'Tropes' (63–4), 'Reward' / 'Bard' (223–4), and, outrageously, 'Great' / '*Billingsgate*' (217–18).

97 For details of Mountjoy (1709–69) and Tullamore (1712–64), see G. E. C[okayne] and others, *The Complete Peerage of England, Scotland, Ireland, Great Britain and the United Kingdom*, rev. edn, 14 vols (London: St. Catherine Press, 1910–59), IX, 351–2, 164.

98 See, e.g., 'The First Ode of the Second Book of Horace Paraphras'd: And Address'd to Richard St[ee]le, Esq;', 'Horace, Lib. 2. Sat. 6, Part of It Imitated', 'Horace, Book I. Ode XIV, Paraphrased and Inscribed to Ir[elan]d', *Poems*, I, 179–84, 197–202; III, 769–72.

99 *Poetical Works*, 2 vols (London: for W. Nicoll, 1774), II, 78–85.

100 *Poetical Works*, II, 83; Jones, *Poems on Several Occasions*, pp. [7], 13. Chesterfield was Jones's patron as well as Dunkin's.

101 *Poetical Works*, II, 86–98; *Select Poetical Works*, 2 vols (Dublin: by W. G. Jones, 1769–70), II, 78–98.

102 *The Field Day Anthology of Irish Writing*, 3 vols, ed. by Seamus Deane, Andrew Carpenter, and Jonathan Williams (Derry: Field Day Publications; London: Faber, 1991), I, 395–499 (ed. by Bryan Coleborne); *Verse in English from Eighteenth-Century Ireland*, pp. 5, 207–21.

103 See, e.g., Boyse's epistles to his dedicatee the Countess of Eglington in *Translations and Poems Written on Several Subjects* (Edinburgh: by Mr. Thomas and Walter Ruddimans, 1731), pp. 56–60, 61–5, and to Sir John Clerk in *Translations and Poems, Written on Several Occasions* (London:

for the Author, 1738), pp. 180–2, 183–4; Cooke's to the Earl of Wilton, the Duke of Somerset and Admiral James Vernon in *Mr. Cooke's Original Poems* (London: for T. Jackson and C. Bathurst, 1742), pp. 71–4, 79–85, 88–91; 92–4; and Woodhouse's to William Shenstone, Lord Lyttelton and several benefactors in a poem entitled 'Gratitude. To ——' in *Poems on Several Occasions*, 2nd edn (London: for the author, 1766), pp. 1–16, 136–61, 164–75, repr. in *Eighteenth-Century Labouring Class Poets*, II, 147–53, 194–204, 205–9.

104 London: for J. Dodsley.

105 See pp. 85–6 above.

106 *Poetical Works*, 2 vols (Edinburgh: Apollo Press, by the Martins, 1780), I, 30–1, 32–3, 22–7, 27–30, the latter two, to Ramsay, repr. with his replies in *Works*, II, 182–9, III, 120–4. Somervile also sent complimentary epistles to, among others, Addison and the Earl of Halifax (*Poetical Works*, I, 5–10, 34–6). Complimentary epistles from Burns to fellow poets include three to John Lapraik and two to David Sillar (*Canongate Burns*, pp. 133–6, 137–40, 568–70, 97–101, 321–2); epistles to Burns from fellow poets include those by David Sillar, Janet Little and Robert Anderson repr. in *Eighteenth-Century Labouring-Class Poets*, III, 173–5, 242–4, 310–15.

107 *Works*, II, 109–12.

108 The epistles between Hamilton and Ramsay are discussed above, pp. 93–6; for those from Burns to Lapraik and Sillar, see note 106 above.

109 *Poems on Several Occasions*, pp. 102–6, 107–8, repr. in Dodsley's *Collection* (1782 edn), II, 262–6, 266–7, the texts cited here. On Hoadly, see the biographical note in Suarez, 'Who's Who in the *Collection*', 169–70.

110 William Mason, 'Memoirs of the Life and Writings of Mr. William White-head', in *Poems by William Whitehead*, Vol. III (York: by A. Ward, 1788), 1–129 (p. 42).

111 *Poems on Several Occasions*, pp. 75–84, repr. in *Plays and Poems* (1774), II, 147–56. Whitehead also addressed to 'Mrs. Wright of Romely, in Derbyshire' his dedication for *Ann Boleyn to Henry the Eighth*, referring to her as 'fair Bride' (London: for R. Dodsley, 1743, p. 5).

112 *Poems on Several Occasions*, pp. 118–21.

113 Dodsley's *Collection* (1782 edn), VI, 337–9.

114 In Pilgrim Plowden (pseudonym for George Farewell), *Farrago* (London: for the author, 1733 [1734?]), pp. 72–3; repr. in *New Oxford Book of Eighteenth-Century Verse*, pp. 268–9, the text cited here.

Appendix 2

1 Steven Hall, 'Literature Online: Building a Home for English and American Literature on the World Wide Web', *Computers and the Humanities*, 32 (1998), 285–301 (p. 285).

List of Works Cited

Primary Sources

Adams, Jane (Jean Adam), *Miscellany Poems* (Glasgow: for James Duncan, 1734)

Addison, Joseph, *A Letter from Italy, to the Right Honourable Charles Lord Halifax* (London: by H. Hills, 1709)

——, *The Miscellaneous Works of Joseph Addison*, ed. by A. C. Guthkelch (London: G. Bell and Sons, 1914)

Akenside, Mark, *The Poetical Works of Mark Akenside*, ed. by Robin Dix (Cranbury, NJ, and London: Associated University Presses, 1996)

Amatory Pieces ([Ludlow]: by George Nicholson, 1799)

Amhurst, Nicholas, *A Congratulatory Epistle from his Holiness the Pope to the Reverend Dr. Snape* (London: for E. Curll, 1718; Foxon A188)

Anderson, Robert, *Poems on Various Subjects* (Carlisle: by J. Mitchell for the author, 1798)

Annual Register, The, 1760 (London: for R. and J. Dodsley, 1761)

Annual Register, The, 1762 (London: for R. and J. Dodsley, 1763)

Annual Register, The, 1766 (London: for J. Dodsley, 1767)

Anonymous, 'Abelard to Eloisa', in John Hughes, *Letters of Abelard and Heloise* (London: for B. Law and others, [1777?]), pp. 192–4

——, *The Art of Preaching* (London: for R. Dodsley, [1738], sometimes attributed to George Smalridge)

——, *The Art of Wenching* (Dublin: by George Faulkner, 1737; Foxon A328)

——, 'Charles Brandon, Duke of Suffolk, to Mary Queen of France', *Gentleman's Magazine*, XII (1742), 439, 489

——, 'An Epistle to a Lady', in *A Collection of Poems by Several Hands*, 6 vols (London; for J. Dodsley, 1782), III, 207–9

——, *An Epistle from Mr. Banks, Voyager, Monster-Hunter, and Amoroso, to Oberea, Queen of Otaheite* ([London]: n. p., [1773]; 'Batavia, for Jacobus Opano')

——, *The Golden Age* (London: for F. and C. Rivington; Oxford: for J. Cooke, 1794)

——, *An Historic Epistle, from Omiah, to the Queen of Otaheite; Being his Remarks on the English Nation* (London: for T. Evans, 1775)

——, *Letters from Zilia to Aza* (Dublin: by and for Henry Saunders, 1753; ms attribution to 'Col. Beaver')

——, 'Mary, Dowager Queen of France, to Charles Brandon, Duke of Suffolk', *Gentleman's Magazine*, XIII (1743), 99–100, 153

——, *The Mistakes of Men in Search of Happiness. An Ethic Epistle, to Mrs. ******* (London: for R. and J. Dodsley, 1761)

Anonymous, *The Royal African: Or, Memoirs of the Young Prince of Annamaboe* (London: for W. Reeve, G. Woodfall and J. Barnes, [1749])

——, *Two Epistles on Happiness: To a Young Lady* (Salisbury: for Edward Easton, 1754)

——, *Yarico to Inkle. An Epistle* (London: for Lawton Gilliver; Foxon M434; dubiously attributed to Edward Moore)

Anstey, Christopher, *An Election Ball*, 2nd edn (Bath: for the author by S. Hazard, 1776)

——, *The New Bath Guide* ([London etc: for J. Dodsley and others], 1766)

——, *The New Bath Guide*, ed. by Gavin Turner (Bristol: Broadcast Books, 1994)

Armstrong, John, *The Art of Preserving Health* (London: for A. Millar, 1744)

——, *A Day: An Epistle to John Wilkes, of Aylesbury, Esq.* (London: for A. Millar, 1761)

——, *The Oeconomy of Love* (London: for T. Cooper, 1736)

Arno Miscellany, The (Florence: printed in the Stamperia Bonducciana, 1784)

Asylum for Fugitives, An, 2 vols [London; for J. Almon, 1776–9]

Ayre, William, *Four Ethic Epistles Opposing Some of Mr. Pope's Opinions of Man* (London: for Samuel Paterson, 1753)

——, *Memoirs of the Life and Writings of Alexander Pope, Esq;*, 2 vols (London: for the author, 1745)

——, *Truth. A Counterpart to Mr. Pope's Essay on Man. Epistle the First* (London: for the author, 1739; Foxon A375)

——, *Truth. A Counterpart to Mr. Pope's Essay on Man. Epistle the Second* (London: for the author, 1739; Foxon A377)

Bancks, John, *Love Atones for Little Crimes: An Ethic Epistle, by Way of Apology for a Darling Passion* (London: for J. Torbuck, 1738; Foxon B51)

——, *Miscellaneous Works, in Verse and Prose*, 2 vols (London: by T. Aris, for the author, 1738)

——, *Miscellaneous Works, in Verse and Prose*, 2 vols (London: for James Hodges, 1739)

——, *Poems on Several Occasions* (London: for the author, [1733])

——, *The Weaver's Miscellany* (London: n. p., 1730)

Barber, Mary, *Poems on Several Occasions* (London: C. Rivington, 1734 [1735])

Barford, Richard, *Abelard to Eloisa* (London: by J. Bettenham, 1725)

Barker, Jane, *Poetical Recreations* (London: for Benjamin Crayle, 1688)

Beckingham, Charles, 'Fragment of an Epistle from Abelard to Eloisa', in *The Pleasures of Coition* (London: for E. Curll, 1721), pp. 47–50

Behn, Aphra, *Oroonoko*, Bedford Cultural Edition, ed. by Catherine Gallagher (Houndmills, Basingstoke, and London: Macmillan; Boston, MA: Bedford/St. Martin's Press, 2000)

——, *Oroonoko*, Norton Critical Edition, ed. by Joanna Lipking (New York: W. W. Norton, 1997)

——, *The Works of Aphra Behn*, ed. by Janet Todd, 7 vols (London: William Pickering, 1992–6), I, *Poetry* (1992)

Bell, John (pub.), *Bell's Classical Arrangement of Fugitive Poetry*, 18 vols

(London: vols 1–16 by John Bell, 1789–94; vols 17–18 by and for James Cawthorn, 1796, 1797)

Bell, John (pub.), *The Poets of Great Britain Complete from Chaucer to Churchill*, 109 vols (Edinburgh: Apollo Press, by the Martins, 1776–82)

Birch, Elizabeth, *Poems on Various Subjects* (Manchester: by C. Wheeler and Son, 1800)

Birch, Samuel, 'Abelard to Eloisa', in *Letters of Abelard and Heloise* (London: for W. Lowndes and others, 1787)

Blamire, Susanna, *The Poetical Works of Miss Susanna Blamire*, [ed. by Henry Lonsdale and Patrick Maxwell] (Edinburgh: John Menzies, 1842; repr. London and New York: Woodstock Books, 1994)

Bland, John, *Genuine Happiness: A Poetical Essay* (London: for J. Townsend, 1759)

Boyse, Samuel, *Translations and Poems Written on Several Subjects* (Edinburgh: by Mr. Thomas and Walter Ruddimans, 1731)

——, *Translations and Poems, Written on Several Occasions* (London: for the Author, 1738)

Bramston, James, *The Art of Politicks* (London: for Lawton Gilliver, 1729)

——, *The Man of Taste* (London: by J. Wright for Lawton Gilliver, 1733)

Brereton, Charlotte, 'To Miss A[nn]a M[ari]a Tra[ver]s. An Epistle from Scotland', *Gentleman's Magazine*, 12 (1742), 103

Brereton, Jane, *An Expostulatory Epistle to Sir Richard Steele upon the Death of Mr. Addison* (London: for W. Hinchliffe, 1720; Foxon R273)

——, *The Fifth Ode of the Fourth Book of Horace Imitated: And Apply'd to the King* (London: for William Hinchliffe: 1716; Foxon B408)

——, *Merlin: A Poem* (London: for Edward Cave, 1735; Foxon B409)

——, *Poems on Several Occasions* (London: by Edward Cave, 1744)

British Apollo, The, [2 vols?], 3rd edn (London: for John Isted and Richard King, 1718)

British Women Poets 1660–1800: An Anthology, ed. by Joyce Fullard (Troy, NY: Whitston Publishing, 1990)

Broome, William, *Poems on Several Occasions* (London: by J. Roberts, 1739)

Browne, Isaac Hawkins, *A Pipe of Tobacco* (London: for L. Gilliver, 1736)

——, *The Fire-Side: A Pastoral Soliloquy* (London: for Henry Carpenter, [1746]; Foxon B517)

Broxholme, Noel, *A Letter from a Lady to her Husband Abroad* (London: for J. Roberts; Foxon B541)

Burgess, D., *The Entertainer; Or, Youth's Delightful Preceptor* (Berwick: by R. Taylor, 1759)

Burns, Robert, *The Canongate Burns*, ed. by Andrew Noble and Patrick Scott Hogg (Edinburgh: Canongate Books, 2001)

Burrell, Lady Sophia, *Poems*, 2 vols (London: by J. Cooper, 1793)

Byrom, John, *Miscellaneous Poems*, 2 vols (Manchester: by J. Harrop, 1773)

——, *The Poems of John Byrom*, ed. by Adophus William Ward, 3 vols (Manchester: Charles E. Simms for the Chetham Society)

Canning, George, *An Epistle from Lord William Russel, to William Lord Cavendish* (Newcastle: n. p., 1775)

Carey, Henry, *Namby Pamby: Or, a Panegyrick on the New Versification Address'd to A----- P---- ([Dublin: n. p., 1725])

Caribbeana, 2 vols (London: for T. Osborne and others, 1741)

Carpenter, Andrew (ed.), *Verse in English from Eighteenth-Century Ireland* (Cork: Cork University Press, 1998)

Cawthorn, James, *Abelard to Eloisa* (London: for M. Cooper, 1747)

——, *Poems* (London: by W. Woodfall, 1771)

Chambers, Sir William, *A Dissertation on Oriental Gardening* (London: by W. Griffin, 1772)

Chandler, *The Description of Bath, A Poem*, 4th edn (London: for James Leake, 1738)

Chillingworth, William, *The Works of William Chillingworth* (London: by M. Clark for A. and J. Churchill, 1704); repr. 2 vols (Dublin: for William Brien, 1752)

Chudleigh, Lady Mary, *Poems on Several Occasions* (London: by W. B. for Bernard Lintott, 1703)

——, *The Poems and Prose of Mary, Lady Chudleigh*, ed. by Margaret J. M. Ezell (New York and Oxford: Oxford University Press, 1993)

Churchill, Charles, *Epistle to William Hogarth* (London: for the author, 1763)

Clarke, Adam, *Memoirs of the Wesley Family* (London: by J. and T. Clarke, 1823)

Claudero (pseudonym for James Wilson), *Miscellanies in Prose and Verse, on Several Occasions*, 4th edn (Edinburgh: for the author, 1771)

Cole, Thomas, *The Life of Hubert* (London: for the author by Samson Low, 1795)

Coleridge, Samuel Taylor, *Poetical Works*, ed. by J. C. C. Mays, vol. 16 (2001) in *The Collected Works of Samuel Taylor Coleridge*, 16 vols (Princeton, NJ: Princeton University Press; London: Routledge & Kegan Paul), 1969–2002)

Collection of Poems by Several Hands, A (London: for R. Dodsley), 3 vols, 1748; 3 vols, 1748 (2nd edn); 4 vols, 1755; 6 vols, 1758, 1763 etc; 6 vols (London: for J. Dodsley, 1782)

Collection of Poems by Several Hands, A, ed. by Michael F. Suarez, SJ, 6 vols (London: Routledge/Thoemmes Press, 1997)

Collection of Poems in Four Volumes, A (London: for G. Pearch, 1770, 1775; for J. Dodsley, 1783)

Collection of Scarce, Curious, and Valuable Pieces, A (Edinburgh: for T. Ruddiman, 1785)

Collington, Charles, *Happiness: an Epistle to a Friend* (Cambridge: by J. Bentham, 1763)

Combe, William, *An Heroic Epistle to the Right Honourable the Lord Craven* (London: for John Wheble, 1775)

——, *An Heroic Epistle to Sir James Wright* (London: for J. Bew, 1779)

——, *An Heroic Epistle to an Unfortunate Monarch* (London: n.p., [1778])

——, *A Poetical Epistle to Sir Joshua Reynolds* (London: for Fielding and Walker, 1777)

Congreve, William, *The Complete Works of William Congreve*, 4 vols, ed. by Montague Summers (London: Nonesuch Press, 1923)

——, *A Letter from Mr. Congreve to the Right Honourable the Lord Viscount Cobham* (London: for A. Dodd and E. Nutt, 1729; Foxon C375)

——, *The Poetical Works of William Congreve* (London: for C. Cooke, [1796])

Cooke, Thomas, *Mr. Cooke's Original Poems* (London: for T. Jackson and C. Bathurst, 1742)

Cooper, John Gilbert, *The Call of Aristippus. Epistle IV. To Mark Akenside, M. D.* (London, for R. and J. Dodsley, 1758)

——, *Epistles to the Great, from Aristippus in Retirement* (London: for R. and J. Dodsley, 1757)

——, *Poems on Several Subjects* (London: for R. and J. Dodsley, 1764)

—— (trans.), *Ver-Vert: Or, the Nunnery Parrot. [. . .] Translated from the French of Monsieur Gresset* (London: for R. and J. Dodsley, 1759)

Correspondence between Frances, Countess of Hartford, (Afterwards Duchess of Somerset,) and Henrietta Louisa, Countess of Pomfret, between the Years 1738 and 1741, 3 vols (London: for Richard Phillips, 1805; 2nd edn, 1806)

Court and City Register for the Year 1746, The (London: for R. Amey and others, 1746)

Courtenay, John, *An Poetical Epistle (Moral and Philosophical) from an Officer at Otaheite to Lady Gr[os]v[e]n[o]r* (London: for T. Evans, 1774)

Cowper, Judith (later Madan), 'Abelard to Eloisa', in William Pattison, *Poetical Works* (London: for H. Curll, 1728 [1727]), pp. 67–77, and *Poems by Eminent Ladies*, 2 vols (London: for R. Baldwin, 1755), II, 137–43

Cunningham, John, *Poems, Chiefly Pastoral* (London: for the author, 1766)

Cupid Triumphant (London: by J. Jefferies, 1747; by M. Hope, 1747)

Curtis, Ann (née Kemble, later Hatton), *Poems on Miscellaneous Subjects* (London: for the author, 1783)

Dallas, Robert Charles, *Miscellaneous Writings* (London: for T. N. Longman, 1797)

Dalton, John, *A Descriptive Poem, Addressed to Two Ladies, at their Return from Viewing the Mines near Whitehaven. To Which Are Added, Some Thoughts on Building and Planting, to Sir James Lowther* (London: for J. and J. Rivington, and R. and J. Dodsley, 1755)

Darwin, Erasmus, *The Golden Age; The Temple of Nature*, repr. with Introduction by Donald H. Reiman (New York: Garland, 1978)

Day, Thomas, and John Bicknell, *The Dying Negro, A Poetical Epistle* (London: for W. Flexney, 1773)

——, *The Dying Negro, A Poetical Epistle* (London: for W. Flexney, 1774)

De-La-Cour (also Delacour, Dalacour, Delacourt), James, *Abelard to Eloisa* (Dublin: by S. Powell, for Abraham Bradley, 1730)

——, *Poems by the Revd. James De-La-Cour* (Cork: by Thomas White, 1778)

Delany, Patrick, *Epistle to his Excellency John Lord Carteret* (Dublin: by George Grierson, [1729])

Dermody, Thomas, *Poems, Consisting of Essays, Lyric, Elegiac, &c.* (Dublin: J. Jones, 1792)

Derrick, Samuel, *A Collection of Original Poems* (London: for the author, 1755)

Desaguliers, John Theophilus, 'John Theophilus Desaguliers to John Thurloe Brace', Bodleian Mss Add B105

Dodd, William, *The African Prince, When in England, to Zara, at his Father's Court; and Zara's Answer*, 2nd edition (London: for Mr. Waller and Mr. Ward, 1755)

——, *Poems* (London: by Dryden Leach for the author, 1767)

Dodsley, Robert, *An Epistle to Mr. Pope, Occasion'd by his Essay on Man* (London: for L. Gilliver, 1734)

——, *A Muse in Livery* (London: for the author, 1732)

Drayton, Michael, *The Works of Michael Drayton*, ed. by J. William Hebel, Kathleen Tillotson and Bernard Newdigate, 5 vols (Oxford: Basil Blackwell for the Shakespeare Head Press, 1931–41)

Dryden, John, *The Comedies, Tragedies, and Operas Written by John Dryden*, 2 vols (London: for Jacob Tonson, Thomas Bennet, and Richard Wellington, 1701)

——, *The Dramatic Works of John Dryden, Esq.*, 6 vols, [ed. by William Congreve] (London: J. and R. Tonson, 1717)

——, *The Miscellaneous Works of John Dryden, Esq;*, 4 vols (London: for J. and R. Tonson, 1760)

——, *Original Poems, by John Dryden, Esq.*, 2 vols (Edinburgh: by Rob. and And. Foulis, 1756)

——, *The Poems of John Dryden*, 5 vols, ed. by Paul Hammond and David Hopkins (London and New York: Longman, 1995–2005)

——, *The Satires of Decimus Junius Juvenalis [. . .] Together with the Satires of Aulus Persius Flaccus* (London: for Jacob Tonson, 1692 [1693])

Duck, Stephen, *Poems on Several Occasions* (London: for the author, 1736)

Duncan, John, *An Essay on Happiness* (London: for R. and J. Dodsley, 1762; rev. edn, London: for T. Cadell, 1772)

Duncombe, John, *The Works of Horace in English Verse. By Several Hands*, 2 vols (London: for R. and J. Dodsley, 1759)

Dunkin, William, *An Epistle to the Right Honourable James Lord Visct. Charlemont. With a Translation of the Sixth Satire of the Second Book of Horace* (Dublin: by and for George Faulkner, 1744; Foxon D519)

——, *Poetical Works*, 2 vols (London: for W. Nicoll, 1774)

——, *Select Poetical Works*, 2 vols (Dublin: by W. G. Jones, 1769–70)

Egerton, Sarah Fyge, *Poems on Several Occasions* (London: for J. Nutt, [1703])

Etherege, Sir George, *The Poems of Sir George Etherege*, ed. by James Thorpe (Princeton, NJ: Princeton University Press, 1963)

Eusden, Laurence, *A Letter to Mr. Addison, on the King's Accession to the Throne* (London: for Jacob Tonson, 1714; Foxon E492)

Evans, Abel, *Vertumnus: An Epistle to Mr. Jacob Bobart* (Oxford: by L[eonard] L[ichfield] for Stephen Fletcher, 1713)

Evans, Nathaniel, *Poems on Several Occasions* (Philadelphia: John Dunlap, 1772)

Examen Poeticum (London: by R. E. for Jacob Tonson, 1693)

Fairer, David, and Christine Gerrard (eds), *Eighteenth-Century Poetry: An*

Annotated Anthology (Oxford and Malden, MA: Blackwell, 1999; 2nd edn, 2004)

Fergusson, Robert, *The Poems of Robert Fergusson*, ed. by Matthew P. McDiarmid, 2 vols, Scottish Text Society, 3rd ser., 21, 24 (Edinburgh and London: William Blackwood & Sons, 1956)

Field Day Anthology of Irish Writing, The, 3 vols, ed. by Seamus Deane, Andrew Carpenter, and Jonathan Williams (Derry: Field Day Publications; London: Faber, 1991)

Fielding, Henry, *Miscellanies by Henry Fielding, Esq*, 3 vols, Welseyan Edition of the Works of Henry Fielding, vol. 1 ed. by Henry Knight Miller (Oxford: Clarendon Press, 1972), vols 2 and 3 by Hugh Amory with introduction and commentary by Bertrand A. Goldgar (Oxford: Clarendon Press, 1993, 1997)

Finch, Anne, Countess of Winchilsea, *The Anne Finch Wellesley Manuscript Poems: A Critical Edition*, ed. by Barbara McGovern and Charles H. Hinnant (Athens and London: University of Georgia Press, 1998)

——, *Miscellany Poems, on Several Occasions: Written by a Lady* (London: for John Barber, 1713)

——, *The Poems of Anne, Countess of Winchilsea*, ed. by Myra Reynolds (Chicago: University of Chicago Press, 1903; repr. New York: AMS Press, 1974)

Fitzgerald, Gerald, *The Injured Islanders, Or the Influence of Art upon the Happiness of Nature* (London: for J. Murray, 1779)

Fowke, Martha (later Sansom), *Clio: Or, a Secret History of the Life and Amours of the Late Celebrated Mrs. S---n---m* (London: for M. Cooper, 1752)

——, *Clio: The Autobiography of Martha Fowke Sansom (1689–1736)*, ed. by Phyllis J. Guskin (Newark, NJ: University of Delaware Press; London: Associated University Presses, 1997)

——, and William Bond, *The Epistles of Clio and Strephon* (London: for J. Hooke, F. Gyles, and W. Boreham, 1720)

Francis, Philip, *The Epistles and Art of Poetry of Horace*, 4 vols (London: for A. Millar, 1746)

Fullard, Joyce (ed.), *British Women Poets 1660–1800: An Anthology* (Troy, NY: Whitston Publishing, 1990)

Gay, John, *An Epistle to her Grace Henrietta, Dutchess of Marlborough* (London: for Jacob Tonson, 1722)

——, *John Gay: Poetry and Prose*, 2 vols, ed. by Vinton A. Dearing and Charles E. Beckwith (Oxford: Clarendon Press, 1974)

Gay, John, *Poems on Several Occasions*, 2 vols (London: for Jacob Tonson and Bernard Lintot, 1720)

Gerrard, John, *Poems* (London: for the author, 1769)

Gentleman's Magazine, 128 vols (London, 1731–1858)

Gilbert, Thomas, *Poems on Several Occasions* (London: for Charles Bathurst, 1747)

Godfrey, Thomas, *Juvenile Poems on Various Subjects* (Philadelphia: by Henry Miller, 1765)

Goodridge, John (gen. ed.), *Eighteenth-Century English Labouring Class Poets*, 3 vols (London: Pickering & Chatto, 2003); vol. 1 (1700–1740) ed. by William Christmas, vol. 2 (1740–1770) Bridget Keenan, vol. 3 (1770–1800) Tim Burke

Hall-Stevenson, John, *The Works of John Hall-Stevenson*, 3 vols (London: by J. Nichols for J. Debrett and T. Beckett, 1795)

Hammond, Anthony (comp.), *A New Miscellany of Original Poems, Translations and Imitations* (London: for T. Jauncy, 1720)

Hardy, Thomas, *Thomas Hardy: The Complete Poems*, ed. by James Gibson (London: Macmillan, 1976)

Harte, Walter, *An Essay on Satire* (London: for Lawton Gilliver, 1730)

Hawkesworth, John, *An Account of the Voyages Undertaken by the Order of his Present Majesty for Making Discoveries in the Southern Hemisphere*, 3 vols (London: for W. Strahan and T. Cadell, 1773)

Hayes, Daniel, *The Works in Verse of Daniel Hayes* (London: n. p., 1769)

Hayley, William, *Epistle to Admiral Keppel* (London: for Fielding and Walker, 1779)

——, *An Essay on Epic Poetry; in Five Epistles to the Revd. Mr. Mason* (London: for J. Dodsley, 1780)

——, *An Essay on History; in Three Epistles to Edward Gibbon, Esq.* (London: for J. Dodsley, 1780)

——, *A Poetical Epistle to an Eminent Painter* (London: for T. Payne and Son, J. Dodsley, and Robson and Co., 1778)

Hill, Bridget (ed.), *Eighteenth-Century Women: An Anthology* (London: Unwin Hyman, 1984)

Honeywood, St John, *Poems* (New York: by T. and J. Swords, 1801)

Horace (Quintus Horatius Flaccus), *The Epistles of Horace*, trans. by David Ferry (New York: Farrar, Straus and Giroux, 2001)

——, *Horace: Satires, Epistles, Ars Poetica*, Loeb Classical Library, ed. with trans. by H. Rushton Fairclough, rev. edn (London: William Heinemann; Cambridge, MA: Harvard University Press, 1929)

Hughes, John, *Letters of Abelard and Heloise*, 3rd edn (London: for J. Watts, 1718; Dublin: for J. Williams, 1769; London: for B. Law etc, [1777?]; London: for T. Lowndes and others, 1781; London: for W. Lowndes etc, 1787)

Husbands, John, *A Miscellany of Poems by Several Hands* (Oxford: by Leon. Lichfield, 1731)

Irwin, Lady Anne, 'An Epistle to Mr Pope. By a Lady. Occasioned by his Characters of Women', *Gentleman's Magazine*, 6 (1736), 745; repr. in *British Women Poets 1660–1800: An Anthology*, ed. by Joyce Fullard (Troy, NY: Whitston Publishing, 1990), pp. 303–5.

Jacob, Giles, *The Rape of the Smock* (London: for R. Burleigh, 1717; Foxon J23)

Jenyns, Soame, *Poems. By ****** (London: for R. Dodsley, 1752)

Jerningham, Edward, *Abelard to Eloisa: A Poem* (London: for J. Robson, 1792)

——, *Poems*, 2 vols (London: for J. Robson, 1796)

——, *Yarico to Inkle: An Epistle* (London: for J. Dodsley, 1766)

Johnson, Samuel, *The Lives of the Most Eminent English Poets*, 4 vols, ed. by Roger Lonsdale (Oxford: Clarendon Press, 2006)

Johnson, Samuel, *The Poems of Samuel Johnson*, ed. by David Nicol Smith and Edward L. McAdam, 2nd edn. rev. by J. D. Fleeman (Oxford: Clarendon Press, 1974)

Jones, Christopher, *The Miscellaneous Poetic Attempts of C. Jones, an Uneducated Journeyman Wool-comber* (Exeter: for the author, 1782)

Jones, Henry, *Poems on Several Occasions* (London: for R. Dodsley and W. Owen, 1749)

Jones, Mary, *Miscellanies in Prose and Verse* (Oxford: by Mr Dodsley, Mr Clements, and Mr Frederick, 1750)

Jones, Vivien (ed.), *Women in the Eighteenth Century: Discourses of Femininity* (London and New York: Routledge, 1990)

Jonson, Ben, *The Complete Poems*, ed. by George Parfitt (Harmondsworth: Penguin Books, 1975)

——, *Works* (London: by Will. Stansby, 1616)

Keate, George, *An Epistle from Lady Jane Gray to Lord Guilford Dudley* (London: for R. and J. Dodsley, 1762)

King, William, *The Art of Cookery, in Imitation of Horace's Art of Poetry* (London: for Bernard Lintott, 1708 [1707])

Leapor, Mary, *The Works of Mary Leapor*, ed. by Richard Greene and Ann Messenger (Oxford: Oxford University Press, 2003)

Learmont, John, *Poems Pastoral, Satirical, Tragic, and Comic* (Edinburgh: for the author, by Alexander Chapman and Company, 1791)

Letters, by Several Eminent Persons Deceased. Including the Correspondence of John Hughes, 2 vols [ed. by John Duncombe] (London: for J. Johnson, 1772)

Lewis, Esther, *Poems Moral and Entertaining* (Bath: by S. Hazard, 1789)

Lloyd, Evan, *Epistle to David Garrick, Esq.* (London: for the author, 1773)

Lloyd, Robert, *Poetical Works*, 2 vols (London: for T. Evans, 1774)

London Magazine. Or, Gentleman's Monthly Intelligencer, 51 vols (London, 1732–83)

Lonsdale, Roger (ed.), *Eighteenth-Century Women Poets: An Oxford Anthology* (Oxford and New York: Oxford University Press, 1989)

——, *The New Oxford Book of Eighteenth-Century Verse* (Oxford and New York: Oxford University Press, 1984)

——, *The Poems of Gray, Collins, and Goldsmith* (London and Harlow: Longmans, Green, 1969)

Lovibond, Edward, *Poems on Several Occasions* (London: for J. Dodsley, 1785)

Lucke, Robert, *A Miscellany of New Poems, on Several Occasions* (London: by Edward Cave, 1736)

Luscious Poet: Or, Venus's Miscellany, The (London: for T. Dormer, 1732)

Lyttelton, George, Baron, *An Epistle to Mr. Pope, from a Young Gentleman at Rome* (London: for J. Roberts, 1730)

Manners, Lady Catharine, *Review of Poetry, Ancient and Modern* (London: for J. Booth, 1799)

Mason, William, *Heroic Epistle to Sir William Chambers* (London: for J. Almon, 1773)

Mason, William, *An Heroic Postscript* (London: for J. Almon, 1774)

Masters, Mary, *Familiar Letters and Poems on Several Occasions* (London: for the author, by D. Henry and R. Cave, 1755)

Masters, Mary, *Poems on Several Occasions* (London: by T. Browne for the author, 1733)

Maxwell, James, *Happiness. A Moral Essay* (Paisley: by John Neilson for the author, 1786)

May, Thomas, *Poems on Various Subjects* (Henley: by and for the author, [1790?])

Meen, Henry, *Happiness: A Poetical Essay* (London: by T. and J. W. Pasham, for J. Johnson and Co., Mr. Dodsley, and Mr. White, 1766)

Miscellany Poems (London: for Jacob Tonson, 1684)

Miscellany Poems, 4th edn, 6 vols (London: for Jacob Tonson, 1716)

Mitchell, Joseph, *A Familiar Epistle to the Right Honourable Sir Robert Walpole; Concerning Poets, Poverty, Promises, Places, &c.* (London: for Alexander Cruden, 1735)

——, *Poems on Several Occasions*, 2 vols (London: for Harmen Noorthouck, 1732)

——, *The Promotion, and the Alternative: Two Poetical Petitions to the Right Honourable Sir Robert Walpole* (Westminster: by A. Campbell, for J. Millan, 1726)

——, *The Sine-Cure. A Poetical Petition to the Right Honourable Robert Walpole, Esq;* (London: n. p., 1725)

——, *Three Poetical Epistles to Mr. Hogarth, Mr. Dandridge, and Mr. Lambert, Masters in the Art of Painting* (London: for John Watts, 1731; Foxon M331)

Montagu, Lady Mary Wortley, *The Complete Letters of Lady Mary Wortley Montagu*, ed. by Robert Halsband, 3 vols (Oxford: Clarendon Press, 1965–7)

——, *Essays and Poems, and Simplicity, a Comedy*, ed. by Robert Halsband and Isobel Grundy (Oxford: Clarendon Press, 1977, repr. 1993)

——, *Works*, [ed. by James Dallaway] (London: by R. Phillips, 1803)

Montgomery, James, *Prison Amusements, and Other Trifles [. . .]. By Paul Positive* (London: for J. Johnson, 1797)

Monthly Review; or, Literary Journal, The, 81 vols (London: for R. Griffiths etc, 1749–89)

Moore, Edward (attrib.), *Yarico to Inkle: An Epistle* (London: for Lawton Gilliver, 1736)

More, Hannah, *Florio: A Tale, for Fine Gentlemen and Fine Ladies: And, the Bas Bleu; Or Conversation* (London: for T. Cadell, 1786)

New Foundling Hospital for Wit, The, 6 vols [London; for J. Debrett, 1784]

New Miscellany: Being a Collection of Pieces of Poetry, A (London: for T. Warner, [1725?])

Newbery, John, *The Art of Poetry Made Easy. [. . .] Being the Seventh Volume of the Circle of the Sciences* (London: for J. Newbery, 1746)

——, *The Art of Poetry on a New Plan*, 2 vols (London: for J. Newbery, 1762)

Nichols, John (ed.), *A Select Collection of Poems*, 8 vols (London: by and for J. Nichols, 1780–2)

Nicol, Alexander, *Nature Without Art: Or, Nature's Progress in Poetry*

(Edinburgh: by P. Matthie, 1739)

Nicol, Alexander, *Poems on Several Subjects, Both Comical and Serious* (Dundee: for the author and James Stark, 1766)

Nugent, Robert, *An Essay on Happiness. In an Epistle to the Right Honourable the Earl of Chesterfield* (London: for J. Walthoe, 1737)

——, *An Essay on Justice. A Poem. In a Letter to the Right Hon. the Lord Viscount Cornberry* (Dublin: repr. by Geo. Faulkner, 1737; Foxon N347)

——, *Odes and Epistles*, 2nd edn (London: for R. Dodsley, 1739)

——, *Political Justice. A Poem. In a Letter to the Right Hon. the Lord* **** (London: for J. Walthoe, 1736)

Oldmixon, John, *Amores Britannici* (London: for J. Nutt, 1703)

Ottley, Adam, 'In a Letter to Mr J. Philips in Christ Church Oxon', in Juan Christian Pellicer, *John Philips (1676–1709): Life, Works, and Reception* (Oslo: Unipub AS, 2002), pp. 342–5

Overton, Bill (ed.), *A Letter to my Love: Love Poems by Women First Published in the Barbados Gazette, 1731–1737* (Newark, NJ: University of Delaware Press; London: Associated University Presses, 2001)

Ovid (Publius Ovidius Naso), *Heroides*, trans. by Harold Isbell (London and New York: Penguin Books, 1990)

——, *Heroides and Amores*, Loeb Classical Library, ed. with trans. by Grant Showerman, 2nd edn. rev. by G. P. Gould (Cambridge, MA: Harvard University Press; London: William Heinemann, 1977)

——, *Ovid's Epistles, Translated by Several Hands* (London: for Jacob Tonson, 1680)

——, 8th edn (London: for Jacob Tonson, 1712)

——, *Ovid's Heroines: A Verse Translation of the Heroides*, trans. by Daryl Hine (New Haven, CT, and London: Yale University Press, 1991)

Ozell, John, *The Rape of the Bucket* (London: for E. Curll, 1715; Foxon O288)

——, *La Secchia Rapita: The Trophy-Bucket* (London: by J. D. for Egbert Sanger, 1710; Foxon O286)

Pack, Richardson, *Miscellanies in Verse and Prose* (London: for E. Curll, 1719 [1718])

Pagett, Thomas Catesby, *Miscellanies in Prose and Verse* (London: n.p., 1741)

Parnell, Thomas, *Collected Poems of Thomas Parnell*, ed. by Claude Rawson and F. P. Lock (Newark: University of Delaware Press; London: Associated University Presses, 1989)

——, *On the Different Stiles of Poetry* (London: for Benj. Tooke, 1713)

Pasquin, Anthony (pseudonym for John Williams), *The New Bath Guide* (London: for H. D. Symonds and T. Bellamy, 1796)

Pattison, William, *Poetical Works* (London: for E. Curll, 1728 [1727])

Pearson, Thomas, *An Epistle to D[aniel] B[raithwaite] from T[homas] P[earson]* (London: J. Nichols and Son, n.d. [1802–5?])

Philips, Ambrose, *An Epistle to the Honourable James Craggs, Esq., Secretary at War: At Hampton-Court* (London: for Jacob Tonson, 1717)

——, *An Epistle to the Right Honourable Charles Lord Halifax, One of the Lords*

Justices Appointed by his Majesty (London: for J. Tonson, 1714)

Philips, Ambrose, *The Poems of Ambrose Philips*, ed. by M. G. Segar, Percy Reprints, no. 14 (Oxford: Basil Blackwell, 1937)

——, *To the Honourable Miss Carteret* (Dublin: by George Grierson, [1725]; Foxon P221)

Pindar, Peter (pseudonym for John Wolcot), *Brother Peter to Brother Tom. An Expostulatory Epistle* (London: for G. Kearsley, 1788)

Plowden, Pilgrim (pseudonym for George Farewell), *Farrago* (London: for the author, 1733 [1734?])

Poems by Eminent Ladies, 2 vols [comp. by George Colman the elder and Bonnell Thornton] (London: for R. Baldwin, 1755)

Poetical Calendar, The, 12 vols [comp. by Francis Fawkes, and William Woty] (London: by Dryden Leach for J. Coote, 1763–4)

Poetical Dictionary, A, 4 vols [ed. by Samuel Derrick] (London: for J. Newbery and others, 1761)

Poetical Miscellanies, Consisting of Original Poems and Translations. [. . .] Publish'd by Mr. Steele (London: Jacob Tonson, 1714)

Pointon (later Pickering), Priscilla, *Poems on Several Occasions* (Birmingham: for the author, by T. Warren, 1770)

——, *Poems by Mrs. Pickering. To Which are Added Poetical Sketches by the Author, and Translator of Philotoxi Ardenæ* (Birmingham: by E. Piercy, 1794)

Pope, Alexander, *Miscellaneous Poems and Translations by Several Hands*, 3rd edn, 2 vols (London: for Bernard Lintot, 1720)

——, *The Poems of Alexander Pope*, Twickenham Edition, 11 vols (London: Methuen, 1938–68)

——, *The Works of Alexander Pope Esq*, 9 vols, ed. by William Warburton (London: for J. Knapton, H. Lintot, J. and R. Tonson, and S. Draper, 1751)

——, *The Works of Mr. Alexander Pope* (London: by W. Bowyer, for Jacob Tonson and Bernard Lintot, 1717)

——, *The Works of Mr. Alexander Pope* (London [The Hague?]: by T[homas] J[ohnson], 1720)

——, *The Works of Mr. Alexander Pope. Volume II* (London: for L. Gilliver, 1735)

Pott, Joseph Holden, *Poems* (London: for T. Beckett, 1780)

Preston, William, *Poetical Works*, 2 vols (Dublin: for the author by Graisberry & Campbell, 1793)

——, *Seventeen Hundred and Seventy-Seven; Or, a Picture of the Manners and Character of the Age. In An Epistle from a Lady of Quality, in England, to Omiah, at Otaheite* (London: for T. Evans, 1777)

Prior, Matthew, *The Literary Works of Matthew Prior*, ed. by H. Bunker Wright and Monroe K. Spears, 2 vols (Oxford: Clarendon Press, 1959)

Pye, Jael Henrietta, *Poems* (London: for J. Walter, 1772)

Ramsay, Allan, *Familiar Epistles between W–– H–– and A–– R––* [Edinburgh: n. p., 1719?; Foxon R51]

——, *Poems* (Edinburgh: for the author, 1720)

——, *Poems* (Edinburgh: Mr. Thomas Ruddiman, for the author, 1721)

Ramsay, Allan, *Poems by Allan Ramsay. Volume II* (Edinburgh: by Mr. Thomas Ruddiman, for the author, 1728)

——, *The Poems of Allan Ramsay. A New Edition*, 2 vols (London: by A. Strahan, for T. Cadell Jun. and W. Davies, 1800)

——, *The Rise and Fall of Stocks* (Edinburgh: for the author; Foxon R87)

——, *The Works of Allan Ramsay*, 6 vols: 1 and 2 ed. by Burns Martin and John W. Oliver, 3–6 by Alexander M. Kinghorn and Alexander Law, Scottish Text Society, 3rd ser., 19–20, 29; 4th ser., 6–8 (Edinburgh and London: William Blackwood & Sons, [1945]–74)

Ramsay, Charlotte (later Lennox), *Poems on Several Occasions* (London: for S. Paterson, 1747)

Ratcliffe, Alexander, *Ovid Travestie* (London: for Jacob Tonson, 1680)

Relph, Josiah, *A Miscellany of Poems* (Glasgow: by Robert Foulis, 1747)

Retzer, Joseph (pub.), *Choice of the Best Poetical Pieces of the Most Eminent English Poets*, 6 vols (Vienna: for Sonnleithner and Hoerling, 1783–86)

Roberts, William Hayward, *Poems by Dr. Roberts of Eton College* (London: for J. Wilkie, 1774)

Robertson, James, *Poems on Several Occasions* (London: for T. Davies, G. Robinson, and T. Cadell, 1773)

Rousseau, Jean-Jacques, *Julie: Or, the New Heloise: Letters of Two Lovers Who Live in a Small Town at the Foot of the Alps*, trans. by Philip Stewart and Jean Vaché (Hanover, NH, and London: University Press of New England, 1997)

Rowe, Elizabeth, *Friendship in Death* and *Letters Moral and Entertaining* (London: for T. Worrall, 1733; New York: Garland, 1972 [facsimile reprint])

——, *Miscellaneous Works in Prose and Verse*, 2 vols (London: for R. Hett and R. Dodsley, 1739)

Royal Society, *Philosophical Transactions*, 52 (London: for L. Davis and C. Reymers, 1763)

Ryves, Elizabeth, *An Epistle to the Right Honourable Lord John Cavendish* (London: for J. Dodsley, 1784)

Savage, Mary, *Poems on Various Subjects and Occasions*, 2 vols (London: for C. Parker, 1777)

Savage, Richard (comp.), *Miscellaneous Poems and Translations. By Several Hands. Publish'd by Richard Savage* (London: for Samuel Chapman, 1726)

——, *The Poetical Works of Richard Savage*, ed. by Clarence Tracy (Cambridge: Cambridge University Press, 1962)

Scott, John (later Scott-Waring), *An Epistle from Oberea, Queen of Otaheite, to Joseph Banks, Esq.* (London: J. Almon, 1774)

——, *A Second Letter from Oberea* ([London]: by T. J. Carnegy for E. Johnson [1774])

Select Collection of Modern Poems from the Best Authors, A (Edinburgh: n.p., 1759)

Seward, Anna, 'Love Elegies and Epistles', in *Bluestocking Feminism: Writings of the Bluestocking Circle, 1738–1785*, 6 vols (London: Pickering & Chatto: 1999), ed. by Gary Kelly and others, IV, *Anna Seward*, ed. by Jennifer Kelly, 1–22

Seward, Anna, *Poetical Works*, ed. by Walter Scott, 3 vols (Edinburgh: by James Ballantyne and Co. for John Ballantyne and Co.; London: Hurst, Rees and Orme: 1810)

Seymour, Frances, Countess of Hertford, *The Story of Inkle and Yarrico* (London: for J. Cooper, 1738)

Seymour, Mr., 'Abelard to Eloisa', in *Letters of Abelard and Heloise* (London: for W. Lowndes and others, 1787)

Shenstone, William, *Shenstone's Miscellany 1759–1763*, ed. by Ian A. Gordon (Oxford: Clarendon Press, 1952)

Smart, Christopher, *The Works of Horace, Translated into Verse*, 4 vols (London: for W. Flexney; Mess. Johnson and Co., and T. Caslon, 1767)

Smedley, Jonathan, *Gulliveriana* (London: for J. Roberts, 1728)

——, *Poems on Several Occasions* (London: by S. Richardson for the author, 1721)

Smith, John, *Poems upon Several Occasions* (London: for H. Clements, 1713)

Somervile, William, *Poetical Works*, 2 vols (Edinburgh: Apollo Press, by the Martins, 1780)

Spectator, The, ed. by Donald F. Bond, 5 vols (Oxford: Clarendon Press, 1965)

Stillingfleet, Benjamin, *An Essay on Conversation* (London: for L. Gilliver and J. Clarke, 1737; Foxon S757)

Swift, Jonathan, *The Correspondence of Jonathan Swift*, ed. by Harold Williams, 5 vols, 2nd edn (Oxford: Clarendon Press, 1965)

——, *An Epistle upon an Epistle* ([Dublin]: n. p., 1730; Foxon S842)

——, *Jonathan Swift: The Complete Poems*, ed. by Pat Rogers (Harmondsworth and New York: Penguin Books, 1983)

——, *A Libel on D[octor] D[elany], and a Certain Great Lord* ([Dublin]: n. p., 1730; Foxon S877)

——, *The Poems of Jonathan Swift*, ed. by Harold Williams, 2nd edn, 3 vols (Oxford: Clarendon Press, 1958)

Sylvæ: Or, the Second Part of Poetical Miscellanies [3rd edn] (London: for Jacob Tonson, 1702)

Tatersal, Robert, *The Bricklayer's Miscellany* (London: for the author, 1734)

Tatler, The, ed. by Donald F. Bond, 3 vols (Oxford: Clarendon Press, 1987)

Thomas, Ann, *Poems, on Various Subjects* (Plymouth: by M. Haydon and Son, 1784)

Thomas, Elizabeth, *Miscellany Poems on Several Subjects* (London: for Tho. Combes, 1722)

Tickell, Thomas, *An Epistle from a Lady in England, to a Gentleman at Avignon* London: for J. Tonson, 1717; Foxon T272)

Tollet, Elizabeth, *Poems on Several Occasions. With Anne Boleyn to King Henry VIII. An Epistle* (London: for John Clarke, 1724)

——, *Poems on Several Occasions. With Anne Boleyn to King Henry VIII. An Epistle* (London: for John Clarke, 1755; for T. Lownds, [1756?])

Travers, Henry, *Miscellaneous Poems and Translations* (London: for Benj. Motte, 1731; York: by C. Ward and R. Chandler, 1740)

Waller, Bryan, *Poems on Several Occasions* (London: by E. Hodson, 1796)

Ward, Edward, *The London-Spy Compleat* (London: by J. How, 1703)

Warton, Joseph, *Essay on the Writings and Genius of Pope* (London: for M. Cooper, 1756)

——, *Fashion: An Epistolary Satire to a Friend* (London: for R. Dodsley, 1742; Foxon W244)

Warton, Thomas (the younger), *A Companion to the Guide, and a Guide to the Companion* (London: for H. Payne, [1760?])

——, *New-Market, A Satire* (London: for J. Newbery, 1751)

—— [comp.], *The Oxford Sausage* (London: for J. Fletcher and Co., 1764)

——, *Poems on Several Subjects* (London: for G. G. J. and J. Robinson, 1791)

Warwick, Thomas, *Abelard to Eloisa: A Poetic Epistle. Newly Attempted* (London: for J. Bew, 1782)

——, *Abelard to Eloisa. An Epistle. To Which Are Prefixed, Sonnets* (Bath: for R. Cruttwell, 1783)

——, *Abelard to Eloisa, Leonora to Tasso, Ovid to Julia, Spring and Other Poems*, 4th edn (London: n.p., [1785?])

——, *Abelard to Eloisa. An Epistle. With a New Account of their Lives* (Bath: by R. Cruttwell, 1785)

Welsted, Leonard, *Of Dulness and Scandal. Occasion'd by the Character of Lord Timon* (London: for T. Cooper, 1732; Foxon W298)

Wesley, Samuel (the elder), *An Epistle to a Friend Concerning Poetry* (London: by B. Motte for Charles Harper, 1700)

Wesley, Samuel (the younger), *Neck or Nothing: A Consolatory Letter from Mr. D[u]nt[o]n to Mr. C[u]rll upon his Being Tossed in a Blanket* ([London]: n. p., 1716; Foxon W343)

——, *Poems on Several Occasions*, ed. by James Nichols (London: Simpkin, Marshall, 1862)

Whaley, John, *A Collection of Original Poems and Translations* (London: for the author, 1745)

White, Gilbert, *The Natural History of Selborne*, ed. by Roger Mabey (Harmondsworth: Penguin Books, 1977)

Whitehead, Paul, *The State Dunces* (London: for W. Dickenson, 1733)

Whitehead, William, *Ann Boleyn to Henry the Eighth. An Epistle* (London: for R. Dodsley, 1743)

——, *Plays and Poems*, 2 vols (London: for J. Dodsley, 1774)

——, *Poems by William Whitehead [. . .]. Vol. III. To Which Are Prefixed, Memoirs of his Life and Writings. By W. Mason, M.A.* (York: by A. Ward, 1788)

——, *Poems on Several Occasions* (London: for R. and J. Dodsley, 1754)

Whyte, Samuel, *The Shamrock: Or, Hibernian Cresses* (Dublin: by R. Marchbank, 1772)

Wilmot, John, Earl of Rochester, *The Works of John Wilmot, Earl of Rochester*, ed. by Harold Love (Oxford: Oxford University Press, 1999)

Wilson, Alexander, *The Poems and Literary Prose of Alexander Wilson*, 2 vols, ed. by Alexander B. Grosart (Paisley: Alex. Garner, 1876)

Wilson, Peter (comp.), *Wilson's Dublin Directory, for the Year 1766* (Dublin: for Peter Wilson, 1766)

Winstanley, John, *Poems Written Occasionally by the Late John Winstanley*, 2 vols (Dublin: by S. Powell for the editor, 1751)

Woodhouse, James, *Poems on Several Occasions*, 2nd edn (London: for the author, 1766)

Woodward, George, *Poems on Several Occasions* (Oxford: Clarendon Printing-House, 1730)

Wright, George, *The Lady's Miscellany* (London: for Chapman and Co., 1793)

Yearsley, Ann, *Poems on Several Occasions* (London: for T. Cadell, 1785)

——, *Poems on Various Subjects* (London: for the author, 1787)

——, *The Rural Lyre* (London: for G. G. and J. Robinson, 1796)

Young, Edward, *Conjectures on Original Composition* (London: for R. Millar and and R. and J. Dodsley, 1754)

——, *The Poetical Works of the Reverend Edward Young*, 2 vols (London: for Messrs Curll and others, 1741)

——, *Two Epistles to Mr. Pope* (London: for Lawton Gilliver, 1730)

Secondary Sources

Altman, Janet Gurkin, *Epistolarity: Approaches to a Form* (Columbus: Ohio State University Press, 1982)

Ballaster, Ros, 'Women and the Rise of the Novel: Sexual Prescripts', in *Women and Literature in Britain 1700–1800*, ed. by Vivien Jones (Cambridge: Cambridge University Press, 2000), pp. 197–216

Barker, Anthony D., 'Edward Cave, Samuel Johnson and the *Gentleman's Magazine*', DPhil thesis, University of Oxford, 1981

Barnett, Corelli, *Britain and her Army, 1509–1970: A Military, Political and Social Survey* (London: Allen Lane, 1970)

Beer, Gillian, '"Our Unnatural No-voice": The Heroic Epistle, Pope, and Women's Gothic', *Yearbook of English Studies*, 12 (1981), 125–51; repr. in *Modern Essays on Eighteenth-Century Literature*, ed. by Leopold Damrosch, Jr. (New York and Oxford: Oxford University Press, 1988)

Bending, Stephen, 'A Natural Revolution? Garden Politics in Eighteenth-Century England', in *Refiguring Revolutions: Aesthetics and Politics from the English Revolution to the Romantic Revolution*, ed. by Kevin Sharpe and Steven N. Zwicker (Berkeley, Los Angeles and London: University of California Press, 1998), pp. 241–66

Bonnell, Thomas F., 'John Bell's *Poets of Great Britain*: The "Little Trifling Edition" Revisited', *Modern Philology*, 85 (1987), 128–52

——, 'Patchwork and Piracy: John Bell's "Connected System of Biography" and the Use of Johnson's *Prefaces*', *Studies in Bibliography*, 48 (1995), 194–229

Brown, Stephen N., 'Edward Young', in *Eighteenth-Century British Poets, First Series*, ed. by John Sitter, *Dictionary of Literary Biography* (Detroit: Bruccoli Clark Layman, 1990), 95: 353–63

Bourdieu, Pierre, 'Forms of Capital', trans. by Richard Nice, in *Handbook of Theory and Research for the Sociology of Education*, ed. by John G. Richardson (New York and London: Greenwood Press, 1986), pp. 241–58; repr. in *Education: Culture, Economy, Society*, ed. by A. H. Halsey, Hugh Lauder, Philip Brown, and Amy Stuart Wells (Oxford and New York: Oxford University Press, 1997; first published in German, 1983), pp. 47–58

Carlson, C. Lennart, *The First Magazine: A History of the Gentleman's Magazine* (Providence, RI: Brown University Press, 1938)

Carter, Harold B., *Sir Joseph Banks, 1743–1820* (London: British Museum [Natural History], 1988)

Chernaik, Warren, *Sexual Freedom in Restoration Literature* (Cambridge: Cambridge University Press, 1995)

Christmas, William, *The Lab'ring Muses: Work, Writing, and the Social Order in English Plebeian Poetry, 1730–1830* (Newark, NJ: University of Delaware Press; London: Associated University Presses, 2001)

Clery, E. J., *The Feminization Debate in Eighteenth-Century England: Literature, Commerce and Luxury* (Houndmills, Basingstoke, and New York: Palgrave Macmillan, 2004)

C[okayne], G. E., and others, *The Complete Peerage of England, Scotland, Ireland, Great Britain and the United Kingdom*, rev. edn, 14 vols (London: St. Catherine Press, 1910–59)

Cook, Elizabeth Heckendorn, *Epistolary Bodies: Gender and Genre in the Eighteenth-Century Republic of Letters* (Stanford, CA: Stanford University Press, 1996)

Crane, R. S., 'An Early Eighteenth-Century Enthusiast for Primitive Poetry: John Husbands', *Modern Language Notes*, 37 (1922), 27–36

Damico, Helen, 'Sources of Stanza Forms Used by Burns', *Studies in Scottish Literature*, 12 (1975), 207–19

Day, Martin S., 'Anstey and Anapestic Satire in the Late Eighteenth Century', *ELH: A Journal of English Literary History*, 15 (1948), 122–46

——, 'The Influence of Mason's *Heroic Epistle*', *Modern Language Quarterly*, 14 (1953), 235–52

Day, Robert Adams, *Told in Letters: Epistolary Fiction before Richardson* (Ann Arbor: University of Michigan Press, 1966)

Dix, Robin, 'John Gilbert Cooper: A Poet in Search of his Metier and Meter', *The Age of Johnson*, 13 (2002), 255–81

Dowling, William C., *The Epistolary Moment: The Poetics of the Eighteenth-Century Verse Epistle* (Princeton: Princeton University Press, 1991)

Eagleton, Terry, *The Rape of Clarissa: Writing, Sexuality and Class Struggle in Samuel Richardson* (Oxford: Basil Blackwell, 1982)

Elias, A. C., Jr., 'Editing Minor Writers: The Case of Laetitia Pilkington and Mary Barber', in *1650–1850: Ideas, Aesthetics, and Inquiries in the Early Modern Era*, III, ed. by Kevin L. Cope (New York: AMS Press), 129–47

Fairer, David, *English Poetry of the Eighteenth Century, 1700–1789* (Harlow and London: Pearson Education, 2003)

Fairer, David, 'Mary Leapor: "Crumble-Hall"', in *A Companion to Eighteenth-Century Poetry*, ed. by Christine Gerrard (Malden, MA, and Oxford: Blackwell Publishing, 2006), pp. 223–36

Feilla, Cecilia A., 'From "Sainted Maid" to "Wife in all her Grandeur": Translations of Heloise, 1687–1817', *Eighteenth-Century Life*, 28 (2004), 1–16

Felsenstein, Frank (ed.), *English Trader, Indian Maid: Representing Gender, Race, and Slavery in the New World: An Inkle and Yarico Reader* (Baltimore, MD, and London: The Johns Hopkins University Press, 1999)

Forster, Harold, *Supplements to Dodsley's Collection of Poems* (Oxford Bibliographical Society Occasional Publication No. 15 (Oxford: Oxford Bibliographical Society, 1980)

Genette, Gérard, *Fiction and Diction*, trans. by Catherine Porter (Ithaca, NY, and London: Cornell University Press, 1993; first published in French, 1991)

Gerrard, Christine, *Aaron Hill: The Muses' Projector, 1685–1750* (Oxford: Oxford University Press, 2003)

——, *The Patriot Opposition to Walpole: Politics, Poetry, and Myth, 1725–1742* (Oxford: Clarendon Press, 1994)

Gillespie, Stuart, 'The Early Years of the Dryden-Tonson Partnership: The Background to their Composite Translations and Miscellanies of the 1680s', *Restoration*, 12 (1988), 10–19

Greene, Richard, *Mary Leapor: A Study in Eighteenth-Century Women's Poetry* (Oxford: Clarendon Press, 1993)

Griffin, Dustin, 'Akenside's Political Muse', in *Mark Akenside: A Reassessment*, ed. by Robin Dix (Cranbury, NJ, and London: Associated University Presses, 2000), pp. 19–50

——, *Literary Patronage in England, 1650–1800* (Cambridge and New York: Cambridge University Press, 1996)

——, *Satire: A Critical Reintroduction* (Lexington: University Press of Kentucky, 1994)

Grundy, Isobel, *Lady Mary Wortley Montagu* (Oxford: Oxford University Press, 1999)

——, 'Ovid and Eighteenth-Century Divorce: An Unpublished Poem by Lady Mary Wortley Montagu', *Review of English Studies*, n.s., 23 (1972), 417–28

Guerinot, J. V. (ed.), *Pamphlet Attacks on Alexander Pope, 1711–1744: A Descriptive Bibliography* (London: Methuen, 1969)

Guest, Harriet, 'Eighteenth-Century Femininity: "A Supposed Sexual Character"', in *Women and Literature in Britain*, ed. by Vivien Jones (Cambridge: Cambridge University Press, 2000), pp. 46–68

Guskin, Phyllis J., '"Not Originally Intended for the Press": Martha Fowke Sansom's Poems in the *Barbados Gazette*', *Eighteenth-Century Studies*, 34 (2000), 61–91

Habermas, Jürgen, *The Structural Transformation of the Public Sphere: An Enquiry into a Category of Bourgeois Society*, trans. by Thomas Burger and Frederick Lawrence (Cambridge, MA: MIT Press, 1989; first published in German, 1962)

Hammond, Brean, 'Verse Satire', in *A Companion to Eighteenth-Century Poetry*, ed. by Christine Gerrard (Malden, MA, and Oxford: Blackwell Publishing, 2006), pp. 369–85

Hardie, Philip (ed.), *The Cambridge Companion to Ovid* (Cambridge: Cambridge University Press, 2002)

Hardin, Richard F., 'Convention and Design in Drayton's *Heroicall Epistles*', *PMLA*, 83 (1968), 35–41

Haslett, Moira, *Pope to Burney, 1714–1779: Scriblerians to Bluestockings* (Houndmills, Basingstoke, and New York: Palgrave Macmillan, 2003)

Havens, Raymond D. 'Changing Taste in the Eighteenth Century: A Study of Dryden's and Dodsley's Miscellanies', *PMLA*, 44 (1929), 501–36

Hinnant, Charles H., *The Poetry of Anne Finch: An Essay in Interpretation* (Newark: University of Delaware Press; London: Associated University Presses, 1994)

Hobsbaum, Philip, 'The Rise of the Dramatic Monologue', *Hudson Review*, 28 (1975), 227–45

How, James, *Epistolary Spaces: English Letter Writing from the Foundation of the Post Office to Richardson's Clarissa* (Aldershot, Hants, and Burlington, VT: Ashgate, 2003)

Hunt, Clay, 'The Elizabethan Background of Neo-Classic Polite Verse', *ELH*, 8 (1941), 273–304

Ives, Eric, *The Life and Death of Anne Boleyn* (Oxford and Malden, MA: Blackwell Publishers, 2004)

Jones, Vivien, 'Introduction', in *Women and Literature in Britain 1700– 1800*, ed. by Vivien Jones (Cambridge: Cambridge University Press, 2000), pp. 1–13

—— (ed.), *Women and Literature in Britain 1700–1800* (Cambridge: Cambridge University Press, 2000)

Kairoff, Claudia Thomas, 'Classical and Biblical Models: The Female Poetic Tradition', in *Women and Poetry 1660–1750*, ed. by Sarah Prescott and David E. Shuttleton (Houndmills, Basingstoke, and New York: Palgrave Macmillan, 2003), pp. 183–202

Kauffman, Linda S., *Discourses of Desire: Gender, Genre, and Epistolary Fictions* (Ithaca, NY, and London: Cornell University Press, 1986)

Kennedy, Duncan F., 'Epistolarity: the *Heroides*', in *The Cambridge Companion to Ovid*, ed. by Philip Hardie (Cambridge: Cambridge University Press, 2002), pp. 217–32

Lakoff, George, *Women, Fire, and Dangerous Things: What Categories Reveal about the Mind* (Chicago: University of Chicago Press, 1987)

Levine, Jay Arnold, 'The Status of the Verse Epistle before Pope', *Studies in Philology*, 59 (1962), 658–84

Lockwood, Thomas, 'Fielding and the Licensing Act', *Huntington Library Quarterly*, 50 (1987), 379–93

——, *Post-Augustan Satire: Charles Churchill and Satirical Poetry, 1750–1800* (Seattle and London: University of Washington Press. 1979)

MacLaine, Allan H., *Allan Ramsay* (Boston: Twayne Publishers, 1985)

McGovern, Barbara, *Anne Finch and her Poetry: A Critical Biography* (Athens and London: University of Georgia Press, 1992)

McGuirk, Carol, 'Augustan Influences on Allan Ramsay', *Studies in Scottish Literature*, 16 (1981), 97–109

McLaverty, James, '"Of Which Being Publick the Publick Judge": Pope and the Publication of *Verses Address'd to the Imitator of Horace*', *Studies in Bibliography*, 51 (1998), 183–204

——, *Pope, Print and Meaning* (Oxford: Oxford University Press, 2001)

Marotti, Arthur, *John Donne, Coterie Poet* (Madison: University of Wisconsin Press, 1986)

Mason, William, 'Memoirs of the Life and Writings of Mr. William Whitehead', in *Poems by William Whitehead [. . .]. Vol. III* (York: by A. Ward, 1788), III, 1–129

Maurer, Margaret, 'John Donne's Verse Letters', *Modern Language Quarterly*, 37 (1976), 234–59

Maycock, Christopher Hugh, *A Passionate Poet: Susanna Blamire* (Penzance: Hypatia Publications, 2003)

Nugent, Claud, *Memoirs of Robert, Earl Nugent, with Letters, Poems, and Appendices* (London: William Heinemann, 1898)

Nuttall, A. D., *Pope's Essay on Man* (London: George Allen & Unwin, 1984)

Overton, Bill, *Fictions of Female Adultery, 1684–1890: Theories and Circumtexts* (Houndmills, Basingstoke, and New York: Palgrave Macmillan, 2002)

Parfitt, George, *John Donne: A Literary Life* (Houndmills, Basingstoke, and London: Macmillan, 1989)

Paulson, Ronald, *The Life of Henry Fielding: A Critical Biography* (Malden, MA, and Oxford: Blackwell Publishing, 2000)

Pellicer, Juan Christian, *John Philips (1676–1709): Life, Works, and Reception* (Oslo: Unipub AS, 2002)

Pollak, Ellen, *The Poetics of Sexual Myth: Gender and Ideology in the Verse of Swift and Pope* (Chicago and London: University of Chicago Press, 1985)

Poovey, Mary, *The Proper Lady and the Woman Writer: Ideology as Style in the Works of Mary Wollstonecraft, Mary Shelley, and Jane Austen* (Chicago and London: University of Chicago Press, 1985)

Prescott, Sarah, *Women, Authorship and Literary Culture, 1690–1740* (Houndmills, Basingstoke, and New York: Palgrave Macmillan, 2003)

Pretis, Anna de, *'Epistolarity' in the First Book of Horace's Epistles*, Gorgias Dissertations: Classics, I (Piscataway, NJ: Gorgias Press, 2002))

Price, Martin, *To the Palace of Wisdom: Studies in Order and Energy from Dryden to Blake* (New York: Anchor Books, 1964)

Ray, William, *Story and History: Narrative Authority and Social Identity in the Eighteenth-Century French and English Novel* (Cambridge, MA, and Oxford: Basil Blackwell, 1990)

Robinson, F. J. G., and P. J. Wallis, *Book Subscription Lists: A Revised Guide* (Newcastle upon Tyne: Harold Hill and Son, for the Book Subscription List Project, 1975)

Rogers, Pat, *The Alexander Pope Encyclopedia* (Westport, CT, and London: Greenwood Press, 2004)

Rogers, Pat, *The Augustan Vision* (London: Weidenfeld and Nicolson, 1974)

——, *An Introduction to Pope* (London: Methuen, 1975)

Rogers, Shef, 'Composing Conscience: *The Injured Islanders* (1779) and English Sensibility', *The Eighteenth Century*, 38 (1997), 259–65

Roscoe, S[ydney], *John Newbery and his Successors 1740–1814: A Bibliography* (Wormley, Herts: Five Owls Press, 1973)

Røstvig, Maren-Sofie, *The Happy Man: Studies in the Metamorphoses of a Classical Ideal*, 2 vols, 2nd edn (Oslo: Universitetsvorslag; New York: Humanities Press, 1971)

Rothstein, Eric, *Restoration and Eighteenth-Century Poetry 1660–1780* (Boston, London and Henley: Routledge & Kegan Paul, 1981)

Rowland, Jon Thomas, *Faint Praise and Civil Leer: The 'Decline' of Eighteenth-Century Panegyric* (Newark, NJ: University of Delaware Press; London and Toronto, Associated University Presses, 1994)

Rumbold, Valerie, 'The Alienated Insider: Mary Leapor in *Crumble Hall*', *British Journal for Eighteenth-Century Studies*, 19 (1996), 63–76

——, 'The Poetic Career of Judith Cowper: An Exemplary Failure?', in *Pope, Swift, and Women Writers*, ed. by Donald C. Mell (Newark, NJ: University of Delaware Press; London: Associated University Presses, 1996), pp. 48–66

——, *Women's Place in Pope's World* (Cambridge: Cambridge University Press, 1989)

Saintsbury, George, *The Peace of the Augustans* (London: G. Bell and Sons, 1916)

Schuller, Tom, John Field and Stephen Baron, 'Social Capital: A Review and Critique' in *Social Capital: Critical Perspectives* (Oxford and New York: Oxford University Press, 2000), ed. by Stephen Baron, John Field and Tom Schuller, pp. 1–38

Sherbo, Arthur, 'Dryden as a Cambridge Editor', *Studies in Bibliography*, 38 (1985), 251–61

——, 'Isaac Reed and the *European Magazine*', *Studies in Bibliography*, 37 (1984), 210–27

Snider, Alvin, 'Hudibrastic', *Restoration: Studies in English Literary Culture, 1660–1700*, 12 (1988), 1–9

Spencer, Jane, *The Rise of the Woman Novelist: From Aphra Behn to Jane Austen* (Oxford and New York: Basil Blackwell, 1986)

Stone, Lawrence, *The Family, Sex and Marriage in England 1500–1800* (London: Weidenfeld and Nicolson, 1977)

Swettenham, Neal, 'Categories and Catcalls: Cognitive Dissonance in *The Playboy of the Western World*', in *Performance and Cognition: Theatre Studies and the Cognitive Turn*, ed. by Bruce A. McConachie and F. Elizabeth Hart (New York: Routledge, 2006), pp. 207–22

Sypher, Wylie, 'The African Prince in London', *Journal of the History of Ideas*, 2 (1941), 237–47

——, *Guinea's Captive Kings: British Anti-Slavery Literature of the XVIIIth*

Century (Chapel Hill: University of North Carolina Press, 1942; repr. New York: Octagon Books, 1969)

Thomas, Claudia N., *Alexander Pope and his Eighteenth-Century Women Readers* (Carbondale and Edwardsville: Southern Illinois University Press, 1994)

Thomas, Donald, *Henry Fielding* (London: Weidenfeld and Nicolson, 1990)

Thomson, Patricia, 'Donne and the Poetry of Patronage: The *Verse Letters*', in *John Donne: Essays in Celebration*, ed. by A. J. Smith (London: Methuen, 1972), pp. 308–23

Todd, Janet, *The Sign of Angellica: Women, Writing and Fiction 1660–1800* (London: Virago Press, 1989)

Violi, Patrizia, 'Letters', in *Discourse and Literature*, ed. by Teun A. Van Dijk (Amsterdam and Philadelphia: John Benjamins, 1985), pp. 149–67

Wallis, P. J., and R. Wallis, *Book Subscription Lists: Extended Supplement to the Revised Guide* (Newcastle upon Tyne: Project for Historical Biobibliography, 1996)

Wechselblatt, Martin, 'Gender and Race in Yarico's Epistles to Inkle: Voicing the Feminine/Slave', *Studies in Eighteenth-Century Culture*, 19 (1989), 197–223

Weinbrot, Howard, 'Johnson's Poetry', in *The Cambridge Companion to Samuel Johnson*, ed. by Greg Clingham (Cambridge: Cambridge University Press, 1997), pp. 34–50

Williams, Abigail, 'Whig and Tory Poetics', in *A Companion to Eighteenth-Century Poetry*, ed. by Christine Gerrard (Malden, MA, and Oxford: Blackwell Publishing, 2006), pp. 444–57

Williams, Franklin B., Jr., 'Commendatory Verses: The Rise of the Art of Puffing', *Studies in Bibliography*, 19 (1966), 1–15

Williams, Raymond, *Marxism and Literature* (Oxford: Oxford University Press, 1977)

——, *Culture* (Glasgow: Fontana Paperbacks, 1981)

Williamson, Karina, 'Voice, Gender, and the Augustan Verse Epistle', in *Presenting Gender: Changing Sex in Early-Modern Culture*, ed. by Chris Mounsey (Lewisburg, PA: Bucknell University Press; London: Associated University Presses, 2001), pp. 76–93

Yost, Calvin D., Jr., *The Poetry of the Gentleman's Magazine: A Study in Eighteenth-Century Literary Taste* (Philadelphia: University of Pennsylvania, 1936)

Internet Sources

http://www.oxforddnb.com (*Oxford Dictionary of National Biography*)
http://www.oed.com (*Oxford English Dictionary*)
http://www.gale.com/EighteenthCentury (*Eighteenth-Century Collections Online*)
http://www.jimandellen.org/finch/finchtexts.html (Ellen Moody's list of unpublished verse by Anne Finch, Countess of Winchilsea)
http://www.lion.chadwyck.com/marketing/index.jsp (*Literature Online*)

Index

Made in the USA
Las Vegas, NV
26 October 2024